Dressmaking

Dressmaking
The complete step-by-step guide

ALISON SMITH

LONDON, NEW YORK, MUNICH, MELBOURNE, AND DELHI

DK UK
PROJECT EDITOR Laura Palosuo
EDITOR Hilary Mandleberg
SENIOR ART EDITORS Jane Ewart, Glenda Fisher
PROJECT ART EDITOR Hannah Moore
DESIGN ASSISTANT Charlotte Johnson
SENIOR PRODUCTION EDITOR Jennifer Murray
SENIOR PRODUCTION CONTROLLER Seyhan Esen
CREATIVE TECHNICAL SUPPORT Sonia Charbonnier
NEW PHOTOGRAPHY Ruth Jenkinson
ART DIRECTION FOR PHOTOGRAPHY Jane Ewart, Alison Shackleton
SENIOR JACKET CREATIVE Nicola Powling
MANAGING EDITOR Penny Smith
MANAGING ART EDITOR Marianne Markham
PUBLISHER Mary Ling
ART DIRECTOR Jane Bull

DK INDIA
SENIOR EDITOR Alicia Ingty
EDITOR Arani Sinha
ASSISTANT EDITOR Neha Ruth Samuel
ART EDITORS Mansi Nagdev, Ira Sharma, Zaurin Thoidingjam
MANAGING EDITOR Glenda Fernandes
MANAGING ART EDITOR Navidita Thapa
PRODUCTION MANAGER Pankaj Sharma
CREATIVE TECHNICAL SUPPORT MANAGER Sunil Sharma
SENIOR DTP DESIGNER Tarun Sharma
DTP DESIGNERS Nand Kishor Archarya, Manish Chandra Upreti

First published in Great Britain in 2012 by
Dorling Kindersley Limited
80 Strand, London WC2R ORL
Penguin Group (UK)

3 4 5 6 7 8 9 10
006–182909– Sep/2012

A CIP catalogue record for this book is available from the British Library.

ISBN: 978-1-4093-8463-2

Printed and bound in China by Hung Hing Offset Printing Company Ltd

Colour reproduction by Butterfly Creative Services and Opus Multi Media Services

Discover more at www.dk.com

CONTENTS

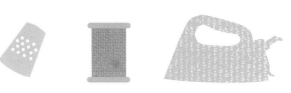

INTRODUCTION

My passion is sewing. I'm never happier than when I'm in front of my sewing machine creating a new garment and I wanted to share that enjoyment with everyone who loves clothes and would like to sew their own. This book offers you twelve basic patterns ranging from skirts and dresses through trousers and tops to jackets. There are full instructions for scaling the patterns up or you can access the patterns via a dedicated website. The bonus is that the basic patterns can be adapted to make a total of thirty-one fabulous garments. If you make them all, you will have a complete wardrobe whatever your age and lifestyle.

Beginners can start with the basic patterns and quickly progress to the more complex ones. For the more experienced sewer, there are plenty of new ideas and techniques to try, or you may feel like making the same pattern several times in different fabrics for a variety of looks. I've also included detailed instructions for the techniques needed to make every garment in the book. This section will also help you to work with any commercial pattern. And finally, there are sections dedicated to mending and customizing, enabling you to prolong the useful life of your clothes.

Happy sewing!

HOW TO USE THIS BOOK

This book contains all the information you need to make your own clothes. There are patterns and step-by-step instructions for twelve classic garments, and variations of each. Additional guidance, if needed, is to be found in sections on key dressmaking techniques, tools, fabrics, and pattern alterations. Finally, sections on mending and customizing show how to prolong the life of your garments, both old and new.

CLASSIC GARMENTS

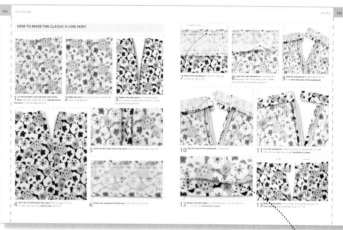

CLASSIC GARMENT OPENERS

Each classic garment is profiled in an introduction spread that tells you what you need to begin your project, including materials, fabric ideas, and information on where to find the patterns.

CLASSIC GARMENT STEP-BY-STEP PAGES

Every step of making each garment is demonstrated with close-up photography and explained with clear text. Where further guidance may be needed, you are directed to the appropriate page in the general techniques section.

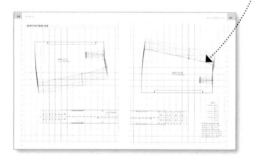

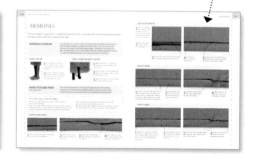

PATTERNS

A pattern for each of the garment projects is printed in the back of the book, and graded for sizes 6–24. Colour-coding helps you find the correct size when using the pattern.

PATTERN GUIDE

A guide to using the patterns shows you how to enlarge, photocopy, or download and print the patterns. A handy size chart helps you find the correct size for you.

GENERAL TECHNIQUES

All key dressmaking techniques are shown and explained, step-by-step, in a self-contained section. Turn to this section for extra guidance when completing a project, or use it as a general reference for dressmaking queries.

CLASSIC GARMENT VARIATIONS

GARMENT OVERVIEWS

An overview of each type of garment showcases the classic garments and all the possible variations you can make with the patterns provided. Use these to see the full range of options available as you plan your next project.

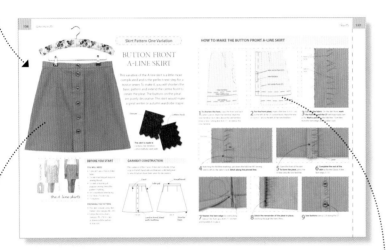

VARIATION PAGES

At least one possible variation is suggested for each classic pattern, along with alternative fabric choices. Variations begin with pattern alterations. Detailed step-by-step instructions then guide you through sewing the garment.

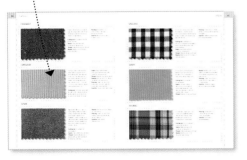

FABRICS

A beautiful gallery showcases more than 30 dressmaking fabrics and explains the uses of each. Use it to find more information on the suggested fabrics for your garment or to find inspiration for future projects.

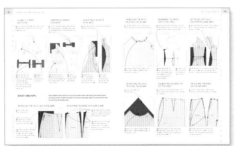

PATTERN ALTERATION

A chapter on pattern alterations teaches you to customize patterns to fit your body shape – for example, shortening arms or lengthening a top. These techniques can be used with the patterns in this book or with commercial patterns.

OTHER USEFUL SECTIONS

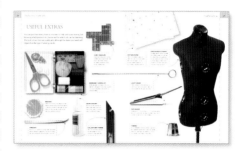

ESSENTIAL TOOLS

All the essential tools and materials you may need are contained in a gallery at the beginning of the book. Full-colour photographs and clear text explain the uses of each.

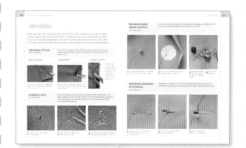

MENDING AND REPAIRS

This section contains all the skills you need to repair worn items. Here you will learn the essentials, such as how to mend tears, darn holes, and replace lost buttons.

CUSTOMIZING

Get inspiration on how to update and personalize your existing pieces in a section on customizing. Six complete projects teach you how to breathe new life into old garments.

TOOLS & MATERIALS

Good-quality basics are essential for successful dressmaking. Scissors, pins, needles and thread are essentials, as is a sewing machine. This section shows the features of your machine and the tools, materials, and extras needed for your project.

BASIC SEWING KIT

A well-equipped sewing kit will include all of the items shown below and many more, depending on the type of sewing that you do regularly. It is important to use a suitable container to keep your tools together, so that they will be readily to hand and to keep them tidy.

TAPE MEASURE
Essential, not only to take body measurements, but also to help measure fabric, seams, etc. Choose one that gives both metric and imperial. A tape made of plastic is best as it will not stretch. See p.18.

SEWING GAUGE
A handy gadget for small measurements. The slide can be set to measure hem depths, buttonhole diameters, and much more. See p.18.

NEEDLES
A good selection of different types of needles for sewing by hand. They will enable you to tackle any hand-sewing project. See p.14.

BUTTONHOLE CHISEL
An exceedingly sharp mini-chisel that gives a clean cut through machine buttonholes. Place a chopping board underneath when using this tool, or you might damage the blade. See p.21.

SAFETY PINS
In a variety of sizes. Useful for emergency repairs as well as threading elastics. See p.15.

CUTTING SHEARS
Required for cutting fabric. When buying, select a pair that feels comfortable in your hand and that is not too heavy. See p.20.

PIN CUSHION
To keep your needles and pins safe and clean. Choose one that has a fabric cover and is firm. See p.15.

ZIPS
It is always a good idea to keep a couple of zips in your sewing kit. Black, cream, and navy are the most useful colours. See pp.119–122.

HABERDASHERY
All the odds and ends a sewer needs, including everything from buttons and snaps to trimmings and elastic. A selection of buttons and snaps in your basic kit is useful for a quick repair. See pp.22–23.

SEAM RIPPER
Also called a stitch ripper, to remove any stitches that have been sewn in the wrong place. Various sizes of seam rippers are available. Keep the cover on when not in use to protect the sharp point. See p.21.

THIMBLE
This is useful to protect the end of your finger when hand sewing. Thimbles are available in various shapes and sizes. See p.25.

PINS
Needed by every sewer to hold the fabric together prior to sewing it permanently. There are different types of pins for different types of work. See p.15.

EMBROIDERY SCISSORS
Small pair of scissors with very sharp points, to clip threads close to the fabric. See p.20.

THREADS
A selection of threads for hand sewing and machine/overlocker sewing in a variety of colours. Some threads are made of polyester, while others are cotton or rayon. See pp.16–17.

BUILD UP YOUR SEWING KIT

CUTTING TOOLS pp.20–21

- Bent-handled shears
- Paper scissors
- Pinking shears
- Snips
- Trimming scissors
- Seam ripper
- Buttonhole chisel
- Cutting shears
- Embroidery scissors

MEASURING TOOLS p.18

- Flexible ruler
- Other tape measures

MARKING AIDS p.19

- Chalk pencil
- Chalk propelling pencil
- Drafting ruler
- Tailor's chalk
- Tracing wheel and carbon paper
- Water/air-soluble pen

USEFUL EXTRAS pp.24–25

- 14-in-1 measure
- Beeswax
- Collar point turner
- Dressmaker's dummy
- Liquid sealant
- Emergency sewing kit
- Loop turner
- Pattern paper
- Tape maker
- Tweezers

NEEDLE THREADERS p.14

- Wire needle threader
- Automatic needle threader

PRESSING AIDS pp.32–33

- Clapper
- Iron
- Ironing board
- Pressing cloth
- Pressing mitten
- Seam roll
- Tailor's ham
- Velvet mat

NEEDLES AND PINS

Using the correct pin or needle for your work is extremely important, as the wrong choice can damage fabric or leave small holes. Needles are made from steel and pins from steel or occasionally brass. Look after them by keeping pins in a pin cushion and needles in a needle case – if kept together in a small container they could become scratched and blunt.

NEEDLES AND THREADERS

Needles are available for all types of fabrics and projects. Keep a good selection of needles at hand at all times, whether it be for emergency mending of tears, or sewing on buttons, or adding trimmings to special-occasion wear. With a special needle threader, inserting the thread through the eye of the needle is simplicity itself.

SHARPS A general-purpose hand-sewing needle, with a small, round eye. Available in sizes 1 to 12. For most hand sewing use a size 6 to 9.

CREWEL Also known as an embroidery needle, a long needle with a long, oval eye that is designed to take multiple strands of embroidery thread.

MILLINER'S OR STRAW A very long, thin needle with a small, round eye. Good for hand sewing and tacking as it doesn't damage fabric. A size 8 or 9 is most popular.

BETWEENS OR QUILTING Similar to a milliner's needle but very short, with a small, round eye. Perfect for fine hand stitches and favoured by quilters.

BEADING Long and exceedingly fine, to sew beads and sequins to fabric. As it is prone to bending, keep it wrapped in tissue when not in use.

DARNER'S A long, thick needle that is designed to be used with wool or thick yarns and to sew through multiple layers.

TAPESTRY A medium-length, thick needle with a blunt end and a long eye. For use with wool yarn in tapestry. Also for darning in overlock threads.

CHENILLE This looks like a tapestry needle but it has a sharp point. Use with thick yarns or wool yarns for darning or heavy embroidery.

BODKIN A strange-looking needle with a blunt end and a large, fat eye. Use to thread elastic or cord. There are larger eyes for thicker yarns.

SELF-THREADING NEEDLE A needle that has a double eye. The thread is placed in the upper eye through the gap, then pulled into the eye below for sewing.

WIRE NEEDLE THREADER
A handy gadget, especially useful for needles with small eyes. Also helpful in threading sewing-machine needles.

AUTOMATIC NEEDLE THREADER
This threader is operated with a small lever. The needle, eye down, is inserted and the thread is wrapped around.

PINS

There is a wide variety of pins available, in differing lengths and thicknesses, and ranging from plain household pins to those with coloured balls or flower shapes on their ends.

HOUSEHOLD
General-purpose pins of a medium length and thickness. Can be used for all types of sewing.

FLOWERHEAD
A long pin of medium thickness with a flat, flower-shaped head. It is designed to be pressed over, as the head lies flat on the fabric.

PEARL-HEADED
Longer than household pins, with a coloured pearl head. They are easy to pick up and use.

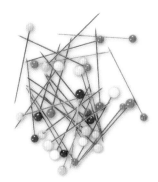

GLASS-HEADED
Similar to pearl-headed pins but shorter. They have the advantage that they can be pressed over without melting.

DRESSMAKER'S
Similar to a household pin in shape and thickness, but slightly longer. These are the pins for beginners to choose.

EXTRA FINE
Extra long and extra fine, this pin is favoured by many professional dressmakers because it is easy to use and doesn't damage finer fabrics.

SAFETY PINS
Available in a huge variety of sizes and made either of brass or stainless steel. Used for holding two or more layers together.

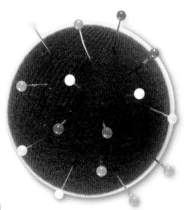

PIN CUSHION
To keep pins clean and sharp. Choose a fabric cover: a foam cushion may blunt pins.

THREADS

There are so many threads available that knowing which ones to choose can be confusing. There are specialist threads designed for special tasks, such as machine embroidery or decorative stitching. Threads also vary in fibre content, from pure cotton to rayon to polyester. Some threads are very fine while others are thick and coarse. Failure to choose the correct thread can spoil your project and lead to problems with the stitch quality of the sewing machine or overlocker.

COTTON THREAD

A 100% cotton thread. Smooth and firm, this is designed to be used with cotton fabrics.

POLYESTER ALL-PURPOSE THREAD

A good-quality polyester thread that has a very slight "give", making it suitable for sewing all types of fabrics and garments. It is the most popular type of thread.

SILK THREAD

A sewing thread made from 100% silk. Used for machining delicate silk garments. Because it can be removed without leaving an imprint, it is also used for tacking or temporary stitching in areas that are to be pressed, such as jacket collars.

ELASTIC THREAD

A thin, round elastic thread normally used on the bobbin of the sewing machine for stretch effects such as shirring.

EMBROIDERY THREAD

Machine embroidery thread is a finer embroidery thread that is usually made from rayon or cotton. Also available on larger reels for economy.

VARIEGATED MACHINE EMBROIDERY THREAD

COTTON MACHINE EMBROIDERY THREAD

LARGE SPOOL OF RAYON EMBROIDERY THREAD

RAYON MACHINE EMBROIDERY THREAD

OVERLOCKER THREAD

A dull yarn on a larger reel designed to be used on the overlocker. This type of yarn is normally not strong enough to use on the sewing machine.

TOP-STITCHING THREAD

A thicker polyester thread used for decorative top-stitching and buttonholes. Also for hand sewing buttons on thicker fabrics.

MEASURING AND MARKING TOOLS

A huge range of tools enables a sewer to measure accurately. Choosing the correct tool for the task in hand is important, so that your measurements are precise. After measuring, the next step is to mark your work using the appropriate marking technique or tool.

MEASURING TOOLS

There are many tools available to help you measure everything from the width of a seam or hem to body dimensions. One of the most basic yet invaluable measuring tools is the tape measure. Be sure to keep yours in good condition – once it stretches or gets snipped on the edges, it will no longer be accurate and should be replaced.

RETRACTABLE TAPE
Very useful to have in your handbag when shopping as you never know when you may need to measure something!

SEWING GAUGE
A handy small tool about 15cm (6in) long, marked in centimetres and inches, with a sliding tab. Use as an accurate measure for small measurements such as hems.

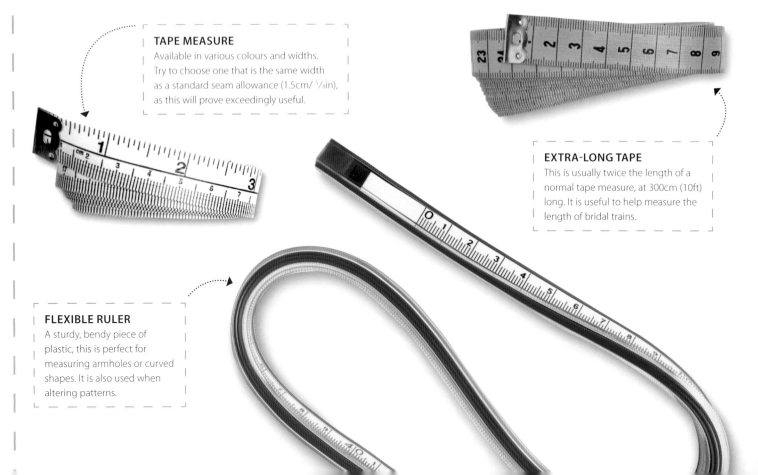

TAPE MEASURE
Available in various colours and widths. Try to choose one that is the same width as a standard seam allowance (1.5cm/ ⅝in), as this will prove exceedingly useful.

EXTRA-LONG TAPE
This is usually twice the length of a normal tape measure, at 300cm (10ft) long. It is useful to help measure the length of bridal trains.

FLEXIBLE RULER
A sturdy, bendy piece of plastic, this is perfect for measuring armholes or curved shapes. It is also used when altering patterns.

MARKING AIDS

Marking certain parts of your work is essential, to make sure that elements such as pockets and darts are placed correctly and seamlines are straight as drawn on the pattern. With some marking tools, such as pens and a tracing wheel and carbon paper, it is always a good idea to test on a scrap of fabric first to make sure that the mark made will not be permanent.

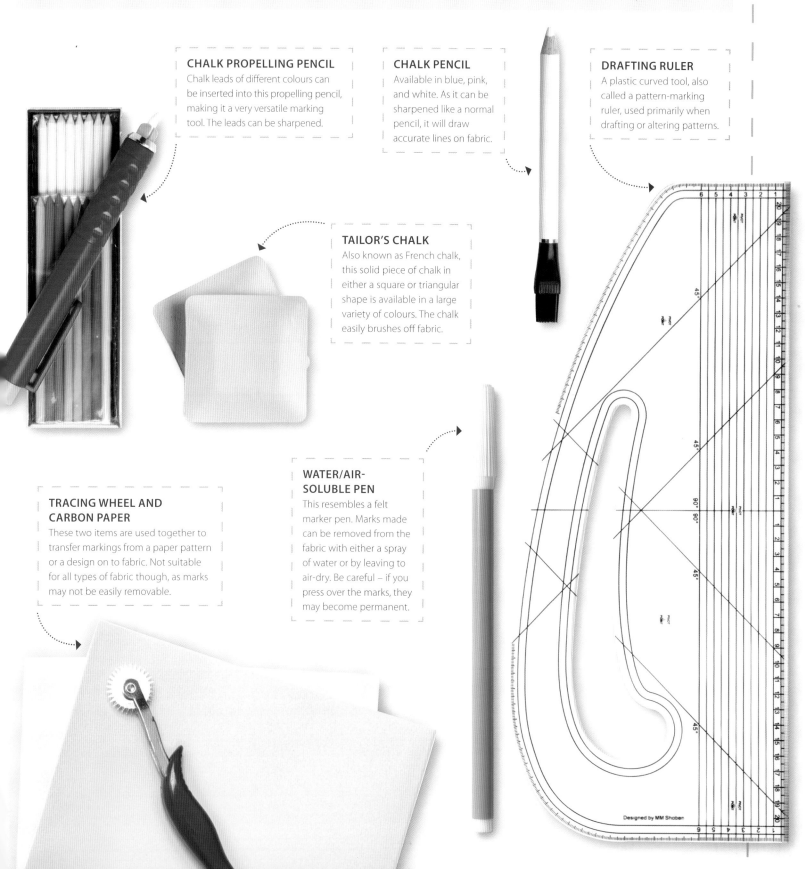

CHALK PROPELLING PENCIL
Chalk leads of different colours can be inserted into this propelling pencil, making it a very versatile marking tool. The leads can be sharpened.

CHALK PENCIL
Available in blue, pink, and white. As it can be sharpened like a normal pencil, it will draw accurate lines on fabric.

DRAFTING RULER
A plastic curved tool, also called a pattern-marking ruler, used primarily when drafting or altering patterns.

TAILOR'S CHALK
Also known as French chalk, this solid piece of chalk in either a square or triangular shape is available in a large variety of colours. The chalk easily brushes off fabric.

TRACING WHEEL AND CARBON PAPER
These two items are used together to transfer markings from a paper pattern or a design on to fabric. Not suitable for all types of fabric though, as marks may not be easily removable.

WATER/AIR-SOLUBLE PEN
This resembles a felt marker pen. Marks made can be removed from the fabric with either a spray of water or by leaving to air-dry. Be careful – if you press over the marks, they may become permanent.

Designed by MM Shoben

CUTTING TOOLS

There are many types of cutting tools, but one rule applies to all: buy good-quality products that can be re-sharpened. When choosing cutting shears, make sure that they fit the span of your hand so that you can comfortably open the whole of the blade with one action. This is very important to allow clean and accurate cutting lines. Shears and scissors of various types are not the only cutting tools required – everyone will at some time need a seam ripper to remove misplaced stitches or to unpick seams for mending.

CUTTING SHEARS
The most popular type of shear, used for cutting large pieces of fabric. The length of the blade can vary from 20 to 30cm (8 to 12in) in length.

SNIPS
A very useful, small, spring-loaded tool that easily cuts the ends of thread. Not suitable for fabrics.

TRIMMING SCISSORS
These scissors have a 10cm (4in) blade and are used to trim away surplus fabric and neaten ends of machining.

EMBROIDERY SCISSORS
A small and very sharp scissor used to get into corners and clip threads close to the fabric.

SEAM RIPPER
A sharp, pointed hook to slide under a stitch, with a small cutting blade at the base to cut the thread. Various sizes of seam ripper are available, to cut through light to heavyweight fabric seams.

BUTTONHOLE CHISEL
A smaller version of a carpenter's chisel, to cut cleanly and accurately through buttonholes. As this is very sharp, use it with a chopping board underneath.

PINKING SHEARS
Similar in size to cutting shears but with a blade that cuts with a zigzag pattern. Used for neatening seams and decorative edges.

PAPER SCISSORS
Use these to cut around pattern pieces – cutting paper will dull the blades of fabric scissors and shears.

BENT-HANDLED SHEARS
This type of blade has an angle between the blade and the handle, which enables the shears to sit flat on the table when cutting out. Popular for cutting long, straight edges.

HABERDASHERY ITEMS

The term haberdashery covers all of the bits and pieces that a sewer will need, for example fasteners such as buttons, snaps, hooks and eyes, and Velcro™. But haberdashery also includes elastics, ribbons, trimmings of all types, and boning.

BUTTONS

Buttons can be made from almost anything – shell, bone, coconut, nylon, plastic, brass, silver. They can be any shape, from geometric to abstract to animal shapes. A button may have a shank or have holes on the surface to enable it to be attached to fabric.

OTHER FASTENERS

Hooks and eyes , snaps, and Velcro™ all come in a wide variety of forms, differing in size, shape, and colour. Some hooks and eyes are designed to be seen, while snaps and Velcro™ are intended to be hidden fasteners.

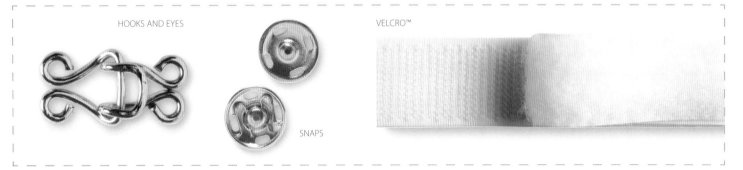

HOOKS AND EYES

VELCRO™

SNAPS

TRIMMINGS, DECORATIONS, FRINGES, AND BRAIDS

Decorative finishing touches – fringes, strips of sequins, ric-rac braids, feathers, pearls, bows, flowers, and beads – can embellish or personalize a garment. Some are designed to be inserted into seams while others are surface-mounted.

RIC-RAC TRIM

RIBBON TRIM

BEADED FRINGE

RIBBONS

From the narrowest strips to wide swathes, ribbons are made from a variety of yarns, such as nylon, polyester, and cotton. They can be printed or plain and may feature metallic threads or wired edges.

ELASTIC

Elastic is available in many forms, from very narrow, round cord elastic to wide strips. The elastic may have buttonhole slots in it or even a decorative edge.

WIDE ELASTIC

NARROW ELASTIC

BUTTONHOLE ELASTIC

BONING

Boning comes in various types and in varying widths. You can sew through polyester boning, used in boned bodices, while nylon boning, also used in boned bodices, has to be inserted into a casing. Specialist metal bones, which may be either spiral or straight, are for corsets and bridal wear.

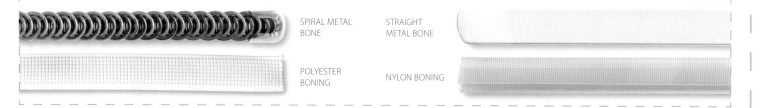

SPIRAL METAL BONE

STRAIGHT METAL BONE

POLYESTER BONING

NYLON BONING

USEFUL EXTRAS

You can purchase many more accessories to help with your sewing, but knowing which products to choose and for which job can be daunting. The tools shown here are useful aids, although the items you need will depend on the type of sewing you do.

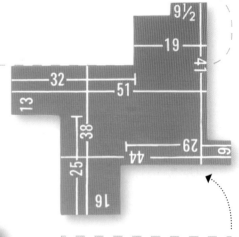

14-IN-1 MEASURE
A strange-looking tool that has 14 different measurements on it. Use to turn hems or edges accurately. Available in both metric and imperial.

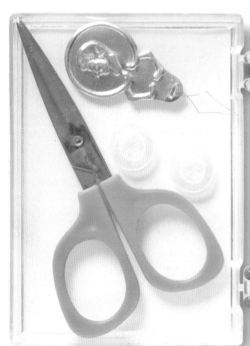

EMERGENCY SEWING KIT
All the absolute essentials to fix loose buttons or dropped hems while away from your sewing machine. Take it with you when travelling.

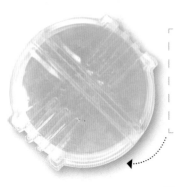

BEESWAX
When hand sewing, this will prevent the thread from tangling, and will strengthen it. First draw the thread through the wax, then press the wax into the thread by running your fingers along it.

LIQUID SEALANT
Used to seal the cut edge of ribbons and trims to prevent fraying. Also useful to seal the ends of overlock stitching.

TWEEZERS
These can be used for removing stubborn tacking stitches that are caught in the machine stitching. Also an essential aid to threading the overlocker.

COLLAR POINT TURNER
This is excellent for pushing out those hard-to-reach corners in collars and cuffs.

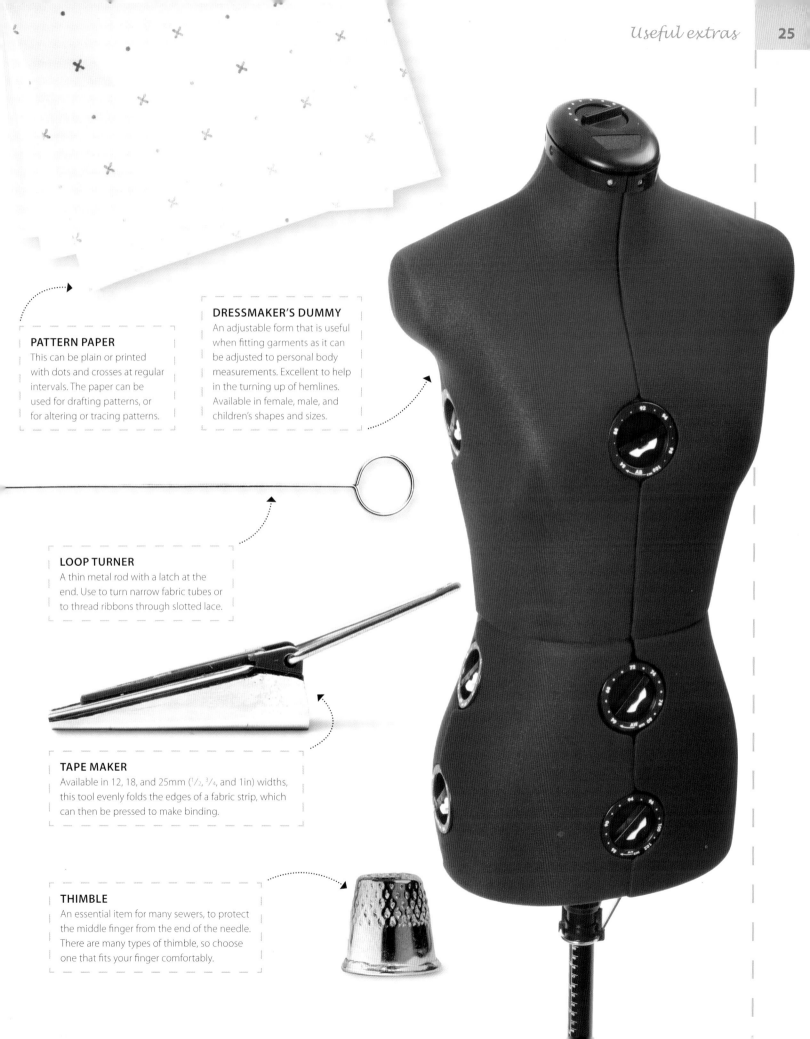

PATTERN PAPER
This can be plain or printed with dots and crosses at regular intervals. The paper can be used for drafting patterns, or for altering or tracing patterns.

DRESSMAKER'S DUMMY
An adjustable form that is useful when fitting garments as it can be adjusted to personal body measurements. Excellent to help in the turning up of hemlines. Available in female, male, and children's shapes and sizes.

LOOP TURNER
A thin metal rod with a latch at the end. Use to turn narrow fabric tubes or to thread ribbons through slotted lace.

TAPE MAKER
Available in 12, 18, and 25mm (1/2, 3/4, and 1in) widths, this tool evenly folds the edges of a fabric strip, which can then be pressed to make binding.

THIMBLE
An essential item for many sewers, to protect the middle finger from the end of the needle. There are many types of thimble, so choose one that fits your finger comfortably.

SEWING MACHINE

A sewing machine will quickly speed up any job, whether it be a quick repair or making a dress for a special occasion. Most sewing machines today are aided by computer technology, which enhances stitch quality and ease of use. Always spend time trying out a sewing machine before you buy, to really get a feel for it.

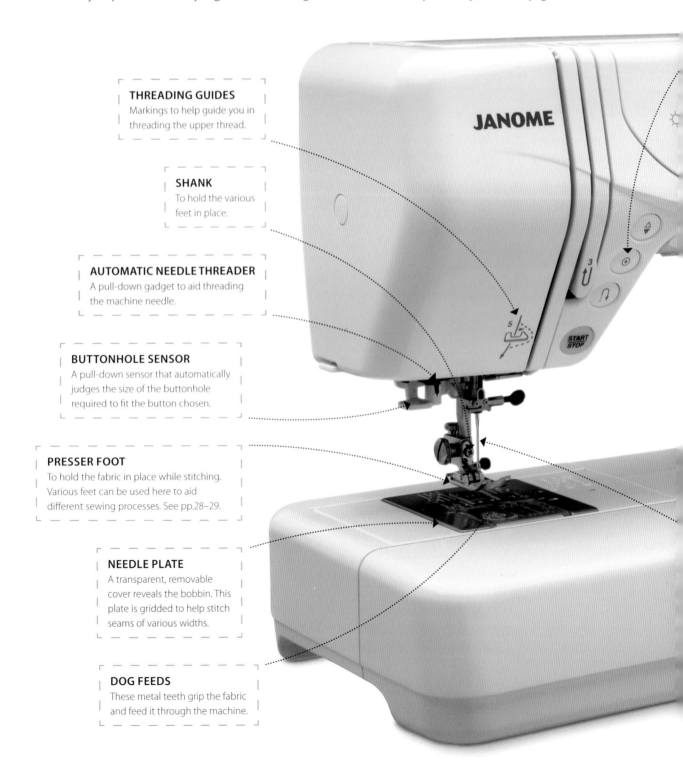

THREADING GUIDES
Markings to help guide you in threading the upper thread.

SHANK
To hold the various feet in place.

AUTOMATIC NEEDLE THREADER
A pull-down gadget to aid threading the machine needle.

BUTTONHOLE SENSOR
A pull-down sensor that automatically judges the size of the buttonhole required to fit the button chosen.

PRESSER FOOT
To hold the fabric in place while stitching. Various feet can be used here to aid different sewing processes. See pp.28–29.

NEEDLE PLATE
A transparent, removable cover reveals the bobbin. This plate is gridded to help stitch seams of various widths.

DOG FEEDS
These metal teeth grip the fabric and feed it through the machine.

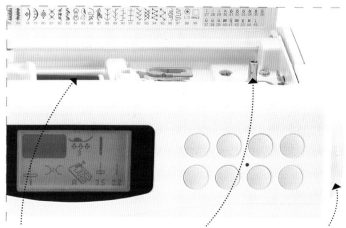

BUTTONS
To provide various functions, such as reverse, locking stitch, and needle-in.

LCD SCREEN
An illuminated screen that displays information such as needle position and stitch type.

SPOOL HOLDER
To hold your sewing thread in place.

BOBBIN WINDER
Winds the thread from the spool on to the bobbin, keeping it under tension. See p.28.

BALANCE WHEEL
This can be turned towards you to move the needle up or down manually.

STITCH SIZE
Used to increase and decrease length and width of stitch.

TOUCH BUTTONS
These quickly select the most popular stitches such as zigzag and buttonhole.

STITCH LIBRARY
All the different stitches this machine can stitch. You just have to key in the number.

SPEED CONTROL
A slide, to control the speed of your machine.

REMOVABLE FREE ARM
This section of the machine will pull away to give a narrow work bed that can be used when inserting sleeves. It also contains a useful storage section.

NEEDLE
The machine needle. Replace it regularly to ensure good stitch quality. See p.28.

SEWING-MACHINE ACCESSORIES

You can purchase a variety of accessories for your sewing machine to make certain sewing processes much easier. There are different machine needles not only for different fabrics but also for different types of threads. There is also a huge number of sewing-machine feet, and new feet are constantly coming on to the market. Those shown here are some of the most popular.

PLASTIC BOBBIN
The bobbin is for the lower thread. Some machines take plastic bobbins, others metal. Always check which sort of bobbin your machine uses as the incorrect choice can cause stitch problems.

METAL BOBBIN
Also known as a universal bobbin, this is used with many types of sewing machines. Be sure to check that your machine requires a metal bobbin before you buy.

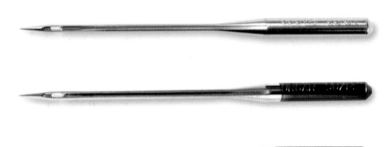

MACHINE NEEDLES
There are different types of sewing machine needles to cope with different fabrics. Machine needles are sized from 60 to 100, a 60 being a very fine needle. There are special needles for machine embroidery and also for metallic threads.

OVEREDGE FOOT
A foot that runs along the raw edge of the fabric and holds it stable while an overedge stitch is worked.

EMBROIDERY FOOT
A clear plastic foot with a groove underneath that allows linear machine embroidery stitches to pass under.

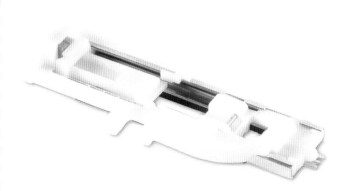

BUTTONHOLE FOOT

This extends so the button can be placed in the back of the foot. The machine will stitch a buttonhole to fit thanks to the buttonhole sensor.

BLIND HEM FOOT

Use this foot in conjunction with the blind hem stitch to create a neat hemming stitch.

WALKING FOOT

This strange-looking foot "walks" across the fabric, so that the upper layer of fabric does not push forward. Great for matching checks and stripes and also for stitching difficult fabrics.

ZIP FOOT

This foot fits to either the right- or left-hand side of the needle to enable you to stitch close to a zip.

CONCEALED ZIP FOOT

A foot that is used to insert a concealed zip – the foot holds the coils of the zip open, enabling you to stitch behind them.

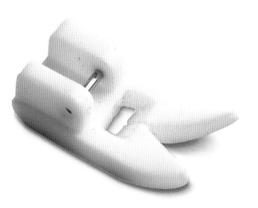

ULTRA-GLIDE FOOT

A foot made from Teflon™ that glides over the fabric. Useful for synthetic leathers.

OVERLOCKER

This machine is often used in conjunction with the sewing machine as it gives a very professional finish to your work. The overlocker has two upper threads and two lower threads (the loopers), with integral knives that remove the edge of the fabric. Used extensively for neatening the edges of fabric, the overlocker can also be used for construction of stretch knits.

OVERLOCKER ACCESSORIES

You can purchase additional feet for the overlocker. Some will speed up your sewing by performing tasks such as gathering.

OVERLOCKER NEEDLES
The overlocker uses a ballpoint needle, which creates a large loop in the thread for the loopers to catch and produce a stitch. If a normal sewing machine needle is used it could damage the overlocker.

OVERLOCKER FOOT
The standard foot used for most processes. Other feet are available for gathering and cording.

OVERLOCKER STITCHES

As the overlocker works, the threads wrap around the edge to give a professional finish. The 3-thread stitch is used primarily for neatening. A 4-thread stitch can also be used for neatening, but its fourth thread makes it ideal for constructing a seam on stretch knits.

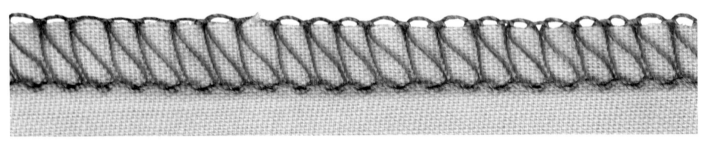

3-THREAD OVERLOCK STITCH

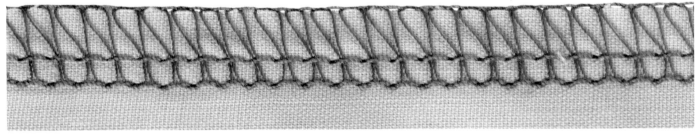

4-THREAD OVERLOCK STITCH

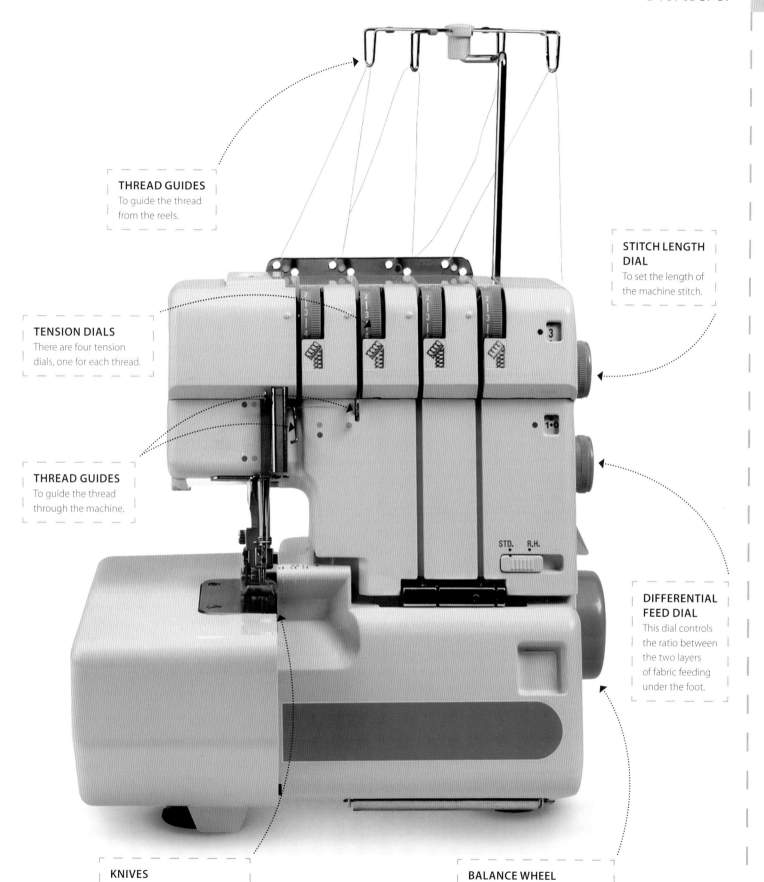

THREAD GUIDES
To guide the thread from the reels.

STITCH LENGTH DIAL
To set the length of the machine stitch.

TENSION DIALS
There are four tension dials, one for each thread.

THREAD GUIDES
To guide the thread through the machine.

DIFFERENTIAL FEED DIAL
This dial controls the ratio between the two layers of fabric feeding under the foot.

KNIVES
Two knives inside the machine cut away the fabric edge.

BALANCE WHEEL
This can be turned manually backwards to disengage a stitch.

PRESSING AIDS

Successful sewing relies on successful pressing. Without the correct pressing equipment, sewing can look too "home-made", whereas if correctly pressed, any sewn item will have a neat, professional finish.

CLAPPER
A wooden aid that pounds creases into a heavy fabric after steaming. The top section is used to help press collar seams and points.

SEAM ROLL
This tubular pressing aid is used to press seams open on fabrics that mark, as the iron only touches the seam on top of the roll. Also used for sleeve and trouser seams.

PRESSING CLOTH
Choose a cloth made from silk organza or muslin as you can see through it. The cloth stops the iron marking the fabric and prevents burning delicate fabrics.

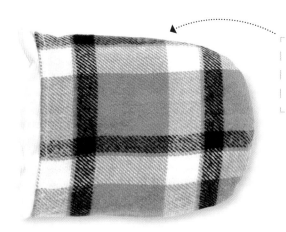

PRESSING MITTEN
Slips on to your hand to give more control over where you are pressing.

VELVET MAT
A pressing mat with a tufted side to aid the pressing of pile fabrics, such as velvet.

IRON
A good-quality steam iron is a wonderful asset. Choose a reasonably heavy iron that has steam and a shot of steam facility.

IRONING BOARD
Essential to iron on. Make sure the board is height-adjustable.

TAILOR'S HAM
A ham-shaped pressing cushion that is used to press darts and press the shape into collar and shoulder curves. Also used in making tailored garments.

FABRICS

Choosing the correct fabric for your dressmaking project is vital. Considerations to bear in mind include the suitability of the fabric for the particular project, whether or not the fabric will need lining, and how easy it will be to care for once it has been made up.

WOOL

A natural fibre, wool comes primarily from sheep – Australian merino sheep's wool is considered to be the best. However, we also get wool fibres from goats (mohair and cashmere), rabbits (angora), camels (camel hair), and llamas (alpaca). A wool fibre is either short and fluffy, when it is known as a woollen yarn, or it is long, strong, and smooth, when it is called worsted. The term virgin (or new) wool denotes wool fibres that are being used for the first time. Wool may be reprocessed or reused and is then often mixed with other fibres.

PROPERTIES OF WOOL

- **Comfortable to wear** in all climates as it is available in many weights and weaves
- **Warm in the winter** and cool in the summer, because it will breathe with your body
- **Absorbs moisture** better than other natural fibres – will absorb up to 30 per cent of its weight before it feels wet
- **Flame-resistant**

- **Relatively** crease-resistant
- **Ideal to tailor** as it can be easily shaped with steam
- **Often blended** with other fibres to reduce the cost of a fabric
- **Felts** if exposed to excessive heat, moisture, and pressure
- **Will be bleached** by sunlight with prolonged exposure
- **Can be damaged** by moths

CASHMERE

Wool from the Kashmir goat, and the most luxurious of all the wools. A soft yet hard-wearing fabric available in different weights.

Cutting out: As cashmere often has a slight pile, use a nap layout
Seams: Plain, neatened with overlocker stitch or pinking shears (a zigzag stitch would curl the edge of the seam)
Thread: A silk thread is ideal, or a polyester all-purpose thread

Needle: Machine size 12/14, depending on the thickness of the fabric; sharps for hand sewing
Pressing: Steam iron on a steam setting, with a pressing cloth and seam roll
Used for: Jackets, coats, men's wear; knitted cashmere yarn for sweaters, cardigans, underwear

CREPE

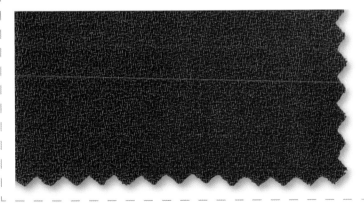

A soft fabric made from a twisted yarn that produces an uneven surface. Crepe will have stretched on the bolt and is prone to shrinkage so it is important to preshrink it by steaming prior to use.

Cutting out: A nap layout is not required
Seams: Plain, neatened with overlocker stitch (a zigzag stitch may curl the edge of the seam)

Thread: Polyester all-purpose thread
Needle: Machine size 12; sharps or milliner's for hand sewing
Pressing: Steam iron on a wool setting; a pressing cloth is not always required
Used for: All types of clothing

COTTON

One of the most versatile and popular of all fabrics, cotton is a natural fibre that comes from the seed pods, or bolls, of the cotton plant. It is thought that cotton fibres have been in use since ancient times. Today, the world's biggest producers of cotton include the United States, India, and countries in the Middle East. Cotton fibres can be filament or staple, with the longest and finest used for top-quality bed linen. Cotton clothing is widely worn in warmer climates as the fabric will keep you cool.

PROPERTIES OF COTTON

- **Absorbs moisture well** and carries heat away from the body
- **Stronger wet** than dry
- **Does not build up** static electricity
- **Dyes** well

- **Prone to shrinkage** unless it has been treated
- **Will deteriorate** from mildew and prolonged exposure to sunlight
- **Creases** easily
- **Soils easily**, but launders well

BRODERIE ANGLAISE

A fine, plain-weave cotton that has been embroidered in such a way as to make small holes.

Cutting out: May need layout to place embroidery at hem edge
Seams: Plain, neatened with overlocker or zigzag stitch; a French seam can also be used
Thread: Polyester all-purpose thread
Needle: Machine size 12/14; sharps for hand sewing

Pressing: Steam iron on a cotton setting; a pressing cloth is not required
Used for: Baby clothes, summer skirts, blouses

CALICO

A plain-weave fabric that is usually unbleached and quite firm. Available in many different weights, from very fine to extremely heavy.

Cutting out: A nap layout is not required
Seams: Plain, neatened with overlocker or zigzag stitch
Thread: Polyester all-purpose thread
Needle: Machine size 11/14, depending on thickness of thread; sharps for hand sewing

Pressing: Steam iron on a steam setting; a pressing cloth is not required
Used for: Toiles (test garments), soft furnishings

CHAMBRAY

A light cotton that has a coloured warp thread and white weft thread. Chambray can also be found as a check or a striped fabric.

Cutting out: A nap layout should not be required
Seams: Plain, neatened with overlocker or zigzag stitch
Thread: Polyester all-purpose thread
Needle: Machine size 11; sharps for hand sewing

Pressing: Steam iron on a cotton setting; a pressing cloth is not required
Used for: Blouses, men's shirts, children's wear

CORDUROY

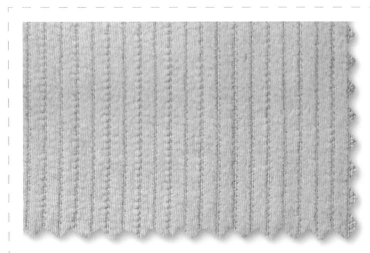

A soft pile fabric with distinctive stripes (known as wales or ribs) woven into it. The name depends on the size of the ribs: baby or pin cord has extremely fine ribs; needle cord has slightly thicker ribs; corduroy has 10–12 ribs per 2.5cm (1in); and elephant or jumbo cord has thick, heavy ribs.

Cutting out: Use a nap layout with the pile on the corduroy brushing up the pattern pieces from hem to neck, to give depth of colour

Seams: Plain, stitched using a walking foot and neatened with overlocker or zigzag stitch
Thread: Polyester all-purpose thread
Needle: Machine size 12/16; sharps or milliner's for hand sewing
Pressing: Steam iron on a cotton setting; use a seam roll under the seams with a pressing cloth
Used for: Trousers, skirts, men's wear

DENIM

Named after Nîmes in France. A hard-wearing, twill-weave fabric with a coloured warp and white weft, usually made into jeans. Available in various weights and often mixed with an elastic thread for stretch. Denim is usually blue, but is also available in a variety of other colours.

Cutting out: A nap layout is not required
Seams: Run and fell or top-stitched
Thread: Polyester all-purpose thread with top-stitching thread for detail top-stitching

Needle: Machine size 14/16; sharps for hand sewing
Pressing: Steam iron on a cotton setting; a pressing cloth should not be required
Used for: Jeans, jackets, children's wear

GINGHAM

A fresh, two-colour cotton fabric that features a check of various sizes. A plain weave made by having groups of white and coloured warp and weft threads.

Cutting out: Usually an even check, so nap layout is not required but recommended; pattern will need matching
Seams: Plain, neatened with overlocker or zigzag stitch
Thread: Polyester all-purpose thread
Needle: Machine size 11/12; sharps for hand sewing

Pressing: Steam iron on a cotton setting; a pressing cloth should not be required
Used for: Children's wear, dresses, shirts, home furnishings

JERSEY

A fine cotton yarn that has been knitted to give stretch, making the fabric very comfortable to wear. Jersey will also drape well.

Cutting out: A nap layout is recommended
Seams: 4-thread overlock stitch; or plain seam stitched with a small zigzag stitch and then seam allowances stitched together with a zigzag
Thread: Polyester all-purpose thread

Needle: Machine size 12/14; a ballpoint needle may be required for overlocker and a milliner's for hand sewing
Pressing: Steam iron on a wool setting as jersey may shrink on a cotton setting
Used for: Underwear, drapey dresses, leisurewear, bedding

MADRAS

A check fabric made from a fine cotton yarn, usually from India. Often found in bright colours featuring an uneven check. An inexpensive cotton fabric.

Cutting out: Use a nap layout and match the checks
Seams: Plain, neatened with overlocker or zigzag stitch
Thread: Polyester all-purpose thread
Needle: Machine size 12/14; sharps for hand sewing

Pressing: Steam iron on a cotton setting; a pressing cloth is not required
Used for: Shirts, skirts, home furnishings

MUSLIN

A fine, plain, open-weave cotton. Can be found in colours but usually sold as natural/unbleached or white. Makes great pressing cloths and interlinings. Washing prior to use is recommended.

Cutting out: A nap layout is not required
Seams: 4-thread overlock stitch or plain seam, neatened with overlocker or zigzag stitch; a French seam could also be used
Thread: Polyester all-purpose thread

Needle: Machine size 11; milliner's for hand sewing
Pressing: Steam iron on a cotton setting; a cloth is not required
Used for: Curtaining and other household uses

SHIRTING

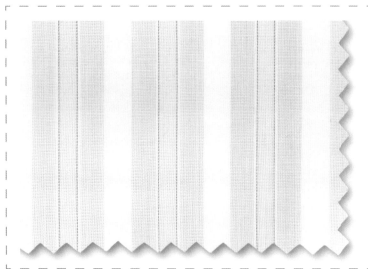

A closely woven, fine cotton with coloured warp and weft yarns making stripes or checks.

Cutting out: Use a nap layout if fabric has uneven stripes
Seams: Plain, neatened with overlocker or zigzag stitch; a run and fell seam can also be used
Thread: Polyester all-purpose thread
Needle: Machine size 12; milliner's for hand sewing

Pressing: Steam iron on a cotton setting; a pressing cloth is not required
Used for: Ladies' and men's shirts

VELVET

A pile-weave fabric, made by using an additional yarn that is then cut to produce the pile. Difficult to handle and can be easily damaged if seams have to be unpicked.

Cutting out: Use a nap layout with the pile brushing up from hem to neck, to give depth of colour
Seams: Plain, stitched using a walking foot (stitch all seams from hem to neck) and neatened with overlocker or zigzag stitch

Thread: Polyester all-purpose thread
Needle: Machine size 14; milliner's for hand sewing
Pressing: Only if you have to; use a velvet board, a little steam, the toe of the iron, and a silk organza cloth
Used for: Jackets, coats

SILK

Often referred to as the queen of fabrics, silk is made from the fibres of the silkworm's cocoon. This strong and luxurious fabric dates back thousands of years to its first development in China, and the secret of silk production was well protected by the Chinese until 300AD. Silk fabrics can be very fine or thick and chunky. They need careful handling as some can be easily damaged.

PROPERTIES OF SILK

- **Keeps you warm** in winter and cool in summer
- **Absorbs moisture** and dries quickly
- **Dyes well**, producing deep, rich colours
- **Static electricity** can build up and fabric may cling
- **Will fade** in prolonged strong sunlight
- **Prone to** shrinkage
- **Best** dry-cleaned
- **Weaker when wet** than dry
- **May** water-mark

CHIFFON

A very strong and very fine, transparent silk with a plain weave. Will gather and ruffle well. Difficult to handle.

Cutting out: Place tissue paper under the fabric and pin the fabric to the tissue, cutting through all layers if necessary; use extra-fine pins
Seams: French
Thread: Polyester all-purpose thread

Needle: Machine size 9/11; fine milliner's for hand sewing
Pressing: Dry iron on a wool setting
Used for: Special-occasion wear, over-blouses

DUCHESSE SATIN

A heavy, expensive satin fabric used almost exclusively for special-occasion wear.

Cutting out: Use a nap layout
Seams: Plain, with pinked edges
Thread: Polyester all-purpose thread
Needle: Machine size 12/14; milliner's for hand sewing
Pressing: Steam iron on a wool setting with a pressing cloth; use a seam roll under the seams to prevent shadowing
Used for: Special-occasion wear

DUPION

Woven using a textured yarn that produces irregularities in the weave.

Cutting out: Use a nap layout to prevent shadowing
Seams: Plain, neatened with overlocker or zigzag stitch
Thread: Polyester all-purpose thread
Needle: Machine size 12; milliner's for hand sewing

Pressing: Steam iron on a wool setting with a pressing cloth as fabric may water-mark
Used for: Dresses, skirts, jackets, special-occasion wear, soft furnishings

HABUTAI

Originally from Japan, a smooth, fine silk that can have a plain or a twill weave. Fabric is often used for silk painting.

Cutting out: A nap layout is not required
Seams: French
Thread: Polyester all-purpose thread
Needle: Machine size 9/11; very fine milliner's or betweens for hand sewing

Pressing: Steam iron on a wool setting
Used for: Lining, shirts, blouses

MATKA

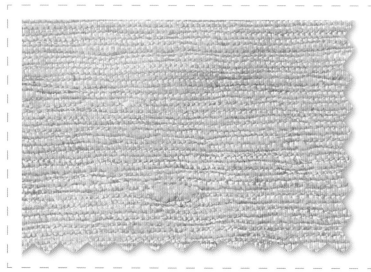

A silk suiting fabric with an uneven-looking yarn. Matka can be mistaken for linen.

Cutting out: Use a nap layout as silk may shadow
Seams: Plain, neatened with overlocker or zigzag stitch or a Hong Kong finish
Thread: Polyester all-purpose thread
Needle: Machine size 12/14; milliner's for hand sewing

Pressing: Steam iron on a wool setting with a pressing cloth; a seam roll is recommended to prevent the seams from showing through
Used for: Dresses, jackets, trousers

ORGANZA

A sheer fabric with a crisp appearance that will crease easily.

Cutting out: A nap layout is not required
Seams: French or use a seam for a difficult fabric
Thread: Polyester all-purpose thread
Needle: Machine size 11; milliner's or betweens for hand sewing
Pressing: Steam iron on a wool setting; a pressing cloth should not be required
Used for: Sheer blouses, shrugs, interlining, interfacing

SATIN

A silk with a satin weave that can be very light to quite heavy in weight.

Cutting out: Use a nap layout in a single layer as fabric is slippery
Seams: French; on thicker satins, use a seam for a difficult fabric
Thread: Polyester all-purpose thread (not silk thread as it becomes weak with wear)
Needle: Machine size 11/12; milliner's or betweens for hand sewing

Pressing: Steam iron on a wool setting with a pressing cloth as fabric may water-mark
Used for: Blouses, dresses, special-occasion wear

TAFFETA

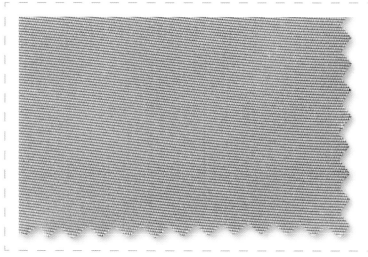

A smooth, plain-weave fabric with a crisp appearance. It makes a rustling sound when worn. Can require special handling and does not wear well.

Cutting out: Use a nap layout, with extra-fine pins in seams to minimize marking the fabric
Seams: Plain; fabric may pucker, so sew from the hem upwards, keeping the fabric taut under the machine; neaten with overlocker or pinking shears

Thread: Polyester all-purpose thread
Needle: Machine size 11; milliner's or betweens for hand sewing
Pressing: Cool iron, with a seam roll under the seams
Used for: Special-occasion wear

LINEN

Linen is a natural fibre that is derived from the stem of the flax plant. It is available in a variety of qualities and weights, from very fine linen to heavy suiting weights. Coarser than cotton, it is sometimes woven with cotton as well as being mixed with silk.

PROPERTIES OF LINEN

- **Cool and comfortable** to wear
- **Absorbs moisture** well
- **Shrinks** when washed
- **Does not** ease well

- **Has a tendency** to crease
- **Prone to** fraying
- **Resists moths** but is damaged by mildew

COTTON AND LINEN MIX

Two fibres may have been mixed together in the yarn or there may be mixed warp and weft yarns. It has lots of texture in the weave.

Cutting out: A nap layout should not be required
Seams: Plain, neatened with overlocker or zigzag stitch
Thread: Polyester all-purpose thread
Needle: Machine size 14; sharps for hand sewing

Pressing: A steam iron on a steam setting with a silk organza pressing cloth
Used for: Summer-weight jackets, tailored dresses

DRESS-WEIGHT LINEN

A medium-weight linen with a plain weave. The yarn is often uneven, which causes slubs in the weave.

Cutting out: A nap layout is not required
Seams: Plain, neatened with overlocker or zigzag stitch or a Hong Kong finish
Thread: Polyester all-purpose thread with a top-stitching thread for top-stitching
Needle: Machine size 14; sharps for hand sewing

Pressing: Steam iron on a cotton setting (steam is required to remove creases)
Used for: Dresses, trousers, skirts

PRINTED LINENS

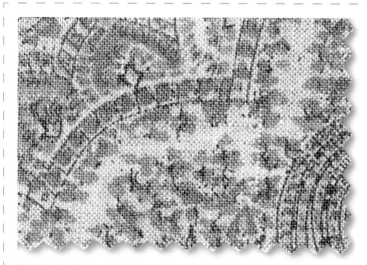

Many linens today feature prints or even embroidery. The fabric may be light to medium weight, with a smooth yarn that has few slubs.

Cutting out: Use a nap layout
Seams: Plain, neatened with overlocker or zigzag stitch
Thread: Polyester all-purpose thread
Needle: Machine size 14; sharps for hand sewing

Pressing: Steam iron on a cotton setting (steam is required to remove creases)
Used for: Dresses, skirts

SUITING LINEN

A heavier yarn is used to produce a linen suitable for suits for men and women. Can be a firm, tight weave or a looser weave.

Cutting out: A nap layout is not required
Seams: Plain, neatened with overlocker or a zigzag stitch
Thread: Polyester all-purpose thread with a top-stitch thread for top-stitching
Needle: Machine size 14; sharps for hand sewing

Pressing: Steam iron on a cotton setting (steam is required to remove creases)
Used for: Men's and women's suits, trousers, coats

FANCY WEAVE LINEN

A linen woven with additional decorative yarns such as metallic or lurex.

Cutting out: A nap layout is not required
Seams: Plain, neatened with overlocker or a zigzag stitch
Thread: Polyester all-purpose thread with a top-stitch thread for top-stitching
Needle: Machine size 14; sharps for hand sewing

Pressing: Press carefully as decorative yarns may melt; use a pressing cloth
Used for: Dresses, jackets

SYNTHETIC FABRICS

The term synthetic applies to any fabric that is not 100 per cent natural. Many of these fabrics have been developed over the last hundred years, which means they are new compared to natural fibres. Some synthetic fabrics are made from natural elements mixed with chemicals, while others are made entirely from non-natural substances. The properties of synthetic fabrics vary from fabric to fabric.

PROPERTIES OF SYNTHETIC FABRICS

- **Durable** and usually launder well
- **Can be prone to static** and "cling" to the body
- **Can dye well** and are often digitally printed
- **Mix well** with natural fibres

ACETATE

Introduced in 1924, acetate is made from cellulose and chemicals. The fabric has a slight shine and is widely used for linings. Acetate can also be woven into fabrics such as acetate taffeta, acetate satin, and acetate jersey.

Properties of acetate:
- Dyes well
- Can be heat-set into pleats
- Washes well

Cutting out: Use a nap layout due to sheen on fabric

Seams: Plain, neatened with overlocker or zigzag stitch, or 4-thread overlock stitch
Thread: Polyester all-purpose thread
Needle: Machine size 11; sharps for hand sewing
Pressing: Steam iron on a cool setting (fabric can melt)
Used for: Special-occasion wear, linings

ACRYLIC

Introduced in 1950, acrylic fibres are made from ethylene and acrylonitrile. The fabric resembles wool and makes a good substitute for machine-washable wool. Often seen as a knitted fabric, the fibres can be mixed with wool.

Properties of acrylic:
- Little absorbency
- Tends to retain odours
- Not very strong

Cutting out: A nap layout may be required

Seams: 4-thread overlock stitch on knitted fabrics; plain seam on woven fabrics
Thread: Polyester all-purpose thread
Needle: Machine size 12/14, but a ballpoint needle may be required on knitted fabrics; sharps for hand sewing
Pressing: Steam iron on a wool setting (fabric can be damaged by heat)
Used for: Knitted yarns for sweaters; wovens for skirts, blouses

POLYESTER

One of the most popular of the man-made fibres, polyester was introduced in 1951 as a man's washable suiting. Polyester fibres are made from petroleum by-products and can take on any form, from a very fine sheer fabric to a thick, heavy suiting.

Properties of polyester:
- Non-absorbent
- Does not crease
- Can build up static
- May "pill"

Cutting out: A nap layout is only required if the fabric is printed
Seams: French, plain, or 4-thread overlock, depending on the weight of the fabric
Thread: Polyester all-purpose thread
Needle: Machine size 11/14; sharps for hand sewing
Pressing: Steam iron on a wool setting
Used for: Workwear, school uniforms

RAYON

Also known as viscose and often referred to as artificial silk, this fibre was developed in 1889. It is made from wood pulp or cotton linters mixed with chemicals. Rayon can be knitted or woven and made into a wide range of fabrics. It is often blended with other fibres.

Properties of rayon:
- Absorbent
- Non-static
- Dyes well
- Frays badly

Cutting out: A nap layout is only required if the fabric is printed
Seams: Plain, neatened with overlocker or zigzag stitch
Thread: Polyester all-purpose thread
Needle: Machine size 12/14; sharps for hand sewing
Pressing: Steam iron on a silk setting
Used for: Dresses, blouses, jackets

SYNTHETIC FURS

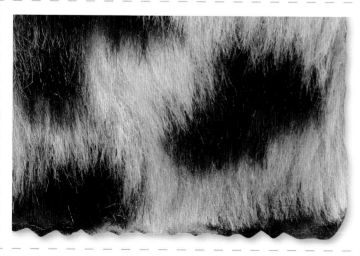

Created using a looped yarn that is then cut on a knitted or a woven base, synthetic fur can be made from nylon or acrylic fibres. The furs vary tremendously in quality and some are very difficult to tell from the real thing.

Properties of synthetic furs:
- Require careful sewing
- Can be heat-damaged by pressing
- Not as warm as real fur

Cutting out: Use a nap layout, with the fur pile brushed from the neck to the hem; cut just the backing carefully and not through the fur pile
Seams: Plain, with a longer stitch and a walking foot; no neatening is required
Thread: Polyester all-purpose thread
Needle: Machine size 14; sharps for hand sewing
Pressing: If required, use a cool iron (synthetic fur can melt under a hot iron)
Used for: Outerwear

PATTERNS &
CUTTING OUT

Any garment pattern, whether a commercial pattern or one from this book, needs
adjusting to suit the wearer's body shape. This section explains the principles of
pattern adjustment, making a toile test garment, and cutting and marking the fabric.

READING PATTERNS

Most dressmakers buy a commercial paper pattern to make a garment. A pattern has three main components: the envelope, the pattern sheets, and the instructions. The envelope gives an illustration of the garment that can be made from the contents, together with fabric suggestions and other requirements. The pattern sheets are normally printed on tissue and contain a wealth of information, while the instructions tell you how to construct the garment.

READING A PATTERN ENVELOPE

The envelope front illustrates the garment that can be made from the contents of the envelope. The illustration may be a line drawing or a photograph. There may be different versions, known as views. On the reverse of the envelope there is usually an illustration of the back view and the standard body measurement chart that has been used for this pattern, plus a chart that will help you purchase the correct amount of fabric for each view. The reverse of the envelope also includes suggestions for suitable fabrics, together with the "notions", or haberdashery, which are all the bits and pieces you need to complete the project.

Number of pattern piece.

Pattern code number for ordering.

Description of garment giving details of style and different views included in pattern.

List of pattern sizes in metric and imperial measurements for bust, waist, and hips in each size.

Suggested fabrics suitable for garment as well as advice on unsuitable fabrics.

Notions required for each view.

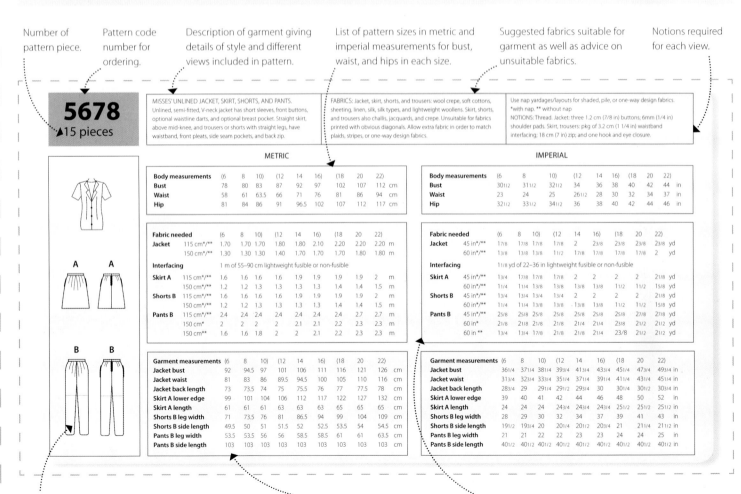

5678
▲15 pieces

MISSES' UNLINED JACKET, SKIRT, SHORTS, AND PANTS. Unlined, semi-fitted, V-neck jacket has short sleeves, front buttons, optional waistline darts, and optional breast pocket. Straight skirt, above mid-knee, and trousers or shorts with straight legs, have waistband, front pleats, side seam pockets, and back zip.

FABRICS: Jacket, skirt, shorts, and trousers: wool crepe, soft cottons, sheeting, linen, silk, silk types, and lightweight woollens. Skirt, shorts, and trousers also challis, jacquards, and crepe. Unsuitable for fabrics printed with obvious diagonals. Allow extra fabric in order to match plaids, stripes, or one-way design fabrics.

Use nap yardages/layouts for shaded, pile, or one-way design fabrics. *with nap. ** without nap. NOTIONS: Thread. Jacket: three 1.2 cm (7/8 in) buttons; 6mm (1/4 in) shoulder pads. Skirt, trousers: pkg of 3.2 cm (1 1/4 in) waistband interfacing; 18 cm (7 in) zip; and one hook and eye closure.

METRIC

Body measurements		(6	8	10)	(12	14	16)	(18	20	22)	
Bust		78	80	83	87	92	97	102	107	112	cm
Waist		58	61	63.5	66	71	76	81	86	94	cm
Hip		81	84	86	91	96.5	102	107	112	117	cm

Fabric needed		(6	8	10)	(12	14	16)	(18	20	22)	
Jacket	115 cm*/**	1.70	1.70	1.70	1.80	1.80	2.10	2.20	2.20	2.20	m
	150 cm*/**	1.30	1.30	1.30	1.40	1.70	1.70	1.70	1.80	1.80	m
Interfacing	1 m of 55–90 cm lightweight fusible or non-fusible										
Skirt A	115 cm*/**	1.6	1.6	1.6	1.6	1.9	1.9	1.9	1.9	2	m
	150 cm*/**	1.2	1.2	1.3	1.3	1.3	1.3	1.4	1.4	1.5	m
Shorts B	115 cm*/**	1.6	1.6	1.6	1.6	1.9	1.9	1.9	1.9	2	m
	150 cm*/**	1.2	1.2	1.3	1.3	1.3	1.3	1.4	1.4	1.5	m
Pants B	115 cm*/**	2.4	2.4	2.4	2.4	2.4	2.4	2.4	2.7	2.7	m
	150 cm*	2	2	2	2	2.1	2.1	2.2	2.3	2.3	m
	150 cm**	1.6	1.6	1.8	2	2	2.1	2.2	2.3	2.3	m

Garment measurements	(6	8	10)	(12	14	16)	(18	20	22)	
Jacket bust	92	94.5	97	101	106	111	116	121	126	cm
Jacket waist	81	83	86	89.5	94.5	100	105	110	116	cm
Jacket back length	73	73.5	74	75	75.5	76	77	77.5	78	cm
Skirt A lower edge	99	101	104	106	112	117	122	127	132	cm
Skirt A length	61	61	61	63	63	63	65	65	65	cm
Shorts B leg width	71	73.5	76	81	86.5	94	99	104	109	cm
Shorts B side length	49.5	50	51	51.5	52	52.5	53.5	54	54.5	cm
Pants B leg width	53.5	53.5	56	56	58.5	58.5	61	61	63.5	cm
Pants B side length	103	103	103	103	103	103	103	103	103	cm

IMPERIAL

Body measurements		(6	8	10)	(12	14	16)	(18	20	22)	
Bust		30 1/2	31 1/2	32 1/2	34	36	38	40	42	44	in
Waist		23	24	25	26 1/4	28	30	32	34	37	in
Hip		32 1/2	33 1/2	34 1/2	36	38	40	42	44	46	in

Fabric needed		(6	8	10)	(12	14	16)	(18	20	22)	
Jacket	45 in*/**	1 7/8	1 7/8	1 7/8	1 7/8	2	2 3/8	2 3/8	2 3/8	2 3/8	yd
	60 in*/**	1 3/8	1 3/8	1 3/8	1 1/2	1 7/8	1 7/8	1 7/8	1 7/8	2	yd
Interfacing	1 1/8 yd of 22–36 in lightweight fusible or non-fusible										
Skirt A	45 in*/**	1 3/4	1 3/4	1 3/4	1 7/8	1 7/8	2	2	2	2 1/8	yd
	60 in*/**	1 1/4	1 1/4	1 3/8	1 3/8	1 3/8	1 3/8	1 1/2	1 1/2	1 5/8	yd
Shorts B	45 in*/**	1 3/4	1 3/4	1 3/4	1 3/4	2	2	2	2	2 1/8	yd
	60 in*/**	1 1/4	1 1/4	1 3/8	- 1 3/8	1 3/8	1 3/8	1 1/2	1 1/2	1 5/8	yd
Pants B	45 in*/**	2 5/8	2 5/8	2 5/8	2 5/8	2 5/8	2 5/8	2 5/8	2 7/8	2 7/8	yd
	60 in*	2 1/8	2 1/8	2 1/8	2 1/8	2 1/4	2 1/4	2 3/8	2 1/2	2 1/2	yd
	60 in **	1 3/4	1 3/4	1 7/8	2 1/8	2 1/8	2 1/4	2 3/8	2 1/2	2 1/2	yd

Garment measurements	(6	8	10)	(12	14	16)	(18	20	22)	
Jacket bust	36 1/4	37 1/4	38 1/4	39 3/4	41 3/4	43 3/4	45 1/4	47 3/4	49 3/4	in
Jacket waist	31 3/4	32 3/4	33 3/4	35 1/4	37 1/4	39 1/4	41 1/4	43 1/4	45 1/4	in
Jacket back length	28 3/4	29	29 1/4	29 1/2	29 3/4	30	30 1/4	30 1/2	30 3/4	in
Skirt A lower edge	39	40	41	42	44	46	48	50	52	in
Skirt A length	24	24	24	24 3/4	24 3/4	24 3/4	25 1/2	25 1/2	25 1/2	in
Shorts B leg width	28	29	30	32	34	37	39	41	43	in
Shorts B side length	19 1/2	19 3/4	20	20 1/4	20 1/2	20 3/4	21	21 1/4	21 1/2	in
Pants B leg width	21	21	22	22	23	23	24	24	25	in
Pants B side length	40 1/2	40 1/2	40 1/2	40 1/2	40 1/2	40 1/2	40 1/2	40 1/2	40 1/2	in

Outline drawing of garment, including back views, showing darts and zip positions.

Garment measurements box gives actual size of finished garment.

Chart to follow for required fabric quantity, depending on size, view, and width of fabric.

SINGLE-SIZE PATTERNS

Some patterns contain a garment of one size only. If you are using a single-size pattern, cut around the tissue on the thick black cutting line before making any alterations.

PATTERN MARKINGS

Each pattern piece will have a series of lines, dots, and other symbols printed on it. These symbols help you to alter the pattern and join the pattern pieces together. The symbols are universal across all major paper patterns.

Zip markings indicate length of seam opening for zip.

Darts are marked with lines, and sometimes with dots or circles that match when darts are folded.

Notches are usually single on front armhole and double on back armhole.

Straight arrow must be placed on straight grain, parallel to selvedges.

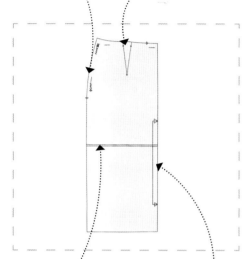

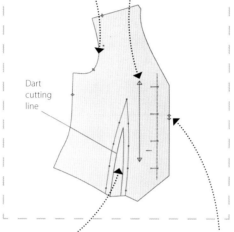

Dart cutting line

Alteration lines indicate best place to lengthen or shorten pattern pieces.

Pattern pieces without grainline have a place-to-fold line, to be positioned directly on fold of fabric, parallel to selvedges.

Open dart is very wide, and fabric is cut away with pattern following cutting line.

Notches on both sides should match to ensure correct edges are joined together.

MULTI-SIZE PATTERNS

Many patterns today have more than one size printed on the tissue. Each size is clearly labelled and the cutting lines are marked with a different type of line for each size.

Where there is one line only, it applies to all sizes.

Straight arrow must be placed along straight grain, parallel to selvedges.

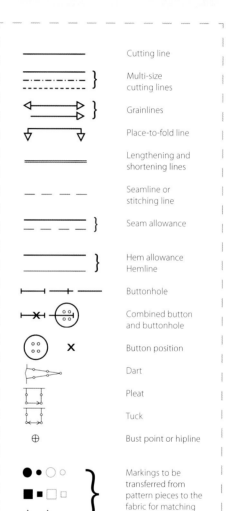

Lengthening and shortening lines

Where there is a choice of size lines, follow the desired size line.

———————	Cutting line
─·─·─·─·─ ┃ - - - - - ┃	Multi-size cutting lines
◁——————▷ ┃	Grainlines
▽————————▽	Place-to-fold line
─ ─ ─ ─ ─ ─	Lengthening and shortening lines
– – – – – –	Seamline or stitching line
— — — — ┃	Seam allowance
——————— ┃	Hem allowance / Hemline
┣━━┃━━┫	Buttonhole
⊕	Combined button and buttonhole
⊙ ✕	Button position
▷———•	Dart
⌐·····⌐	Pleat
⌐·····⌐	Tuck
⊕	Bust point or hipline
●•○◦ ■▪□▫ ▲△ ┃	Markings to be transferred from pattern pieces to the fabric for matching or to indicate detail
◇◆▽▼	Single notches
⬡⬢	Double notches
⬡⬢ ┃	Triple notches
⊏▣─▸·┃·	Zip placement

BODY MEASURING

Accurate body measurements are needed to determine the correct pattern size to use and to know if any alterations are required. Pattern sizes are usually chosen by the hip or bust measurement; for tops follow the bust measurement, but for skirts or trousers use the hip measurement. If you are choosing a dress pattern, go by whichever of your measurements is the largest.

TAKING BODY MEASUREMENTS

You will need a tape measure and ruler as well as a helper for some of the measuring, and a firm chair or stool.

Wear close-fitting clothes such as a leotard and leggings.

Do not wear any shoes.

MEASURING YOUR HEIGHT

Most paper patterns are designed for a woman 165 to 168cm (5ft 5in to 5ft 6in). If you are shorter or taller than this you may need to adjust the pattern prior to cutting out your fabric.

1 Remove your shoes.

2 Stand straight, with your back against the wall.

3 Place a ruler flat on your head, touching the wall, and mark the wall at this point.

4 Step away and measure the distance from the floor to the marked point.

FULL BUST

Make sure you are wearing a good-fitting bra and measure over the fullest part of the bust. If your cup size is in excess of a B, you will probably need to do a bust alteration, although some patterns are now cut to accommodate larger cup sizes.

WAIST

This is the measurement around the smallest part of your waist. Wrap the tape around first to find your natural waist, then measure.

CHEST

Measure above the bust, high under the arms, keeping the tape measure flat and straight across the back.

HIPS

This measurement must be taken around the fullest part of the hips, between the waist and legs.

HIGH HIPS

Take this just below the waist and just above the hip bones to give a measurement across the tummy. Measure around the fullest part of your tummy.

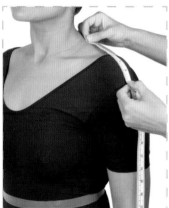

SHOULDER

Hold the end of the tape measure at the base of your neck (where a necklace would lie) and measure to the dent at the end of your shoulder bone. To find this dent raise your arm slightly.

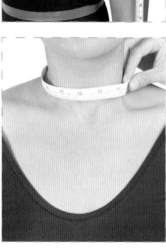

NECK

Measure around the neck – snugly but not too tightly – to determine collar size.

ARM

Bend your elbow and place your hand on your hip, then measure from the end of the shoulder over the elbow to the wrist bone.

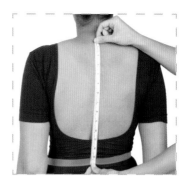

BACK WAIST

Take this measurement down the centre of the back, from the bony bit at the top of the spine, in line with the shoulders, to the waist.

OUTSIDE LEG

Measure the side of the leg from the waist, over the hip, and straight down the leg to the ankle bone.

INSIDE LEG

Stand with your legs apart and measure the inside of one leg from the crotch to the ankle bone.

CROTCH DEPTH

Sit upright on a firm chair or stool and measure from the waist vertically down to the chair.

ALTERING PATTERNS

These alterations relate specifically to commercial patterns; the patterns in this book can be altered in a similar way. Your body measurements are unlikely to be exactly the same as those of your chosen pattern, so you will need to alter the pattern. Here is how to lengthen and shorten pattern pieces, and how to make specific alterations at the bust, waist and hips, shoulders and back, and to sleeves and trousers.

EQUIPMENT

In addition to scissors and pins or tape, you will need a pencil, an eraser, a ruler that is clearly marked, and possibly a set square. For many alterations you will also need some paper. After pinning or taping the pattern to the paper, you can redraw the pattern lines. Trim away the excess paper before pinning the pattern to the fabric for cutting out.

EASY MULTI-SIZE PATTERN ALTERATIONS

Using a multi-size pattern has many advantages, as you can cut it to suit your unique individual shape – for example, to accommodate a hip measurement that may be two sizes different to a waist measurement, if you are not precisely one size or another.

INDIVIDUAL PATTERN ADJUSTMENT

To adjust for a wider hip measurement, cut from the smaller pattern size to the larger, curving the line gently to follow the contours of the body.

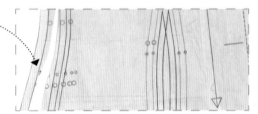

BETWEEN SIZES

If your body measurements fall between two pattern sizes, cut carefully between the two cutting lines for the different sizes.

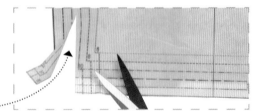

LENGTHENING AND SHORTENING PATTERNS

If you are short or tall, or if your arms or legs are shorter or longer than the pattern allows, you will need to adjust the pattern prior to cutting out. There are lengthening and shortening lines printed on the pattern pieces that will guide you as to the best places. However, you will need to compare your body shape against the pattern. Alter the front and back by the same amount at the same points, and always check finished lengths.

SLEEVE

To keep the wrist area intact on the pattern, alter partway down the sleeve, or at the hem.

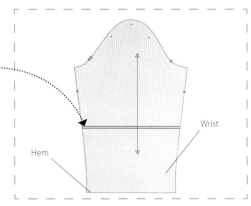

Hem

Wrist

BODICE

Alter the back neck to waist length below the bust dart but above the waist. Alter through the waist dart if there is one.

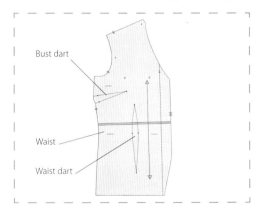

Bust dart

Waist

Waist dart

FITTED DRESS

Mark between the bust and waist to alter the back neck to waist length.

Alter below the hipline if not altering at the hem.

Alter below the hem if not altering at the hipline.

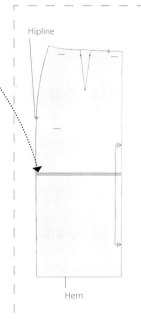

Waist

Bust dart

Hipline

SKIRT

Alter below hipline or at hem.

Hipline

Hem

TROUSERS

Increase crotch depth below the darts, but above the crotchline.

Make length alterations midway down the leg to retain the leg width.

Crotchline

Hem

LENGTHENING A PATTERN PIECE

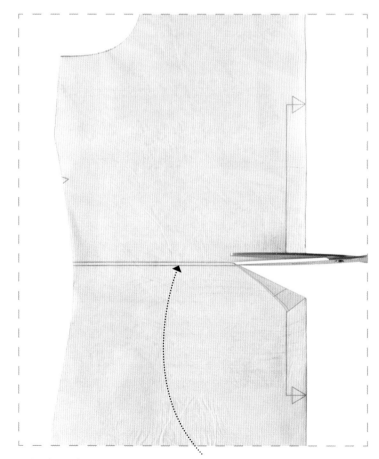

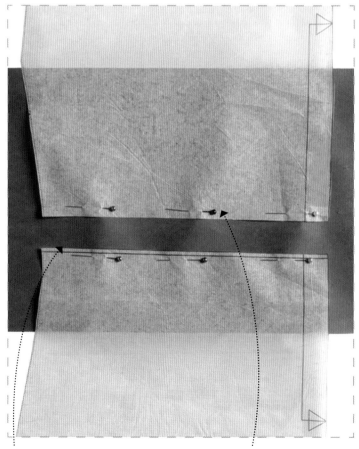

1 Work out the amount you want to lengthen by.

2 Cut through the lengthening and shortening lines on the pattern, following the lines carefully.

3 Place some paper behind the pattern and spread the pattern pieces apart to leave a gap of the required amount. Make sure the gap is level along the cut lines.

4 Pin or tape the pattern pieces to the paper.

SHORTENING A PATTERN PIECE

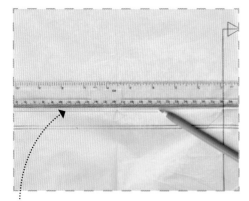

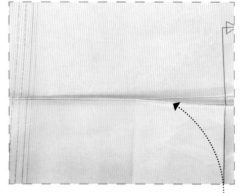

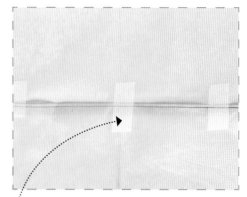

1 Work out the amount you want to shorten by. Mark this amount at intervals above the lengthening and shortening lines, then draw a line through the marks using the ruler as a guide.

2 Fold the lengthening and shortening line on to the drawn line so the two lines meet neatly.

3 Press with your fingers to crease the fold sharply, then secure the fold in the pattern with tape.

LENGTHENING ACROSS DARTS

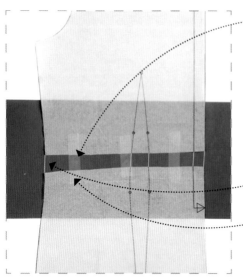

1 If an adjustment is required across a dart, cut and lengthen the pattern piece through the dart.

2 Place paper behind the pattern, making sure that the lines of the dart are smoothly connected.

3 Tape or pin in place.

SHORTENING ACROSS DARTS

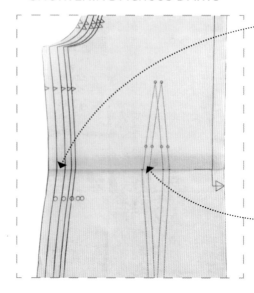

1 Fold the pattern through the dart to shorten the pattern piece.

2 After shortening across a dart, the lines of the dart may not be in line. If this is the case, re-draw the dart from dot to dot, using a ruler to ensure the lines are straight.

LENGTHENING A HEM EDGE

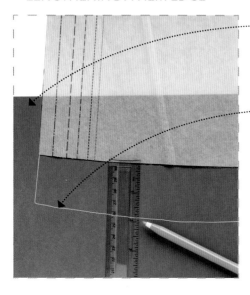

1 Place a sheet of pattern paper under the tissue at the hem edge and tape down.

2 Using a ruler as a guide, add on the required amount, marking dots at intervals along the pattern paper first, then connecting them with a line.

SHORTENING A HEM EDGE

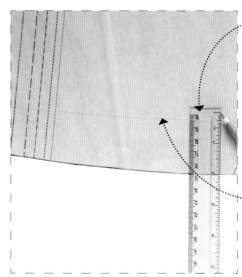

1 Using a ruler as a guide, carefully measure the new hemline at intervals from the original hemline on the pattern piece.

2 Connect the marks with a line, then cut along the line to remove the surplus pattern.

BUST

Some paper patterns today feature various cup sizes, but most are cut to accommodate a B cup, including those in this book. If you are larger than this, you will probably need to adjust your pattern before cutting out. As a general rule, when spreading the pattern pieces apart, try adjusting by 6mm ($\frac{1}{4}$in) per cup size over a B cup.

RAISING A BUST DART

1 If you have a high bust you may need to raise the point of the darts. The bust point is nearly always marked on the pattern. Mark the desired new bust point on the pattern.

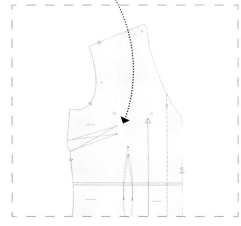

2 Redraw the dart, tapering it to the new, higher, point.

RAISING A BUST DART SUBSTANTIALLY

1 Mark the desired new bust point on the pattern.

2 Cut a rectangle out of the bust dart area and move it up to the new position.

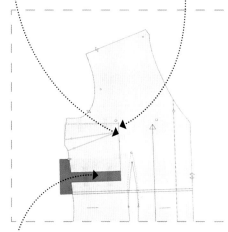

3 Tape paper behind and redraw the side seam.

INCREASING A BUST DART FOR A FULL BUST

1 Cut the pattern vertically and horizontally straight through the bust point.

2 Spread the cut pattern pieces apart by about 6mm ($\frac{1}{4}$in) per cup size over a B cup.

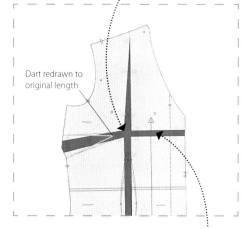

Dart redrawn to original length

3 Tape paper behind and redraw the cutting lines as necessary.

LOWERING A BUST DART

1 Mark the desired new bust point on the pattern.

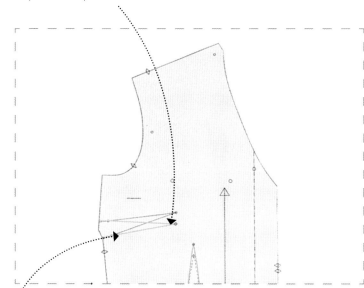

2 Redraw the dart, tapering it to the new, lower, point.

LOWERING A BUST DART SUBSTANTIALLY

1 Mark the desired new bust point on the pattern.

2 Cut a rectangle out of the bust dart area and move it to the new, lower, position.

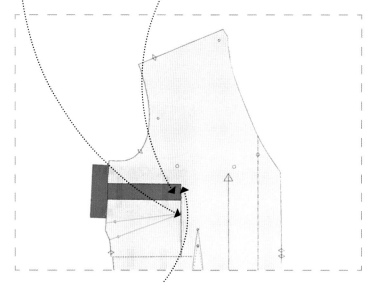

3 Tape paper behind and redraw the side seam.

RAISING A CURVED BUST SEAM

1 Fold a pleat in the shoulder area on the centre front pattern to raise the bust point by the required amount.

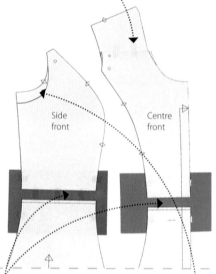

2 Cut both the centre front and side front patterns on the lengthening and shortening lines. Spread the cut pattern pieces apart by the amount in the pleat and tape paper behind them.

3 Redraw the armhole, lowering it by the same amount.

LOWERING A CURVED BUST SEAM

1 Cut the centre front pattern in the shoulder area and spread the cut pattern pieces apart by the required amount. Tape paper behind the pattern pieces.

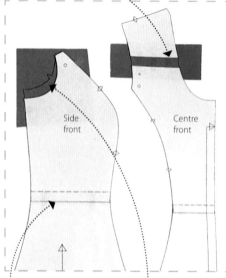

2 Fold both the centre front and the side front patterns on the lengthening and shortening lines by the same amount.

3 Redraw the armhole, raising it by the same amount.

ADJUSTING A SEAM FOR A FULL BUST

1 Tape paper under the centre front and side front patterns in the bust area.

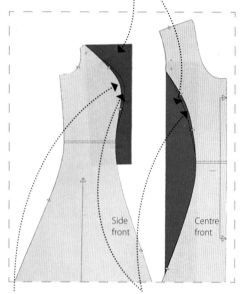

2 Divide the total increase required by two and add this amount at the point of the bust at each seamline.

3 Draw new seamlines from these points, tapering them into the old seamlines.

WAIST AND HIPS

Most people's waists and hips are out of proportion when compared to the measurements of a paper pattern. To alter the pattern to suit your body shape, adjust the pieces for the waist first and then do the hip pieces.

INCREASING THE WAIST ON A FITTED SKIRT

1 Increase the waist at the side seams.

2 Tape paper behind the pattern pieces. Divide the total increase required by four as there are four seamlines.

3 Add this amount on the paper at the waist edge at each seamline. Draw new seamlines from these points, tapering them into the old seamlines.

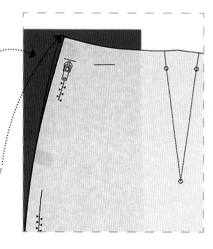

INCREASING THE WAIST ON A GORED SKIRT

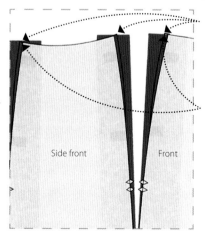

1 Tape paper behind the pattern pieces. As there are many seams, divide the total increase required by the number of seamlines.

2 Add this amount on the paper at the waist edge at each seamline. Draw new seamlines from these points, tapering them into the old seamlines.

INCREASING THE WAIST ON A FULL-CIRCLE SKIRT

1 Carefully check the waist circumference on the pattern against your waist measurement.

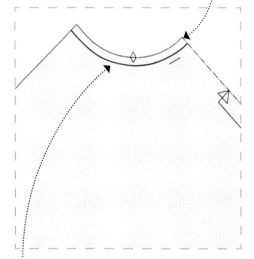

2 Draw a new, lower waist stitching line on the pattern. Adjust the finished length of the skirt if necessary.

INCREASING THE WAIST ON A FITTED DRESS

1 Tape paper behind the waist area of the front and back pattern pieces. Divide the total increase required by four as there are four seamlines.

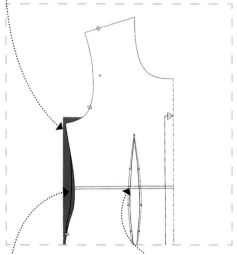

2 Add this amount on the paper at the waist area of each seamline. Draw new seamlines from these points, tapering them into the old seamlines.

3 If more increase is required, the darts can also be made narrower.

INCREASING THE WAIST ON A PRINCESS-LINE DRESS

1 Tape paper behind the waist area of each pattern piece. Divide the total increase required by the number of seamlines.

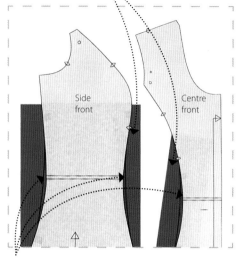

2 Add this amount on the paper at the waist area of each seamline. Draw new seamlines from these points, tapering them into the old seamlines.

DECREASING THE WAIST ON A FULL-CIRCLE SKIRT

1 Tape paper behind each pattern piece.

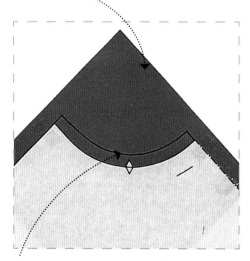

2 Draw a new, higher waist stitching line on the pattern. Adjust the finished length of the skirt if necessary.

DECREASING THE WAIST ON A FITTED SKIRT

1 Decrease the waist at the side seams. Divide the total decrease required by four as there are four seamlines.

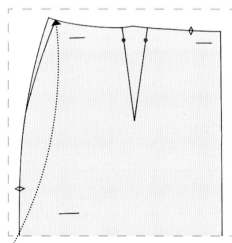

2 Mark this amount on the pattern at the waist edge at each seamline. Draw new seamlines from these points, tapering them into the old seamlines.

DECREASING THE WAIST ON A GORED SKIRT

1 As there are many seams, divide the total decrease required by the number of seamlines.

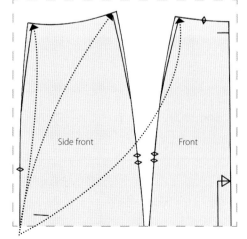

2 Mark this amount on the pattern at the waist edge at each seamline. Draw new seamlines from these points, tapering them into the old seamlines.

DECREASING THE WAIST ON A FITTED DRESS

1 Divide the total decrease required by four as there are four seamlines.

2 Mark this amount on the pattern at the waist on each seamline. Draw new seamlines from these points, tapering them into the old seamlines.

DECREASING THE WAIST ON A PRINCESS-LINE DRESS

1 Divide the total decrease required by the number of seamlines.

2 Mark this amount on the pattern at the waist on each seamline. Draw new seamlines from these points, tapering them into the old seamlines.

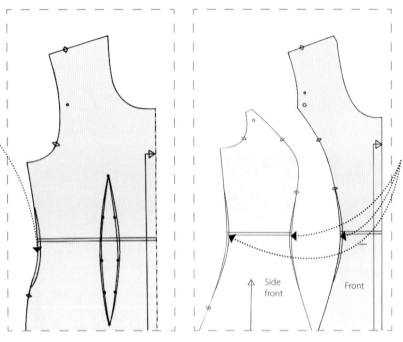

Side front

Front

INCREASING A FITTED SKIRT AT THE HIPLINE

1 Tape paper behind the pattern pieces. Divide the total increase required by four as there are four seamlines.

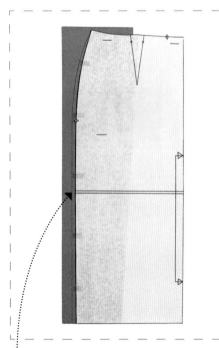

2 Add this amount on the paper at the hipline. Draw new seamlines from these points, tapering them into the old seamlines.

DECREASING A FITTED SKIRT AT THE HIPLINE

1 Divide the total decrease required by four as there are four seamlines.

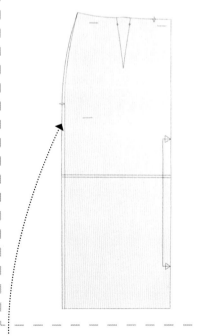

2 Mark this amount on the pattern at the hip on each seamline. Draw new seamlines straight down to the hem from these points, tapering them up into the waist.

ADJUSTING A FITTED SKIRT FOR A LARGE BOTTOM

1 Cut vertically through the dart to the hem on the skirt back pattern.

2 Cut through the hipline, stopping before you reach the side seam.

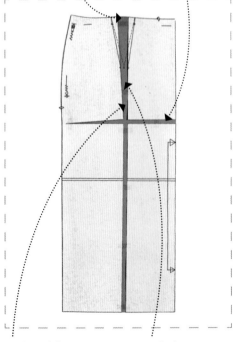

3 Spread the cut pattern pieces apart by the required amount and tape paper behind them.

4 Redraw the dart.

ADJUSTING A FITTED SKIRT FOR EXTRA-LARGE HIPS

1 For an increase over 5cm (2in), cut each pattern piece vertically between the dart and the side seam.

2 Divide the total increase required by four. Spread the cut pattern pieces apart by this amount and tape paper behind them.

3 If the waist is to remain the same, draw in a second dart to remove the increase at the waist.

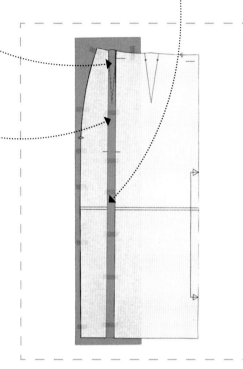

ADJUSTING A GORED SKIRT AT THE HIPLINE

1 As there are many seams, divide the total decrease or increase required by the number of seamlines.

2 If increasing, tape paper behind the pattern pieces.

3 Mark the reduction at the hipline on the pattern or mark the increase on the paper.

4 Draw new seamlines straight down to the hem from these points, tapering them up into the waist.

Side front   Centre

MAKING A LARGE INCREASE AT THE HIPLINE ON A FITTED DRESS

1 Divide the total increase required by four.

2 Make a horizontal cut in each pattern piece the length of this amount and just below the waist.

3 Cut vertically from this point to the hem.

4 Spread the cut pattern pieces apart by the required amount and tape paper behind them.

5 Redraw the side seam.

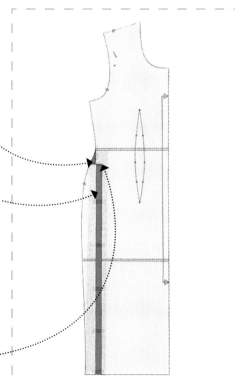

ADJUSTING AT THE HIPLINE TO ALLOW FOR A HOLLOW BACK

1 A hollow back requires a shorter centre back seam. Draw a horizontal line on the pattern from the centre back across the hipline.

2 Fold along the line to make a pleat at the centre back that takes up the required reduction. Taper the pleat to nothing at the side seam. Tape in place.

Centre back seam

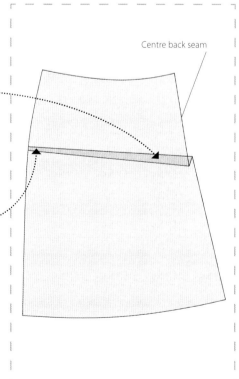

SHOULDERS, BACK, AND SLEEVES

Alterations can be made to accommodate sloping shoulders, square shoulders, and backs that may be wider or narrower than the pattern allowances. It's important to ensure that these alterations have a minimum effect on the armhole. Sleeves need to allow for movement, so should not be too tight; pattern pieces can be enlarged as necessary. Alterations can also be made for thin arms.

ADJUSTING TO FIT SQUARE SHOULDERS

1 Starting at the armhole, slash the pattern about 3cm (1¼in) below and parallel with the shoulder line, stopping before you reach the neck seamline.

2 Spread the cut pattern apart to straighten the shoulder line. Tape paper behind.

3 Redraw the line to close the gap at the armhole.

4 Raise the armhole by the amount added at the shoulder. Mark the new cutting line on the paper.

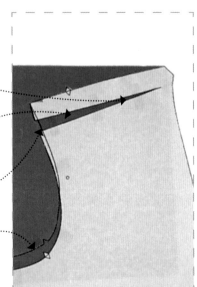

ADJUSTING TO FIT SLOPING SHOULDERS

1 Slash the pattern 3cm (1¼in) below the shoulder line and parallel with it.

2 Overlap the cut pieces by the required amount and tape in place.

3 Lower the armhole by the same amount, marking the new cutting line on the pattern.

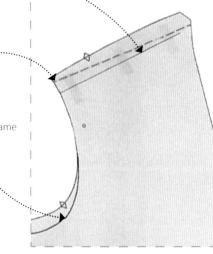

PREPARING THE PATTERN FOR BROAD OR NARROW SHOULDER ALTERATIONS

1 Draw a vertical line 20cm (8in) long on the pattern from the middle of the shoulder.

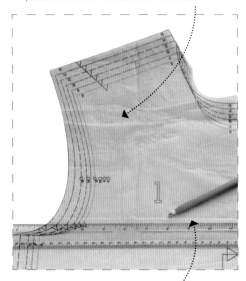

2 Draw a second, horizontal, line from the end of the first line to the armhole.

ADJUSTING TO FIT BROAD SHOULDERS

1 Cut along the two drawn lines (see left).

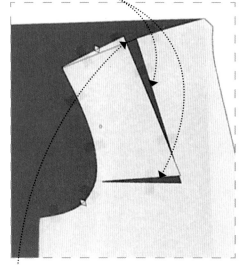

2 Spread the cut pattern pieces apart to accommodate the required increase in shoulder length.

3 Tape paper behind. Redraw the line to close the gap along the shoulder.

ADJUSTING TO FIT NARROW SHOULDERS

1 Cut along the two drawn lines (see far left).

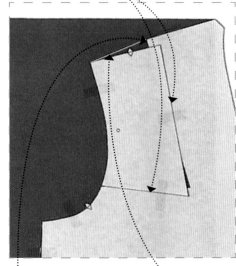

2 Overlap the cut pieces by the amount required to reduce the shoulder length.

3 Tape paper behind. Redraw the shoulder line.

ENLARGING A FITTED SLEEVE

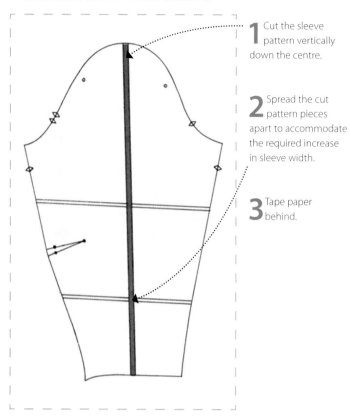

1 Cut the sleeve pattern vertically down the centre.

2 Spread the cut pattern pieces apart to accommodate the required increase in sleeve width.

3 Tape paper behind.

ENLARGING THE HEAD OF A FITTED SLEEVE

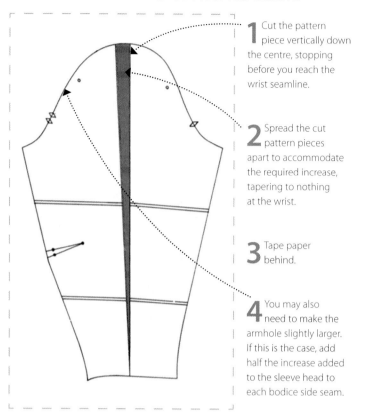

1 Cut the pattern piece vertically down the centre, stopping before you reach the wrist seamline.

2 Spread the cut pattern pieces apart to accommodate the required increase, tapering to nothing at the wrist.

3 Tape paper behind.

4 You may also need to make the armhole slightly larger. If this is the case, add half the increase added to the sleeve head to each bodice side seam.

INCREASING A FITTED SLEEVE AT THE UNDERARM

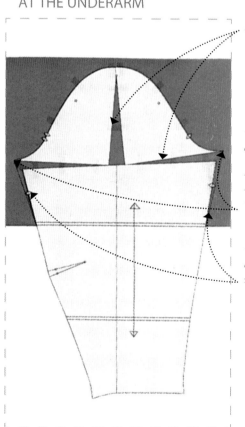

1 Cut the sleeve pattern horizontally from armhole to armhole. Cut a second, vertical, line almost to the sleeve head.

2 Pull the outside points of the horizontal cut upwards to accommodate the required increase in width.

3 Tape paper behind. Redraw the sleeve side seams.

DECREASING A FITTED SLEEVE TO ACCOMMODATE THIN ARMS

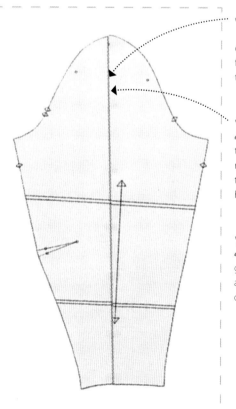

1 Draw a vertical line at the centre of the sleeve pattern from the sleeve head to the wrist.

2 Fold along the line to make a pleat that takes up the required reduction. Taper the pleat to nothing at the sleeve head. Tape in place.

3 Reduce the side seams on the garment by half the amount of the reduction on the sleeve.

TROUSERS

Trouser alterations, to accommodate a large stomach, wide hips, or a prominent or flat bottom, can be more complicated than those on other pattern pieces, and need to be done in the correct order. Crotch depth alterations are done first, followed by width alterations, then crotch length alterations, and finally trouser leg length. The crotch depth line is only marked on the back pattern pieces.

INCREASING DEPTH AT CROTCH SEAM

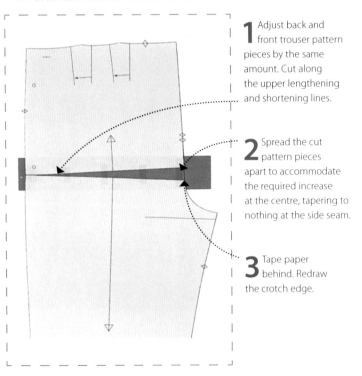

1 Adjust back and front trouser pattern pieces by the same amount. Cut along the upper lengthening and shortening lines.

2 Spread the cut pattern pieces apart to accommodate the required increase at the centre, tapering to nothing at the side seam.

3 Tape paper behind. Redraw the crotch edge.

DECREASING DEPTH AT THE CROTCH SEAM

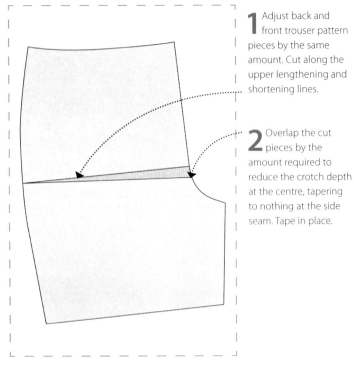

1 Adjust back and front trouser pattern pieces by the same amount. Cut along the upper lengthening and shortening lines.

2 Overlap the cut pieces by the amount required to reduce the crotch depth at the centre, tapering to nothing at the side seam. Tape in place.

INCREASING THE WAISTLINE

1 Tape paper behind the pattern pieces. Divide the total increase required by eight as there are eight seamlines.

2 Add this amount on the paper at the waist edge at each seamline. Draw new seamlines from these points, tapering them into the old seamlines.

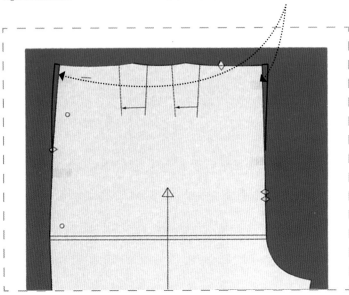

DECREASING THE WAISTLINE

1 Divide the total decrease required by eight as there are eight seamlines.

2 Mark this amount on the pattern at the waist edge at each seamline. Draw new seamlines from these points, tapering them into the old seamlines.

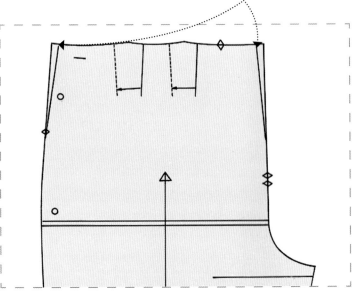

INCREASING AT THE HIPLINE

1 Tape paper behind the pattern pieces. Divide the total increase required by four as there are four seamlines.

2 Add this amount on the paper at the hipline. Draw new seamlines from these points, tapering them into the old seamlines.

3 For straight trousers, draw the new seamlines straight down from the hip to the hem.

DECREASING AT THE HIPLINE

1 Divide the total decrease required by four as there are four seamlines.

2 Mark this amount on the pattern at the hipline. Draw new seamlines from these points, tapering them into the old seamlines.

ADJUSTING FOR A LARGE BOTTOM

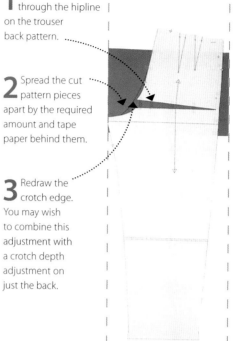

1 Cut horizontally through the hipline on the trouser back pattern.

2 Spread the cut pattern pieces apart by the required amount and tape paper behind them.

3 Redraw the crotch edge. You may wish to combine this adjustment with a crotch depth adjustment on just the back.

INCREASING LENGTH AT CROTCH POINT

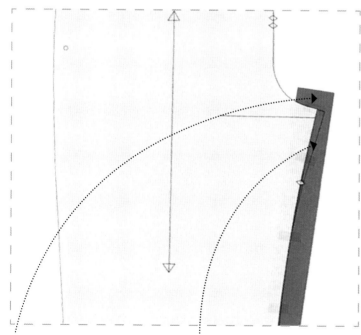

1 If trousers are too tight between the legs, this alteration may be required. The crotch length may need to be increased by a different amount on the front and the back. Tape paper under the crotch seam.

2 Add the required amount to the inside leg seam on the paper. Draw a new seamline from the new crotch point, tapering it into the old seamline.

DECREASING LENGTH AT CROTCH POINT

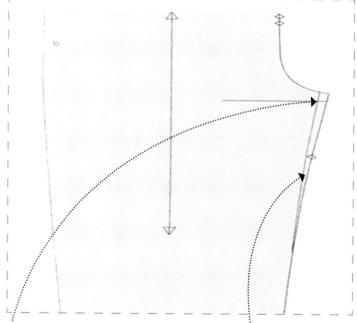

1 If trousers are too loose between the legs, this alteration may be required. Mark the inside leg seam with the position of the new crotch point.

2 Draw a new seamline from the new crotch point, tapering it into the old seamline.

MAKING A TOILE

When using a new pattern for the first time, or if you have made pattern alterations, it is always a good idea to try out the pattern in calico, making a test garment called a toile. This will tell you if the garment is going to fit you, or whether more alterations are required. It is also a good opportunity to confirm that the style suits your figure type. You will need a helper, or failing that, a dressmaker's dummy.

TOILE TOO BIG

When you try the toile on, if it is too big there will be surplus fabric. Pleat and pin out the surplus fabric, making the pleating equal on both the left- and right-hand sides of the garment. Take off the toile and measure the surplus amount. Alter the pattern pieces to match, by pinning out the surplus tissue.

BACK ADJUSTMENT

If the back is too loose, pleat and pin out the surplus fabric parallel to the centre back seam. Do this equally on both sides. Make the alteration down the centre back seam on the appropriate pattern pieces.

SHOULDER ADJUSTMENT

If the shoulder is too wide it will need a sloping shoulder adjustment (see page 64).

THE WAIST ON THE BODICE AND SKIRT

If the waist is too big, this can easily be adjusted by taking more fabric into the bust dart. If you adjust the bust dart on the bodice, you will need to alter the skirt dart too, so they join up.

THE HIP ON THE SKIRT

If the hip is too loose, pleat and pin out the surplus fabric on the side seams. Do this equally on both sides. Measure the surplus amount and take in the hipline on the pattern pieces accordingly (see Decreasing a fitted skirt at the hipline, p.62).

TOILE TOO SMALL

If the toile is too small, the fabric will "pull" where it is tight. The garment shown below is too tight over the bust and also over the high hip area. The pattern will need adjusting to allow more fabric in these areas. This toile is also snug at the top of the sleeve; this needs adjusting, too.

ADJUSTING A TOILE THAT IS TOO SMALL

If the toile is too tight, it will require more fabric to cover the contours of the body and you will need to make further alterations to the pattern pieces. For small increases (up to 4cm/1½in), you can adjust the toile as described below and then alter the pattern pieces accordingly, redrawing the seamlines. For more substantial increases, after altering the pattern pieces you will need to make up a new toile and to try it on.

1 Where the toile is too tight, unpick the side seam on either side, until the garment will hang without pulling.

2 Measure the gap at the fullest point between the stitching lines on the opened-out seam. It should be the same on both sides of the body.

3 Divide this measurement in half – for example, if the gap is 4cm (1½in) at the fullest point, then 2cm (¾in) needs to be added to each side seam seamline.

4 Using a marker pen, mark the top and bottom of the alteration directly on the toile. Also mark the fullest point of the alteration.

5 When the toile has been removed, add calico to the seam in the given area at the fullest point, tapering back to the original seam at either end.

6 Try the toile on again to be sure your alterations have made it fit properly. Then measure the alterations and make adjustments to the relevant pattern pieces.

THE HIP ON THE SKIRT

Unpick the side seams and measure the increase required. When you have adjusted the toile with extra calico and ensured the fit is right, you can alter the pattern pieces accordingly (see pp. 62–63).

THE BUST ON THE BODICE

If a small increase is required in the bust, unpick the side seams and measure the increase required. Then make the required alteration to the pattern pieces. If a larger increase is required, the whole pattern piece will need to be re-cut (see Increasing a bust dart, p.59). To be sure the alteration is successful, make up a new toile bodice.

SHOULDER ADJUSTMENT

If the sleeve is tight at the top or at the underarm, it is best to alter the pattern pieces (see p. 65) and then make up a new sleeve for the toile.

CUTTING OUT

Cutting out can make or break your project. But first you need to examine the fabric in the shop, looking for any flaws, such as a crooked pattern, and checking to see if the fabric has been cut properly from the roll – that is at a right angle to the selvedge. If it has not been cut properly, you will need to straighten the edge before cutting out. If the fabric is creased, press it; if washable, wash it to avoid shrinkage later. After this preparation, you will be ready to lay the pattern pieces on the fabric, pin in place, and cut out.

FABRIC GRAIN AND NAP

It is important that pattern pieces are cut on the correct grain; this will make the fabric hang correctly. The grain is the direction in which the yarns or threads that make up the fabric lie. The majority of pattern pieces need to be placed with the straight of grain symbol running parallel to the warp yarn. Some fabrics have a nap due to the pile, which means the fabric shadows when it is smoothed in one direction. A fabric with a one-way design or uneven stripes is also described as having a nap. Fabrics with nap are generally cut out with the nap running down, whereas those without nap can be cut out at any angle.

GRAIN ON WOVEN FABRICS

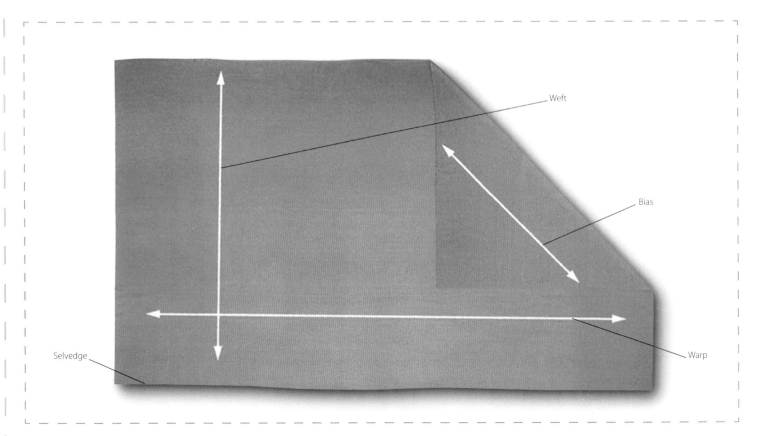

Yarns that run the length of the fabric are called warp yarns. They are stronger than weft yarns and less likely to stretch.

Weft yarns run crossways, over and under the warp yarns.

The bias grain is diagonal – running at 45 degrees to the warp and weft. A garment cut on the bias will follow the contours of the body.

The selvedge is the woven, non-frayable edge that runs parallel to the warp yarn.

NAP DUE TO PILE

Fabrics such as velvet, corduroy, and velour will show a difference in colour, depending on whether the nap is running up or down.

NAP DUE TO ONE-WAY DESIGN

A one-way pattern – in this case flowers – that runs lengthways in the fabric will be upside-down on one side when the fabric is folded back on itself.

NAP DUE TO STRIPES

If the stripes do not match on both sides when the fabric is folded back, they are uneven and the fabric will need a nap layout.

FABRIC PREPARATION

To check if the fabric has been cut properly from the roll, fold it selvedge to selvedge and see if it lies flat. If the cut ends are uneven and do not match, use one of the following methods to make the edge straight. Then press the fabric.

PULLING A THREAD TO OBTAIN A STRAIGHT EDGE

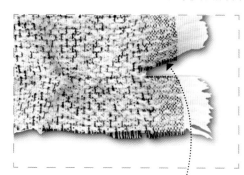

1 On a loose-woven fabric you can pull a weft thread to get a straight edge. First snip the selvedge, then find a single thread and tug it gently to pull it out.

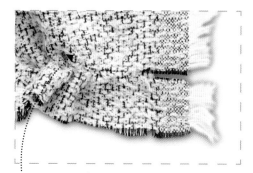

2 The fabric will gather along the pulled weft thread until the thread can be removed completely.

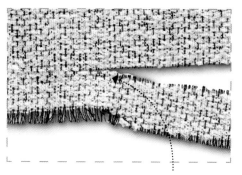

3 Carefully cut along the space left by the pulled-out weft thread.

CUTTING ON A STRIPE LINE TO OBTAIN A STRAIGHT EDGE

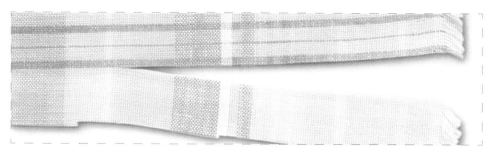

On checks and stripes, cut along the edge of one of the boldest stripes to achieve a straight edge.

PATTERN LAYOUT

For cutting out, fabric is usually folded selvedge to selvedge. With the fabric folded, the pattern is pinned on top, and both the right- and left-side pieces are cut out at the same time. If pattern pieces have to be cut from single layer fabric, remember to cut matching pairs. If a fabric has a design, lay the fabric design-side upwards so that you can arrange the pattern pieces to show off the design. If you have left- and right-side pattern pieces, they are cut on single fabric with the fabric right-side up and the pattern right-side up.

PINNING THE PATTERN TO THE FABRIC

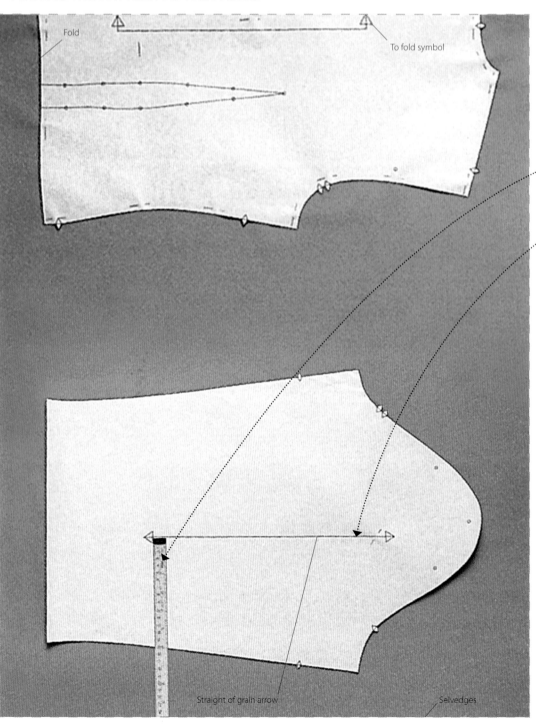

Fold

To fold symbol

Straight of grain arrow

Selvedges

1 The "to fold" symbol indicates the pattern piece is to be pinned carefully to the folded edge of the fabric. To check the straight of grain on the other pattern pieces, place the grain arrow so that it looks parallel to the selvedge, then pin to secure at one end of the arrow.

2 Measure from the pinned end to the selvedge and make a note of the measurement.

3 Measure from the other end of the arrow to the selvedge.

4 Move the pattern piece slightly until both measurements are the same, then pin in place.

5 Once the pattern is straight, pin around the rest of it, placing pins in the seam allowances.

GENERAL GUIDE TO LAYOUT

Place the pattern pieces on the fabric with the printed side uppermost. Some pieces will need to be placed to a fold.

LAYOUT FOR FABRICS WITH A NAP OR A ONE-WAY DESIGN

If your fabric needs to be cut out with a nap, all the pattern pieces need to be placed so the nap will run in the same direction in the made-up garment.

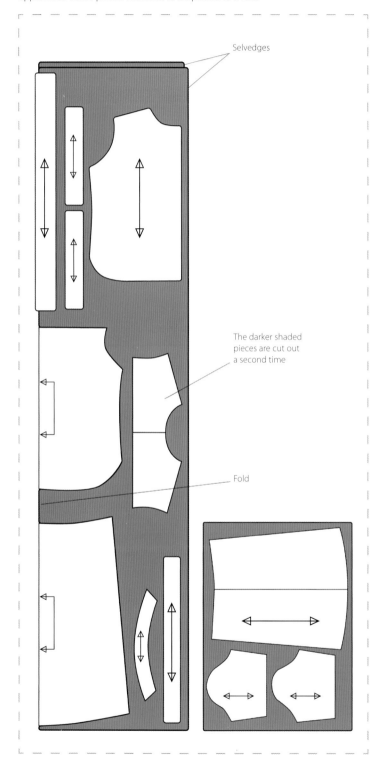

Selvedges

The darker shaded pieces are cut out a second time

Fold

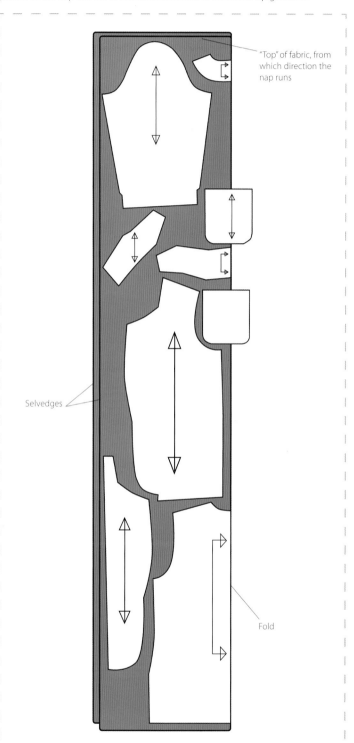

"Top" of fabric, from which direction the nap runs

Selvedges

Fold

If a piece has to be cut twice on a fold, this will need to be done after the other pieces have been cut and the fabric can be refolded.

If using a single layer of fabric, the pieces will need to be cut twice, turning the pattern over for the second piece.

STRIPES AND CHECKS

For fabrics with a stripe or check pattern, a little more care is needed when laying out the pattern pieces. If the checks and stripes are running across or down the length of the fabric when cutting out, they will run the same direction in the finished garment. So it is important to place the pattern pieces to ensure that the checks and stripes match and that they run together at the seams. If possible, try to place the pattern pieces so each has a stripe down the centre. With a checked fabric, be aware of the hemline placement on the pattern.

EVEN AND UNEVEN STRIPES

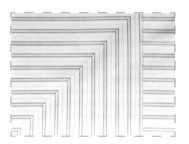 

EVEN STRIPES When a corner of the fabric is folded back diagonally, the stripes will meet up at the fold.

UNEVEN STRIPES When a corner of the fabric is folded back diagonally, the stripes will not match at the fold.

EVEN AND UNEVEN CHECKS

EVEN CHECKS When a corner of the fabric is folded back diagonally, the checks will be symmetrical on both of the fabric areas.

UNEVEN CHECKS When a corner of the fabric is folded back diagonally, the checks will be uneven lengthways, widthways, or both.

MATCHING STRIPES OR CHECKS ON A SKIRT

1 Place one of the skirt pattern pieces on the fabric and pin in place.

2 Mark on the pattern the position of the boldest lines of the checks or stripes.

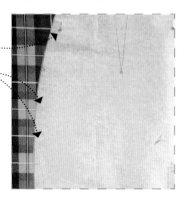

3 Place the adjoining skirt pattern piece alongside, with notches matching and side seams even. Transfer the marks to the second pattern piece.

4 Slide the second pattern piece across, matching up the bold lines. Pin in place.

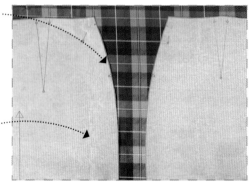

MATCHING STRIPES OR CHECKS AT THE SHOULDER

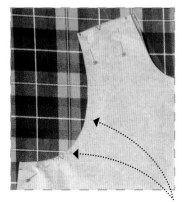 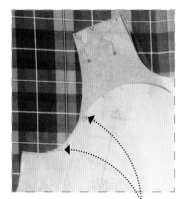 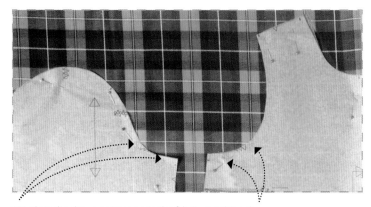

1 Mark the boldest lines of the stripes or checks around the armhole on the front bodice pattern.

2 Place the sleeve pattern on to the armhole, matching the notches, and copy the marks on to the sleeve pattern.

3 Place the sleeve pattern on to the fabric, matching the marks to the corresponding bold lines, and pin in place.

LAYOUT FOR EVEN CHECKS ON FOLDED FABRIC

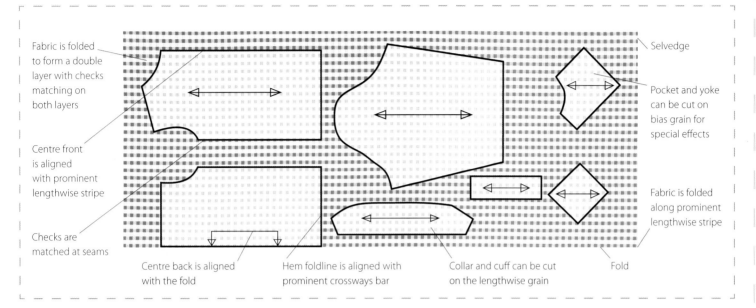

Fabric is folded to form a double layer with checks matching on both layers

Centre front is aligned with prominent lengthwise stripe

Checks are matched at seams

Centre back is aligned with the fold

Hem foldline is aligned with prominent crossways bar

Collar and cuff can be cut on the lengthwise grain

Selvedge

Pocket and yoke can be cut on bias grain for special effects

Fabric is folded along prominent lengthwise stripe

Fold

LAYOUT FOR EVEN STRIPES ON FOLDED FABRIC

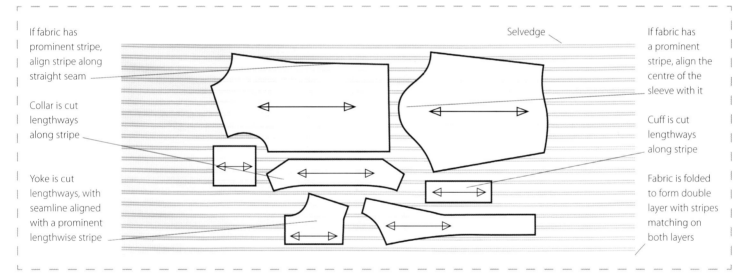

If fabric has prominent stripe, align stripe along straight seam

Collar is cut lengthways along stripe

Yoke is cut lengthways, with seamline aligned with a prominent lengthwise stripe

Selvedge

If fabric has a prominent stripe, align the centre of the sleeve with it

Cuff is cut lengthways along stripe

Fabric is folded to form double layer with stripes matching on both layers

LAYOUT FOR UNEVEN CHECKS OR STRIPES ON UNFOLDED FABRIC

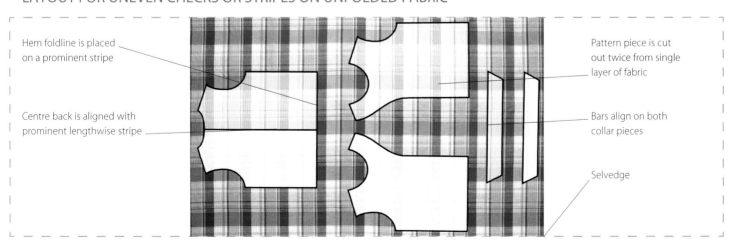

Hem foldline is placed on a prominent stripe

Centre back is aligned with prominent lengthwise stripe

Pattern piece is cut out twice from single layer of fabric

Bars align on both collar pieces

Selvedge

CUTTING OUT ACCURATELY

Careful, smooth cutting around the pattern pieces will ensure that they join together accurately. Always cut out on a smooth, flat surface such as a table – the floor is not ideal – and be sure your scissors are sharp. Use the full blade of the scissors on long, straight edges, sliding the blades along the fabric; use smaller cuts around curves. Do not nibble or snip at the fabric.

HOW TO CUT

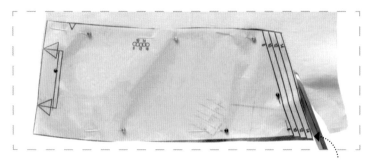

If you are right-handed, place your left hand on the pattern and fabric to hold them in place, and cut cleanly with the scissor blades at a right angle to the fabric.

MARKING NOTCHES

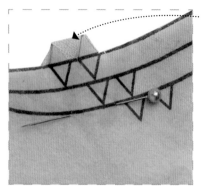

These symbols need to be marked on to the fabric as they are matching points. One of the easiest ways to do this is to cut out the mirror image of the notches in the fabric. Rather than cutting out double or triple notches separately, cut straight across from point to point.

MARKING DOTS

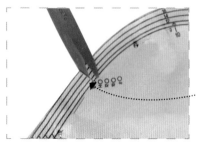

You can cut a small clip into the fabric to mark the dots that indicate the top of the shoulder on a sleeve. Alternatively, these can be marked with tailor's tacks (see opposite).

CLIPPING LINES

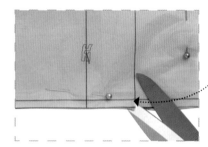

A small clip or snip into the fabric is a useful way to mark some of the lines that appear on a pattern, such as the centre front line and foldlines or notches and dart ends.

PATTERN MARKING

Once the pattern pieces have been cut out, but before you remove the pattern, you will need to mark the symbols shown on the pattern through to the fabric. There are various ways to do this. Tailor's tacks are good for circles and dots, or these can be marked with a water- or air-soluble pen. When using a pen, it's a good idea to test it on a piece of scrap fabric first. For lines, you can use trace tacks or a tracing wheel with dressmaker's carbon paper.

TRACE TACKS

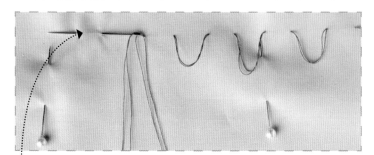

1 This is a really useful technique to mark centre front lines, foldlines, and placement lines. With double thread in your needle, stitch a row of loopy stitches, sewing along the line marked on the pattern.

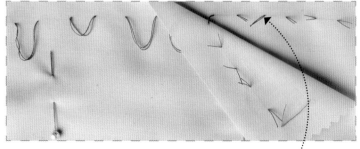

2 Carefully pull away the tissue. Cut through the loops, then gently separate the layers of fabric to show the threads. Snip apart to leave thread tails in both of the fabric layers.

TAILOR'S TACKS

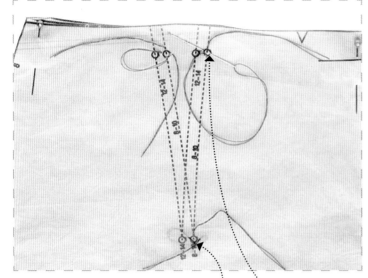

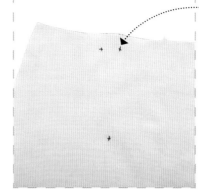

3 Carefully pull the pattern away. On the top side you will have four threads marking each dot. When you turn the fabric over, the dot positions will be marked with an X.

4 Gently turn back the two layers of fabric to separate them, then cut through the threads so that thread tails are left in both pieces of fabric.

1 As there are often dots of different sizes on the pattern, choose a different colour thread for each dot size. It is then easy to match the colours as well as the dots. Have double thread in your needle, unknotted. Insert the needle through the dot from right to left, leaving a tail of thread. Be sure to go through the pattern and both layers of fabric.

2 Now stitch through the dot again, this time from top to bottom to make a loop. Cut through the loop, then snip off excess thread to leave a tail.

TRACING PAPER AND WHEEL

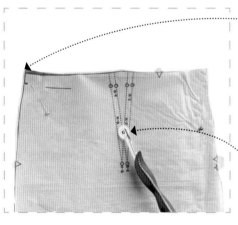

1 This method is not suitable for all fabrics as the marks may not be easy to remove. Slide dressmaker's carbon paper against the wrong side of the fabric.

2 Run a tracing wheel along the pattern lines (a ruler will help you make straight lines).

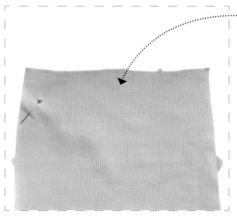

3 Remove the carbon paper and carefully pull off the pattern. There will be dotted lines marked on your fabric.

MARKER PENS

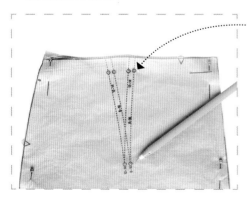

1 This method can only be used with a single layer of fabric. Press the point of the pen into the centre of the dot marked on the pattern.

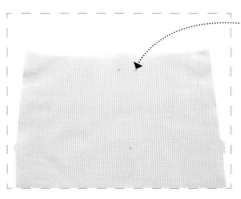

2 Carefully remove the pattern. The pen marks will have gone through the pattern on to the fabric. Be sure not to press the fabric before the pen marks are removed or they may become permanent.

GENERAL TECHNIQUES

Knowing the correct type of seam or stitch to use is essential for making a successful garment. Here the fundamentals of stitches, seams, and darts are described, as well as how to make sleeves, collars, and pockets, and adding zips, buttons, and hooks.

STITCHES FOR HAND SEWING

Although modern sewing machines have eliminated the need for a lot of hand sewing, it is still necessary to use hand stitching to prepare the fabric prior to permanent stitching – these temporary pattern-marking and tacking stitches will eventually be removed. Permanent hand stitching is used to finish a garment and to attach fasteners, as well as to help out with a quick repair.

THREADING THE NEEDLE

When sewing by hand, cut your piece of thread to be no longer than the distance from your fingertips to your elbow. If the thread is much longer than this, it will knot as you sew.

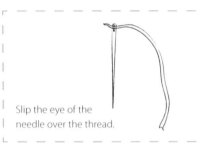

Slip the eye of the needle over the thread.

1 Hold your needle in your right hand and the end of the thread in your left. Keeping the thread still, place the eye of the needle over the thread.

Pull the thread through.

2 If the needle will not slip over the thread, dampen your fingers and run the moisture across the eye of the needle. Pull the thread through.

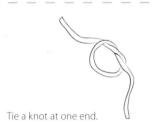

Tie a knot at one end.

3 At the other end of the thread, tie a knot as shown or secure the thread as shown on the right.

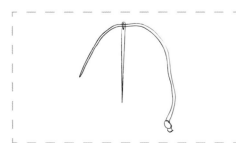

4 You are now ready to start your sewing.

SECURING THE THREAD

The ends of the thread must be secured firmly. A knot (see left) is frequently used and is the preferred choice for temporary stitches. For permanent stitching a double stitch is a better option.

DOUBLE STITCH

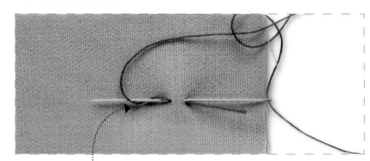

1 Take a stitch.

2 Go back through the stitch with the thread wrapped under the needle.

3 Pull through to make a knot.

BACK STITCH

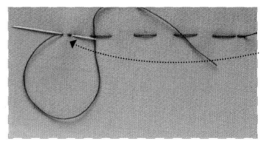

Make two small stitches in the same place.

LOCKING STITCH

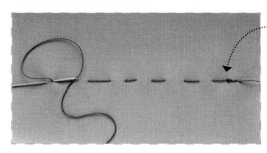

Start the stitching with a knot and finish by working a knot at the end.

HAND STITCHES

There are a number of hand stitches that can be used during the construction of a garment. Some are for decorative purposes while others are more functional.

RUNNING STITCH

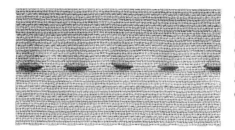

Very similar to tacking (see below), but used more for decorative purposes. Work from right to left. Run the needle in and out of the fabric to create even stitches and spaces.

PRICK STITCH

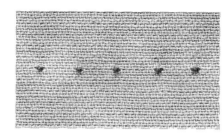

Often used to highlight the edge of a completed garment, such as a collar. Work from right to left. Make small stitches about 2mm (¹⁄₁₆in) long, with spaces between of at least three times that length.

TACKING STITCHES

Each of the many types of tacking stitches has its own individual use. Basic tacks hold two or more pieces of fabric together. Long and short tacks are an alternative version of the basic tacking stitch, often used when the tacking will stay in the work for some time.

BASIC TACKS

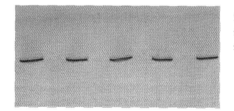

Starting with a knot and, using single thread, make straight stitches, evenly spaced.

LONG AND SHORT TACKS

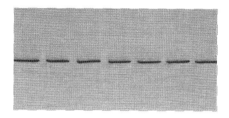

Make long stitches with a short space between each one.

HEM STITCHES

There are various hand stitches that can be used to hold a hem in place. Whichever of these you choose, ensure the stitches do not show on the right side.

FLAT FELL STITCH

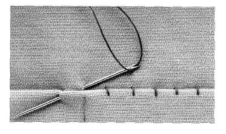

A strong, secure stitch to hold two layers permanently together. As well as being used for hems, this stitch is often used to secure bias bindings and linings. Work from right to left. Make a short, straight stitch at the edge of the fabric.

BLIND HEM STITCH

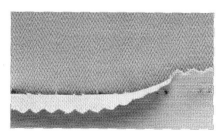

This stitch gives a very discreet finish to a hem. Working from right to left, fold the top edge of the fabric down and use a slip hem stitch (below left).

SLIP HEM STITCH

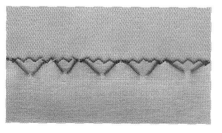

Also called a catch stitch, this is used primarily for securing hems. It looks similar to herringbone (right). Work from right to left. Take a short horizontal stitch into one layer and then the other.

HERRINGBONE STITCH

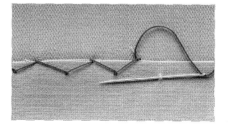

A very useful stitch as it is secure yet has some movement in it. It is used to secure hems and interlinings. Work from left to right. Take a small horizontal stitch into one layer and then the other, so the thread crosses itself.

MACHINE STITCHES AND SEAMS

When making a garment, fabric is joined together using seams. The most common seam is a plain seam, which is suitable for a wide variety of fabrics and garments. However, there are many other seams to be used as appropriate, depending on the fabric and garment being constructed.

SECURING THE THREAD

Machine stitches need to be secured at the end of a seam to prevent them from coming undone. This can be done by hand, tying the ends of the thread, or using the machine with a reverse stitch or a locking stitch, which stitches three or four stitches in the same place.

TIE THE ENDS

1 Pull on the top thread and it will pull up a loop – this is the bobbin thread.

2 Pull the loop through to the top.

3 Tie the two threads together.

REVERSE STITCH

1 When starting to machine, stitch a couple of stitches forward, then hold in the reverse button and reverse over them. Continue forward again.

2 At the end of the seam, reverse again to secure the stitches.

LOCKING STITCH

1 When starting to machine, press the locking stitch and stitch, then continue forward.

2 At the end of the seam, press the locking stitch again.

STITCHES MADE WITH A MACHINE

The sewing machine will stitch plain seams and decorative seams as well as buttonholes of various styles. The length and width of buttonholes can be altered to suit the garment.

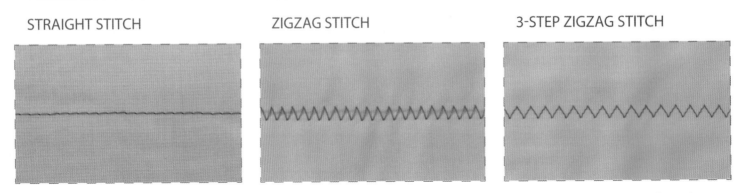

STRAIGHT STITCH

Used for most applications. The length of the stitch can be altered from 0.5 to 5.0 on most sewing machines.

ZIGZAG STITCH

To neaten seam edges and for securing and decorative purposes. Both the width and the length of this stitch can be altered.

3-STEP ZIGZAG STITCH

Made up of small, straight stitches. This stitch is decorative as well as functional. The stitch length and width can be altered.

BLIND HEM STITCH

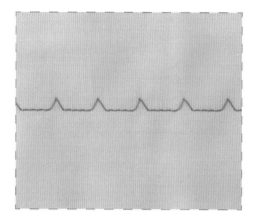

Made in conjunction with the blind hem foot. A combination of straight stitches and a zigzag stitch (see opposite page). Used to secure hems.

OVEREDGE STITCH

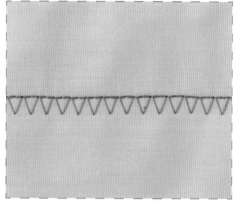

Made in conjunction with the overedge foot. The stitch is used for neatening the edge of fabric. The width and length of the stitch can be altered.

STRETCH STITCH

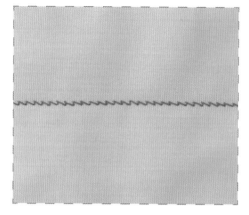

Also known as a lightening stitch. This stitch is recommended for stretch knits but is better used to help control difficult fabrics.

BASIC BUTTONHOLE STITCH

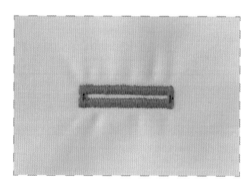

Square on both ends. Used on all styles of garment.

ROUND-END BUTTONHOLE STITCH

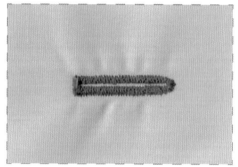

One square end and one round end. Used on jackets.

KEYHOLE BUTTONHOLE STITCH

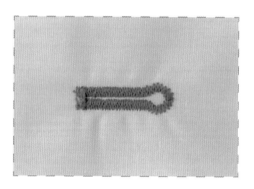

One square end and one end shaped like a loop. Used on jackets.

DECORATIVE STITCHES

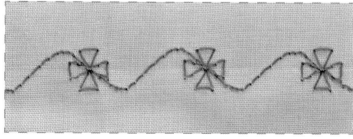

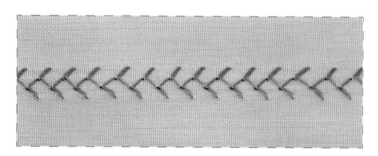

Sewing machines are capable of producing decorative linear stitches. These can be used to enhance a seam or the surface of a garment. Or, when worked as many rows together, they can be used to create a piece of embroidered fabric.

PLAIN SEAM
LEVEL OF DIFFICULTY *

A plain seam is 1.5cm (⁵/₈in) wide. It is important that the seam is stitched accurately at this measurement, otherwise the garment will end up being the wrong size and shape. There are guides on the plate of the sewing machine to help align the fabric correctly.

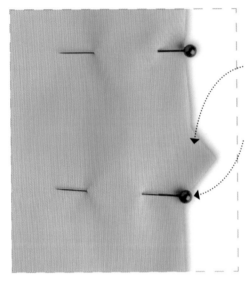

1 Pin the two pieces of fabric together, right side to right side, matching notches.

2 Place the pins at right angles to the raw edge at approx 5–8cm (2–3in) intervals.

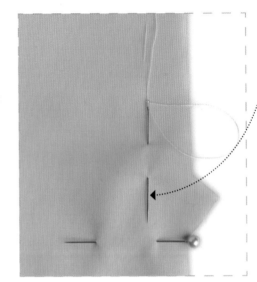

3 Tack the two pieces of fabric together about 1cm (³/₈in) from the raw edge, removing the pins as you reach them.

4 Machine the seam at 1.5cm (⁵/₈in), securing it at either end by your chosen technique.

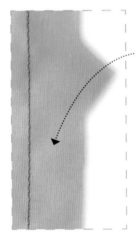

5 Carefully remove the tacking stitches.

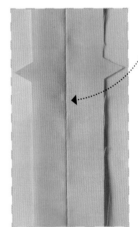

6 Press the seam open on the wrong side.

SEAM NEATENING
LEVEL OF DIFFICULTY *

It is important that the raw edges of the seam are neatened or finished – this will make the seam hard-wearing and prevent fraying. The method of neatening will depend on the style of garment that is being made and the fabric you are using.

PINKED

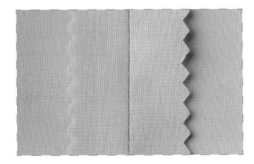

This method of neatening is ideal for fabrics that do not fray badly. Using pinking shears, trim as little as possible off the raw edge.

ZIGZAGGED

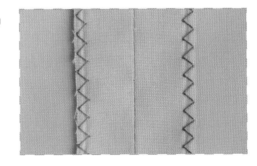

All sewing machines will make a zigzag stitch. It is an ideal stitch for stopping the edges fraying and is suitable for all types of fabric. Stitch in from the raw edge, then trim back to the zigzag stitch. Use a stitch width of 2.0 and a stitch length of 1.5.

3-THREAD OVERLOCK STITCH

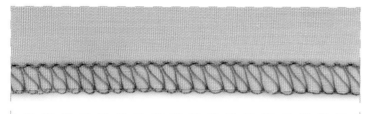

Stitched using three threads on the overlocker. Used to neaten the edge of fabric to prevent fraying.

4-THREAD OVERLOCK STITCH

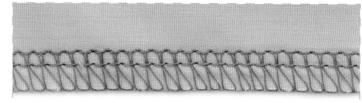

Made using four threads on the overlocker. Used to neaten edges on difficult fabrics or to construct a seam on stretch knits.

FRENCH SEAM
LEVEL OF DIFFICULTY **

A French seam is stitched twice, first on the right side of the work and then on the wrong side, enclosing the first seam. It is traditionally used on delicate garments and on sheer and silk fabrics.

1 Stitch a seam 5mm (³/₁₆in) from the edge of the fabric, with the fabric wrong side to wrong side so the seam is on the right side of the garment.

2 Trim the seam slightly, then press open.

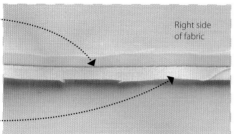

Right side of fabric

5 The first seam will be enclosed by the second seam.

3 Fold the fabric right side to right side.

4 Machine the stitched edge again using a 1cm (³/₈in) seam allowance.

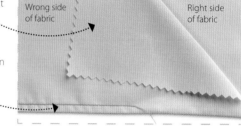

Wrong side of fabric

Right side of fabric

6 Press the completed seam flat on the right side.

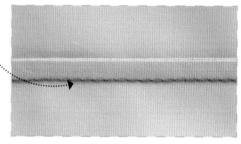

RUN AND FELL SEAM
LEVEL OF DIFFICULTY **

Some garments require a strong seam that will withstand frequent washing and wear and tear. A run and fell seam, also known as a flat fell seam, is very strong. It is made on the right side of a garment and is used on the inside leg seam of jeans, and on men's tailored shirts.

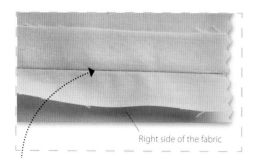

Right side of the fabric

1 Stitch a 1.5cm (⁵/₈in) seam on the right side of the fabric. Press open.

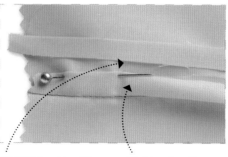

2 Trim the side of the seam allowance that is towards the back of the garment to one-third of its width.

3 Wrap the other side of the seam allowance around the trimmed side and pin in position.

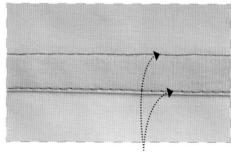

4 Machine along the folded pinned edge through all layers. Press.

5 When you turn to the right side, there will be two rows of parallel stitching.

HONG KONG FINISH

LEVEL OF DIFFICULTY **

This is a great finish to use to neaten the seams on unlined jackets made from wool or linen. It is made by wrapping the raw edge with bias-cut strips.

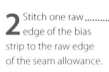
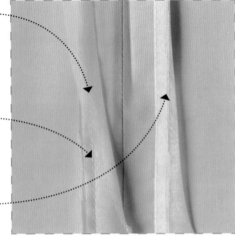
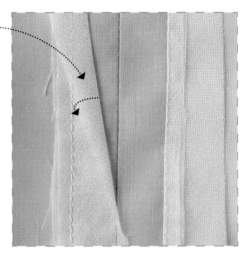

1 Cut bias strips of silk organza 2cm (³/₄in) wide. Good-quality lining fabric or 2cm (³/₄in) bias binding can also be used.

2 Stitch one raw edge of the bias strip to the raw edge of the seam allowance.

3 Press the other raw edge across the stitching.

4 Wrap the pressed raw edge over the stitching to the wrong side of the seam allowance.

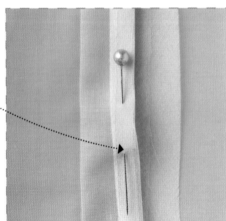
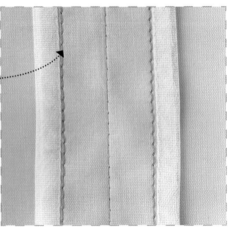

5 Pin the wrapped bias strip to the fabric, then press the folded edge.

6 Machine the wrapped bias strip to the seam, from the upper side of the seam, stitching alongside the edge of the bias.

A SEAM FOR SHEER FABRICS

LEVEL OF DIFFICULTY **

Sheer fabrics require specialist care for seam construction because they are very soft and delicate. The seam shown below is an alternative to a French seam; it is very narrow when finished and presses very flat so is less visible on sheer fabrics.

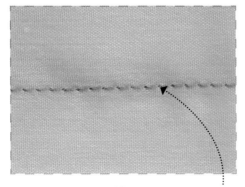
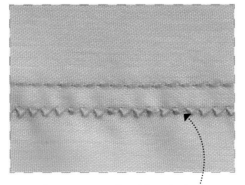
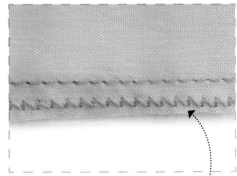

1 Join the two pieces of fabric on the wrong side with a 1.5cm (⁵/₈in) seam.

2 Machine again 5mm (³/₁₆in) from the first stitching, using either a very narrow zigzag stitch or a stretch stitch. Press.

3 Trim the raw edge of the fabric close to the second row of stitching.

STITCHING CORNERS AND CURVES

LEVEL OF DIFFICULTY **

Not all sewing is straight lines. The work will have curves and corners that require negotiation to produce sharp clean angles and curves on the right side. The technique for stitching a corner shown below applies to corners of all angles. On a thick fabric, the technique is slightly different, with a stitch taken across the corner, and on a fabric that frays badly the corner is reinforced with a second row of stitches.

STITCHING A CORNER

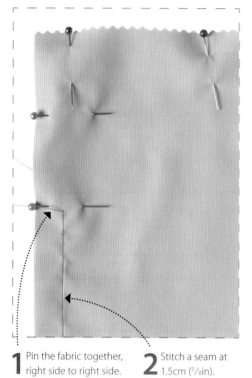

1 Pin the fabric together, right side to right side.

2 Stitch a seam at 1.5cm (⅝in).

3 On reaching the corner, insert the machine needle into the fabric.

4 Raise the presser foot and turn the fabric through 90 degrees to pivot at the corner.

5 Lower the presser foot and continue stitching along the other side.

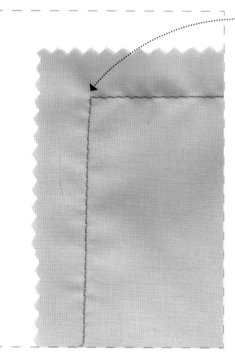

6 The stitching lines are at right angles to each other, which means the finished corner will have a sharp point when turned through to the right side.

STITCHING A CORNER ON HEAVY FABRIC

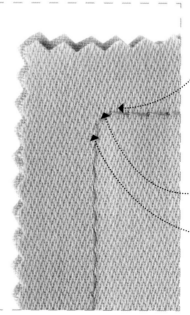

1 On a thick fabric it is very difficult to achieve a sharp point, so instead a single stitch is taken across the corner. First, stitch to the corner.

2 At the corner, insert the needle into the fabric, then lift the presser foot. Turn the fabric 45 degrees. Put the foot down again and make one stitch.

3 With the needle in the fabric, lift the foot and turn the fabric 45 degrees again. Lower the foot and continue stitching along the other side.

STITCHING A REINFORCED CORNER

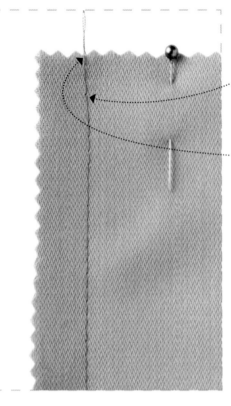

1 On the wrong side of the fabric, stitch along one side of the corner to make a 1.5cm (⅝in) seam.

2 Take the machining through to the edge of the fabric.

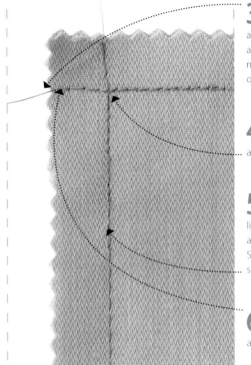

3 Stitch the other side of the corner at a 1.5cm (⅝in) seam allowance, again machining to the edge of the fabric.

4 The two stitching lines will overlap at the corner.

5 Stitch exactly over the first two stitching lines, this time pivoting at the corner (see Stitching a corner, steps 3–5, p.87).

6 Remove the surplus stitches in the seam allowance by unpicking.

STITCHING AN INNER CORNER

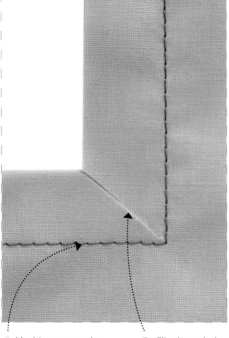

1 Machine accurately at 1.5cm (⅝in) from the edge, pivoting at the corner (see Stitching a corner, steps 3–5, p.87).

2 Clip through the seam allowance into the corner.

STITCHING AN INNER CURVE

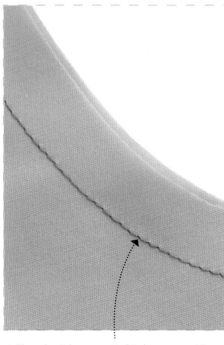

1 Place the right sides of the fabric together.

2 Stitch a seam at 1.5cm (⅝in) from the edge. Be sure the stitching line follows the curve (use the stitching guides on the needle plate to help).

STITCHING AN OUTER CURVE

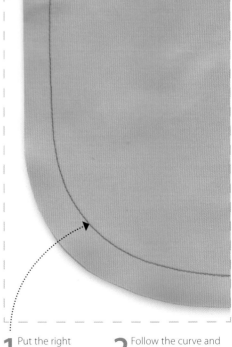

1 Put the right sides of the fabric together and stitch a 1.5cm (⅝in) seam.

2 Follow the curve and keep the stitching line at a uniform distance from the edge.

REDUCING SEAM BULK

It is important that the seams used for construction do not cause bulk on the right side. To make sure this does not happen, the seam allowances need to be reduced in size by a technique known as layering a seam. They may also require V shapes to be removed, which is known as notching, or the seam allowance may be clipped.

LAYERING A SEAM

On the majority of fabrics, if the seam is on the edge of the work, the amount of fabric in the seam needs reducing. Leave the seam allowance that lies closest to the outside of the garment full width, but reduce the seam allowance that lies closest to the body.

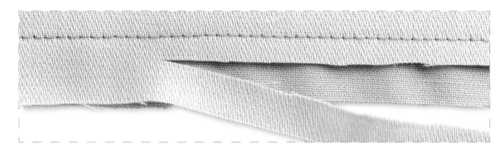

Cut along one side of the seam allowance to reduce the fabric in the seam allowance by half to one-third of its original width.

REDUCING SEAM BULK ON AN INNER CURVE

For an inner curve to lie flat, the seam will need to be layered and notched, then understitched to hold it in place (see p.90).

LEVEL OF DIFFICULTY *

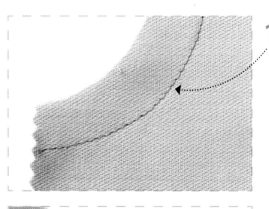

1 Stitch the seam on the inner curve.

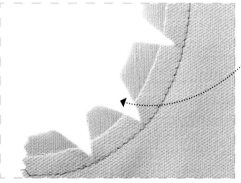

2 Layer the seam (see above), then cut out V notches to reduce the bulk.

3 Turn to the right side and press.

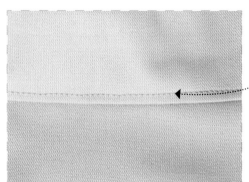

4 Understitch by machining the seam allowances on to the wrong side (see p.90).

REDUCING SEAM BULK ON AN OUTER CURVE

LEVEL OF DIFFICULTY *

An outer curve also needs layering and notching or clipping to allow the seam to be turned to the right side, after which it is understitched.

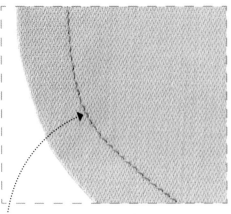

1 Make the seam, stitching along the outer curve.

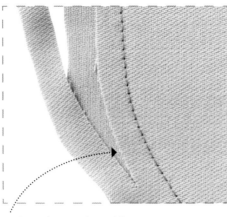

2 Layer the seam (see p.89).

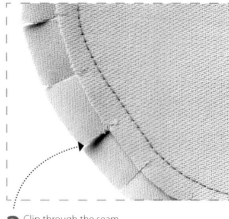

3 Clip through the seam allowances to reduce bulk.

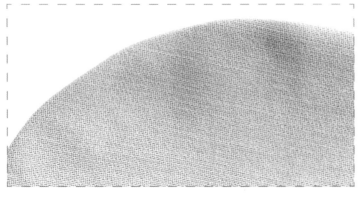

4 Turn through to the right side and press.

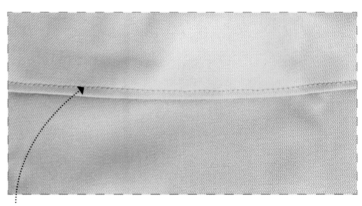

5 Understitch the seam allowances (see below) to finish.

FINISHING EDGES

LEVEL OF DIFFICULTY **

Top-stitching and understitching are two methods to finish edges. Top-stitching is meant to be seen on the right side of the work, whereas understitching is not visible from the right side.

TOP-STITCHING

A top-stitch is a decorative, sharp finish to an edge. Use a longer stitch length, of 3.0 or 3.5, and machine on the right side of the work, using the edge of the machine foot as a guide.

UNDERSTITCHING

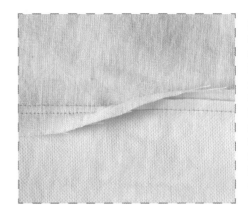

Understitching is used to secure a seam that is on the edge of a piece of fabric. It helps to stop the seam from rolling to the right side. First make the seam, then layer (see p.89), turn to the right side and press. Working from the right side, machine the seam allowance to the facing or to the lining side of the fabric.

DARTS

A dart is used to give shape to a piece of fabric so that it can fit around the contours of the body. Some darts are stitched following straight stitching lines and other darts are stitched following a slightly curved line. Always stitch a dart from the point to the wide end as then you will be able to sink the machine needle into the point accurately and securely.

PLAIN DART
LEVEL OF DIFFICULTY *

This is the most common type of dart and is used to give shaping to the bust in the bodice. It is also found at the waist in skirts and trousers to give shape from the waist to the hip.

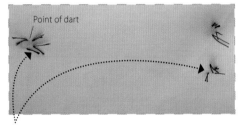

Point of dart

1 Tailor tack the dart as marked on the pattern, making one tack at the point and two at the wide ends.

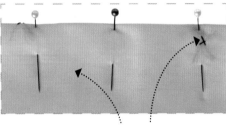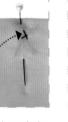

2 Fold the fabric right side to right side, matching the tailor's tacks.

3 Pin through the tailor's tacks to match them.

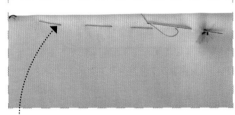

4 Tack along the dart line, joining the tailor's tacks. Remove the pins.

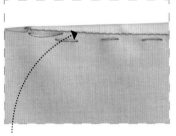

5 Machine stitch alongside the tacking line. Remove the tacks.

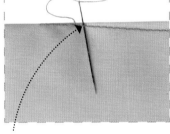

6 Sew the machine threads back into the stitching line of the dart to secure them.

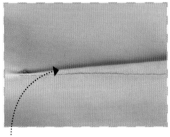

7 Press the dart to one side (see p.92).

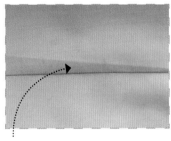

8 The finished dart on the right side.

SHAPING DARTS TO FIT
LEVEL OF DIFFICULTY **

Our bodies have curves, and the straight line of the dart may not sit closely enough to our own personal shape. The dart can be stitched slightly concave or convex so it follows our contours. Do not curve the dart by more than 3mm (⅛in) from the straight line.

CONVEX DART

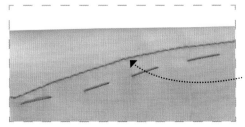

Use this for fuller shapes. Stitch the dart slightly inside the normal stitching line, to make a smooth convex curve.

CONCAVE DART

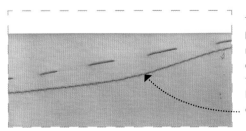

This is for thinner bodies as it takes up more fabric. Stitch the dart slightly outside the normal stitching line, in a smooth concave curve.

CONTOUR OR DOUBLE-POINTED DART

LEVEL OF DIFFICULTY **

This type of dart is like two darts joined together at their wide ends. It is used to give shape at the waist of a dress. It will contour the fabric from the bust into the waist and then from the waist out towards the hip.

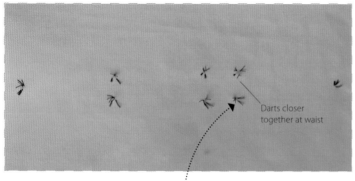

Darts closer together at waist

1 Tailor tack the dots on the pattern that mark the dart.

2 Cut through the loops in the tailor's tacks and remove the pattern.

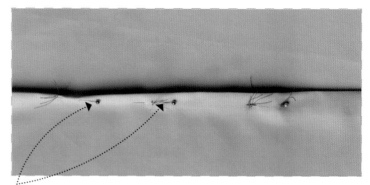

3 Bring the tailor's tacks together, keeping the fabric right side to right side, and pin the tacks together.

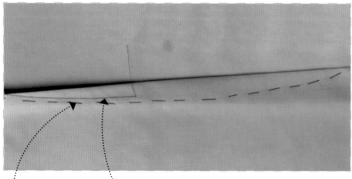

4 Make a row of tacking stitches just outside the pin line.

5 Machine stitch following the tailor-tack line, starting at one end and curving out to the widest point, then in to the other end. Secure the machine stitching at both ends.

6 Remove the tacking.

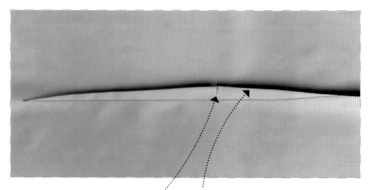

7 Clip across the fold in the fabric at the widest point, to allow the dart to be pressed to one side.

8 Press the dart to one side. Contour darts are normally pressed towards the centre front or centre back.

PRESSING A DART

If a dart is pressed incorrectly it can spoil the look of a garment. For successful pressing you will need a tailor's ham and a steam iron on a steam setting. A pressing cloth may be required for delicate fabrics such as silk, satin, and chiffon, and for lining fabrics.

1 Place the fabric, right side down, on the tailor's ham. The point of the dart should be over the end of the ham.

2 Press the fabric around the point of the dart.

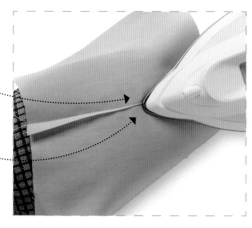

3 Move the iron from the point towards the wide end of the dart to press the dart flat, open, or to one side, depending on the type of dart.

GATHERS

Gathers are an easy way to draw up a piece of larger fabric so that it will fit on to a smaller piece of fabric. They often appear at waistlines or yoke lines. The gather stitch is inserted after the major seams have been constructed. Gathers are best worked on the sewing machine using the longest available stitch length. On the majority of fabrics, two rows of gather stitches are required, but for very heavy fabrics it is advisable to have three rows. Try to stitch the rows so that the stitches line up under one another.

MAKING AND FITTING GATHERS

LEVEL OF DIFFICULTY *

Once all the main seams have been sewn, stitch the two rows of gathers so that the stitches are inside the seam allowance. This should avoid the need to remove them because doing so after they have been pulled up can damage the fabric. In the example below, we attach a skirt to a bodice.

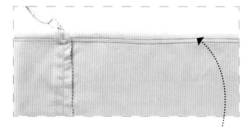

1 Stitch two rows of gathers around the waist of the skirt. Stitch the first at 1cm (³/₈in) and the second at 1.2cm (¹/₂in). Leave long tails of thread for gathering. Do not stitch over the seams.

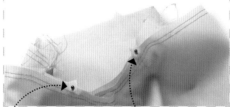

2 Place the skirt against the bodice section, right side to right side.

3 Match the notches and seams, and hold in place with pins.

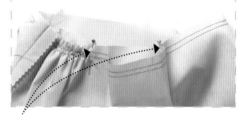

4 Gently pull on the two long tails of thread on the wrong side of the skirt – the fabric will gather along the threads.

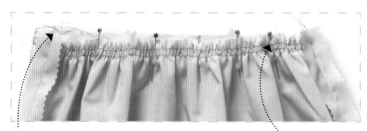

5 Secure the threads at one end to prevent the stitches from pulling out.

6 Even out the gathers and pin.

7 When all the gathers are in place, use a standard machine stitch to stitch a 1.5cm (⁵/₈in) wide seam.

8 Stitch with the gathers uppermost and keep pulling them to the side to stop them creasing up.

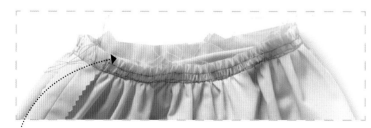

9 Turn the bodice of the garment inside. Press the seam very carefully to avoid creasing the gathers.

10 Neaten the seam by stitching both edges together. Use either a zigzag stitch or a 3-thread overlock stitch.

11 Press the seam up towards the bodice.

INTERFACINGS

An interfacing may be non-fusible (sew-in) or fusible and is only attached to certain parts of a garment. Parts that are normally interfaced include the collar and cuffs and the facings.

NON-FUSIBLE INTERFACINGS

All of these interfacings need to be tacked to the main fabric around the edges prior to construction of the work or seam neatening.

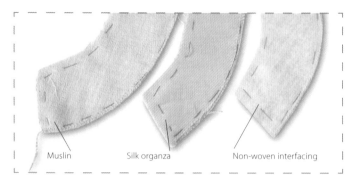

Muslin   Silk organza   Non-woven interfacing

FUSIBLE INTERFACINGS

A fusible interfacing is used in the same areas as a sew-in interfacing. To prevent the fusible interfacing from showing on the right side of the work, use pinking shears on the edge of the interfacing.

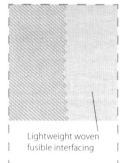

Lightweight woven fusible interfacing

Knitted fusible interfacing

Non-woven fusible interfacing

HOW TO APPLY A NON-FUSIBLE INTERFACING

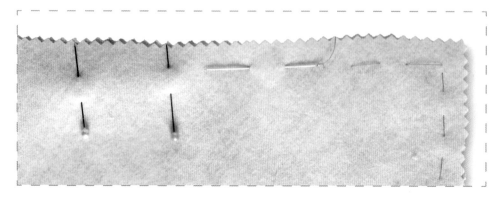

1 Place the interfacing on to the wrong side of the fabric, aligning the cut edges.

2 Pin in place.

3 Using a basic tacking stitch, tack the interfacing to the fabric or facing at 1cm (³⁄₈in) within the seam allowance.

HOW TO APPLY A FUSIBLE INTERFACING

1 Place the fabric on the pressing surface, wrong side up, making sure it is straight and not wrinkled.

2 Place the sticky side (this feels gritty) of the chosen interfacing on the fabric.

3 Cover with a dry pressing cloth and spray the cloth with a fine mist of water.

4 Place a steam iron, on a steam setting, on top of the pressing cloth.

5 Leave the iron in place for at least 10 seconds before moving it to the next area of fabric.

6 Check to see if the interfacing is fused to the fabric by rolling the fabric. If the interfacing is still loose in places, repeat the pressing process.

7 When the fabric has cooled down, the fusing process will be complete. Then pin the pattern back on to the fabric and transfer the pattern markings as required.

FACINGS

The simplest way to finish the neck or armhole of a garment is to apply a facing. The neckline can be any shape to have a facing applied, from a curve to a square to a V, and many more. Some facings and necklines can add interest to the centre back or centre front of a garment.

APPLYING INTERFACING TO A FACING

LEVEL OF DIFFICULTY *

All facings require interfacing. The interfacing is to give structure to the facing and to hold it in shape. A fusible interfacing is the best choice and should be cut on the same grain as the facing. Choose an interfacing that is lighter in weight than the main fabric.

INTERFACING FOR HEAVY FABRIC

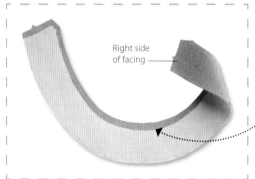

Right side of facing

For a heavy-weight fabric use a medium-weight fusible interfacing. Remove the seam allowance on the interfacing on the inner curve to reduce bulk.

INTERFACING FOR LIGHT FABRIC

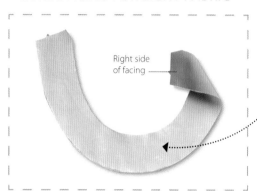

Right side of facing

For a light- to medium-weight fabric, choose a lightweight interfacing and fuse it over the complete facing.

CONSTRUCTION OF A FACING

LEVEL OF DIFFICULTY *

The facing may be in two or three pieces in order to fit around a neck or armhole edge. The facing sections need to be joined together prior to being attached. The photographs here show an interfaced neck facing in three pieces.

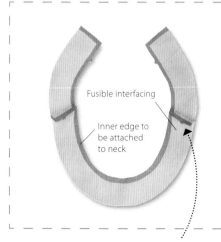

Fusible interfacing

Inner edge to be attached to neck

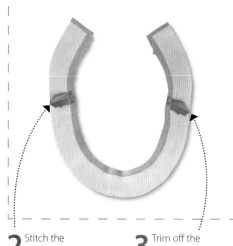

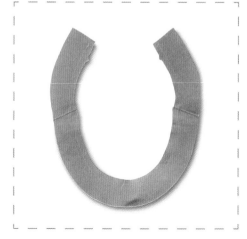

1 Tack together the pieces of the facing at the shoulder seams.

2 Stitch the shoulder seams and press open.

3 Trim off the outer corners on the shoulder seams.

4 The right side of the facing, ready to attach to the neckline.

NEATENING THE EDGE OF A FACING

LEVEL OF DIFFICULTY **

The outer edge of a facing will require neatening to prevent it from fraying, and there are several ways to do this. Binding the lower edge of a facing with a bias strip makes the garment a little more luxurious and can add a designer touch inside the garment. Alternatively, the edge can be stitched or pinked (see opposite).

CUTTING BIAS STRIPS

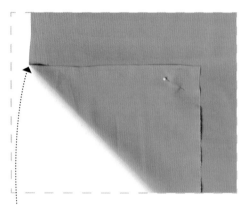
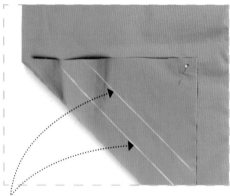
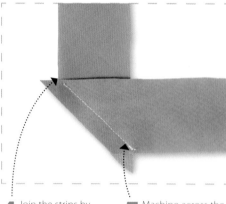

1 Fold the fabric on to itself at 45 degrees so the selvedge edges are at right angles to each other. Pin in place.

2 Using tailor's chalk and a ruler, mark lines 4cm (1½in) apart.

3 Cut along these lines to make bias strips.

4 Join the strips by placing them together right side to right side at 90 degrees to each other.

5 Machine across the join. There should be a triangle of fabric at either end of the seam.

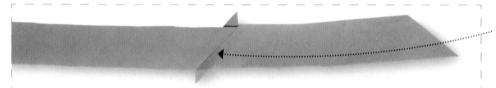

6 Press the seam open.

7 Press under the edges of the bias strip with the iron by running the bias strip through a 25mm (1in) tape maker.

NEATENING THE EDGE OF A FACING WITH A BIAS STRIP

1 Making your own bias strip is easy (see above). Open out one folded edge of the bias strip and place to the outer edge of the facing, right side to right side.

2 Machine along the crease line in the bias.

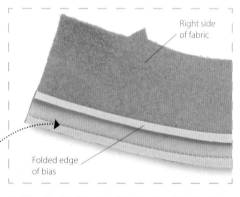

Right side of fabric

Folded edge of bias

3 Wrap the bias around to the wrong side of the work. Tack to hold in place.

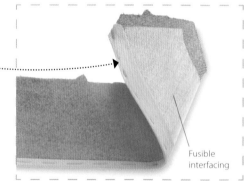

Fusible interfacing

4 Working from the right side of the facing, stitch in the ditch made by the bias-to-facing stitching.

5 On the right side of the facing, the bias-bound edge has a neat, professional finish.

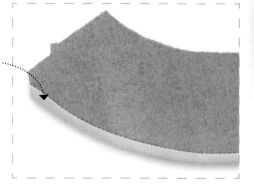

OTHER NEATENING METHODS

The following techniques are popular alternative ways to neaten the edge of a facing. The one you choose depends upon the garment being made and the fabric used.

LEVEL OF DIFFICULTY *

OVERLOCKED

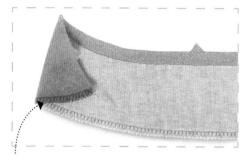

Neaten the outer edge with a 3-thread overlock stitch.

ZIGZAGGED

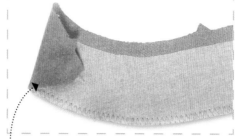

Neaten the outer edge with a zigzag stitch.

PINKED

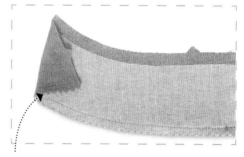

Machine stitch 1cm (³/₈in) from the edge and trim the raw edge with pinking shears.

ATTACHING A NECK FACING

This technique applies to all shapes of neckline, from round to square to sweetheart.

LEVEL OF DIFFICULTY **

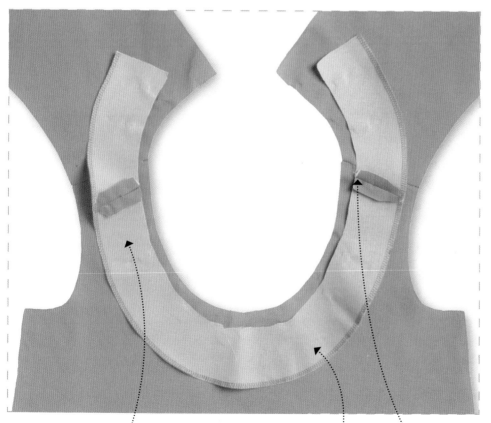

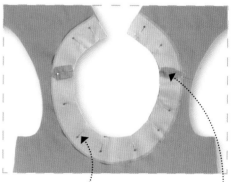

4 Pin the facing in place, matching around the neck edge.

5 Match the shoulder seams on the facing and the bodice.

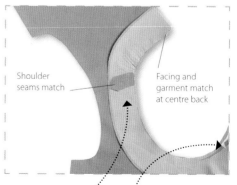

Shoulder seams match

Facing and garment match at centre back

1 Apply fusible interfacing to the facing and join the three pieces at the shoulder seams (see p.95).

2 Lay the neckline area flat, right side up. Place the facing on top, right side to right side.

3 Match the shoulder seams.

6 Machine in place using a 1.5cm (⁵/₈in) seam allowance.

7 Trim the facing down to half its width.

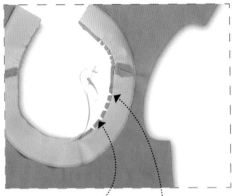

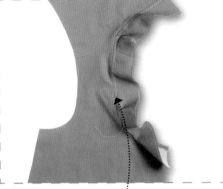

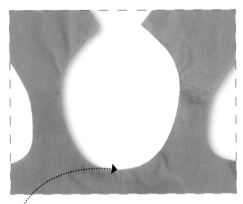

8 Clip out V notches around the neck edge.

9 Clip into the facing as well.

10 Press the seam allowance towards the facing.

11 Understitch by machining the seam allowance to the facing about 5mm (³/₁₆in) from the first stitching line.

12 Turn the facing to the wrong side and press the finished neck edge.

ATTACHING AN ARMHOLE FACING

LEVEL OF DIFFICULTY **

On sleeveless garments, a facing is an excellent way of neatening an armhole because it is not bulky. Also, as the facing is made in the same fabric as the garment, it does not show.

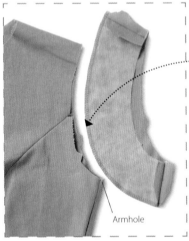

Armhole

1 Construct the interfaced armhole facing and neaten the long edge by your preferred method.

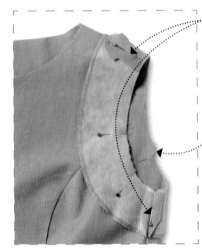

2 Place the facing to the armhole, right side to right side. Match at the shoulder seam and at the underarm seam.

3 Match the single notches at the front and the double notches at the back. Pin the facing in place.

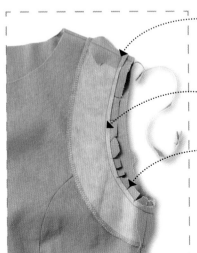

4 Machine around the armhole to attach the facing, taking a 1.5cm (⁵/₈in) seam allowance.

5 Layer the seam allowance by trimming the facing down to half its width.

6 Clip out some V shapes in the seam allowance to reduce bulk.

7 Turn the facing into position on the wrong side. Understitch by machining the seam allowance to the facing.

Understitching

8 On the underarm and shoulder seams, secure the facing to the seam allowance with cross stitches.

9 Press the stitched edge. On the right side the armhole will have a neat finish.

BIAS-BOUND NECK EDGE
LEVEL OF DIFFICULTY **

Binding is another way to finish a raw neck edge, especially on bulkier fabrics. In this method the bias strip is cut from the same fabric as the garment.

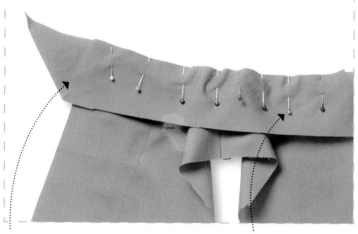

1 Cut a bias strip 7cm (2³/₄in) wide (see p.96).

2 Pin to the neck edge.

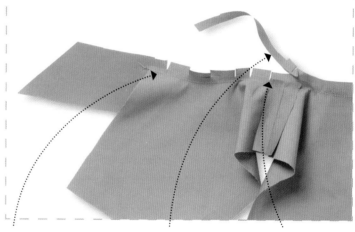

3 Machine along the neck edge using a 1.5cm (⁵/₈in) seam allowance.

4 Trim off half the seam allowance on the garment side.

5 Clip the seam allowance on the bias strip.

6 Fold the raw edge of the bias strip to the wrong side, to touch the line of machining.

7 Fold the bias strip again to the same machine stitches and pin.

8 Stitch permanently in position using a flat fell stitch.

A WAIST WITH A FACING

LEVEL OF DIFFICULTY **

Many waistlines on skirts and trousers are finished with a facing, which will follow the contours of the waist but will have had the dart shaping removed to make the facing smooth. A faced waistline always sits comfortably to the body. The facing is attached after all the main sections of the skirt or trousers have been constructed.

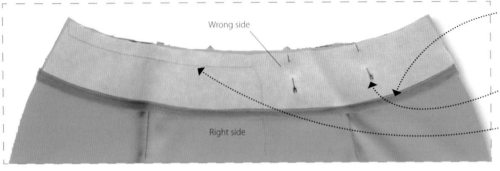

Wrong side

Right side

1 Apply a fusible interfacing to the facing. Neaten the lower edge of the facing with bias binding.

2 Pin the interfaced facing to the waist edge, matching notches.

3 Stitch the facing in place using a 1.5cm (⁵⁄₈in) seam allowance.

4 Layer the seam allowance by trimming the facing down to half its width.

5 Clip the seam allowance using straight cuts at 90 degrees to the stitching line.

6 Press seam allowance towards the facing.

7 Understitch by machining the seam allowance to the facing about 3mm (¹⁄₈in) from the first stitching line.

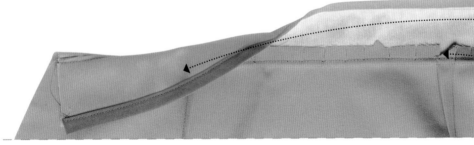

8 Turn the facing to the inside of the garment and press the waist edge.

9 Clip to reduce the bulk at the top of the dart.

10 The right side of the waistline.

COLLARS

All collars consist of a minimum of two pieces, the upper collar (which will be on the outside) and the under collar. Interfacing, which is required to give the collar shape and structure, is often applied to the upper collar to give a smoother appearance to the fabric.

TWO-PIECE SHIRT COLLAR
LEVEL OF DIFFICULTY ***

A traditional-style shirt has a collar that consists of two pieces: a collar and a stand, both of which require interfacing. The stand fits close around the neck and the collar is attached to the stand. This type of collar is found on men's and ladies' shirts. On a man's shirt, the stand accommodates the tie.

1 Cut the upper and under collar. Apply interfacing to the upper collar.

2 Machine the upper and under collar together, right side to right side, stitching around the sides and the outside edge. Stitch a sharp point by pivoting at the corners.

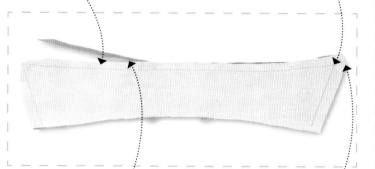
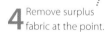
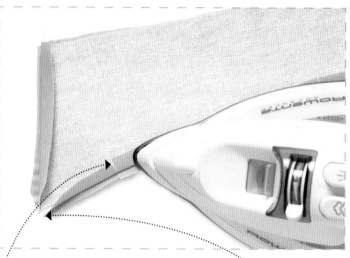

3 Trim the seam allowance from the under collar.

4 Remove surplus fabric at the point.

5 Press the seam open, pressing the upper collar seam allowance on to the collar. Clip as required.

6 The fabric at the point should not be bulky. If it is, remove more.

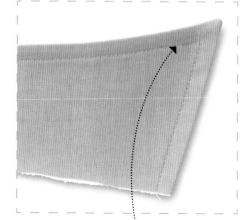

Collar fits between the tailor's tacks

7 Turn the collar to the right side and press.

8 Top-stitch the sides and outside edge using the edge of the machine foot as a guide.

9 Apply interfacing to one side of the stand.

10 Place the non-interfaced side of the collar to the interfaced side of the stand. Match the notches, then pin in place.

11 Machine the collar to the stand.

12 Place the stand to the shirt neck, matching the notches. The seam allowance on the stand will extend at the centre front. Pin and tack the stand to the shirt neck.

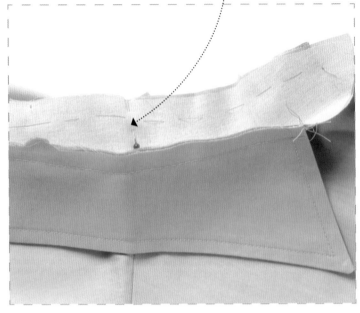

13 Pin the non-interfaced side of the stand to the shirt neck, so that there is a collar stand on the right and wrong side of the shirt.

14 Tack the collar stand to the shirt neck.

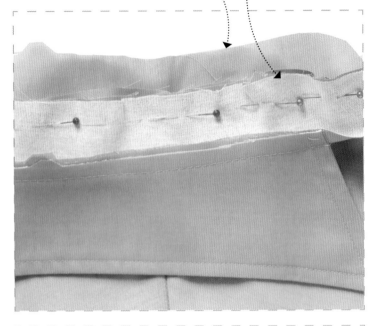

15 Reposition the stand so that the front edges come together right side to right side.

16 Machine along the shirt neck and around the centre front curve to the collar.

17 Trim away the non-interfaced side of the stand.

18 Remove surplus fabric from the corner.

19 Turn and press.

20 Bring the raw edge of the stand to the collar and turn under. Pin in place.

21 Secure this edge with a flat fell stitch.

22 Top-stitch the stand, if required. The stand fits snugly under the collar at the centre front.

WAISTBANDS

A waistband is designed to fit snugly but not tight to the waist. Whether it is shaped, straight, or slightly curved, it will be constructed and attached in a similar way. Every waistband will require a fusible interfacing to give it structure and support.

FINISHING THE EDGE OF THE WAISTBAND

LEVEL OF DIFFICULTY *

One long edge of the waistband will be stitched to the garment waist. The other edge will need to be finished, to prevent fraying and reduce bulk inside.

TURNING UNDER

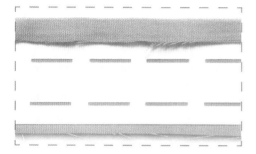

This method is suitable for fine fabrics only. Turn under 1.5cm (⅝in) along the edge of the waistband and press in place. After the waistband has been attached to the garment, hand stitch the pressed-under edge in place.

OVERLOCK STITCHING

This method is suitable for heavier fabrics as it lies flat inside the garment after construction. Neaten one long edge of the waistband with a 3-thread overlock stitch.

BIAS BINDING

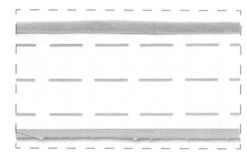

This method is ideal for fabrics that fray badly and can add a feature inside the garment. It lies flat inside the garment after construction. Apply a 2cm (¾in) bias binding to one long edge of the waistband.

ATTACHING A STRAIGHT WAISTBAND

LEVEL OF DIFFICULTY **

Special waistband interfacings are available, usually featuring slot lines that will guide you where to fold the fabric. Make sure the slots on the outer edge correspond to a 1.5cm (⅝in) seam allowance. If a specialist waistband fusible interfacing is not available you can use any medium-weight fusible interfacing.

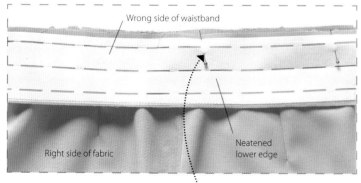

Wrong side of waistband

Right side of fabric

Neatened lower edge

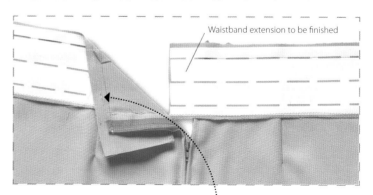

Waistband extension to be finished

1 Cut the waistband and apply the interfacing. Neaten one long edge.

2 Pin the waistband to the skirt waist edge, right side to right side. Match the notches.

3 Stitch the waistband to the waist edge using a 1.5cm (⅝in) seam allowance. The waistband will extend beyond the zip by 1.5cm (⅝in) on the left and by 5cm (2in) on the right.

4 Press the waistband away from the skirt.

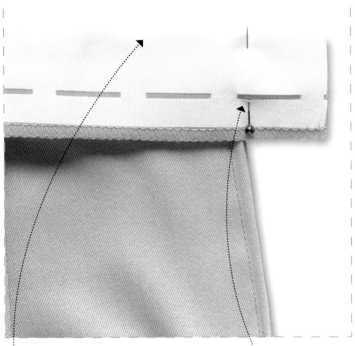

5 Fold the waistband along the crease in the interfacing, right side to right side. The neatened edge of the waistband should extend 1.5cm (⅝in) below the stitching line.

6 Pin and stitch the left-hand back of the waistband, as worn, in line with the centre back.

7 On the right-hand back, as worn, extend the waist/skirt stitching line along the waistband and pivot to stitch across the end.

8 Turn the ends of the waistband to the right side. The extension on the waistband should be on the right-hand back.

9 Add your chosen fasteners.

10 To complete the waistband, stitch through the band to the skirt seam. This is known as stitching in the ditch.

11 The finished straight waistband.

SLEEVES

Sleeves come in all shapes and lengths, and form an important part of the design of a garment. A set-in sleeve should always hang from the end of the wearer's shoulder, without wrinkles. The lower end of the sleeve is normally finished by means of a cuff or a facing.

INSERTING A SET-IN SLEEVE

LEVEL OF DIFFICULTY ***

A set-in sleeve should feature a smooth sleeve head that fits on the end of your shoulder accurately. This is achieved by the use of ease stitches, which are long stitches used to tighten the fabric but not gather it.

Armhole with notches

1 Machine the side seams and the shoulder seams on the garment and press them open.

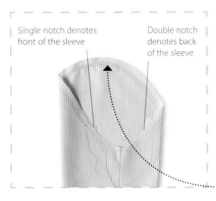

Single notch denotes front of the sleeve

Double notch denotes back of the sleeve

2 Machine the sleeve seam and press open. Turn the sleeve to the right side.

3 Around the sleeve head, machine two rows of long stitches between the notches – one row at 1cm ($^3/_8$in) from the edge and the second row at 1.2cm ($^1/_2$in). These are the ease stitches.

4 Place the sleeve into the armhole, right side to right side. Match the underarm seams and the notches.

5 Match the highest point of the sleeve to the shoulder.

6 Pull up the ease stitches until the sleeve fits neatly in the armhole.

7 Pin from the sleeve side.

8 Machine the sleeve in place, starting at the underarm seam and using a 1.5cm ($^5/_8$in) seam allowance. When you machine, have the sleeve on top and keep the machining straight over the shoulder.

9 Overlap the machining at the underarm to reinforce the stitching.

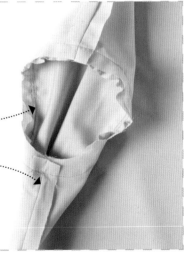

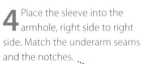

10 Stitch around the sleeve again inside the seam allowance.

11 Trim the raw edges of the sleeve.

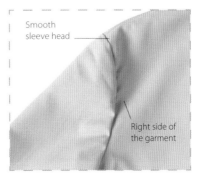

Smooth sleeve head

Right side of the garment

12 Neaten the seam with a zigzag or overlock stitch, then turn the sleeve through the armhole. Do not press or you will flatten the sleeve head.

INSERTING A PUFF SLEEVE

LEVEL OF DIFFICULTY **

A sleeve that has a gathered sleeve head is referred to as a puff sleeve or gathered sleeve. It is one of the easiest sleeves to insert because the gathers take up any spare fabric.

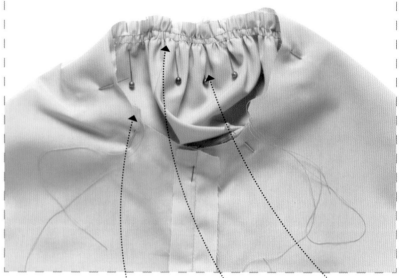

1 Machine the sleeve seam, right side to right side, using a 1.5cm (⅝in) seam allowance. Press the seam open.

2 Machine two rows of gather stitches between the sleeve notches, one row at 1cm (⅜in) from the raw edge and the second row at 1.2cm (½in).

3 Place the sleeve into the armhole, right side to right side.

4 Match the underarm seams and the notches.

5 Pull up the gather stitches to make the sleeve head fit the armhole.

6 Pin from the sleeve side.

7 Working with the sleeve on top, machine the sleeve to the armhole. Use a 1.5cm (⅝in) seam allowance. Overlap the machining at the underarm.

8 Stitch around the sleeve seam again between the first row of stitching and the raw edge.

9 Trim away the surplus fabric by 5mm (³⁄₁₆in).

10 Neaten the seam with a zigzag or overlock stitch.

11 Turn right side out – all the gathers will be at the top of the sleeve.

SLEEVE HEMS
LEVEL OF DIFFICULTY **

The simplest way to finish a sleeve is with a self hem. Here the edge of the sleeve is turned up onto itself. Alternative finishes include inserting elastic into a casing or attaching a cuff.

SELF HEM

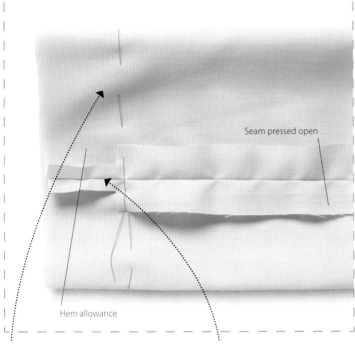

Seam pressed open

Hem allowance

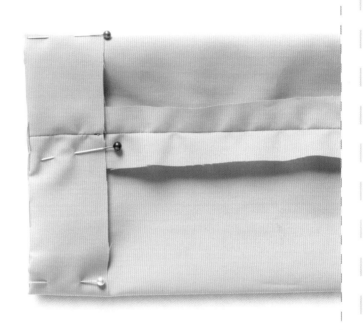

1 Mark the final length of the sleeve with a row of tacking stitches.

2 Remove the excess seam allowance in the hem area.

3 Turn up the hem along the tacked line.

4 Match the seams. Pin in place.

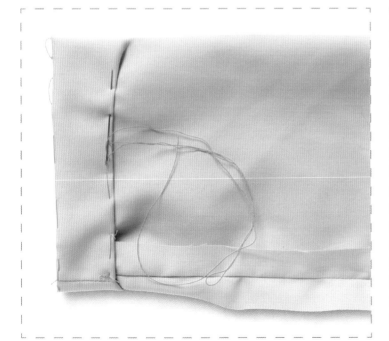

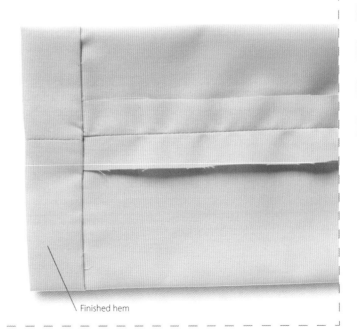

Finished hem

5 Turn under the top edge of the hem allowance by 1cm (³/₈in) and pin.

6 Tack to secure.

7 Hand stitch the sleeve hem in place using a slip stitch.

ELASTICATED SLEEVE EDGE

1 Make up the sleeve and press the seam open.

2 Work a row of tacking stitches on the foldline of the hem.

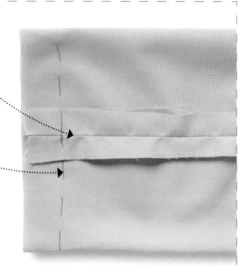

3 Turn up 5mm (³/₁₆in) at the raw edge and press.

4 Turn again on to the tacking line.

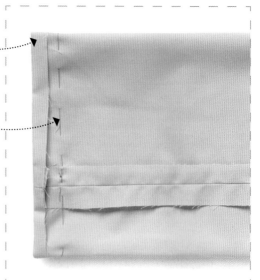

5 Machine to hold the turn-up in place, 2mm (¹/₁₆in) from the folded edge. Leave a gap either side of the seam allowance through which you will insert the elastic.

Gap to insert the elastic.

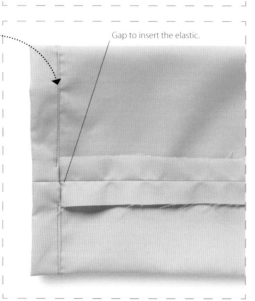

6 Machine the bottom of the sleeve 2mm (¹/₁₆in) from the edge, to give a neat finish. This will also help prevent the elastic from twisting.

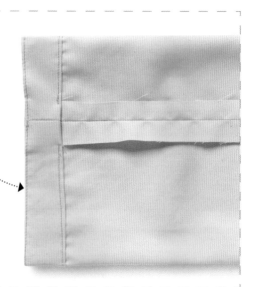

7 Cut a piece of elastic to fit the arm or wrist and insert it into the sleeve end between the two rows of machining.

8 Secure the ends of the elastic together, stitching an X for strength.

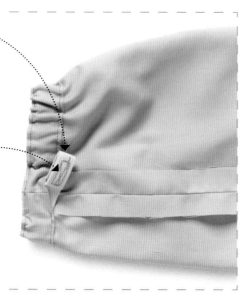

9 Turn the sleeve to the right side and check that the elasticated edge is even.

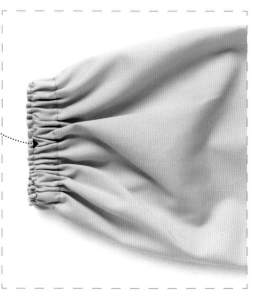

OPENINGS
LEVEL OF DIFFICULTY **

The following finishes can both be used to complete the opening that accompanies a cuff. Use the bound opening on fabrics that fray easily.

BOUND OPENING

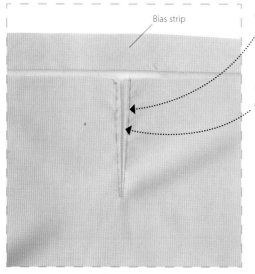
Bias strip

1 Stay stitch the split in the sleeve.

2 Slash between the stay stitching lines.

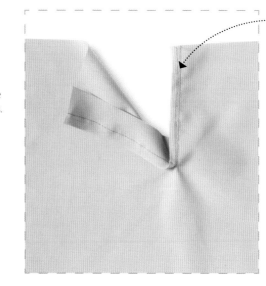

3 Working on the right side of the sleeve, pin the bias strip along the stay stitching lines. To stitch around the end of the split, open the split out into a straight line.

4 Wrap the bias strip, edge turned under, to the wrong side and pin in place.

5 Hand stitch to secure.

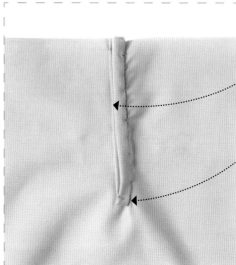

6 Allow the bias strip to close. One side of the strip will fold under and the other will extend over it.

7 Secure the top fold in the bias strip with a double stitch.

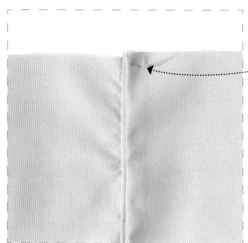

8 Tailor tack the cuff end of the bias strip to aid the placement of the cuff.

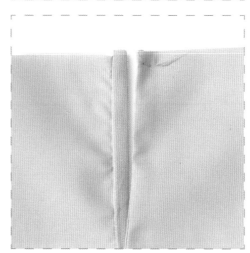

9 The finished bias-bound opening.

FACED OPENING

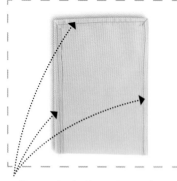

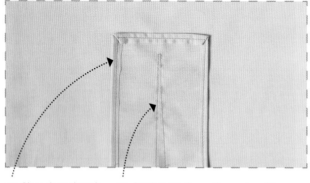

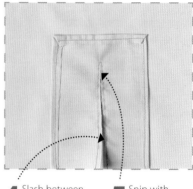

1 Turn under the long edges and one short edge on the facing by about 3mm (¹/₈in). Machine stitch to secure.

2 Place the right side of the facing to the right side of the sleeve at the appropriate sleeve markings.

3 Stitch vertically up the centre of the facing. Take one stitch across the end and then stitch down the other side with about 5mm (³/₁₆in) between the stitching lines at the raw edge of the sleeve.

4 Slash between the stitching lines.

5 Snip with small scissors into the end.

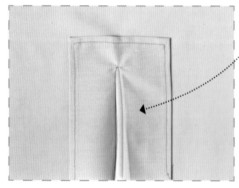

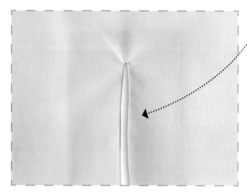

6 Turn the facing to the wrong side of the sleeve and press.

7 The finished opening on the right side.

ATTACHING A CUFF
LEVEL OF DIFFICULTY **

There are various types of cuff that can be attached to sleeve openings. The one-piece cuff and the one-piece lapped cuff are both – as their names suggest – cut from the fabric in one piece. Both work well with either a bound or faced opening.

ONE-PIECE CUFF

1 Apply fusible interfacing to the half of the cuff that will be the upper cuff.

2 Turn under a seam allowance on the non-interfaced side and tack to secure.

3 Fold the cuff along the centre line, right side to right side.

4 Machine stitch down the two short ends.

5 Layer the seam by trimming one edge, and clip the corners.

6 Turn the cuff through to the right side and press.

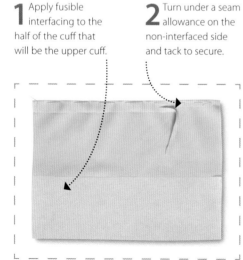

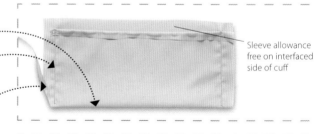

Sleeve allowance free on interfaced side of cuff

Seam allowance ready to stitch on to sleeve

ONE-PIECE LAPPED CUFF

1 Apply fusible interfacing to the upper half of the cuff. Pin the interfaced half of the cuff to the sleeve end, right side to right side.

2 Machine the cuff to the sleeve using a 1.5cm ($^5/_8$in) seam allowance.

3 Trim the sleeve side of the seam allowance to half its width. Press the seam towards the cuff.

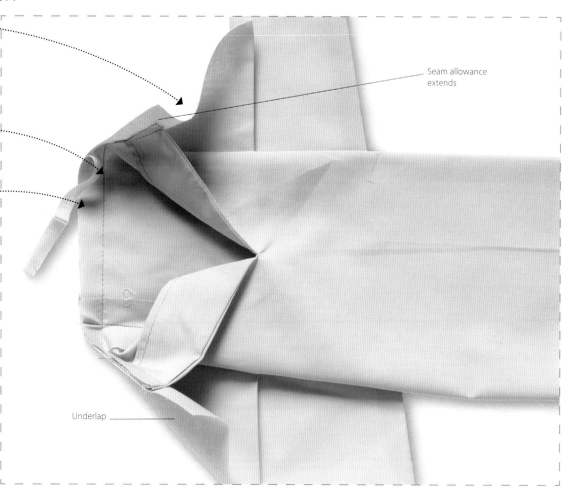

Seam allowance extends

Underlap

4 Fold the non-interfaced edge of the cuff over to the wrong side by 1.5cm ($^5/_8$in).

5 Fold the cuff to itself, right side to right side, so the folded edge of the cuff comes to the sleeve-to-cuff seamline.

6 Stitch one short end in line with the opening.

7 Stitch the other short end along from the sleeve-to-cuff seamline and then down the cuff.

8 Trim away the corners. Press the seams open.

9 Turn the cuff to the right side. Push the corners out to points.

10 On the inside, hand stitch the folded edge with a flat fell or blind hem stitch.

11 Make a buttonhole on the upper side of the cuff.

12 Sew a button on the underside of the cuff.

POCKETS

Pockets come in lots of shapes and formats. Some, such as patch pockets, are external and can be decorative, while others, including front hip pockets, are more discreet and hidden from view. You can also have a pocket flap that is purely decorative. This can be made from the same fabric as the garment or from a contrasting fabric. Whether casual or tailored, all pockets are functional.

POCKET FLAP
LEVEL OF DIFFICULTY **

This pocket flap is sewn where the pocket would be, but there is no opening beneath it. This is to reduce the bulk that would arise if there was a complete pocket.

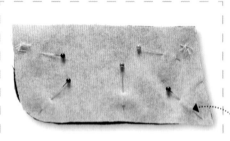

1 The flap consists of two pieces – a piece of lining and a piece of interfaced fabric. Place the two pieces together, right side to right side.

2 Match the tailor's tacks, then pin to secure.

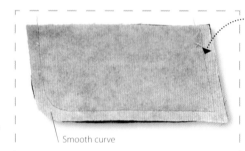

Smooth curve

3 Stitch the pieces together along three sides, using a 1cm (³⁄₈in) seam allowance. Stitch through the tailor's tacks. Leave the upper edge open.

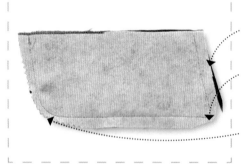

4 Layer the seam allowance, trimming from the lining only.

5 Remove the fabric from the point.

6 Use pinking shears to reduce the bulk through the curve. Press.

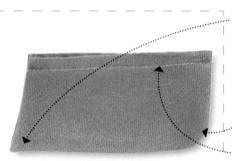

7 Turn the flap through to the right side. Push out the point.

8 Press the lining towards the back so that it does not show. Press a smooth curve.

9 Stitch across the upper open edge to hold together.

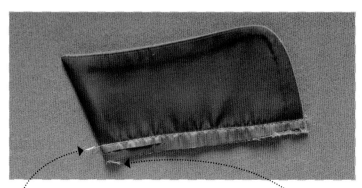

10 Place the flap to the garment, right side to right side. Match the edges of the flap to the tailor's tacks on the garment.

11 Machine in place over the stitching line.

12 Reduce the seam allowance by half. Press.

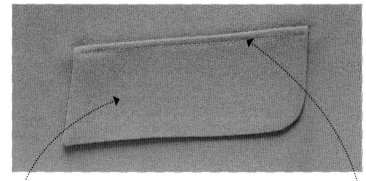

13 Press the flap into place. Allow the fabric at the top of the flap to roll gently downwards.

14 Top-stitch across the upper edge to secure.

LINED PATCH POCKET
LEVEL OF DIFFICULTY **

If a self-lined patch pocket is likely to be too bulky, then a lined pocket is the answer. It is advisable to interface the pocket fabric.

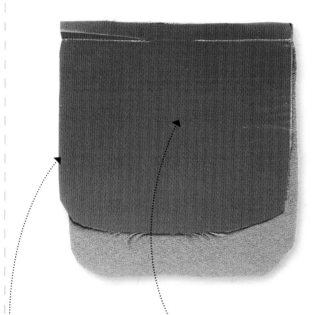

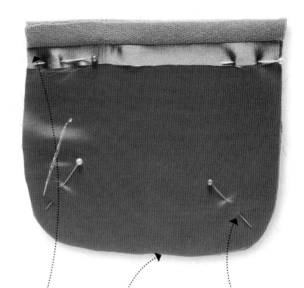

1 Cut the pocket fabric and apply interfacing. Cut the lining fabric. The lining should be shorter than the pocket.

2 Place the lining top edge to the pocket top edge and machine together. Leave a gap of about 3cm (1¼in) in the seam for turning through.

3 Press the pocket-to-lining seam open.

4 Bring the bottom edges of pocket and lining together.

5 Pin through the corners and along the sides.

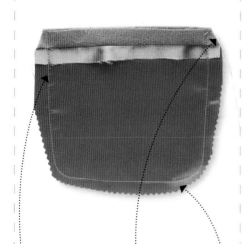

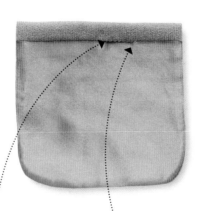

6 Stitch around the three open sides of the pocket to attach the lining to the pocket fabric.

7 Trim away the corners.

8 Use pinking shears to trim the curves.

9 Turn the pocket to the right side through the gap left in the seam. Press.

10 Hand stitch the gap with a flat fell or blind hem stitch.

11 The lined patch pocket is ready to be attached.

IN-SEAM POCKET

LEVEL OF DIFFICULTY **

In trousers and skirts, the pocket is sometimes disguised in the seam line. In the method below, a separate pocket is attached to the seam, but the pocket shape could also be cut as part of the main fabric.

1 Neaten the seam allowance on the front of the garment.

2 Neaten the straight edge of the pocket.

3 Place the pocket to the garment, right side to right side. Match the tailor's tacks and the neatened edges. Pin in place.

4 Machine the pocket in place using a 1cm (³/₈in) seam allowance. Only stitch between the tailor's tacks.

5 Repeat the process for the back of the garment.

6 Open the pocket out and press the seam towards the pocket.

7 Place the back section of the garment to the front, right side to right side. Match the seams above and below the pocket.

8 Stitch a 1.5cm (⁵/₈in) seam to join the front and back of the garment together. Extend the seam stitching 1.5cm (⁵/₈in) beyond the pocket stitching.

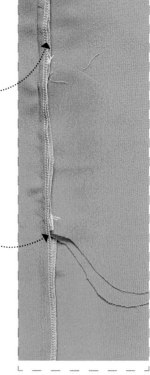

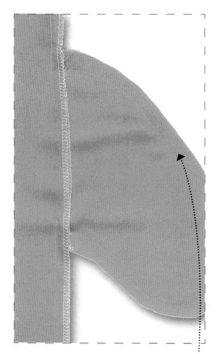

9 Stitch around the pocket to join the two pieces together stopping the stitching at the pocket-to-garment stitching line.

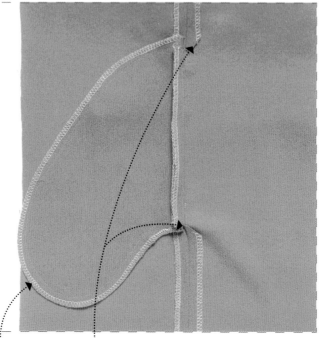

10 Neaten the raw edges of the pocket.

11 On the garment back, clip the seam allowance to the pocket-to-garment stitching line.

12 Press the side seam open. Press the pocket towards the front of the garment.

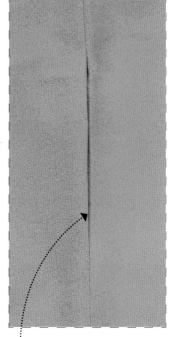

13 On the right side, the pocket opening is discreet.

FRONT HIP POCKET
LEVEL OF DIFFICULTY **

On many trousers and casual skirts, the pocket is placed on the hipline. It can be low on the hipline or cut quite high, as on jeans. The construction is the same for all types of hip pockets. When inserted at an angle, hip pockets can slim the figure.

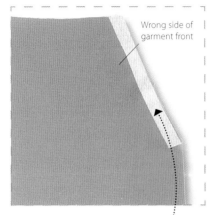

Wrong side of garment front

1 Apply a piece of fusible tape on the garment along the line of the pocket.

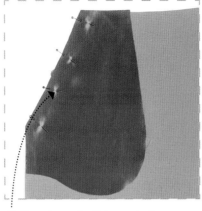

2 Place the pocket lining to the front of the garment, right side to right side. Match any notches that are on the seam. Pin in place.

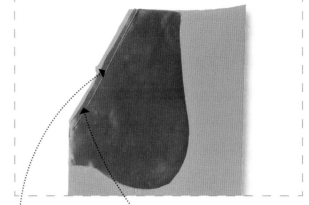

3 Machine the lining in place, taking a 1.5cm (⁵/₈in) seam allowance.

4 Trim the lining side of the seam allowance down to half its width.

5 Open out the lining and press the seam towards it.

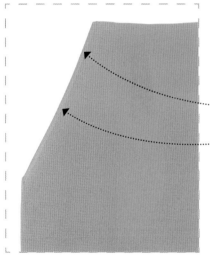

6 Turn the lining to the inside. Press so that the lining is not visible on the outside.

7 Top-stitch 5mm (³/₁₆in) from the edge.

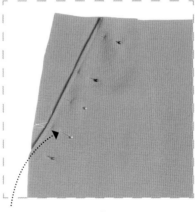

8 On the right side of the garment, pin the front to the side front along the placement lines.

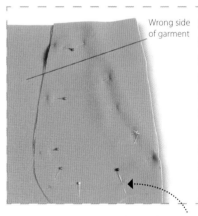

Wrong side of garment

9 On the wrong side, pin the side front to the lining to create the pocket.

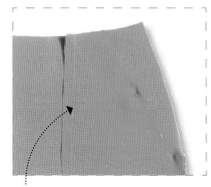

10 Machine the pocket and lining together using a 1.5cm (⁵/₈in) seam allowance. Press.

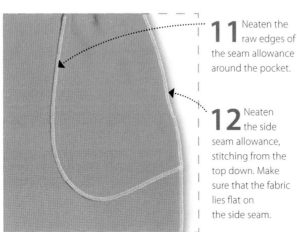

11 Neaten the raw edges of the seam allowance around the pocket.

12 Neaten the side seam allowance, stitching from the top down. Make sure that the fabric lies flat on the side seam.

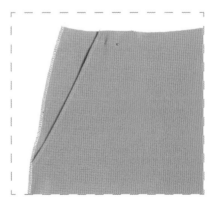

13 The angled front hip pocket from the right side.

HEMLINES

The lower edge of a garment is normally finished with a hem. Sometimes the style of the garment dictates the type of hem used, and sometimes the fabric.

MARKING A HEMLINE

On a garment such as a skirt or a dress it is important that the hemline is level all around. Even if the fabric has been cut straight, some styles of skirt – such as A-line or circular – will "drop", which means that the hem edge is longer in some places. This is due to the fabric stretching where it is not on the straight of the grain. Hang the garment for 24 hours in a warm room before hemming so you do not end up with an uneven hem.

USING A RULER

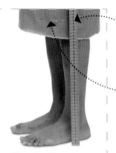

1 Put on the skirt or dress but no shoes. With the end of the ruler on the floor, have a helper measure and mark.

2 Use pins to mark the crease line of the proposed hem. Ensure the measurement from floor to pin line is the same all the way round.

USING A DRESSMAKER'S DUMMY

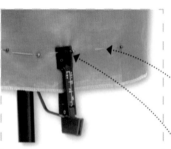

1 Adjust the dummy to your height and measurements. Place the skirt or dress on the dummy.

2 The hem marker on its stand will hold the fabric. Use the marker to mark the crease line of the proposed hem.

3 Slide a pin through the slot in the marker, then gently release the marker.

HAND-STITCHED HEMS

LEVEL OF DIFFICULTY *

One of the most popular ways to secure a hem edge is by hand. Hand stitching is discreet and, if a fine hand-sewing needle is used, the stitching should not show on the right side of the work. Always finish the raw edge before stitching the hem.

TIPS FOR SEWING HEMS BY HAND

1 Always use a single thread in the needle – a polyester all-purpose thread is ideal for hemming.
2 Once the raw edge of the hem allowance has been neatened by one of the methods below, secure it using a slip hem stitch. Take half of the stitch into the neatened edge and the other half into the wrong side of the garment fabric.

3 Start and finish the hand stitching with a double stitch, not a knot, because knots will catch and pull the hem down.
4 It is a good idea to take a small back stitch every 10cm (4in) or so to make sure that if the hem does come loose in one place it will not all unravel.

OVERLOCKED FINISH

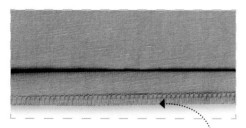

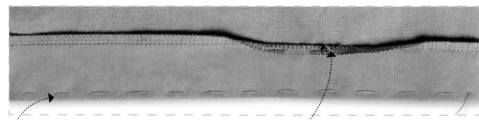

1 Using a 3-thread overlock stitch, stitch along the raw edge of the hem allowance.

2 Gently press the hem up into position and tack close to the crease.

3 Roll back the overlocked edge. Using a slip hem stitch, stitch the hem in place.

4 Press carefully to prevent the overlocking from being imprinted on the right side.

BIAS-BOUND FINISH

1 This is a good finish for fabrics that fray or that are bulky. Turn up the hem on to the wrong side of the garment and tack close to the crease line.

2 Pin the bias binding to the raw edge of the hem allowance.

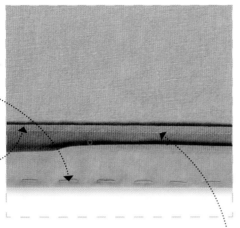
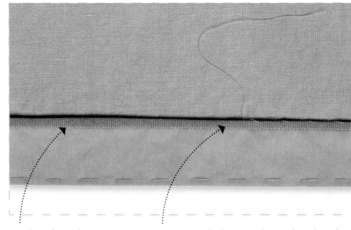

3 Open out the crease in the bias and stitch along the crease line, keeping the raw edges level.

4 Turn down the bias over the raw edge and press.

5 Using a slip hem stitch, join the edge of the bias to the wrong side of the fabric. Remove the tacking and press lightly.

ZIGZAG FINISH

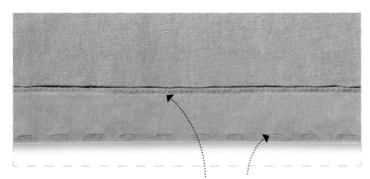
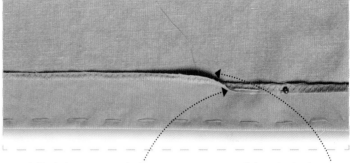

1 Use this to neaten the edge of the hem on fabrics that do not fray too badly. Set the sewing machine to a zigzag stitch, width 4.0 and length 3.0. Machine along the raw edge. Trim the fabric edge back to the zigzag stitch.

2 Turn up the hem on to the wrong side of the garment and tack in place close to the crease line.

3 Fold back the zigzag-stitched edge. Using a slip hem stitch, stitch the hem into place.

4 Roll the edge back into position. Remove the tacking and press lightly.

PINKED FINISH

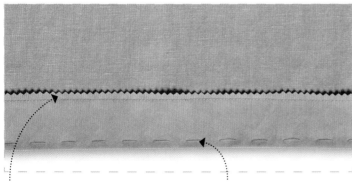
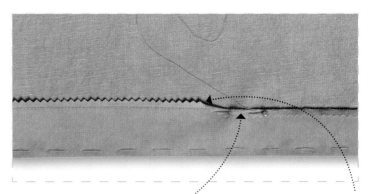

1 Pinking shears can give an excellent hem finish on difficult fabrics. Machine a row of straight stitching along the raw edge, 1cm (³/₈in) from the edge. Pink the raw edge.

2 Turn up the hem on to the wrong side of the garment and tack in place close to the crease line.

3 Fold back the edge along the machine stitching line. Using a slip hem stitch, stitch the hem in place.

4 Roll the hem edge back into position. Remove the tacking and press lightly.

CURVED HEM FINISH

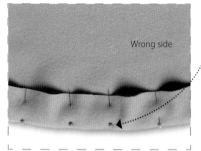

Wrong side

1 Fold up the hemline and pin, placing the pins vertically to avoid squashing the fullness out of the raw upper edge.

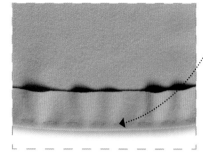

2 Tack the hem into position close to the crease line. Remove the pins.

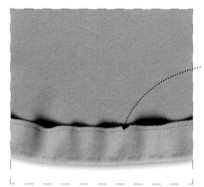

3 Make a row of long machine stitches, length 5.0, close to the raw upper edge of the turned-up hem.

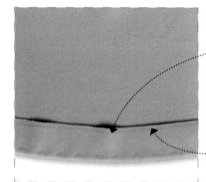

4 Pull on one of the threads of the long stitches to tighten the fabric and ease out the fullness.

5 Use the steam iron to shrink out the remainder of the fullness. The hem is now ready to be stitched in place by hand or machine.

MACHINED HEMS

LEVEL OF DIFFICULTY *

On many occasions , the hem or edge of a garment or other item is turned up and secured using the sewing machine. It can be stitched with a straight stitch, a zigzag stitch, or a blind hem stitch. Hems can also be made on the overlocker.

DOUBLE-TURN HEM

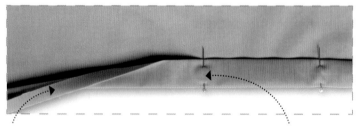

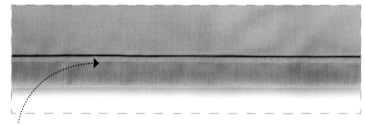

1 This hem will add weight at the edge. Fold up the raw edge of the fabric once and then fold again.

2 Pin in place, then press.

3 Machine using a straight stitch, close to the upper fold.

HEMS ON DIFFICULT FABRICS

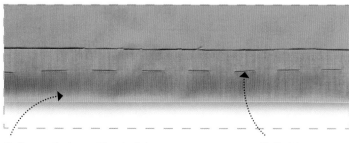

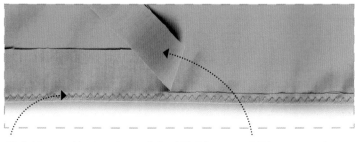

1 Turn up the hem with a single turn.

2 Tack to secure.

3 Set the machine to a zigzag stitch, width 3.5 and length 2.0, and zigzag close to the fold.

4 Trim away surplus hem allowance. Press.

ZIPS

The zip is probably the most used of all fastenings. There are a great many types available, in a variety of lengths, colours, and materials, but they all fall into one of five categories: skirt or trouser zips, metal or jeans zips, concealed zips, open-ended zips, and decorative zips.

LAPPED ZIP
LEVEL OF DIFFICULTY **

A skirt zip in a skirt or a dress is usually put in by means of a lapped technique or a centred zip technique (see p.120). For both of these techniques you will require the zip foot on the sewing machine. A lapped zip features one side of the seam – the left-hand side – lapping over the teeth of the zip to conceal them.

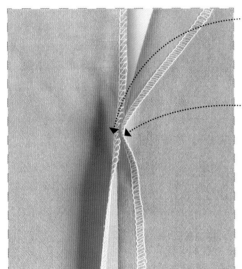

1 Stitch the seam, leaving enough of it open to accommodate the zip.

2 Secure the end of the stitching.

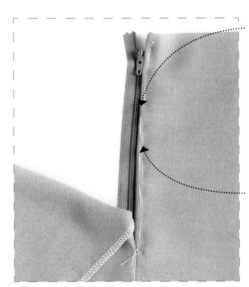

3 Insert the right-hand side of the zip first. Fold back the right-hand seam allowance by 1.2cm (¹/₂in). This folded edge will not be in line with the seam.

4 Place the folded edge against the zip teeth. Tack.

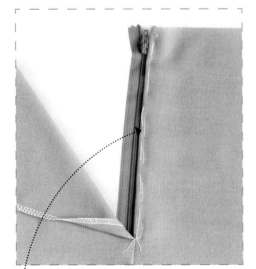

5 Using the zip foot, stitch along the tack line to secure the zip tape to the fabric. Stitch from the bottom of the zip to the top.

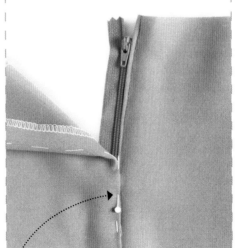

6 Fold back the left-hand seam allowance by 1.5cm (⁵/₈in). Place the folded edge over the machine line of the other side. Pin and then tack.

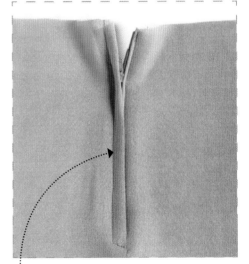

7 Starting at the bottom of the zip, stitch across from the centre seamline and then up the left side of the zip. The finished zip should have its teeth covered by the fabric.

CENTRED ZIP
LEVEL OF DIFFICULTY **

With a centred zip, the two folded edges of the seam allowances meet over the centre of the teeth, to conceal the zip completely.

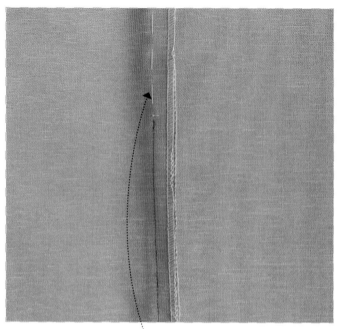

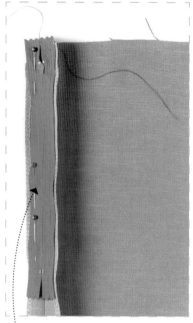

1 Stitch the seam, leaving a gap for the zip.

2 Tack the rest of the seam.

3 Press the seam open lightly.

4 Centre the zip behind the tacked part of the seam. Pin and then tack in place along both sides.

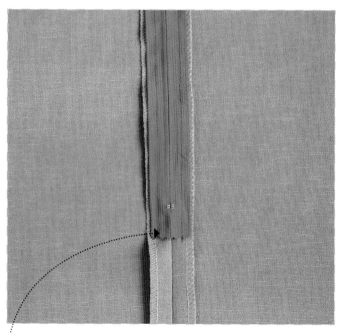
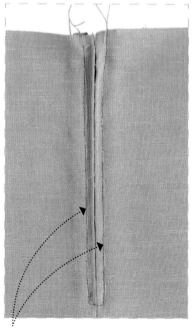

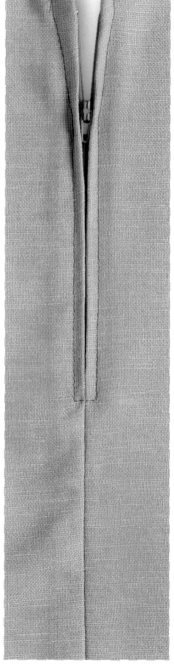

5 Machine the zip tape to the seam allowance. Make sure both sides of the tape are secured to the seam allowances. Stitch right to the end of the zip tape.

6 Working from the right side, stitch down one side of the zip, across the bottom, and up the other side through all the layers.

7 Remove the tacks.

8 The finished zip from the right side.

FACED FLY-FRONT ZIP
LEVEL OF DIFFICULTY ***

Whether it be for a classic pair of trousers or a pair of jeans, a fly front is the most common technique for inserting a trouser zip. The zip usually has a facing behind it to prevent the zip teeth from catching.

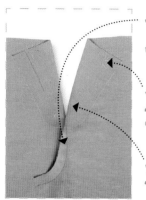

1 Stitch the seam, leaving a gap for the zip.

2 Using tailor's tacks, mark the centre front lines.

3 Trace tack the foldlines.

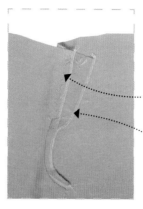

4 Trim the left-hand front of the opening straight, to measure 1.5cm (⁵/₈in) from the centre line.

5 Neaten the edges on both sides.

6 Fold the left-hand front along the foldline.

7 Place the fold adjacent to the zip teeth and pin in place. The zip may be too long; if so, it will extend beyond the top of the fabric.

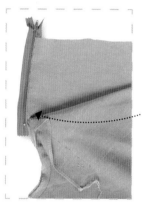

8 Machine along the foldline using the zip foot. Extend the machining past the seam stitching line.

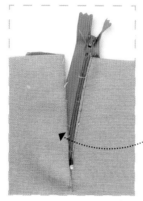

9 Fold the right-hand front along the foldline. Place the foldline over the zip and pin to the machine stitching on the left-hand side.

10 On the inside, pin the zip tape to the fabric extension.

11 Machine the zip tape to the fabric along the centre of the tape.

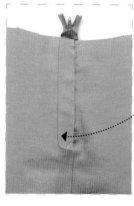

12 On the right side, top-stitch around the zip. Start stitching at the centre front. Stitch a smooth curve.

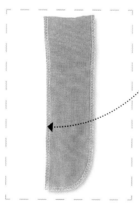

13 Neaten all the edges of the fly-front facing, leaving the top edge raw.

14 On the wrong side, pin the facing to the left-hand side seam allowance. Ensure that the facing covers the zip fully.

15 Machine to the seam allowance on the left-hand side.

16 Attach the waistband over the zip and the facings. Trim facing and zip.

17 Secure the lower edge of the facing on the right-hand side to the right-hand seam allowance.

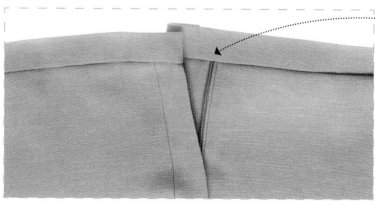

18 The waistband goes over the zip and acts as the zip stop. Attach a trouser hook and eye.

CONCEALED OR INVISIBLE ZIP

LEVEL OF DIFFICULTY **

This type of zip looks different from other zips because the teeth are on the reverse and nothing except the pull is seen on the front. The zip is inserted before the seam is stitched. A special concealed zip foot is required for stitching this zip in position.

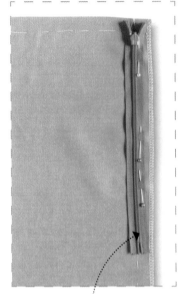

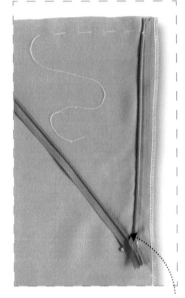

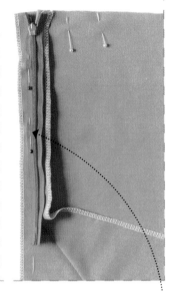

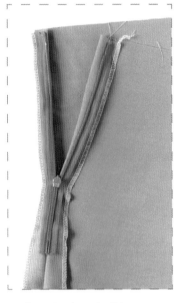

1 Mark the seam allowance with tacking stitches.

2 Centre the zip over the tack line, right side of zip to right side of fabric. Pin in place down one side.

3 Undo the zip. Using the concealed zip foot, stitch under the teeth from the top of the zip. Stop when the foot hits the zip pull and do two reverse stitches.

4 Do the zip up. Place the other side of the fabric to the zip. Match along the upper edge. Pin the other side of the zip tape in place.

5 Open the zip again. Using the concealed zip foot, stitch down the other side of the zip to attach to the other side of the fabric. Remove any tacking stitches.

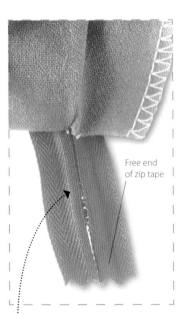

Free end of zip tape

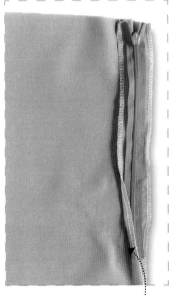

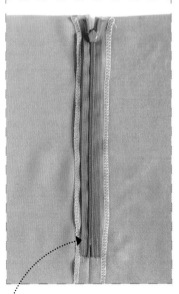

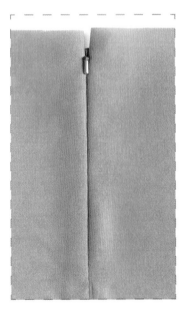

6 Close the zip. On the wrong side at the bottom of the zip, the two rows of stitching that hold in the zip should finish at the same place.

7 Stitch the seam below the zip using the normal machine foot. There will be a small gap of about 3mm (1/8in) between the stitching line for the zip and that for the seam.

8 Stitch the last 3cm (1¼in) of the zip tape to just the seam allowances. This will stop the zip pulling loose.

9 On the right side, the zip is completely concealed, with only the pull visible at the top. Apply waistband or facing.

BUTTONS

Buttons are one of the oldest forms of fastening. They come in many shapes and sizes, and can be made from a variety of materials including shell, bone, plastic, nylon, and metal. Buttons are sewn to the fabric either through holes on their face, or through a hole in a stalk called a shank, which is on the back. Buttons are normally sewn on by hand, although a two-hole button can be sewn on by machine.

SEWING ON A TWO-HOLE BUTTON

LEVEL OF DIFFICULTY **

This is the most popular type of button and requires a thread shank to be made when sewing in place. A cocktail stick on top of the button will help you to make the shank.

1 Position the button on the fabric. Start with a double stitch and double thread in the needle.

2 Place a cocktail stick on top of the button. Stitch up and down through the holes, going over the stick.

3 Remove the cocktail stick.

4 Wrap the thread around the thread loops under the button to make a shank.

5 Take the thread through to the back of the fabric.

6 Buttonhole stitch over the loop of threads on the back of the work.

SEWING ON A FOUR-HOLE BUTTON

LEVEL OF DIFFICULTY **

This is stitched in the same way as a two-hole button except that the threads make an X over the top of the button.

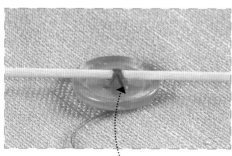  

1 Position the button on the fabric. Place a cocktail stick on the button.

2 Using double thread, stitch diagonally between the holes of the button to make an X on top of the cocktail stick.

3 Remove the cocktail stick.

4 Wrap the thread around the thread loops under the button to make the shank.

5 On the reverse of the fabric, buttonhole stitch over the X-shaped thread loops.

SEWING ON A SHANKED BUTTON

LEVEL OF DIFFICULTY **

When sewing this type of button in place, use a cocktail stick under the button to enable you to make a thread shank on the underside of the fabric.

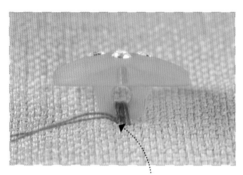
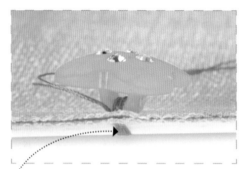
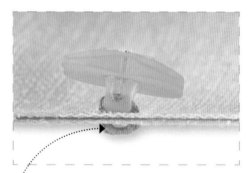

1 Position the button on the fabric. Hold a cocktail stick beneath the fabric, behind the button.

2 Using double thread, stitch the button to the fabric, through the shank.

3 Be sure each stitch goes around the cocktail stick beneath the fabric.

4 Remove the cocktail stick. Work buttonhole stitching over the looped thread shank beneath the fabric.

OVERSIZED AND LAYERED BUTTONS

LEVEL OF DIFFICULTY **

There are some huge buttons available, many of which are really more decorative than functional. By layering buttons of varying sizes together, you can make an unusual feature on a garment.

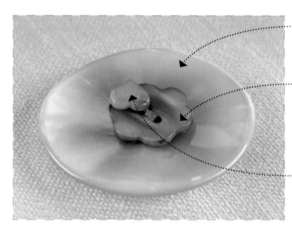

1 First position the oversized button on the fabric.

2 Top with a smaller button and stitch the two together to the fabric.

3 Place a small one-hole button on the layered buttons and attach to the thread using a buttonhole stitch.

POSITIONING BUTTONHOLES

LEVEL OF DIFFICULTY *

Whether the buttonholes are to be stitched by machine or another type of buttonhole is to be made, the size of the button will need to be established in order to work out the position of the buttonhole on the fabric.

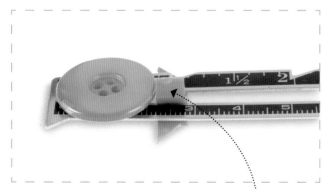
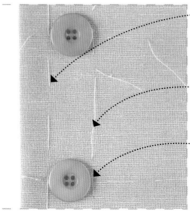

1 Place the button on a sewing gauge and use the slider to measure the button's diameter.

2 Work a row of tacking stitches along the centre front line of the right-hand side of the garment, as worn.

3 Work a second row of tacks the diameter of the button away.

4 Lay the buttons between the tack lines. Stitch lines of tacking at right angles to the first two tacked rows, to mark the buttonhole positions.

VERTICAL OR HORIZONTAL?

Generally, buttonholes are only placed vertically on a garment with a placket or strip to contain the buttonhole. All other buttonholes should be horizontal. Any strain on the buttonhole will then be taken by the end stop and prevent the button from coming undone.

HORIZONTAL BUTTONHOLES

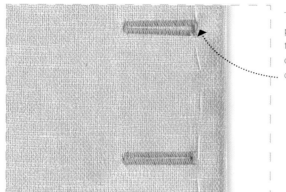

These are positioned with the end stop on the tacked centre line.

VERTICAL BUTTONHOLES

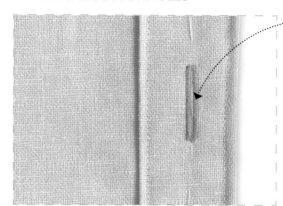

These are positioned with the buttonhole centred on the tacked centre line.

STAGES OF A BUTTONHOLE

A sewing machine stitches a buttonhole in three stages. The stitch can be varied slightly in width and length to suit the fabric, but the stitches need to be tight and close together.

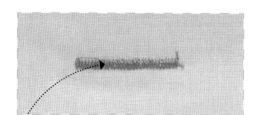

1 Machine the first side of the buttonhole.

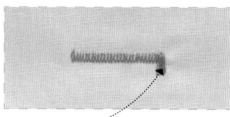

2 Stitch a bar tack at one end.

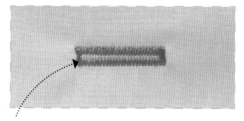

3 Machine the second side and bar tack at the other end.

MACHINE-MADE BUTTONHOLES

LEVEL OF DIFFICULTY *

Modern sewing machines can stitch various types of buttonhole, suitable for all kinds of garments. On many machines the button fits into a special foot, and a sensor on the machine determines the correct size of buttonhole. The width and length of the stitch can be altered to suit the fabric. Once the buttonhole has been stitched, always use a buttonhole chisel to slash through, to ensure that the cut is clean.

BASIC BUTTONHOLE

The most popular shape for a buttonhole is square on both ends.

ROUND-END BUTTONHOLE

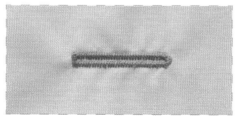

A buttonhole featuring one rounded end and one square end is used on lightweight jackets.

KEYHOLE BUTTONHOLE

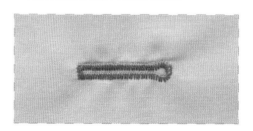

This is also called a tailor's buttonhole. It has a square end and a keyhole end, and is used on jackets and coats.

HOOKS AND EYES AND SNAPS

There are many alternative ways to fasten a garment. The different hooks and eyes shown below are normally used to finish the top end of a zip to help prevent it from pulling open, but a row of hooks and eyes can also be used on its own as a decorative way of closing and opening a garment. Snap fasteners are good for children's clothing and uniforms, as they are easy to use. They also feature commonly on lightweight jackets, cardigans, and fleece jackets.

HOOKS AND EYES
LEVEL OF DIFFICULTY **

There are a multitude of different types of hook and eye fasteners. Purchased hooks and eyes are made from metal and are normally silver or black in colour. Different-shaped hooks and eyes are used on different garments – large, broad hooks and eyes can be decorative and stitched to show on the outside, while tiny fasteners are meant to be discreet. A hook with a hand-worked eye produces a neat, close fastening.

ATTACHING HOOKS AND EYES

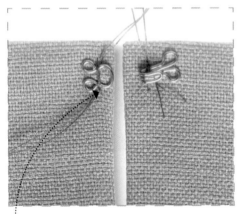

1 Secure the hook and eye in place with a tacking stitch. Make sure they are in line with each other.

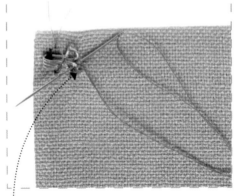

2 Stitch around each circular end with a buttonhole stitch.

3 Place a few over-stitches under the hook to stop it moving.

HAND-WORKED EYE

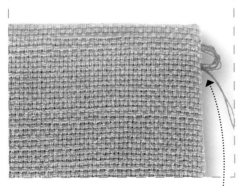

1 Using a double thread, work several small loops into the edge of the fabric.

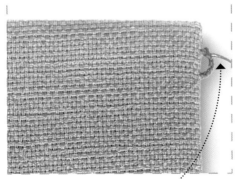

2 Buttonhole stitch over these loops.

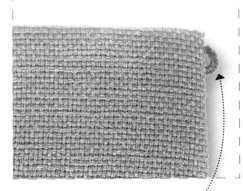

3 The completed loop will have a neat row of tight buttonhole stitches.

TROUSER HOOK AND EYE

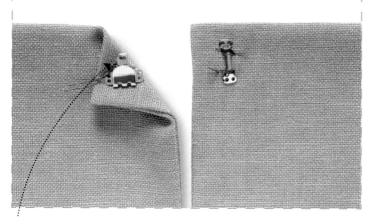

1 A hook and eye fastener for trouser and skirt waistbands is large and flat. Tack both the hook and eye in position. Do not tack through their securing holes.

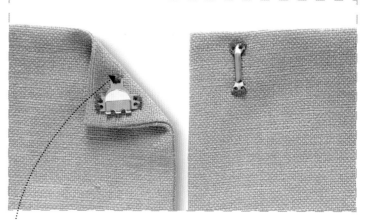

2 Buttonhole stitch through all the securing holes on both hook and eye.

SNAPS
LEVEL OF DIFFICULTY **

A snap is a ball and socket fastener that is used to hold two overlapping edges closed. The ball side goes on top and the socket side underneath. Snaps can be round or square and can be made from metal or plastic.

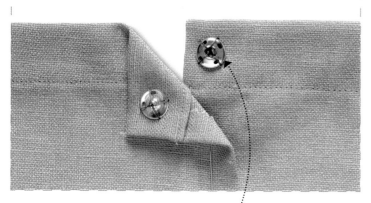

1 Tack the ball and socket halves of the snap in place.

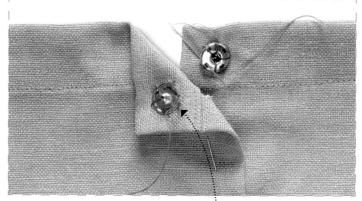

2 Secure permanently using a buttonhole stitch through each hole in the outer edges of the snap halves.

3 Remove the tacks.

PLASTIC SNAPS

A plastic snap may be white or clear plastic and is usually square in shape. Stitch in place as for a metal snap.

the
GARMENTS

The twelve basic patterns in this section can be used to make thirty-one different garments. Details are given for making up the basic patterns, followed by the adaptations that are required to produce the variations.

the
SKIRTS

This section is the perfect place for a beginner to start. It gives instructions for making three fabulous skirts and one simple variation of each. These stylish garments are straightforward and use a minimum of pattern pieces.

Skirt pattern one

Classic A-line skirt

>> p.132

Skirt pattern one variation

Button front A-line skirt

>> p.136

Skirt pattern two

Classic tailored skirt

>> p.138

Skirt pattern two variation

Tailored evening skirt

>> p.143

Skirt pattern three

Classic pleated skirt

>> p.146

Skirt pattern three variation

Topstitched pleated skirt

>> p.152

A simple A-line skirt with a narrow waistband will flatter all figure types and all ages

SKIRT PATTERN

1

>> p.134

>> p.136

the A-line skirts

Skirt Pattern One

CLASSIC A-LINE SKIRT

This A-line skirt will never go out of fashion and can be worn at all times of the year and to all occasions. It is also one of the easiest garments for a beginner to make. It has only three pattern pieces – a front, a back, and a waistband. The skirt needs to fit comfortably around the waist and across the tummy, so check your measurements carefully against the pattern.

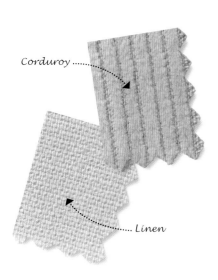

Corduroy

Linen

This skirt is made in a cotton print, but works well in a wide range of fabrics. For winter you could choose a cosy corduroy, while for summer, linen will keep you cool and fresh.

BEFORE YOU START

YOU WILL NEED
- 1.3m (51in) x 150cm (59in) fabric
- 1 x reel matching all-purpose sewing thread
- 1 x reel contrasting all-purpose sewing thread for pattern marking
- 1m x waistband interfacing
- 1 x 22cm (8$\frac{1}{2}$in) skirt zip
- 1 x button

PREPARING THE PATTERN
- This skirt is made using Skirt Pattern One (see pp. 280–281)
- Follow the instructions (see pp.278–279) to copy or download the pattern in your size

GARMENT CONSTRUCTION

This A-line skirt is shaped by the two darts in the front and back. There is a zip in the left-hand side. The narrow waistband is fastened with a button and buttonhole fastening. The finished skirt should sit just above the knee.

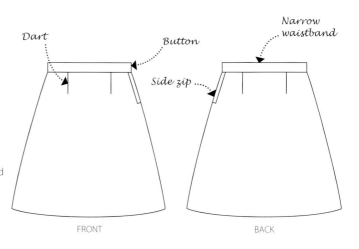

Dart

Button

Narrow waistband

Side zip

FRONT

BACK

HOW TO MAKE THE CLASSIC A-LINE SKIRT

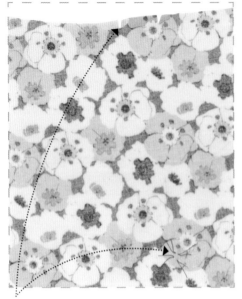

1 **Cut out the fabric and mark the start of the darts** with tailor's tacks (see p.91). **Clip the end of the darts** on the raw edge (see p.76).

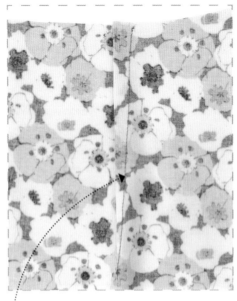

2 **Make the darts** (see p.91) and press towards the centre of the garment.

3 **Neaten the side seams** on the back and the front using a 3-thread overlock stitch or a small zigzag stitch (see pp.84–85).

4 **Stitch the LH (left hand) side seam,** leaving a gap for the zip. Press the seam open then **insert a zip** (see p.119).

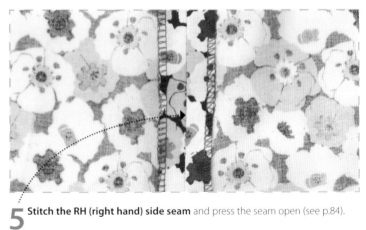

5 **Stitch the RH (right hand) side seam** and press the seam open (see p.84).

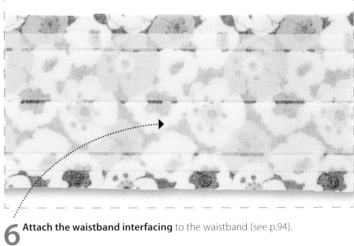

6 **Attach the waistband interfacing** to the waistband (see p.94).

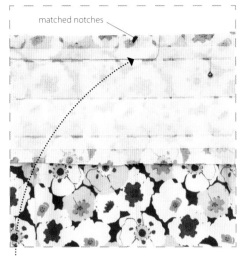

matched notches

7 **Attach the waistband** to the skirt, matching the notches (see p.103).

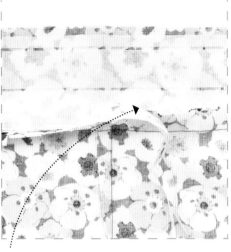

8 **Layer the seam allowance** by trimming the waistband side of the seam to half its width (see p.89). Press towards the waistband.

9 **Fold the waistband** RS (right side) to RS. Pin then **stitch the ends of the waistband**.

10 **Clip the ends of the waistband** to reduce bulk.

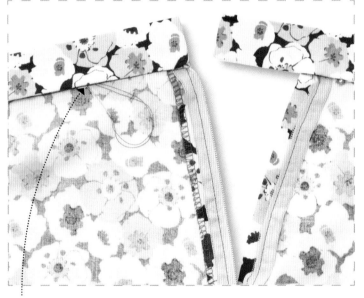

11 **Turn the waistband** to the RS, pushing the clipped ends out. Fold under the raw edge, then pin and **handstitch in place**.

12 **Neaten the hem edge** by overlocking (see p.116). Turn up a 4cm (1¹⁄₂in) hem and **handstitch in place**.

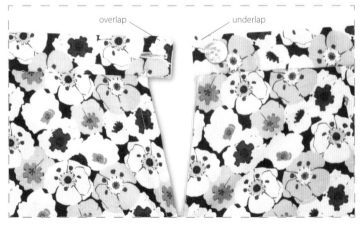

overlap   underlap

13 **Make a buttonhole** on the overlap of the waistband (see p.125). **Sew a button** on the underlap (see pp.123–124).

SKIRT PATTERN **1**

the A-line skirts

>> p.132

>> p.137

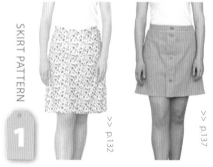

Skirt Pattern One Variation

BUTTON FRONT A-LINE SKIRT

This variation of the A-line skirt is a little more complicated and is the perfect next step for a novice sewer. To make it, you will shorten the basic pattern and extend the centre front to create the pleat. The buttons on the pleat are purely decorative. This skirt would make a great winter or autumn wardrobe staple.

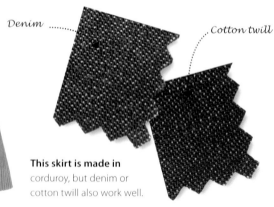

Denim

Cotton twill

This skirt is made in corduroy, but denim or cotton twill also work well.

BEFORE YOU START

YOU WILL NEED

- 1.2m (47¼in) x 150cm (59in) fabric
- 1 x reel matching all-purpose sewing thread
- 1 x reel contrasting all-purpose sewing thread for pattern marking
- 1m x waistband interfacing
- 1 x 18cm (7in) skirt zip
- 7 x buttons

PREPARING THE PATTERN

- This skirt is made using Skirt Pattern One (see pp.280–281)
- Follow the instructions (see pp.278–279) to copy or download the pattern in your size

GARMENT CONSTRUCTION

This variation of the Classic A-line skirt is shorter. It has a zip in the left-hand side and features a stitched pleat to which buttons have been sewn for decoration.

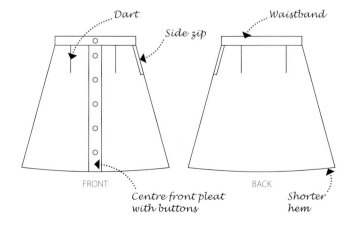

Dart

Side zip

Waistband

FRONT

Centre front pleat with buttons

BACK

Shorter hem

HOW TO MAKE THE BUTTON FRONT A-LINE SKIRT

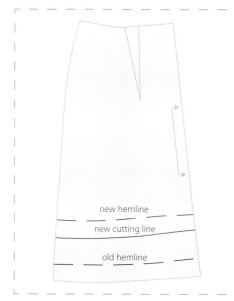

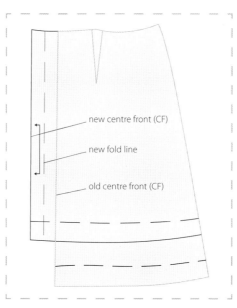

new centre front (CF)

new fold line

old centre front (CF)

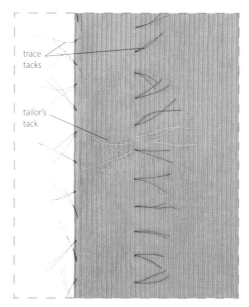

trace tacks

tailor's tack

1 **To shorten the hem,** copy the front and back pattern pieces. Mark the hemline. Mark the new hemline 10cm (4in) above the old hemline. Draw a new cutting line 4cm (1½in) below the new hemline.

2 **For the front pleat,** mark a fold line 3cm (1¼in) to the left of the CF (centre front). Mark the new CF 3cm (1¼in) to the left of the new fold line.

3 **Cut out the fabric.** On the skirt front, **mark the fold line and the CF** with trace tacks (see p.76). **Mark a point** on the fold line, 15cm (6in) from the hem edge, with a tailor's tack.

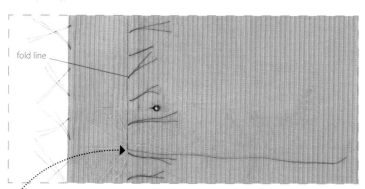

fold line

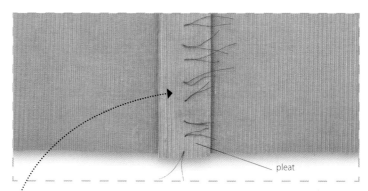

pleat

4 Matching the fold line markings, pin down the fold line WS (wrong side) to WS to the tailor's tack. **Stitch along the pinned line.**

5 Open the front of the skirt. **To form the pleat,** press the CF line onto the stitched line.

6 **Complete the rest of the skirt** as for the Classic A-line Skirt steps 1–11.

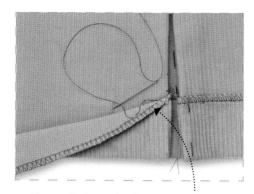

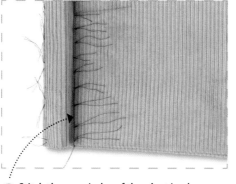

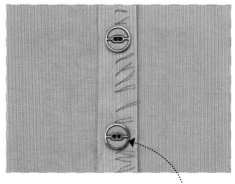

7 **Neaten the hem edge** by overlocking (see p.116). Turn up a 4cm (1½in) hem and handstitch in place.

8 **Stitch the remainder of the pleat in place,** stitching through the hem. Press.

9 **Sew buttons** (see p.123) along the CF.

HOW TO MAKE THE CLASSIC TAILORED SKIRT

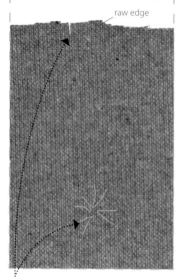

raw edge

1 **Cut out the fabric and mark the darts** using tailor's tacks (see p.91). **Clip the end of the darts** on the raw edge (see p.76).

2 **Make the darts** (see p.91) and press towards the centre of the garment.

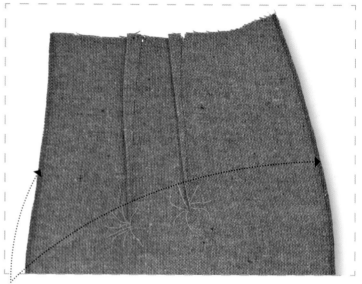

3 **Neaten the side and CB (centre back) seams** using a 3-thread overlock stitch or a small zigzag stitch (see pp.84–85).

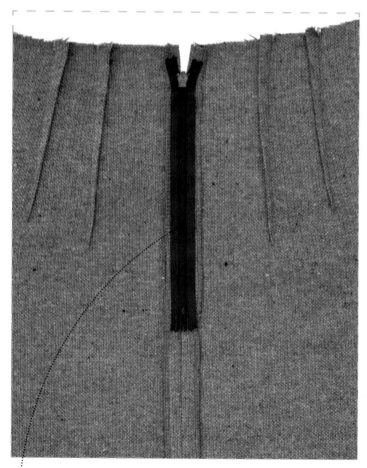

4 **Insert a concealed zip** at the CB (see p.122).

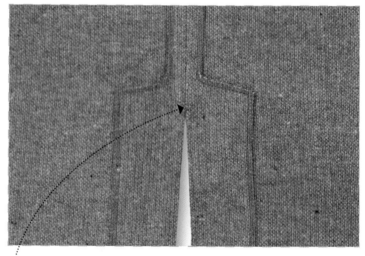

5 **Stitch the remainder of the CB seam,** stopping at the dot marking the top of the vent. Press the seam open.

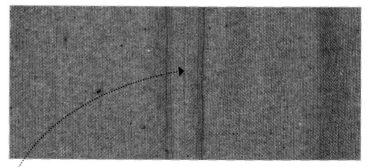

6 **Join the front to the back** at the side seams and press the seams open.

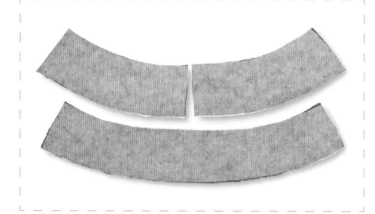

7 **Attach a lightweight fusible interfacing** to the waist facing pieces (see p.94).

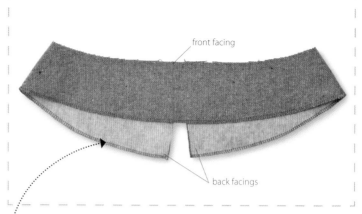

front facing

back facings

8 **Join the front and back facings** and press the seams open. Neaten the lower edge of the facing using a 3-thread overlock stitch or a small zigzag stitch.

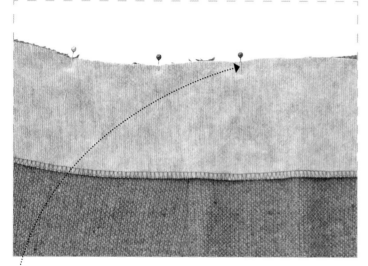

9 **Place the facing to the skirt** at the waist edge RS (right side) to RS, matching the side seams and matching at the top of the zip. Pin and machine.

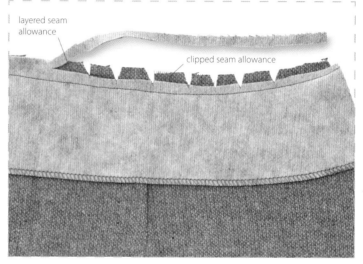

layered seam allowance

clipped seam allowance

10 **Layer the seam allowance** by trimming the facing side of the seam to half its width. **Clip the seam allowance** to reduce bulk (see p.89).

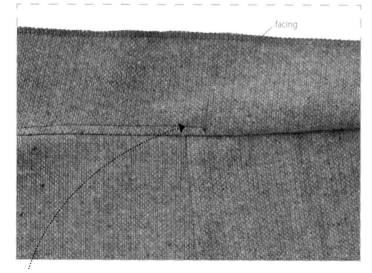

facing

11 **Press the seam** towards the facing and **understitch** (see p.90).

12 **Turn the facing** to the inside then, at the CB, fold the edge of the facing in to meet the zip tape. Pin and **handstitch in place**.

13 **At the vent,** snip through the seam allowance on the LH (left hand) side and press the seam extension to the RH (right hand) side.

14 Machine the extension in place.

15 From the RS, the top of the vent can be seen as a line of stitching.

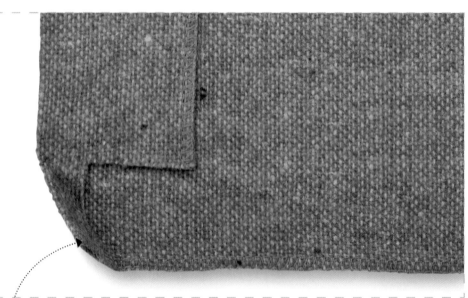

16 **Neaten the hem edge** (see pp.116–117). On each side of the vent, **remove the surplus fabric** in the hem allowance.

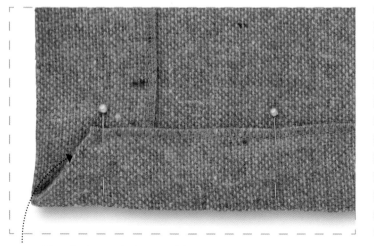

17 **Mitre the hem** at the bottom of the vent. Pin.

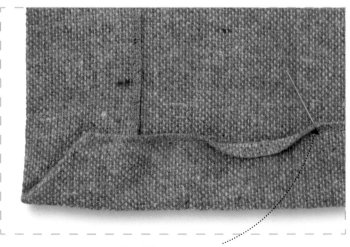

18 **Turn up the remainder of the hem,** pin and handstitch in place.

TAILORED EVENING SKIRT

For this version of the skirt you will add a lining for a more luxurious finish. You will also shorten the skirt, which means you no longer need a centre back vent to make walking easier. This skirt has been made in silk for an evening out, but would also work well in a heavier fabric worn with thick tights.

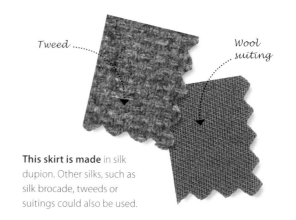

Tweed ......

Wool suiting

This skirt is made in silk dupion. Other silks, such as silk brocade, tweeds or suitings could also be used.

SKIRT PATTERN

2

>> p.138

>> p.144

the tailored skirts

BEFORE YOU START

YOU WILL NEED

- 90cm (36in) x 150cm (59in) fabric
- 90cm (36in) x 150cm (59in) lining fabric
- 1 x reel matching all-purpose sewing thread
- 1 x reel contrasting all-purpose sewing thread for pattern marking
- 50cm (20in) lightweight fusible interfacing
- 1 x 18cm (7in) skirt zip

PREPARING THE PATTERN

- This skirt is made using Skirt Pattern Two (see pp. 282–283)
- Follow the instructions (see pp.278–279) to copy or download the pattern in your size

GARMENT CONSTRUCTION

This lined variation of the Classic Tailored Skirt is shorter without a back vent. There is a zip in the centre back. The waistline is finished with a facing. The lining is cut from the same pattern pieces as the skirt.

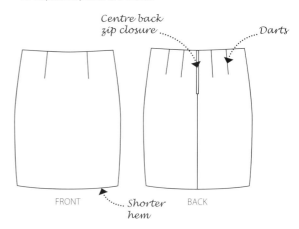

Centre back zip closure

Darts

FRONT

Shorter hem

BACK

HOW TO MAKE THE TAILORED EVENING SKIRT

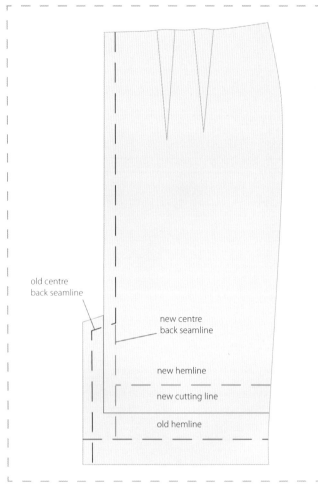

old centre
back seamline

new centre
back seamline

new hemline

new cutting line

old hemline

new hemline

new cutting line

old hemline

1 **To shorten the front of the skirt,** copy the skirt front pattern piece. Mark the hemline. Mark the new hemline 8cm (3¼in) above the old hemline. Draw a new cutting line 4cm (1½in) below the new hemline.

2 **To shorten the back of the skirt,** copy the skirt back pattern piece. Shorten the skirt as for step 1. **To remove the vent,** extend the CB (centre back) seamline to the hemline.

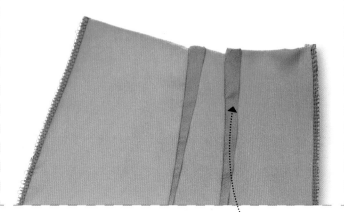

3 **Cut out the fabric and lining** using the new pattern pieces.

4 **Make up the skirt** in the silk fabric as for the Classic Tailored Skirt steps 1–6.

5 **For the lining:** make the darts and neaten the side and CB seams as for the skirt.

6 **Stitch the CB (centre back) seam** in the lining between the marked dots, leaving the seam above open for the zip. Press open.

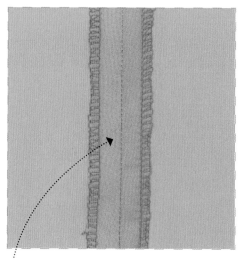

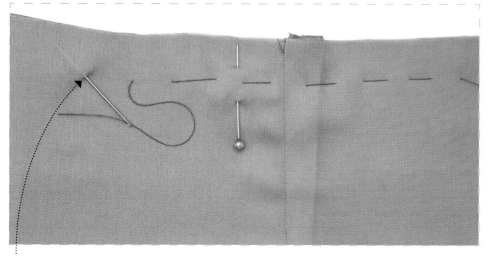

7 **Join the side seams** in the lining and press open.

8 **Pin and tack the lining to the skirt** at the waist edge WS (wrong side) to WS, matching the darts and seams.

9 **Attach the facing** to the skirt and lining as for the Classic Tailored Skirt steps 7–11.

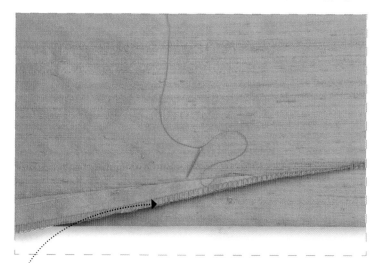

10 **Neaten the hem edge** on the skirt (see pp.116–117). Turn up the hem and handstitch in place.

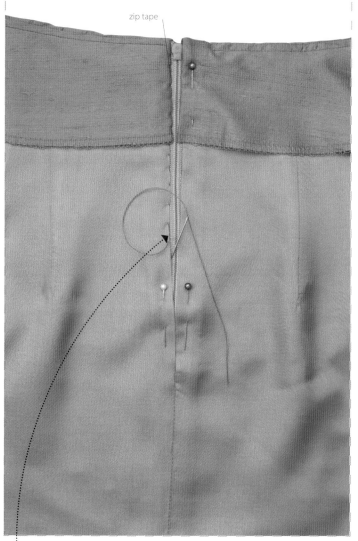

zip tape

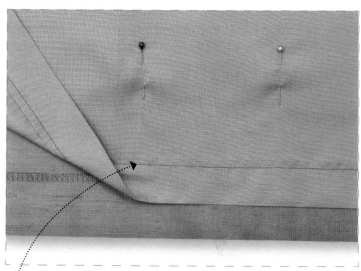

11 **Trim the lining** level to the finished hem of the skirt and machine a 2cm (³⁄₄in) double-turn hem (see p.118).

12 At the CB, **fold the edge of the lining** in to meet the zip tape. Pin and handstitch in place.

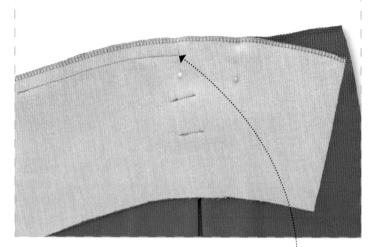

15 **Place the yoke** to the skirt front and back. Pin and machine. Press the seam open.

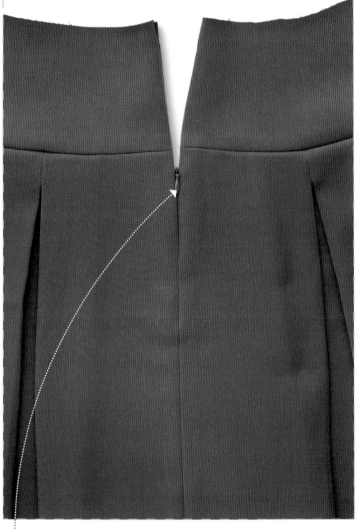

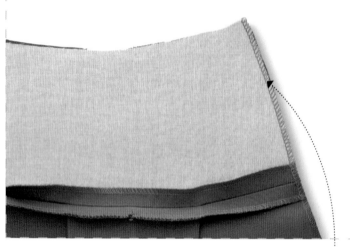

16 **Press the skirt-to-yoke seam** open, then neaten the side seams using a 3-thread overlock stitch or a small zigzag stitch.

17 **Insert a zip** of your choice on the LH (left hand) side (see pp.119–122). Stitch the remainder of the side seam and press open.

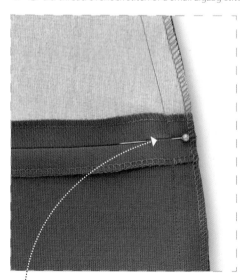

18 **Join the RH side seam,** matching at the skirt-to-yoke seam. Press open.

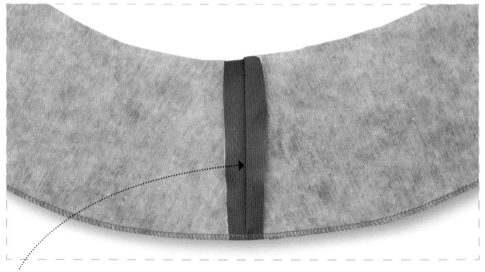

19 **Attach a lightweight interfacing** to the remaining set of yokes to make the yoke facing (see p.94). Join the facings at the RH side and press the seam open. Neaten the lower edge using either a 3-thread overlock stitch or a small zigzag stitch.

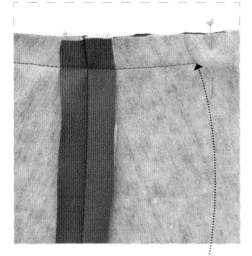

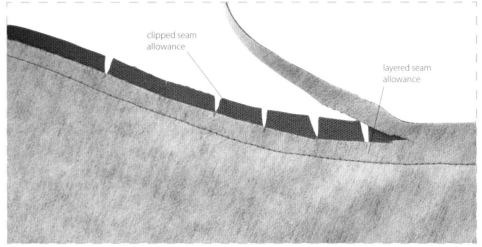

20 **Place the yoke facing to the yoke** RS (right side) to RS, matching at the side seam. Pin and machine.

21 **Layer the seam allowance** by trimming the facing side of the seam to half its width. **Clip the seam allowance** to reduce bulk (see p.89).

clipped seam allowance

layered seam allowance

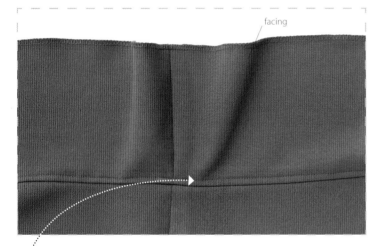

facing

22 **Press the seam** towards the facing and understitch (see p.90).

23 **Turn the facing to the inside** then fold the edge of the facing in to meet the zip tape. Pin. Pin the facing to the skirt-to-yoke seam.

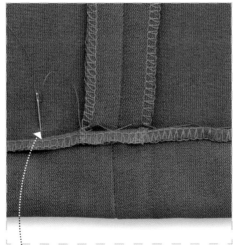

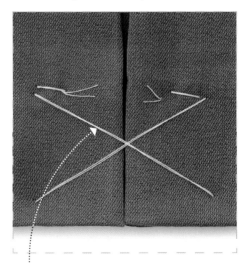

24 Working from the RS (right side) of the skirt **stitch in the ditch** – the line produced by the skirt-to-yoke seam – through all layers. This will secure the facing on the inside.

25 **Neaten the hem edge** (see pp.116–117). Turn up and handstitch in place. Remove the tacks in the pleats.

26 **Fold the pleats** at the hem edge back into place and tack together with a large X. Press. Remove any remaining tacks and trace tacks.

Skirt Pattern Three Variation

TOPSTITCHED PLEATED SKIRT

With its contrast topstitching and shorter length, this skirt is rather youthful. The pleats swing out from the thigh and the deep, topstitched hem gives the skirt a casual feel. Try this version in a chunky winter tweed worn with thick tights or leggings; for the summer, a crisp linen would be ideal.

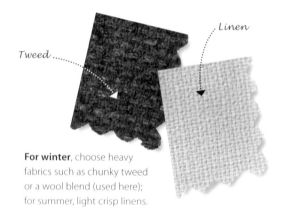

Tweed

Linen

For winter, choose heavy fabrics such as chunky tweed or a wool blend (used here); for summer, light crisp linens.

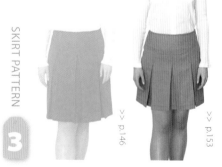

SKIRT PATTERN

3

the pleated skirts

>> p.146   >> p.153

BEFORE YOU START

YOU WILL NEED

- 1.2m (47¼in) x 150cm (59in) fabric
- 1 x reel matching all-purpose sewing thread
- 2 x reels contrasting all-purpose sewing thread in two different colours for pattern marking
- 1 x reel contrasting all-purpose sewing thread for topstitching
- 50cm medium-weight interfacing
- 1 x 18cm (7in) skirt zip

PREPARING THE PATTERN

- This skirt is made using Skirt Pattern Three (see pp. 284–285)
- Follow the instructions (see pp.278–279) to copy or download the pattern in your size

GARMENT CONSTRUCTION

This variation of the Classic Pleated Skirt is shorter. The pleats start lower and they are topstitched below the yoke in a contrast colour. The yoke and the deep hem are also topstitched.

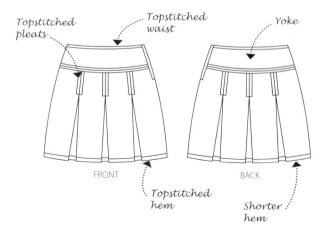

Topstitched pleats

Topstitched waist

Yoke

Topstitched hem

Shorter hem

FRONT   BACK

HOW TO MAKE THE TOPSTITCHED PLEATED SKIRT

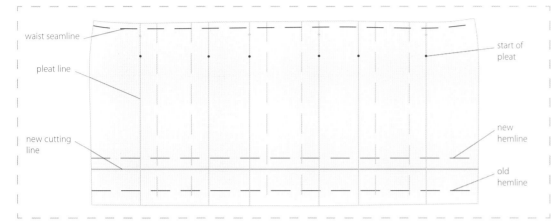

waist seamline

pleat line

new cutting line

start of pleat

new hemline

old hemline

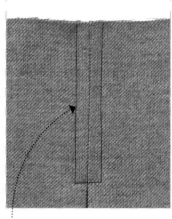

1 **Copy the front and back pattern pieces** and mark the waist seamline, the hemline, and the pleat lines. Mark the new hemline 9cm (3¹⁄₂in) above the old hemline. Draw a new cutting line 4cm (1¹⁄₂in) below the new hemline. Mark the start of the pleats on the pleat line and 8cm (3¹⁄₄in) below the waist seamline.

2 **Cut out the fabric** and make up as for the Classic Pleated Skirt steps 1–6.

3 Working from the RS (right side) of the skirt, **topstitch around the pleats in a contrasting thread** using the edge of the presser foot as a guide.

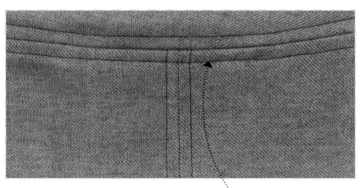

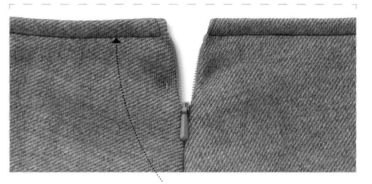

4 **Continue as for the Classic Pleated Skirt** steps 7, 8, 9, and 15 (i.e. omitting the belt carriers).

5 **Topstitch the skirt-to-yoke seam** in a contrasting thread.

6 **Continue as for the Classic Pleated Skirt steps 16–21** to make and attach the yoke facing.

7 **Fold the facing** to the inside of the skirt and topstitch around the waist. Fold the edge of the facing in to meet the zip tape and handstitch in place.

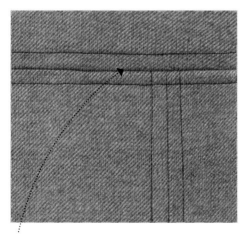

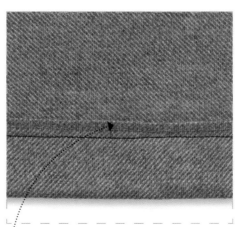

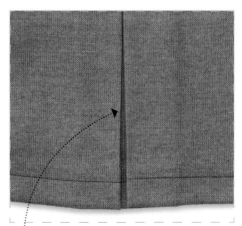

8 **Pin the facing** to the skirt-to-yoke seam as in step 23 of the Classic Pleated Skirt. Working from the RS of the skirt **stitch in the ditch** through all layers to secure the facing on the inside.

9 **Neaten the hem edge** (see pp.116–117) and topstitch in place using contrasting thread 3cm (1¹⁄₄in) from the fold.

10 **Press the pleats** from the top to the hem.

the DRESSES

The three classic dresses in this section can be adapted to make a total of twelve styles, some unlined and some lined. The dresses suit all ages and can take you to any occasion at any time of the year, depending on the fabric you choose.

1

Dress
pattern one
*Classic shift
dress*
>> p.156

2

Dress
pattern two
*Classic
waisted
dress*
>> p.174

3

Dress
pattern three
*Classic
empire line
dress*
>> p.190

Dress pattern
one variation
*Short-
sleeved
shift dress*
>> p.161

Dress pattern
one variation
*Square-
neck shift
dress*
>> p.164

Dress pattern
one variation
*Sleeveless
shift dress*
>> p.167

Dress pattern
one variation
*Short
sleeveless
shift dress*
>> p.170

Dress pattern
two variation
*Short-
sleeved
waisted
dress*
>> p.179

Dress pattern
two variation
*Sleeveless
waisted
dress*
>> p.181

Dress pattern
two variation
*Waisted
cocktail
dress*
>> p.185

Dress pattern
three variation
*Sleeveless
empire line
dress*
>> p.195

Dress pattern
three variation
*Long empire
line dress*
>> p.198

This simple yet stylish dress can be worn by any age and on any occasion, depending on the fabric you choose

DRESS PATTERN

1

>> p.158

>> p.161

>> p.164

>> p.167

>> p.170

the shift dresses

Dress Pattern One

CLASSIC SHIFT DRESS

A classic fitted dress like this never goes out of fashion and you can make it in almost any fabric. In fact, you'll love it so much that you'll want it in several different ones. The dress must fit well across the bust and in the hip area, so choose your pattern by your bust measurement and alter the waist and hip as required. As with any fitted style, it's best to make the pattern up in calico first and try it out.

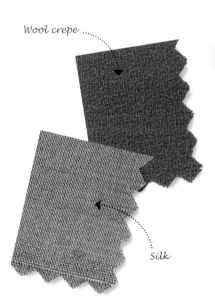

Wool crepe

Silk

This dress is made in wool crepe but any fabric from tweed to silk to cotton could be used. Fine suiting works well for the office and printed stretch cotton makes a great summer wedding outfit.

BEFORE YOU START

YOU WILL NEED

- 1.7m (67in) x 150cm (59in) fabric
- 1 x reel matching all-purpose sewing thread
- 1 x reel contrasting all-purpose sewing thread for pattern marking
- 50cm (20in) lightweight interfacing
- 1 x 56cm (22in) zip

PREPARING THE PATTERN

- This dress is made using Dress Pattern One (see pp.286–287)
- Follow the instructions (see pp.278–279) to copy or download the pattern in your size

GARMENT CONSTRUCTION

This unlined one-piece fitted dress has darts at the bust and waist to ensure a fitted silhouette. It also has a zip in the centre back and a centre-back vent. It features a high round neck and long set-in sleeves. The hemline just brushes the knee.

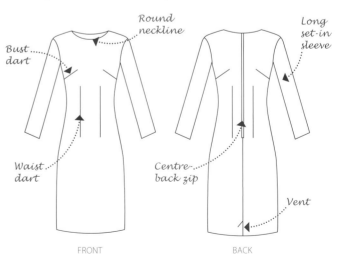

Round neckline

Bust dart

Long set-in sleeve

Waist dart

Centre-back zip

Vent

FRONT

BACK

HOW TO MAKE THE CLASSIC SHIFT DRESS

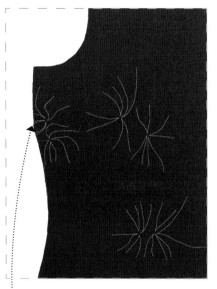

1 **Cut out the fabric and mark the darts** using tailor's tacks (see p.77).

2 **Make the plain and the contour darts** (see pp.91–92).

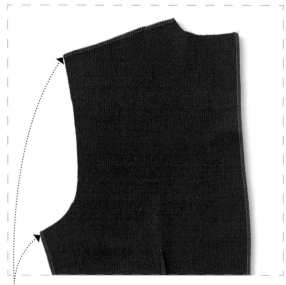

3 **Neaten the shoulder seam, side seams on the front and back, and the CB (centre back) seams**, using either a 3-thread overlock stitch or a small zigzag stitch (see pp.84–85).

4 **Insert a zip** of your choice in the CB. A concealed zip is used here (see p.122).

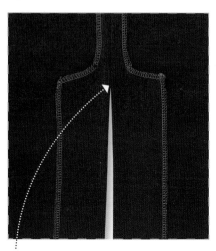

5 **Stitch the remainder of the CB seam** stopping at the dot marking the top of the vent. Press the seam open.

6 **Join the front to the back** at the shoulder and side seams. Press the seams open.

7 **Neaten the sides and lower edge of both sleeves** using either a 3-thread overlock stitch or a small zigzag stitch.

8 **Machine the sleeve seam** and press it open.

ease stitches

9 Using the longest stitch available, **machine two rows of ease stitches** through the sleeve head (see p.105).

10 **Insert the sleeve into the armhole**, RS (right side) to RS, remembering to pin and stitch from the sleeve side (see p.105).

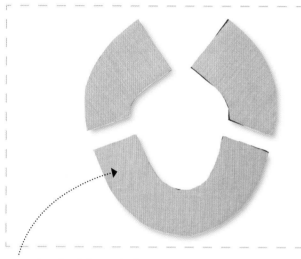

11 **Attach a lightweight fusible interfacing** to the neck facing pieces (see p.94).

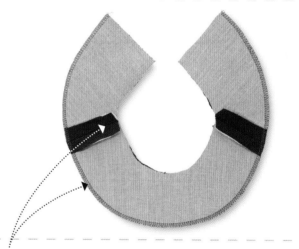

12 **Join the facings at the shoulder seams** and press the seams open. Neaten the lower edge (see pp.95–97).

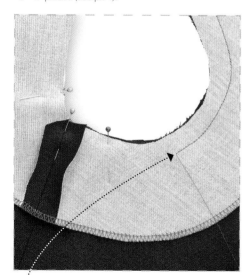

13 **Place the facings to the neck edge of the dress** RS to RS, matching the seams. Pin and machine.

layered seam allowance

clipped seam allowance

14 **Layer the seam allowance** by trimming the facing side of the seam to half its width. **Clip the seam allowance** to reduce bulk (see p.89).

15 **Press the seam** towards the facing and understitch (see p.90).

16 **Pin and handstitch** the facing to the seam allowance at the shoulder seams.

17 At the CB, **fold the edge of the facing in to meet the zip tape.** Pin and handstitch in place.

18 From the RS, the back neck edge should now look neatly finished.

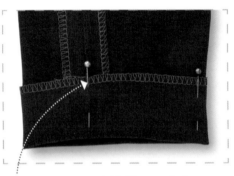

19 **Turn up a 4cm (1½in) hem at the bottom of each sleeve**. Pin and handstitch in place.

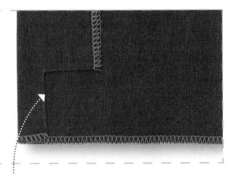

20 **Neaten the hem edge** (see pp.116–117). On each side of the vent, **remove a square of surplus fabric in the hem allowance.**

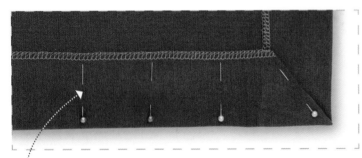

21 **Mitre the hem** at the bottom of the vent and pin. **Turn up the remainder of the hem** and pin.

22 **Handstitch the mitre and hem** in place.

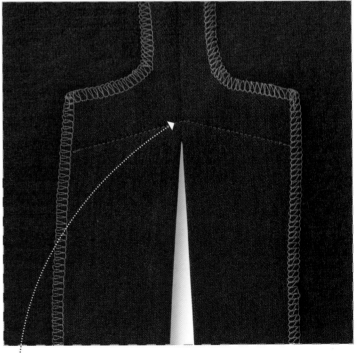

23 **Machine through all layers** at the top of the vent to secure.

the shift dresses

Dress Pattern One Variation

SHORT-SLEEVED SHIFT DRESS

With this garment you'll be introduced to the techniques of lining a dress and shortening a sleeve. A lined dress is a pleasure to wear. The lining also helps prevent fabrics with a looser weave from stretching. With fine cottons or linens, the lining will help prevent see-through.

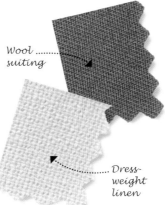

Wool suiting

Dress-weight linen

This dress is made in tweed, but bouclé wools, suiting or linen and cotton would also work well.

BEFORE YOU START

YOU WILL NEED

- 1.7m (67in) x 150cm (59in) fabric
- 1.7m (67in) lining fabric
- 1 x reel matching all-purpose sewing thread
- 1 x reel contrasting all-purpose sewing thread for pattern marking
- 50cm (20in) lightweight interfacing
- 1 x 56cm (22in) zip

PREPARING THE PATTERN

- This dress is made using Dress Pattern One (see pp.286–287)
- Follow the instructions (see pp.278–279) to copy or download the pattern in your size

GARMENT CONSTRUCTION

This lined variation of the Classic Shift Dress has a lower neckline and a short set-in sleeve. It has a zip in the centre back and a centre-back vent. The lining is cut from the same pattern pieces as the dress.

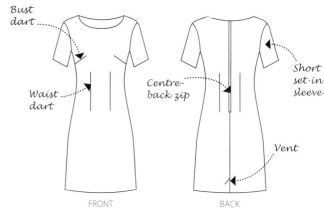

Bust dart

Waist dart

Centre-back zip

Short set-in sleeve

Vent

FRONT

BACK

HOW TO MAKE THE SHORT-SLEEVED SHIFT DRESS

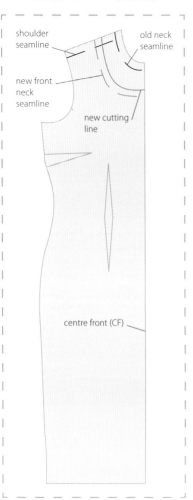

1 **Copy the pattern front and mark the seamlines.** Mark a point on the CF (centre front) 4cm (1½in) below the neck seamline and another point 5.5cm (2in) from the neck seamline along the shoulder seamline. Join the points for the new neck seamline. Measure a 1.5cm (⅝in) seam allowance from the new neck seamline and mark a new cutting line.

2 **Copy the pattern back and mark the seamlines.** Mark a point on the CB (centre back) 2cm (¾in) below the neck seamline and another point 5.5cm (2in) from the neck seamline along the shoulder seamline. Join the points for the new neck seamline. Measure a 1.5cm (⅝in) seam allowance from the new neck seamline and mark a new cutting line.

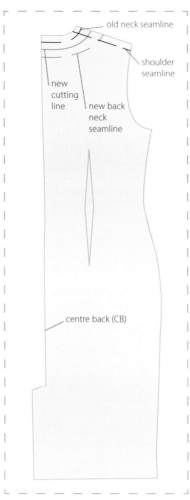

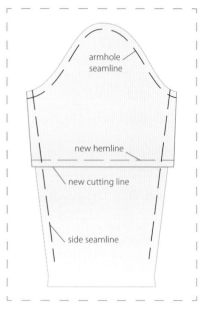

3 **To shorten the sleeve,** copy the sleeve and mark the seamlines. Mark a point either side of the sleeve, 15cm (6in) below the armhole seamlines. Join these points together to make a new hemline. Draw a new cutting line 1.5cm (⅝in) below the new hemline. (If you have a slightly fuller arm you may need to extend the new hemline by 1.5cm (⅝in) on each side. Draw new cutting lines, allowing a 1.5cm (⅝in) seam allowance).

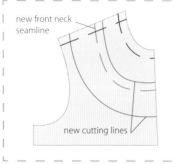

4 **To make the new front neck facing pattern piece,** copy the new front neck seamline and cutting line from step 1 onto a piece of paper. Measure points 5cm (2in) from the seamline. Join these points together to create a new cutting line. Cut out along these lines.

5 **To make the new back neck facing pattern piece,** copy the new back neck seamline and cutting line from step 2 onto a piece of paper. Measure points 5cm (2in) from the seamline. Join these points together to create a new cutting line. Cut out along these lines.

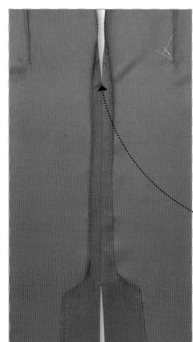

6 **Cut out the dress fabric** using the new pattern pieces and **cut the lining** using the front, back, and sleeve pieces. Mark the darts in both fabrics with tailor's tacks (see p.77).

7 **Make up the dress fabric** as for The Classic Shift Dress steps 2–10.

8 **Make up the lining** as for The Classic Shift Dress steps 2–3.

9 **Stitch the lining together** at the CB seam leaving a gap for the zip and another for the vent as marked on the pattern. Press the seam open.

10 **Make up the remaining lining** as for The Classic Shift Dress steps 6–10.

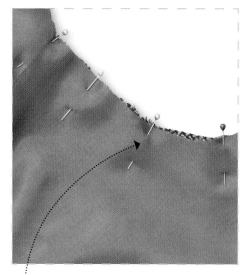

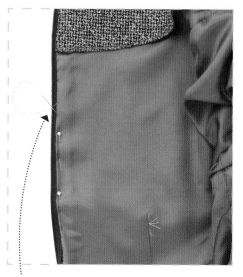

11 **Pin the lining and dress together** WS (wrong side) to WS at the neck edge, matching the seams.

12 **Make the facings** as for The Classic Shift Dress steps 11–16.

13 **Handstitch the lining to the dress** on the shoulder seam and side seam, adjacent to the armhole.

14 At the CB, **fold the edge of the lining in to meet the zip tape.** Pin and handstitch in place.

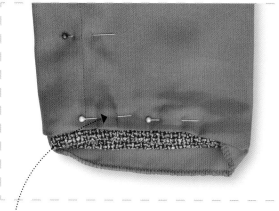

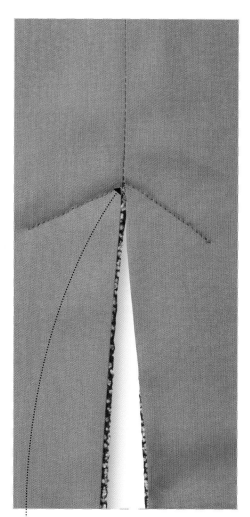

15 From the RS (right side), the back neck edge should now look neatly finished.

16 **Turn up a 1.5cm (⅝in) hem** at the bottom of each sleeve. Pin and handstitch in place. **Turn up the hem of the sleeve lining** by 1.5cm (⅝in) and place the fold 1cm (⅜in) above the fold of the sleeve hem. Handstitch in place.

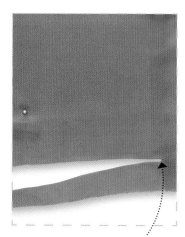

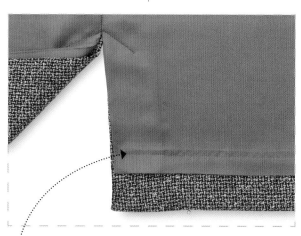

17 **Turn up the dress hem** 4cm (1½in) and handstitch in place. **Trim the lining** level to the hem of the skirt.

18 **Machine a 1.5cm (⅝in) double-turn hem** in the lining (see p.118). Fold the lining under around the vent and hand stitch in place

19 **Machine through all layers** at the top of the vent to secure the lining to the dress.

DRESS PATTERN

1

the shift dresses

Dress Pattern One Variation

SQUARE-NECK SHIFT DRESS

This dress features a flattering low, square neck. After altering the pattern, make the dress up in calico to check the fit and ensure that the neckline isn't too low or wide. This would make a great dress for a supper party or a slightly more formal occasion.

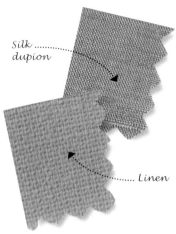

Silk dupion

Linen

This dress is made in a wool/polyester blend. Other good alternatives include silk dupion, linen, cotton, and wool crepe

BEFORE YOU START

YOU WILL NEED

- 2.20m (87in) x 150cm (59in) fabric for sizes 8–14 and 3.40m (134in) x 150cm (59in) for sizes 16–22
- 2.20m (87in) x 150cm (59in) lining fabric for sizes 8–14 and 3.40m (134in) x 150cm (59in) for sizes 16–22
- 1 x reels matching all-purpose sewing thread
- 1 x reel contrasting all-purpose sewing thread for pattern marking
- 1 x 56cm (22in) zip

PREPARING THE PATTERN

- This dress is made using Dress Pattern One (see pp.286–287)
- Follow the instructions (see pp. 278–279) to copy or download the pattern in your size

GARMENT CONSTRUCTION

The skirt of this second, lined variation of the Classic Shift Dress has been widened into an A-line. The dress also features a squared-off neckline, long, set-in sleeves, and a zip in the centre back. The lining is cut from the same pattern pieces as the dress.

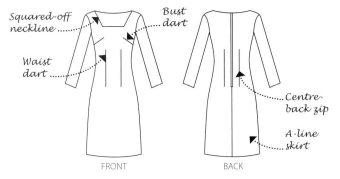

Squared-off neckline

Bust dart

Waist dart

Centre-back zip

A-line skirt

FRONT   BACK

HOW TO MAKE THE SQUARE-NECK SHIFT DRESS

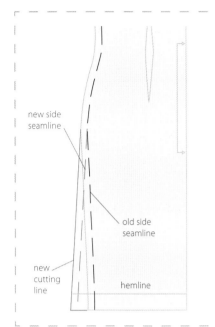

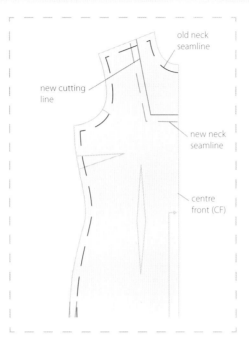

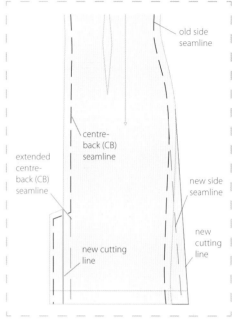

1 **Copy the dress front and mark the side seamline.** At the bottom of the side seamline, mark a point 4cm (1¹/₂in) to the left. **Extend the hemline** to this point. Join to the existing side seamline, just below the hip line to make a new side seamline. **Measure a 1.5cm (⅝in) seam allowance** from the new side seamline and mark a new cutting line.

2 **Mark a point** 12cm (5in) below the old neck seamline at the CF (centre front) and another 5cm (2in) along the shoulder seamline. Draw an 8cm (3¹/₄in) horizontal line from the CF mark towards the armhole and a second line down from the point on the shoulder to join it to make a new neck seamline. **Measure a 1.5cm (⅝in) seam allowance** from the new neck seamline and mark a new cutting line.

3 **Copy the dress back and mark the CB (centre back) and side seamlines.** Extend the CB seamline to the hem to remove the vent. Extend the CB cutting line to match. **Widen at the hem** at the side seamline as in step 1.

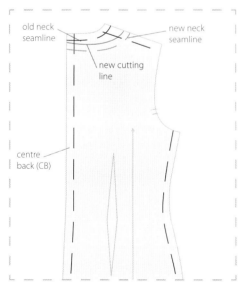

4 **Mark a point on the CB** 2cm (³/₄in) below the neck seamline and another point 5cm (2in) from the neck seamline along the shoulder line. Join the points to make a new neck seamline. **Measure a 1.5cm (⅝in) seam allowance from the new neck seamline** and mark a new cutting line.

5 **Cut out the fabric and the lining** using the new pattern pieces. **Mark the darts** with tailor's tacks (see p.77).

6 **Make the plain and the contour darts** (see pp.91–92) in the lining and dress fabric. Press the contour darts towards the centre of the body.

7 **Neaten the side, shoulder, and CB seams** in the dress fabric and lining using either a 3-thread overlock stitch or a small zigzag stitch (see pp.84–85).

8 **Make up the dress fabric** as for The Classic Shift Dress steps 4–10.

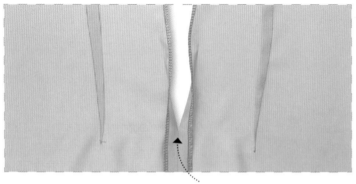

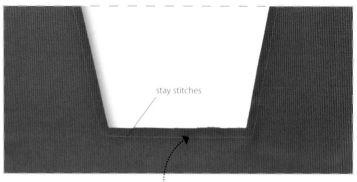

stay stitches

10 **Make up the lining fabric** as for The Classic Shift Dress steps 6–10.

11 **Stitch the lining together** at the CB seam leaving a gap for the zip as marked on the pattern.

12 You should now have one dress made in dress fabric and one made in lining fabric.

13 **Machine a row of stay stitches** (stitch length approximately 3.5), 1.3cm (¹/₂in) from the raw edge of the fabric dress around the neckline, pivoting at the corners (see p.87).

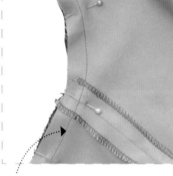

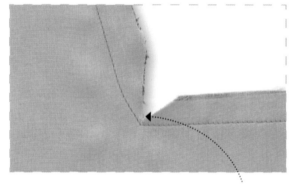

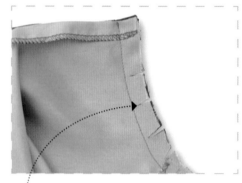

14 **Place the neck of the lining dress to the neck of the fabric dress** RS (right side) to RS, matching the shoulder seams. Pin and machine.

15 **Clip the seam** right into the corners of the front of the neckline.

16 **Clip around the back of the neckline.**

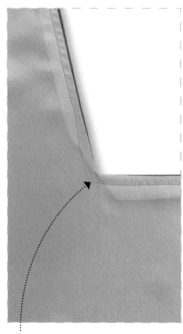

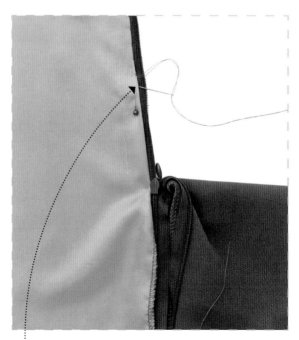

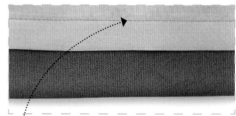

17 **Turn the lining** to the WS (wrong side) and press around the neck edge. Top-stitch around the neck, using a longer stitch length.

18 At the CB, **fold the edge of the lining in to meet the zip tape**. Pin and handstitch in place.

19 Neaten the hem edge of the dress (see pp.116–117). **Turn up a 4cm (1½ in) hem** and handstitch in place. **Trim the lining level to the finished hem** of the dress and machine a 2cm (³/₄in) double-turn hem (see p.118).

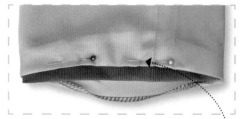

20 **Turn up a 2.5cm (1in) hem at the bottom of each sleeve.** Pin and handstitch in place. Turn up the hem of the sleeve lining by 1.5cm (⁵/₈in) and place the fold 1cm (³/₈in) above the fold of the sleeve hem. Handstitch in place.

Dress Pattern One Variation

SLEEVELESS SHIFT DRESS

This sleeveless, lined dress with its top-stitched neck and armholes will happily take you from the office straight to a smart summer's evening do. Its simple lines can quickly be dressed up with clever accessorizing. A really easy way to insert a lining in this style of garment is shown here.

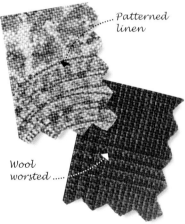

Patterned linen

Wool worsted

This dress is wool crepe. Lightweight suitings, cottons, and linens all work well.

BEFORE YOU START

YOU WILL NEED

- 1.5m (59in) x 150cm (59in) fabric
- 1.5m (59in) x 150cm (59in) lining fabric
- 1 x reels matching all-purpose sewing thread
- 1 x reel contrasting all-purpose sewing thread for pattern marking
- 1 x 56cm (22in) zip

PREPARING THE PATTERN

- This dress is made using Dress Pattern One (see pp.286–287)
- Follow the instructions (see pp.278–279) to copy or download the pattern in your size

GARMENT CONSTRUCTION

This third, lined variation of the Classic Shift Dress is shorter so there is no need for a back vent. This dress has a zip in the centre back and features top-stitching at the neck and armhole edges. The lining is cut from the same pattern as the dress.

the shift dresses

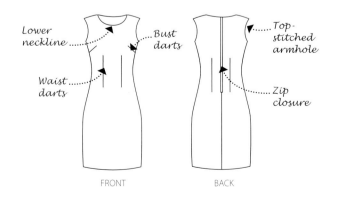

Lower neckline   *Bust darts*   *Top-stitched armhole*

Waist darts   *Zip closure*

FRONT   BACK

HOW TO MAKE THE SLEEVELESS SHIFT DRESS

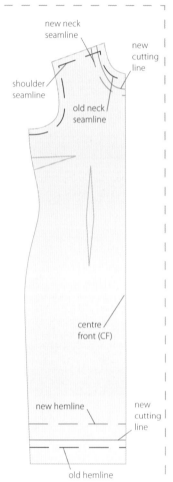

new neck seamline

new cutting line

shoulder seamline

old neck seamline

centre front (CF)

new hemline

new cutting line

old hemline

1 **Copy the pattern front and mark the seamlines and hemline.** Draw a new hemline 6cm (2³⁄₈in) above the old hemline. Measure 4cm (1¹⁄₂in) below the new hemline to mark a new cutting line. Mark a point on the CF (centre front) 4cm (1¹⁄₂in) below the old neck seamline and another point 2cm (³⁄₄in) from the old neck seamline along the shoulder seamline. Join the points to make a new neck seamline. Measure a 1.5cm (⁵⁄₈in) seam allowance from the new neck seamline and mark a new cutting line.

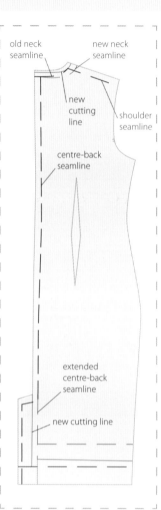

old neck seamline

new neck seamline

new cutting line

shoulder seamline

centre-back seamline

extended centre-back seamline

new cutting line

2 **Copy the pattern back and mark the seamlines and hemline.** Extend the CB (centre back) seamline to the hem to remove the vent. Extend the CB cutting line to match. Shorten the dress as in step 1.

3 Mark a point 2cm (³⁄₄in) along the shoulder seamline from the neck edge and **draw a new neck seamline**, tapering it into the old neck seamline at the CB. Measure a 1.5cm (⁵⁄₈in) seam allowance from the new neck seamline and mark a new cutting line.

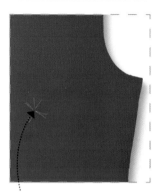

4 **Cut out the dress fabric and the lining** using the new pattern pieces. Mark the darts on the fabric using tailor's tacks (see p.76–77).

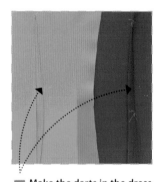

5 **Make the darts in the dress fabric and lining** (see pp.91–92) and press towards the centre of the garment.

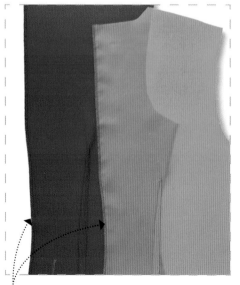

6 **Neaten the side and CB seams in the dress fabric and lining** using either a 3-thread overlock stitch or a small zigzag stitch (see pp.84–85).

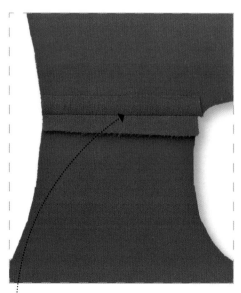

7 **Join the front to the back** at the shoulders in both the dress fabric and the lining. Press open.

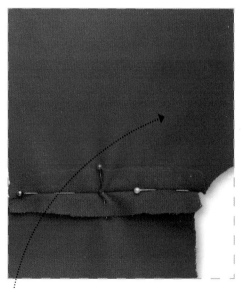

8 On the shoulder seam of the dress fabric **make a 2mm (¹⁄₁₆in) tuck** and pin in place. This slightly shortens the shoulder seam and prevents the lining from showing on the finished dress.

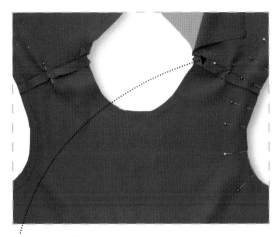

9 Place the lining to the dress fabric at the neck and armholes, RS (right side) to RS and matching at the shoulder seams. Pin and machine.

10 Clip and trim the neck and armhole seams as for the Classic Shift Dress step 14. **To turn through to the right side,** pull the back of the dress through the shoulders to the front.

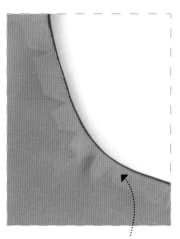

11 Roll the lining to the inside and press.

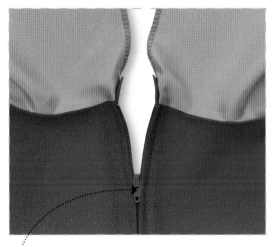

12 Insert a zip of your choice in the CB of just the dress fabric (see pp.119–122). Stitch the remainder of the CB seam. Stitch the CB seam in the lining leaving a gap for the zip.

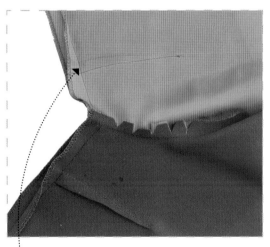

13 With RS to RS place the front to the back. Join the side seams by stitching through the fabric and lining in one continuous seam. Press the seams open.

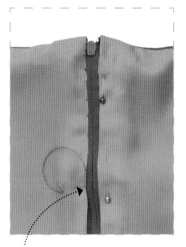

14 At the CB, fold the edge of the lining in to meet the zip tape. Pin and handstitch in place.

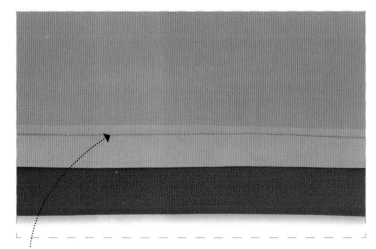

15 Neaten the hem edge of the dress (see pp.116–117). Turn up a 4cm (1¹⁄₂in) hem and handstitch in place. **Trim the lining level to the finished hem** of the dress and machine a 1.5cm (⁵⁄₈in) double-turn hem (see p.118).

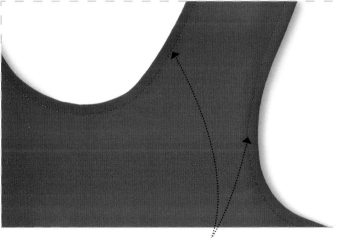

16 Topstitch around the neck and armholes.

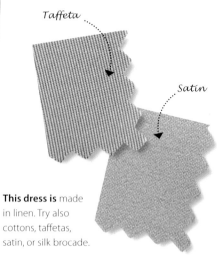

Dress Pattern One Variation

SHORT SLEEVELESS SHIFT DRESS

Omitting the darts and shortening the pattern gives us a simple sun dress or, in a sparkly fabric, it would become a teriffic little cocktail dress. Alternatively, try making the pattern even shorter and you'll have a tunic top to wear with trousers.

Taffeta

Satin

This dress is made in linen. Try also cottons, taffetas, satin, or silk brocade.

BEFORE YOU START

YOU WILL NEED

- 1.2m (47in) x 150cm (59in) fabric
- 1 x reel matching all-purpose sewing thread
- 1 x reel contrasting all-purpose sewing thread for pattern marking

PREPARING THE PATTERN

- This dress is made using Dress Pattern One (see pp.286–287)
- Follow the instructions (see pp. 278–279) to copy or download the pattern in your size

GARMENT CONSTRUCTION

This fourth variation of the Classic Shift Dress omits the waist darts and the zip, and is sleeveless. It is also wider at the hem and shorter than the Classic Shift Dress, so again there is no need for a back vent. The dress is unlined and has no facings, but instead features a bias-binding trim at the neck and armhole edges.

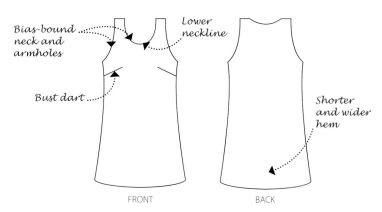

Bias-bound neck and armholes

Lower neckline

Bust dart

Shorter and wider hem

FRONT

BACK

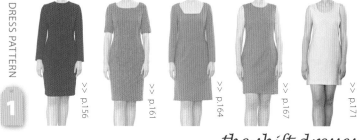

the shift dresses

HOW TO MAKE THE SHORT SLEEVELESS SHIFT DRESS

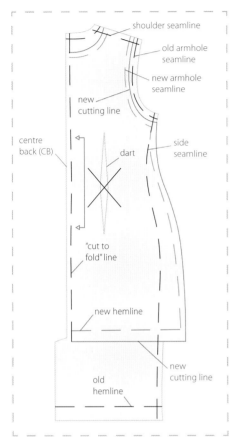

1 **Copy the pattern back and mark the seamlines and hemline.** Mark a new hemline 21cm (8¼in) above the old hemline and draw a new cutting line 3cm (1¼in) below this. **Cross out the dart marking** to remove the dress shaping.

2 **At the CB (centre back) draw a straight line through the old seamline** and mark this as a "cut to fold" line.

3 **Mark a point** 2cm (¾in) from the shoulder seamline at the armhole edge and another point on the side seamline 2.5cm (1in) below the armhole seamline. **Join the points to make a new armhole seamline.** Measure a 1.5cm (⅝in) seam allowance from the new armhole seamline and mark a new cutting line.

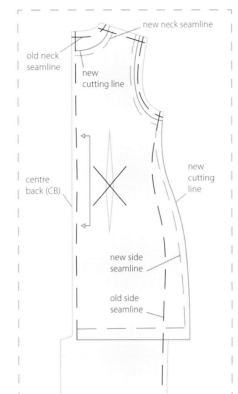

4 **Mark a point** on the CB 5cm (2in) below the neck seamline and another point 3cm (1¼in) from the neck seamline along the shoulder seamline. **Join the points to make a new neck seamline.** Measure a 1.5cm (⅝in) seam allowance from the new neck seamline and mark a new cutting line.

5 **At the bottom of the side seamline, mark a point** 6cm (2⅜in) to the right. Extend the hemline to this point. Join to the old side seamline, just below the armhole to make a new side seamline. Measure a 1.5cm (⅝in) seam allowance from the new side seamline and mark a new cutting line.

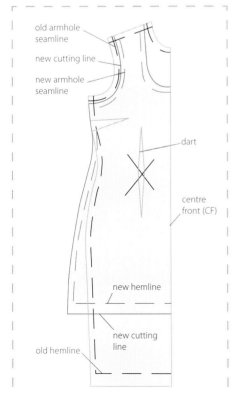

6 **Copy the pattern front and mark the seamlines and hemline.** Shorten the hem and cross out the dart as in step 1.

7 **Alter the armhole** as in step 3.

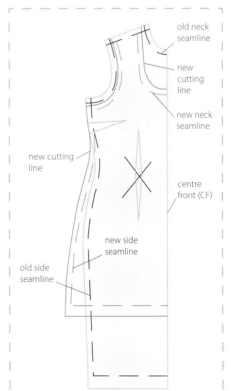

8 **Mark a point on the CF (centre front)** 12cm (5in) below the neck seamline and another point 3cm (1¼in) from the neck seamline along the shoulder seamline. **Join the points to make a new neck seamline.** Measure a 1.5cm (⅝in) seam allowance from the new neck seamline and mark a new cutting line.

9 **Widen at the side seam** as in step 5.

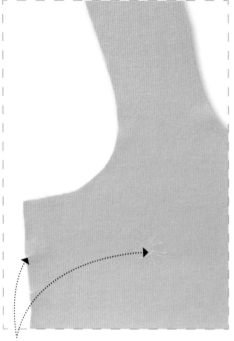

10 **Cut out the fabric** using the new pattern pieces. Mark the bust darts using tailor's tacks (see p.77) and by clipping the raw edge.

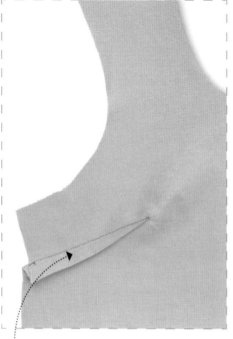

11 **Make the darts** (see p.91) and press towards the waist.

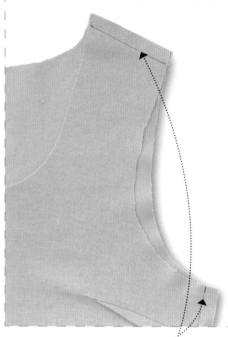

12 **Join the front to the back** at the shoulder and side seams. Press the seam allowances together.

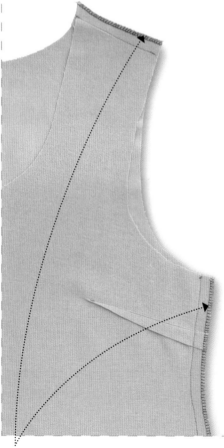

13 **Neaten the seam allowances** together using either a 3-thread overlock stitch or a small zigzag stitch (see pp.84–85). Press towards the back.

14 **Cut 4cm (1½in) wide bias strips** (see p.96). Make enough strips to go around the armholes and neck.

15 **Join the strips** RS (right side) to RS (see p.96). Press the seams open.

16 **Cut one end of a bias strip square** and fold it over WS (wrong side) to WS by ½cm (³/₁₆in). Pin the bias strip RS to RS around the armhole, starting at the underarm.

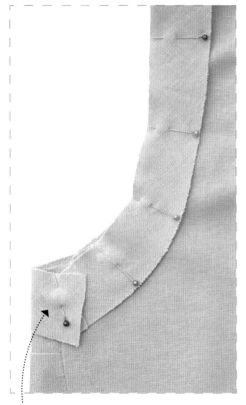

17 When you reach the underarm again, **overlap the end of the bias strip** onto the folded end. Repeat for the other armhole and the neck edge.

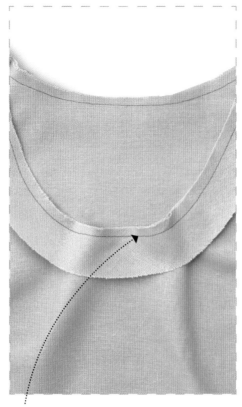

18 **Machine the bias strips** around the armholes and the neck using the edge of the presser foot as a guide.

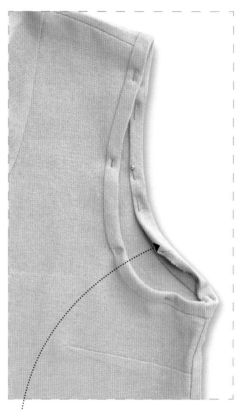

19 **Press the seams** towards the bias strips and wrap the strips over to the wrong side. **Turn the raw edges under and pin.**

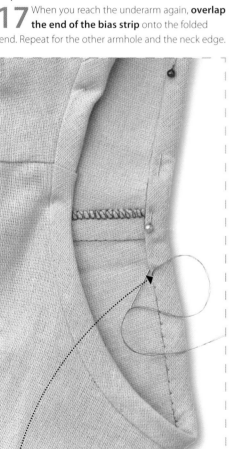

20 Handstitch in place.

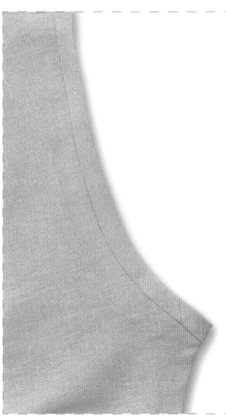

21 The finished binding, as seen from the RS, gives the edges a neat finish.

22 **Machine a 1.5cm (⅝in) double-turn hem** (see p.118). Press.

The gently flaring A-line skirt of this long-sleeved dress is sure to turn heads as you sashay by

DRESS PATTERN

2

>> p.176

>> p.179

>> p.181

>> p.185

the waisted dresses

> Dress Pattern Two

CLASSIC WAISTED DRESS

This dress has a darted bodice fitted into the waist for a smooth, flattering line at the waist and hips. Choose your pattern by your bust measurement and adjust the waist and hips if necessary. It is recommended to make the pattern up in calico first to ensure a good fit through the bust and waist, and to check the fit of the sleeve in the shoulder area. Lightweight fabrics work well for this dress and will ensure that the slightly A-line skirt moves with a nice swirl as you walk.

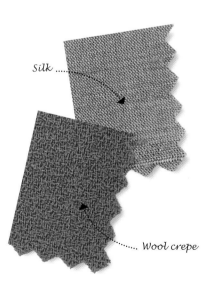

Silk

Wool crepe

This dress is made in polyester brocade, but this style of dress could be made in a variety of fabrics from cotton prints to lightweight wools, or silk.

BEFORE YOU START

YOU WILL NEED

- 2.5m (98in) x 150cm (59in) fabric
- 1 x reel matching all-purpose sewing thread
- 1 x reel contrasting all-purpose sewing thread for pattern marking
- 50cm (20in) lightweight interfacing
- 1 x 56cm (22in) zip

PREPARING THE PATTERN

- This dress is made using Dress Pattern Two (see pp.288–290)
- Follow the instructions (see pp.278–279) to copy or download the pattern in your size

GARMENT CONSTRUCTION

This unlined two-piece dress has waist darts in the bodice and in the skirt. It has long, fitted set-in sleeves and a lower neckline finished with a facing. There is a zip in the centre back and the A-line skirt sits just on the knee.

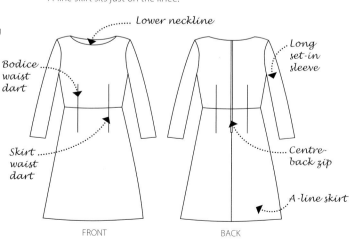

Lower neckline

Bodice waist dart

Skirt waist dart

Long set-in sleeve

Centre-back zip

A-line skirt

FRONT

BACK

HOW TO MAKE THE CLASSIC WAISTED DRESS

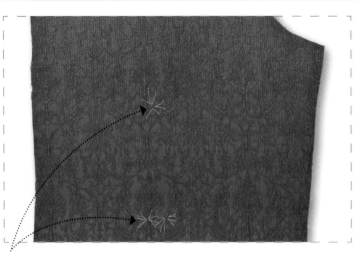

1 **Cut out the fabric** and mark all the darts using tailor's tacks (see p.77).

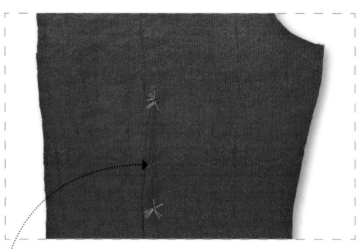

2 **Make all the darts** (see p.91) and press towards the centre of the garment.

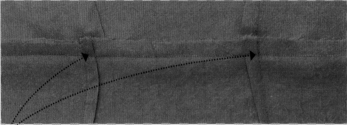

3 **Join the front and back skirts to the front and back bodices,** matching the darts. To ensure they match, you may have to ease the skirt to the bodice by stretching the bodice slightly. Press the seam allowances together.

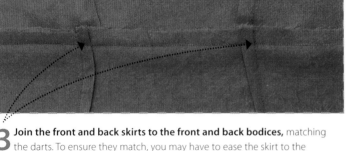

4 **Neaten the seam allowances** together using either a 3-thread overlock stitch or a small zigzag stitch (see pp.84–85). Press up towards the bodice.

5 Using either a 3-thread overlock stitch or a small zigzag stitch, **neaten the CB (centre back) seam, the side seams, and the shoulder seams** on both the front and the back.

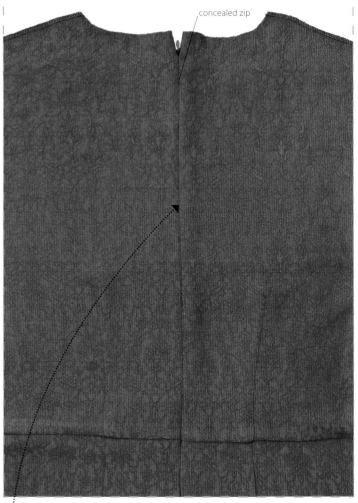

concealed zip

6 Making sure the waist seams match on either side, **insert a zip** of your choice in the CB (see pp.119–122). **Stitch the remainder of the CB seam** and press open.

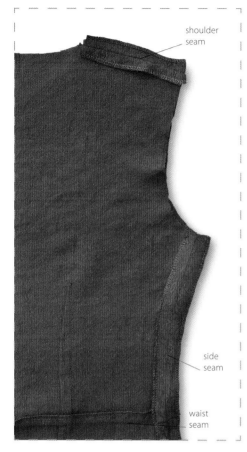

shoulder seam

side seam

waist seam

7 **Join the front to the back** at the shoulder and side seams, matching at the waist seam. Press the seams open.

8 **Neaten the sides and lower edge of both sleeves** using either a 3-thread overlock stitch or a small zigzag stitch.

ease stitches

9 **Machine the sleeve seam** and press open. Using stitch length 5, machine two rows of ease stitches through the sleeve head (see p.105).

10 **Insert the sleeve** (see p.105) and neaten the raw edges using either a 3-thread overlock stitch or a small zigzag stitch.

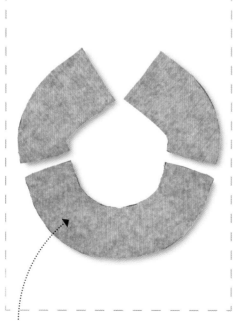

11 **Attach a lightweight fusible interfacing** to the neck facing pieces (see p.94).

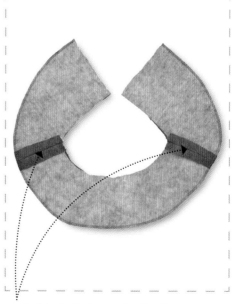

12 **Join the facings at the shoulder seams** and press the seams open. Neaten the lower edge using either a 3-thread overlock stitch or a small zigzag stitch.

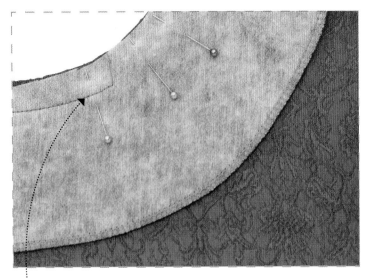

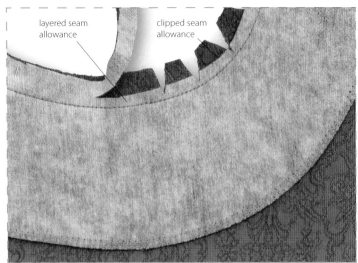

layered seam
allowance

clipped seam
allowance

13 **Place the facings** to the neck edge of the dress RS (right side) to RS, matching the seams. Pin and machine.

14 **Layer the seam allowance** by trimming the facing side of the seam to half its width. **Clip the seam allowance** to reduce bulk (see p.89).

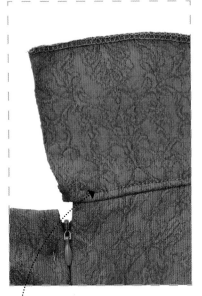

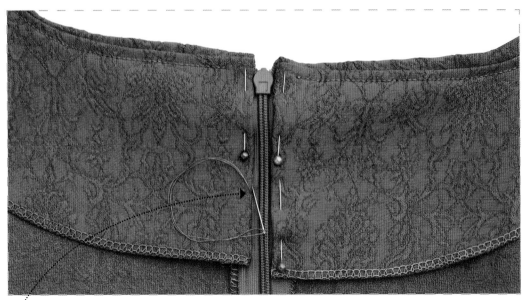

15 **Understitch the seam allowances** to the facing (see p.90).

16 **Turn the facing to the inside** then, at the CB, **fold the edge of the facing** in to meet the zip tape. Pin and handstitch in place.

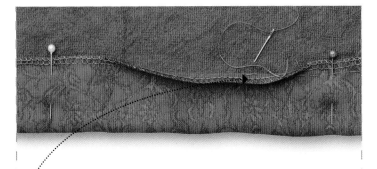

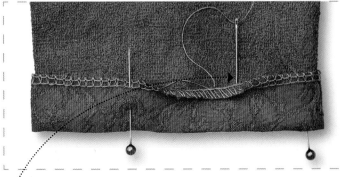

17 **Neaten the hem edge** (see pp.116–117) and turn up by 4cm (1½in). To ease the fullness out of the hem, **make a row of running stitches** close to the neatened edge (see p.81). Pull the thread to tighten the fabric. Handstitch, then remove the running stitches.

18 **Turn up a 2.5cm (1in) hem** at the bottom of each sleeve. Pin and handstitch in place.

Dress Pattern Two Variation

SHORT-SLEEVED WAISTED DRESS

For a dress with a gathered skirt, your choice of fabric is key. Don't go for anything too heavy: it won't gather evenly and could be very bulky at the waist. The skirt should sit neatly into the fitted darted bodice.

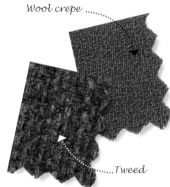

Wool crepe

Tweed

This dress is made in a cotton tweed mix, but lightweight wools such as tweed or wool crepe are also suitable, as are cottons and silks.

BEFORE YOU START

YOU WILL NEED

- 2.2m (87in) x 150cm (59in) fabric
- 1 x reel matching all-purpose sewing thread
- 1 x reel contrasting all-purpose sewing thread for pattern marking
- 50cm (20in) lightweight interfacing
- 1 x 56cm (22in) zip

PREPARING THE PATTERN

- This dress is made using Dress Pattern Two (see pp.288–290)
- Follow the instructions (see pp. 278–279) to copy or download the pattern in your size

GARMENT CONSTRUCTION

In this variation of the Classic Waisted Dress, a gathered skirt is attached to the fitted darted bodice. It has short set-in sleeves, a scoop neck, and a zip in the centre back.

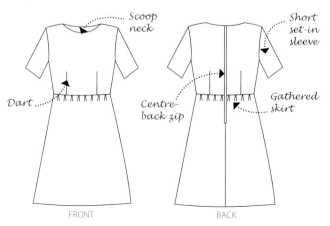

Scoop neck

Short set-in sleeve

Dart

Centre back zip

Gathered skirt

FRONT   BACK

DRESS PATTERN

2

>> p.174   >> p.179   >> p.181   >> p.185

the waisted dresses

HOW TO MAKE THE SHORT-SLEEVED WAISTED DRESS

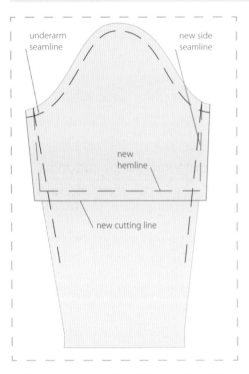

underarm seamline

new side seamline

new hemline

new cutting line

1 **Copy the sleeve and mark the seamlines.** Mark a point either side of the sleeve and 17cm (6½in) below the underarm seamlines. Join these points together to make a new hemline. Draw a new cutting line 1.5cm (⅝in) below the new hemline. (If you have a slightly fuller arm you may need to extend the new hemline by 1.5cm (⅝in) on each side. Draw new side seamlines and cutting lines allowing a 1.5cm (⅝in) seam allowance.)

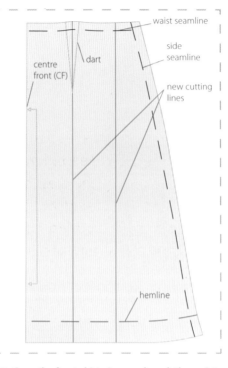

waist seamline

side seamline

centre front (CF)

dart

new cutting lines

hemline

2 **Copy the front skirt piece and mark the waist and side seam seamlines.** Draw a vertical line parallel to the CF (centre front) through the dart from waist to hem. Draw a second line 9cm (3½in) away from this line (solid red lines). Repeat on the back skirt piece, drawing the vertical line parallel to the CB (centre back) seam.

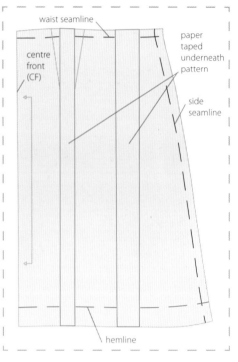

waist seamline

paper taped underneath pattern

centre front (CF)

side seamline

hemline

3 **Cut through the vertical lines.** Spread the pattern pieces apart at the dart by 3cm (1½in) at the waist and 2cm (¾in) at the hem, and at the second cut by 5cm (2in) at the waist, and 4cm (1½in) at the hem. **Place paper behind the pattern pieces and tape them down.** Repeat on the back.

4 **Cut out the fabric** using the new pattern pieces and mark and stitch the bodice darts as for The Classic Waisted Dress steps 1 and 2.

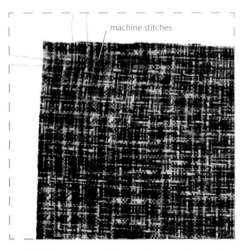

machine stitches

5 **Stitch two rows** of long machine stitches at the waist edge of the front and back skirt pieces (see p.93). Start and finish the stitching 2.5cm (1in) from the CB and side seams.

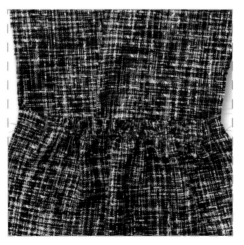

6 **Place the front skirt to the front bodice** RS (right side) to RS, and the back bodice pieces to the back skirts, RS to RS. Match the notches, pull up the two rows of stitches, and pin (see p.93).

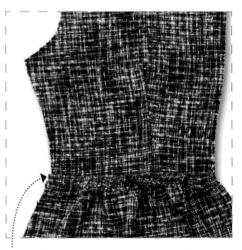

7 **Machine the waist seam** and neaten the seam allowances together using either a 3-thread overlock stitch or a small zigzag stitch (see pp.84–85).

8 **Complete the dress** as for The Classic Waisted Dress steps 5–17.

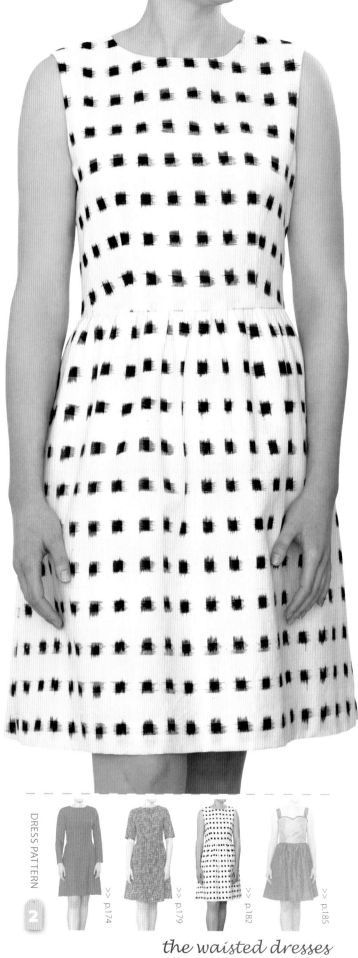

Dress Pattern Two Variation

SLEEVELESS WAISTED DRESS

In this version of the Classic Waisted Dress the sleeves have been removed and a lining added. The dress has the same skirt as the Short-Sleeved Waisted Dress. In a patterned fabric, it would be lovely for a summer wedding or even an evening function; in plain it would be ideal for office wear.

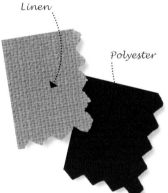

Linen

Polyester

This dress is made in a linen ikat weave, but heavy cotton, linen, polyester, and poly-viscose fabrics are all suitable.

BEFORE YOU START

YOU WILL NEED

- 2.2m (87in) x 150cm (59in) fabric
- 2.2m (87in) x 150cm (59in) lining fabric
- 1 x reel matching all-purpose sewing thread
- 1 x reel contrasting all-purpose sewing thread for pattern marking
- 1 x 56cm (22in) zip

PREPARING THE PATTERN

- This dress is made using Dress Pattern Two (see pp.288–290)
- Follow the instructions (see pp.278–279) to copy or download the pattern in your size

GARMENT CONSTRUCTION

This lined dress has a gathered A-line skirt and a fitted bodice with waist darts. The dress is sleeveless and has a scoop neck. There is a CB (centre back) zip.

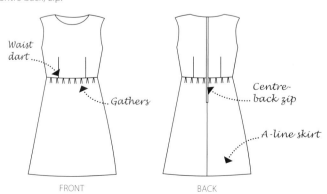

Waist dart

Gathers

Centre-back zip

A-line skirt

FRONT

BACK

DRESS PATTERN

2

>> p.174

>> p.179

>> p.182

>> p.185

the waisted dresses

HOW TO MAKE THE SLEEVELESS WAISTED DRESS

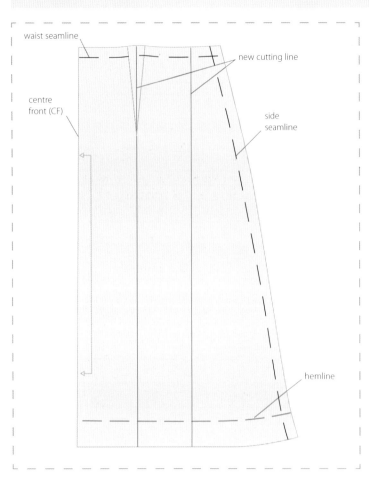

1 **Copy the front skirt piece and mark the waist and side seamlines.** Draw a vertical line parallel to the CF (centre front) through the dart from waist to hem. Draw a second line 9cm (3½in) away from this line (solid red lines). Repeat on the back skirt piece, drawing the vertical line parallel to the CB (centre back) seam.

2 **Cut through the vertical lines.** Spread the cut pattern pieces apart through the dart by 3cm (1½in) at the waist and 2cm at the hem, and at the second cut by 5cm (2in) at the waist and 4cm (1½in) at the hem. **Place paper behind the pattern pieces and tape them down.** (For sizes over a size 14 or for more fullness, double these measurements.) Repeat on the back.

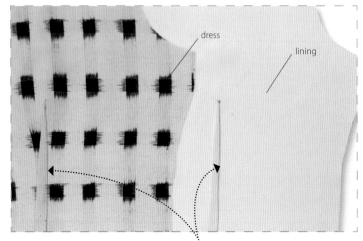

3 **Cut out** the bodice front, bodice back, skirt front and skirt back from both the dress fabric and the lining.

4 **Mark the darts** in both fabrics with tailor's tacks (see p.77). Make the darts (see p.91) and press towards the centre of the garment.

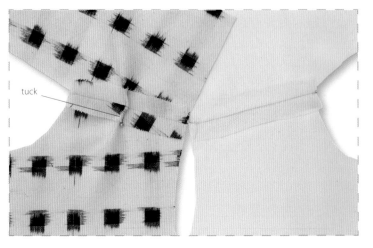

5 **Join the front bodice to the back bodice** RS (right side) to RS at the shoulder seam in both the dress fabric and the lining. Press the seams open. On the shoulder seam of the dress fabric make a 2mm (¹⁄₁₆in) tuck and pin in place.

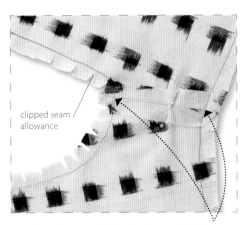

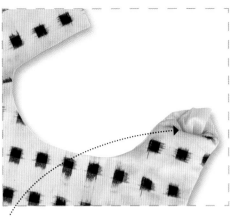

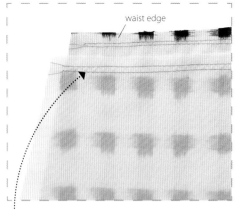

clipped seam allowance

waist edge

6 **Place the dress fabric bodice to the lining bodice** RS to RS matching at the shoulder seams. Pin and machine around the armholes and the neck. **Clip the seam allowance.**

7 Remove the pin in each shoulder. **To turn through to the right side**, pull the back of the dress through the shoulders to the front. Roll the lining to the inside and press.

8 **Stitch two rows of long machine stitches,** length 5, at the waist edge of the front and back skirt pieces in both the dress fabric and the lining (see p.93). Start and finish the stitching 2.5cm (1in) from the CB and side seams.

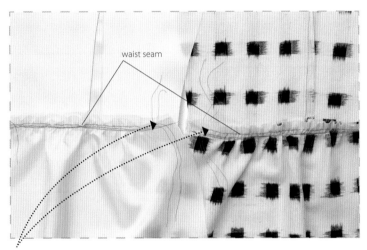

waist seam

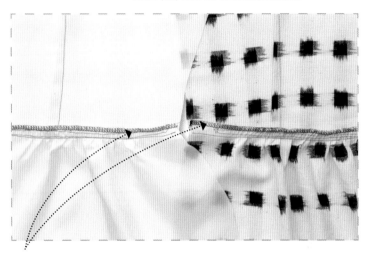

9 In both the dress fabric and the lining **place the front skirt to the front bodice** RS to RS, and the **back bodice pieces to the back skirts**, RS to RS. Match the notches, pull up the two rows of stitches, and pin (see p.93). Machine the waist seam.

10 **Neaten the seam allowances** together using either a 3-thread overlock stitch or a small zigzag stitch (see pp.84–5). Press the seam towards the bodice.

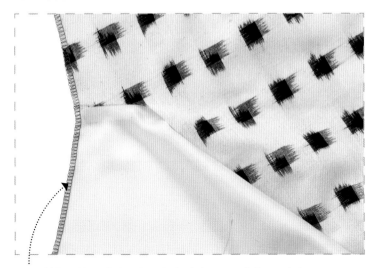

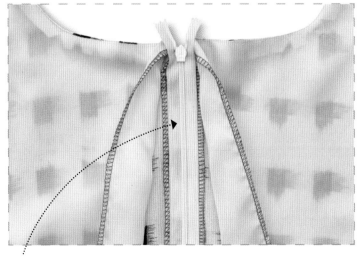

11 Using either a 3-thread overlock stitch or a small zigzag stitch, **neaten the CB seam and the side seam allowances** in both the dress fabric and the lining.

12 **Insert a zip** of your choice in the CB of just the dress fabric (see pp.119–122). Stitch the remainder of the CB seam in the dress fabric.

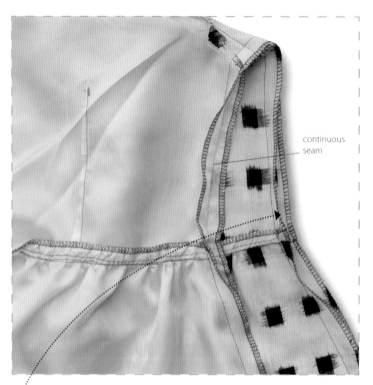

continuous seam

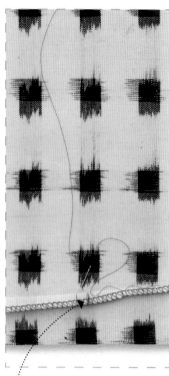

13 **Stitch the CB seam in the lining** leaving a gap for the zip.

14 With RS to RS **place the front to the back**. Join the side seams by stitching through the fabric and lining in one continuous seam. **Match the seams** at the waist and armholes.

15 **Neaten the hem edge of** the dress (see pp.116–117). Turn up a 4cm (1½in) hem and handstitch in place.

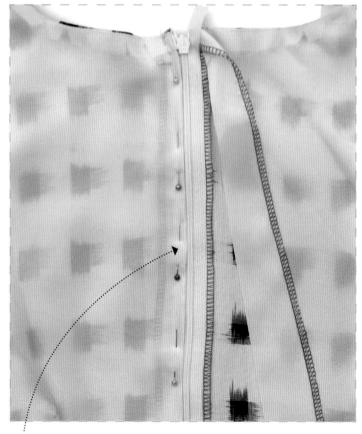

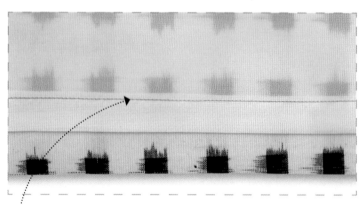

17 **Trim the lining level to the finished hem** of the dress and machine a 1.5cm (⅝in) double-turn hem (see p.118).

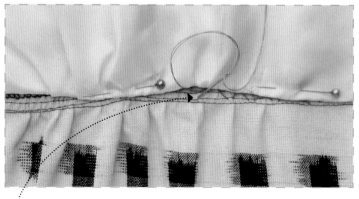

16 At the CB, **fold the edge of the lining** in to meet the zip tape. Pin and handstitch in place.

18 At the waist, **turn under the raw edge of the bodice lining**. Pin and handstitch to the waist seam.

>> p.174   >> p.179   >> p.181   >> p.186

DRESS PATTERN 2

the waisted dresses

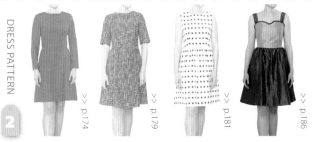

Dress Pattern Two Variation

WAISTED COCKTAIL DRESS

This great little dress could be a cocktail or prom dress or just a sundress. If you like a vintage look you can wear a net petticoat underneath. The dress requires some complex pattern alterations. The skirt has been widened to accommodate more gathers and the bodice has been re-shaped.

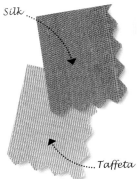

Silk

Taffeta

This dress is made in polyester crinkle taffeta, but this pattern suits any lightweight taffeta, satin, silk dupion or crepe.

BEFORE YOU START

YOU WILL NEED

- 1m (39in) x 150cm (59in) bodice fabric
- 1.5m (59in) x 150cm (59in) skirt fabric
- 60cm (36in) x 150cm (59in) lining fabric
- 1 x reel matching all-purpose sewing thread
- 1 x reel contrasting all-purpose sewing thread for pattern marking
- 1m x 115cm (46in) woven medium-weight interfacing
- 1 x 40cm (16in) zip
- 1 x hook and eye fastener

PREPARING THE PATTERN

- This dress is made using Dress Pattern Two (see pp.288–290)
- Follow the instructions (see pp.278–279) to copy or download the pattern in your size

GARMENT CONSTRUCTION

This dress in two contrasting fabrics has a full, gathered skirt, a sweetheart neckline and straps. The darted bodice with centre back (CB) zip is lined and trimmed around its upper edge with the skirt fabic.

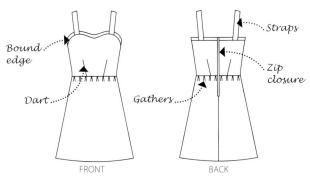

Bound edge

Dart

Gathers

Straps

Zip closure

FRONT   BACK

HOW TO MAKE THE WAISTED COCKTAIL DRESS

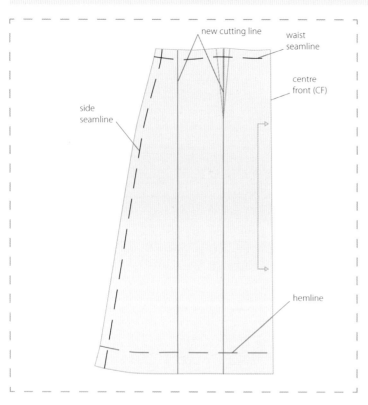

1 **Copy the front skirt piece and mark the waist and side seamlines.** Draw a vertical line parallel to the CF (centre front) through the dart from waist to hem. Draw a second line 9cm (3½in) away from this line. Repeat on the back skirt piece, drawing the vertical line parallel to the CB (centre back).

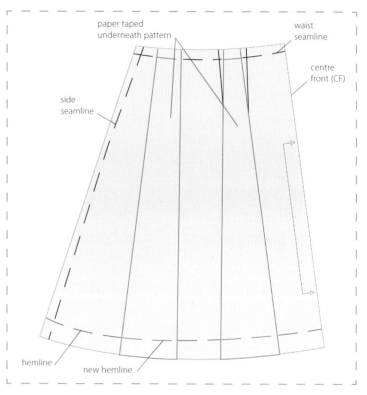

2 **Cut through the vertical lines.** Spread the cut pattern pieces apart through the dart by 3cm (1½in) at the waist and by 12cm (5in) at the hem, and at the second cut by 6cm (2⅜in) at the waist and 12cm (5in) at the hem. **Place paper behind the pattern pieces and tape them down.** (For sizes over a size 14 or for more fullness, double these measurements.) Repeat on the back skirt piece.

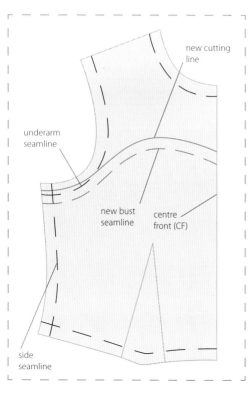

3 **Copy the bodice front pattern and mark the seamlines.** At the side seamline mark a point 1cm (½in) below the underarm seamline. At the CF line mark a point approx 9cm (3½in) below the neck seamline. Join these two points together to make the new bust seamline in a curve over the top of the bust. Measure a 1.5cm (⅝in) seam allowance from this line and mark a new cutting line.

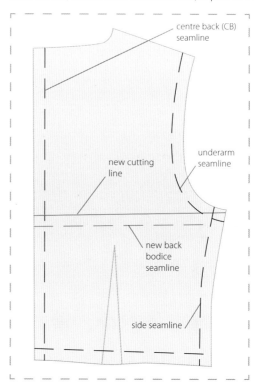

4 **Copy the bodice back pattern and mark the seamlines.** At the side seamline mark a point 1cm (½in) below the underarm seamline. Draw a horizontal line across the back to the CB seamline to make a new back bodice seamline. Measure a 1.5cm (⅝in) seam allowance from this line and mark a new cutting line.

5 **Cut out the dress fabric** using the new pattern pieces. **Cut out the lining fabric** using the bodice pattern pieces.

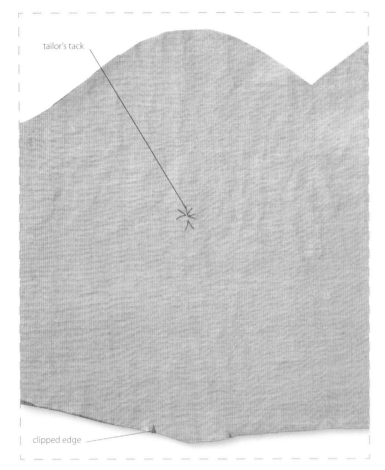

tailor's tack

clipped edge

6 **Apply fusible interfacing to the front and back bodice pieces** (see p.94). Mark the darts using tailor's tacks (see p.77) and by clipping the raw edge.

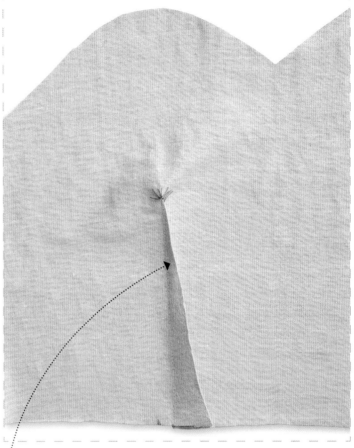

7 **Make the darts in the in the front and back bodice pieces** (see p.91) and press towards the centre of the garment.

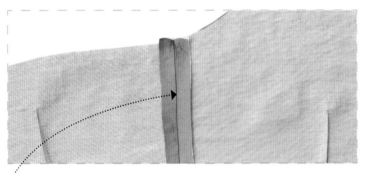

8 **Join the bodice front to the bodice back at the side seams.** Press the seams open.

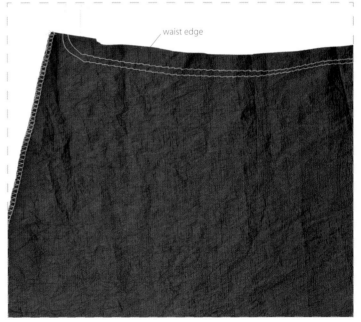

waist edge

10 **Stitch two rows of long machine stitches,** stitch length 5, at the waist edge of the front and back skirt pieces (see p.93). Start and finish the stitching 2.5cm (1in) from the CB and side seams. **Neaten the side seams** on the skirt using either a 3-thread overlock stitch or a small zigzag stitch (see pp.84–85).

dart   side seam

9 **Mark and make the darts** in the front and back bodice lining pieces and join the side seams.

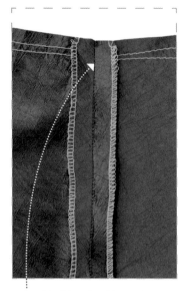

11 **Machine the skirt sections** together at the side seams and press open.

12 **Place the skirt to the bodice** RS (right side) to RS. Match the side seams, pull up the two rows of stitches and pin (see p.93). **Machine the waist seam** and neaten the seam allowances together using either a 3-thread overlock stitch or a small zigzag stitch. **Neaten the CB seams.**

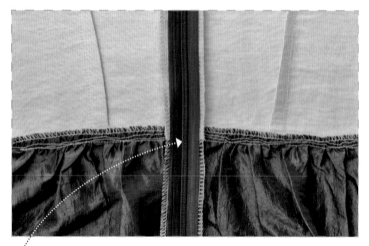

13 **Insert a zip** of your choice in the CB (see pp.119–122). Stitch the remainder of the CB seam. Press the seam open.

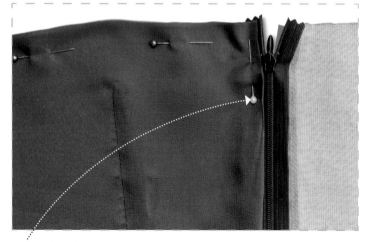

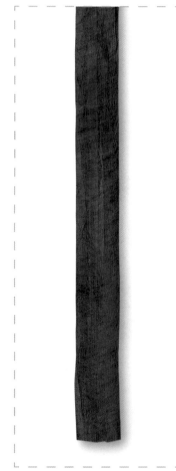

14 **Place the lining to the bodice** WS (wrong side) to WS and pin then tack around the top edge. At the CB, **fold the edge of the lining in to meet the zip tape.** Pin in place.

15 **To make the straps,** cut two pieces of fabric 45cm x 10cm (17³/₄in x 4in). Fold each in half lengthways RS to RS and machine along the long edge. Trim the seam allowance close to the seamline.

16 **Turn the straps to the RS** using a loop turner (see p. 25). Press flat ensuring that the seam is at the CB of the strap.

17 **Pin one end of each strap to the front bodice,** just to the armhole side of the dart. Try the dress on to ensure the strap will cover your bra strap. Reposition if necessary.

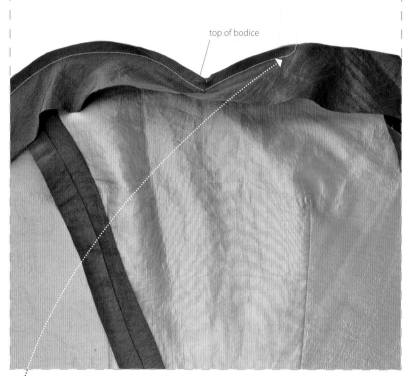

top of bodice

18 **To finish the top edge of the dress,** cut 6cm (2¹/₂in) wide bias strips from the skirt fabric (see p.96). Make a strip that is long enough to go around the top of the bodice. Pin the bias strip RS (right side) to RS to the top edge of the bodice and tack down. Machine using the edge of the presser foot as a guide. Pivot (see p.87) and clip the seam allowance at the CF. Remove the tacking stitches.

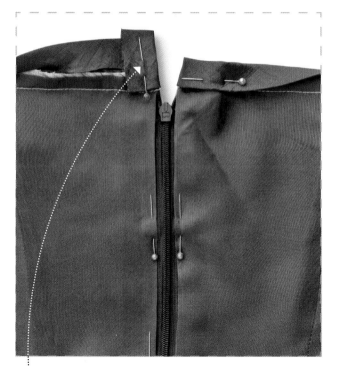

19 Trim the top of the zip tape. Fold the bias strip to the WS of the bodice and fold the raw edge under. At the CB, trim the top of the zip tape, and fold the end of the strip in line with the folded edge of the lining. Pin and handstitch. **Attach a hook and eye** to the bias strip.

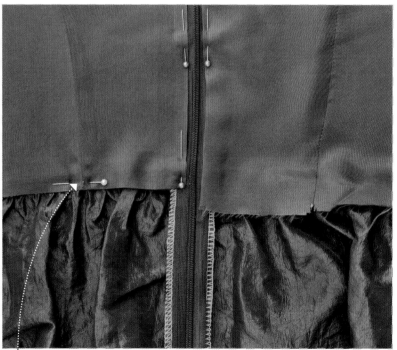

20 **To finish the bodice,** turn under the raw edge of the bodice lining. Pin and handstitch to the waist seam. Handstitch the lining to the zip tape.

21 **Finish the hem** as for the Classic Waisted Dress step 17. Try the dress on and **attach the straps** to the back of the bodice to fit. Handstitch the straps to the binding.

The flattering silhouette of this empire line dress with its gently flaring A-line skirt will hide a multitude of sins

DRESS PATTERN

3

>> p.192

>> p.195

>> p.198

the empire line dresses

CLASSIC EMPIRE LINE DRESS

Those ladies of The First French Empire certainly knew a thing or two about how to flatter the figure. The high waist of an Empire Line Dress helps to conceal a fuller waistline and the low neck of this version sets off the face and neck. Choose your pattern size by your bust measurement and check for fit in the hip and waist areas. This is an easy-to-wear day dress that can take you from work to dinner.

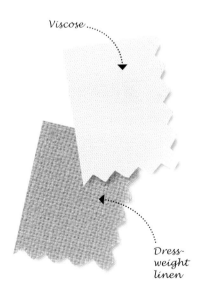

Viscose

Dress-weight linen

This dress has been made in a cotton print, but many fabrics suit this style including lightweight tweeds, wool suiting, silks, linens, viscose, or polyester.

BEFORE YOU START

YOU WILL NEED

- 2.50m (98½in) x 150cm (59in) fabric
- 1 x reel matching all-purpose sewing thread
- 1 x reel contrasting all-purpose sewing thread for pattern marking
- 50cm (20in) lightweight interfacing
- 1 x 56cm (22in) zip

PREPARING THE PATTERN

- This dress is made using Dress Pattern Three (see pp.291–293)
- Follow the instructions (see pp.278–279) to copy or download the pattern in your size

GARMENT CONSTRUCTION

This unlined dress has wrist-length sleeves and a wide, low neckline finished with a facing. The waist darts of the bodice meet the skirt darts at an under-bust seamline. There is a centre back (CB) zip and a vent in the gently shaped A-line skirt.

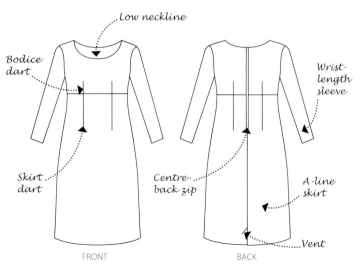

Low neckline

Bodice dart

Wrist-length sleeve

Skirt dart

Centre-back zip

A-line skirt

Vent

FRONT

BACK

HOW TO MAKE THE CLASSIC EMPIRE LINE DRESS

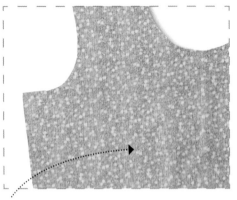

1 **Cut out the fabric** and mark the darts using tailor's tacks (see p.77).

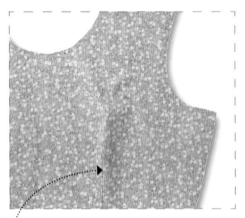

2 **Make the darts** (see p.91) in the bodice and skirt and press towards the centre of the garment.

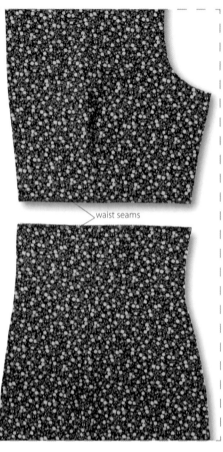

waist seams

3 **Neaten the waist seams** on all the bodice and skirt pieces using a 3-thread overlock stitch or a small zigzag stitch (see pp.84–85).

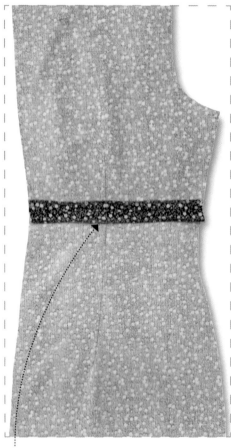

4 **Join the front bodice to the front skirt** and the back bodice pieces to the back skirts at the waist. Press the seams open.

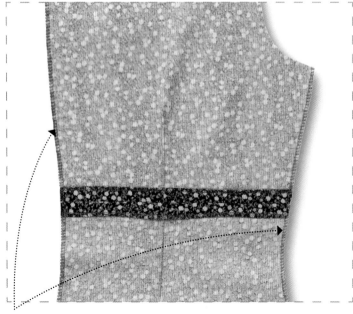

5 **Neaten all the side seams, shoulder seams, and the CB (centre back) seam** using a 3-thread overlock stitch or a small zigzag stitch.

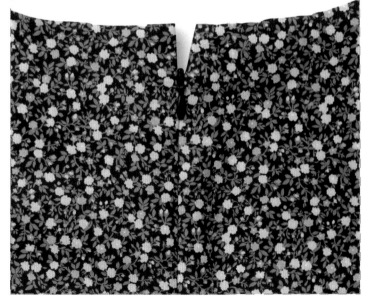

6 **Insert a zip** of your choice in the CB (see pp.119–122). Stitch the remainder of the CB seam stopping at the dot marking the top of the vent.

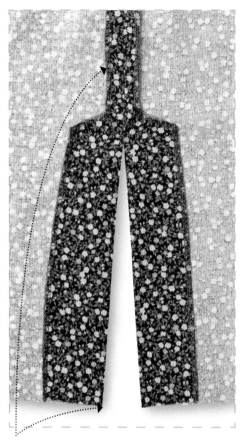

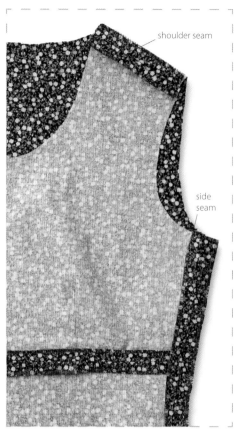

shoulder seam

side seam

7 Press the seam and the vent open.

8 Join the front to the back pieces at the shoulder and side seams. Press the seams open.

9 Neaten the sides and lower edge of both sleeves using either a 3-thread overlock stitch or a small zigzag stitch.

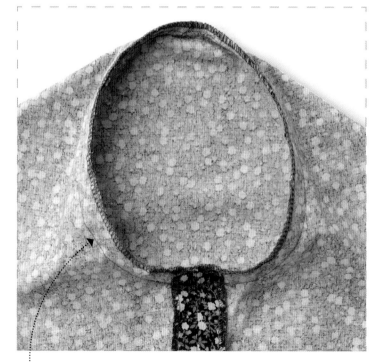

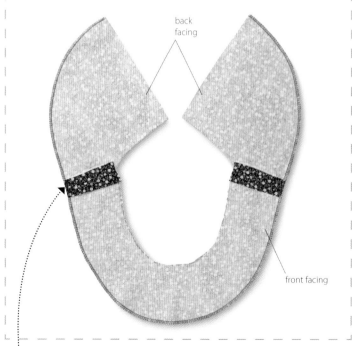

back facing

front facing

10 Machine the sleeve side seam and press it open. Using the longest stitch available, machine two rows of ease stitches through the sleeve head (see p.105). Fit the sleeve into the armhole, RS (right side) to RS. Pin, then stitch the sleeve into place from the sleeve side (see p.105).

11 Attach a lightweight fusible interfacing to the neck facing pieces (see p.94). Join the facings at the shoulder seams and press the seams open. Neaten the lower edge of the facing pieces (see pp.95–97).

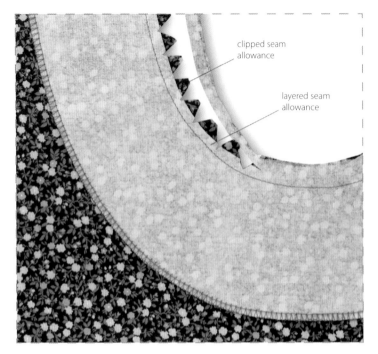

clipped seam allowance

layered seam allowance

topstitching

12 **Place the facings to the neck edge of the dress** RS to RS, matching the seams. Pin and machine. **Layer the seam allowance** by trimming the facing side of the seam to half its width. **Clip the seam allowance** to reduce bulk (see p.89).

13 **Turn the facing to the WS** (wrong side), press and topstitch to hold in place.

hem edge   mitre

15 **Turn up the sleeve hem** by 3cm (1¹⁄₂in), pin and handstitch in place.

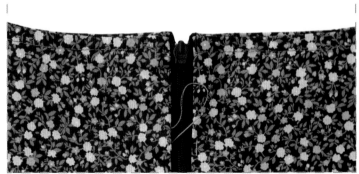

14 **Neaten the hem edge** (see pp.116–117). On each side of the vent, **remove the surplus fabric** in the hem allowance. Mitre the hem at the bottom of the vent and pin. Turn up the remainder of the hem and pin. Handstitch the mitre and hem in place.

16 At the CB, **fold the edge of the facing in to meet the zip tape**. Pin and handstitch in place.

DRESS PATTERN 3

>> p.190   >> p.196   >> p.198

the empire line dresses

Dress Pattern Three Variation

SLEEVELESS EMPIRE LINE DRESS

This version of the Classic Empire Line Dress features tucks in the skirt, which give a full yet sleek, smooth line. The dress is lined but also has facings in order to show an alternative way of inserting a lining into a sleeveless dress. Made in silk, this dress is ideal for a party, or try a poly-cotton mix for daywear.

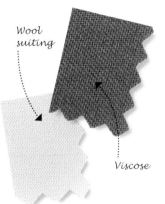

Wool suiting

Viscose

This dress is silk dupion but it could also be made in poly-cotton, viscose, or wool suiting.

BEFORE YOU START

YOU WILL NEED

- 1.75m (69in) x 150cm (59in) fabric
- 1.75m (69in) x 150cm (59in) lining fabric
- 1 x reel matching all-purpose sewing thread
- 1 x reel contrasting all-purpose sewing thread for pattern marking
- 50cm (20in) x lightweight fusible interfacing
- 1 x 56cm (22in) zip

PREPARING THE PATTERN

- This dress is made using Dress Pattern Three (see pp.291–293)
- Follow the instructions (see pp.278–279) to copy or download the pattern in your size

GARMENT CONSTRUCTION

This sleeveless empire line dress has front and back bodice darts at the waist that line up with tucks in the skirt. The tucks give a fuller skirt. The dress is lined and the neckline is faced.

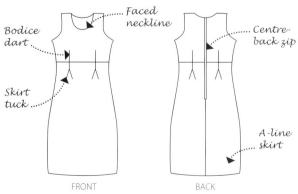

Faced neckline

Bodice dart

Skirt tuck

Centre-back zip

A-line skirt

FRONT   BACK

HOW TO MAKE THE SLEEVELESS EMPIRE LINE DRESS

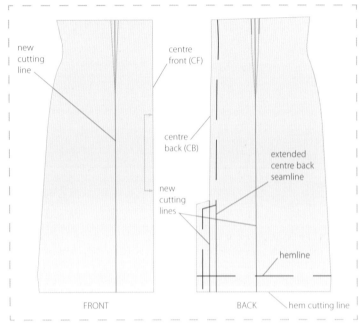

new
cutting
line

centre
front (CF)

centre
back (CB)

extended
centre back
seamline

new
cutting
lines

hemline

FRONT

BACK — hem cutting line

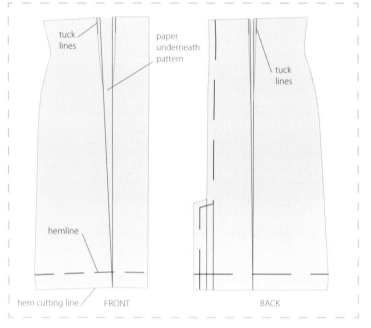

tuck
lines

paper
underneath
pattern

tuck
lines

hemline

hem cutting line — FRONT

BACK

1 **Copy the skirt front and back and mark the seamlines and hemlines.** On the front, draw a vertical line parallel to the CF (centre front). On the back, draw a vertical line parallel to the CB (centre back) seam through the dart to the hem cutting line. **To remove the vent,** extend the CB seamline to the hemline. Draw a new cutting line 1.5cm (⁵⁄₈in) to the left of it.

2 **Cut through the vertical lines** to within 3mm (¹⁄₈in) of the hem cutting line. **Place paper underneath,** and spread the cut pattern pieces apart through the front waist by 3cm (1¹⁄₂in) and through the back waist by 1.5cm (⁵⁄₈in). **Tape the pattern pieces** to the paper. **Mark the tuck lines** at points 4cm (1¹⁄₂in) below the waist, following the original dart seamlines.

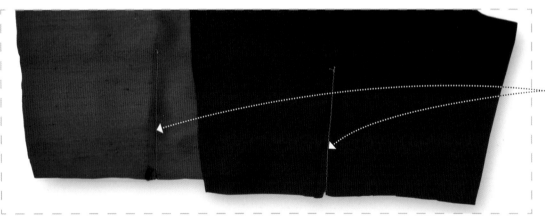

3 **Cut out the fabric and the lining** using the new skirt pieces and the bodice pieces.

4 **Mark the darts** in both the fabric and the lining bodices with tailor's tacks (see p.77). Make the darts (see p.91) and press towards the centre of the body.

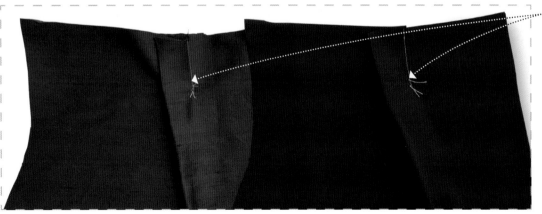

5 **Make the tucks** in both the fabric and lining skirt front and skirt backs by bringing the tuck lines at the waist edge together RS (right side) to RS. **Stitch along the tuck lines** 4cm (1¹⁄₂in). Press towards the side seamlines.

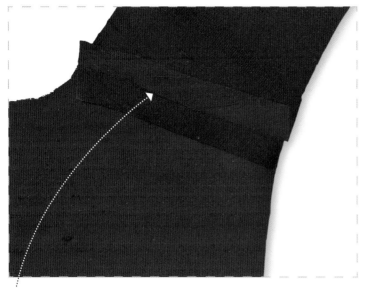

6 **Join the front to the back at the shoulder seams** in both the fabric and the lining bodices. Press the seams open.

clipped seam allowance

7 **Place the fabric bodice to the lining bodice** RS to RS and matching at the shoulder seams. Pin and machine just around the armholes. Clip the seam.

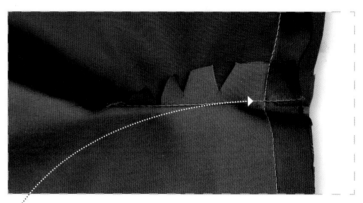

10 With RS to RS **place the front to the back. Join the side seams** by stitching through the fabric and lining in one continuous seam. Press the seams open.

11 **Make and attach the neck facing** to the tacked raw neck edge as for the Classic Empire Line Dress steps 11–12.

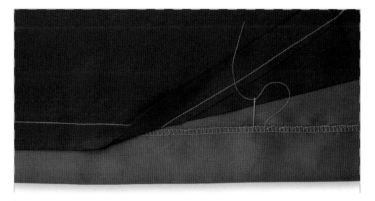

8 **Turn through to the right side,** roll the lining to the inside and press. **Tack the raw edges together** around the neck.

9 Working separately on the fabric and the lining, **follow steps 3–7 of the Classic Empire Line Dress**, leaving a gap corresponding to the zip in the lining. Do not neaten the bodice seams and ignore the reference to the CB vent.

12 **Neaten the hem edge** of the dress (see pp.116–117). Turn up a 4cm (1½in) hem and handstitch in place. Trim the lining level to the finished hem of the dress and machine a 2cm (¾in) double-turn hem (see p.118).

LONG EMPIRE LINE DRESS

Here the strapless bodice has been interlined and boned, and the skirt extended to floor length with a small "puddle" train. The bodice requires a snug fit, so you should definitely test your pattern in calico first. Try this dress in a crepe or satin for evening wear or a prom, or in silk and lace for a wedding.

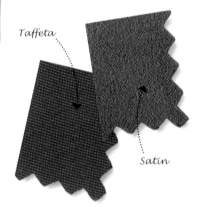

Taffeta

Satin

This dress is made in polyester crepe, but satin, silk, taffeta, and satin-backed crepe are all good fabric choices.

BEFORE YOU START

YOU WILL NEED

- 3.5m (138in) x 150cm (59in) fabric
- 3.5m (138in) x 150cm (59in) lining fabric
- 75cm (30in) x 150cm (59in) calico
- 2 x reels matching all-purpose sewing thread
- 1 x reel contrasting all-purpose sewing thread for pattern marking
- 75cm (30in) x medium-weight fusible woven interfacing
- 2m (79in) x sew-in polyester boning 12mm (1/2in) wide
- 1 x 40cm (16in) concealed zip

PREPARING THE PATTERN

- This dress is made using Dress Pattern Three (see pp.291–293)
- Follow the instructions (see pp.278–279) to copy or download the pattern in your size

GARMENT CONSTRUCTION

The high-waisted, strapless fitted bodice is boned, interfaced, and interlined. The full-length skirt has been widened and falls into a small "puddle" train. The dress has a centre-back (CB) zip.

DRESS PATTERN

3

>> p.190 <<

>> p.195 <<

>> p.199 <<

the empire line dresses

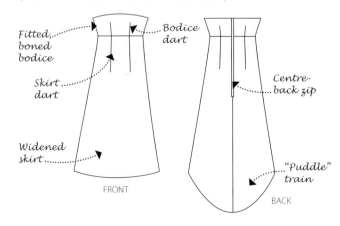

Fitted, boned bodice

Bodice dart

Skirt dart

Widened skirt

Centre-back zip

"Puddle" train

FRONT

BACK

HOW TO MAKE THE LONG EMPIRE LINE DRESS

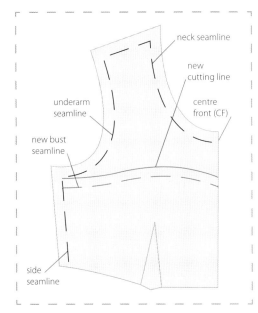

1 **Copy the bodice front pattern and mark the seamlines.** At the side seamline mark a point 1.5cm ($^5/_8$in) below the underarm seamline. At the CF (centre front) line mark a point 7cm ($2^3/_4$in) below the neck seamline. Join these two points together to make the new bust seamline in a curve over the top of the bust. Measure a 1.5cm ($^5/_8$in) seam allowance from this line and mark a new cutting line.

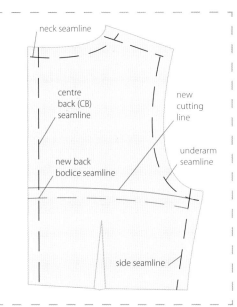

2 **Copy the bodice back pattern and mark the seamlines.** At the side seamline mark a point 1.5cm ($^5/_8$in) below the underarm seamline. Mark another point on the CB (centre back) seamline 21cm ($8^1/_4$in) below the neck seamline. Join these two points together with a slightly curving line to make the new back bodice seamline. Measure a 1.5cm ($^5/_8$in) seam allowance from this line and mark a new cutting line.

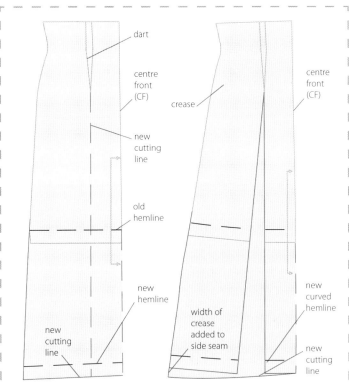

3 **Copy the front skirt piece.** See p.58 to extend the pattern by 46cm (18in) to make the skirt floor length. Add a 4cm ($1^1/_4$in) hem allowance and mark a new cutting line. Draw a vertical line parallel to the CF through the dart from the waist to the new hem cutting line. **Slash along this line and spread the pattern** at the hem by 9cm ($3^1/_2$in). **Measure the width of the crease** that forms on the side seamline in the hip area and add this amount to the hem on the side seam. **Draw in a new curved hemline and cutting line.**

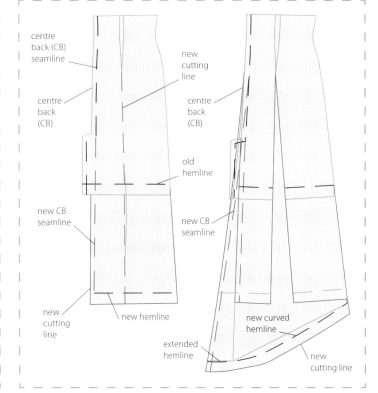

4 **Copy the back skirt pieces and mark the CB seamlines and the hemlines.** Extend the pattern at the hemline as in step 3. **Remove the vent** by extending the CB seamline to the new hemline. **Slash and spread the pattern** as in step 3. **To create the train,** extend the CB seamline by 30cm (12in). At the hemline extend the hemline horizontally by 6cm ($2^3/_8$in). Join this point with a straight line to the CB seamline in the hip area and extend the other way by at least 30cm (12in). On the extended hem, join these new points with straight lines and then draw in curved lines to create the train. **Draw in a new cutting line** 4cm ($1^1/_2$in) below this line.

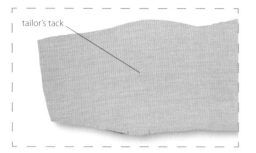

tailor's tack

5 **Cut out the bodice front and back pieces** from fabric, calico, medium-weight interfacing, and lining. **Cut the skirt front and back pieces** from fabric and lining. **Mark the darts** with tailor's tacks (see p.77).

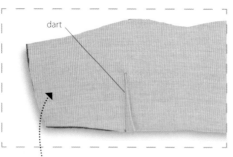

dart

6 **Attach fusible interfacing** (see p.94) to the fabric bodice pieces. **Make the darts** (see p.91) and press towards the centre of the body.

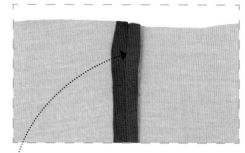

7 **Join the interfaced bodice front to the interfaced bodice back** at the side seams. Press the seams open.

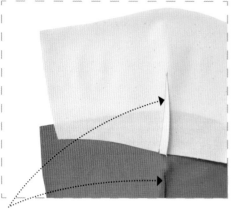

8 **Make the darts** in the calico and lining bodice sections.

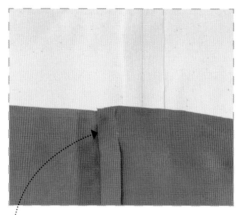

9 **Join the side seams** in the calico bodice and in the lining bodice sections. Press open.

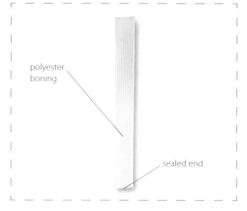

polyester boning

sealed end

10 **Cut the polyester boning** to fit the bodice (see step 11) and seal the ends if required.

11 **Place the boning on the calico bodice** as shown, leaving 2cm (³/₄in) clearance at the top and bottom. Attach with a zigzag stitch (see p.82).

12 **Place the WS (wrong side) of the fabric bodice to the RS (right side) of the boned bodice.** Tack around the edges.

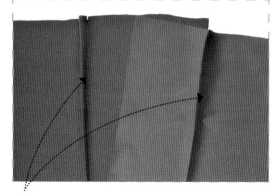

13 **Cut out the skirt front and back pieces** from fabric and lining. **Mark and make the darts** in both.

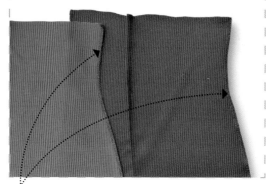

14 **Neaten the side and CB seams** in the fabric and the lining skirt pieces using either a 3-thread overlock stitch or a small zigzag stitch (see pp.84–85).

15 **Join the side seams** in both the fabric and the lining skirt pieces. Press the seams open.

trimmed seam allowance

16 **Attach just the fabric skirt to the boned bodice.** Cut away the calico from the seam and press the seam allowances up towards bodice.

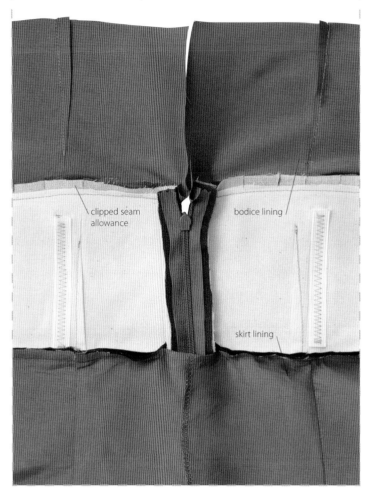

clipped seam allowance

bodice lining

skirt lining

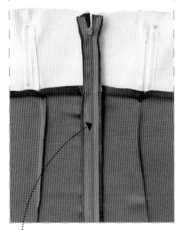

17 **Insert a 40cm (16in) concealed zip** in the CB (see p.122). Stitch the remainder of the CB seam.

18 **Machine the lining skirt to the skirt-to-bodice seam** allowances, stopping 3cm (1¼in) from the zip.

19 **Attach the bodice lining to the top edge of the boned bodice** RS to RS. Cut away the calico from the seam and clip the seam allowance.

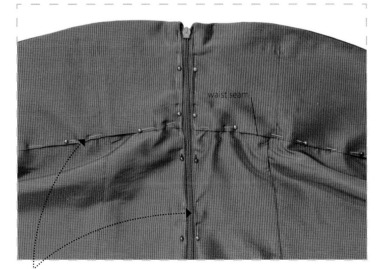

waist seam

20 **Turn the lining bodice to the inside** and press. **At the CB,** fold the edge of the lining in to meet the zip tape. Pin and handstitch in place. **At the waist,** turn under the raw edge of the bodice lining. Pin and handstitch to the waist seam.

21 **Neaten the hem edge of the dress** (see pp.116–117) and turn up a 4cm (1½in) hem, placing the pins vertically in the area of the train to ease out any fullness. Handstitch in place.

22 **Trim the lining level to the finished hem** of the dress and machine a 2cm (¾in) double-turn hem (see p.118).

the
TROUSERS

Every woman needs at least a couple of pairs of trousers in her wardrobe. Here are two basic styles and a variation of each that will work well for most occasions. Making trousers may appear daunting, but the steps are all clearly explained.

Trouser pattern one
Classic tailored
trousers
>> p.204

Trouser pattern one
variation
Tapered capri
trousers
>> p.208

Trouser pattern two
Classic palazzo
trousers
>> p.210

Trouser pattern two
variation
Wide-leg shorts
>> p.216

These go-anywhere trousers are sure to appeal. The flat front ensures a smooth line over the tummy area

Gabardine

We made our trousers in a wool flannel but you can also try them in a gabardine or a polyester and wool mix. They would also work well in a fabric with a 2 or 3 per cent stretch.

Stretch cotton

TROUSER PATTERN

1

>> p.206

>> p.208

the tailored trousers

Trouser Pattern One

CLASSIC TAILORED TROUSERS

These classic trousers with their slanted hip pockets and shaped waistband have a timeless appeal and can be worn by any age. Choose your pattern according to your full hip measurement (see pp.54–55). To ensure the trousers fit well in the crotch area, check your crotch measurements carefully against the pattern and make the trousers in calico first, altering where necessary before cutting them out of your fabric. Wearing trousers like this, you can go absolutely anywhere.

BEFORE YOU START

YOU WILL NEED

- 2.5m (98$\frac{1}{2}$in) x 150cm (59in) fabric
- 30cm (12in) x 150cm lining fabric
- 1 x reel matching all-purpose sewing thread
- 1 x reel contrasting all-purpose sewing thread for pattern marking
- 50cm (20in) x medium-weight fusible interfacing
- 1 x 18cm (7$\frac{1}{4}$in) trouser zip
- 1 x trouser hook and eye

PREPARING THE PATTERN

- These trousers are made using Trouser Pattern One (see pp.294–295)
- Follow the instructions (see pp.278–279) to copy or download the pattern in your size

GARMENT CONSTRUCTION

The trousers feature a flat front with a fly-front zip opening and a slightly tapered leg. They have slanted pockets on the hip and a shaped waistband that sits just below the natural waistline.

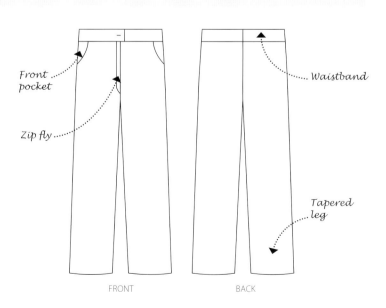

Front pocket

Zip fly

Waistband

Tapered leg

FRONT

BACK

HOW TO MAKE THE CLASSIC TAILORED TROUSERS

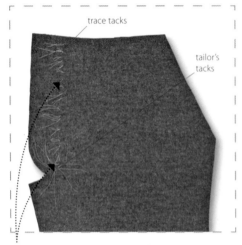

trace tacks

tailor's tacks

1 **Cut out the fabric** and transfer the pattern markings using tailor's tacks (see p.91). **Mark the CF (centre front) line** with trace tacks (see p.76).

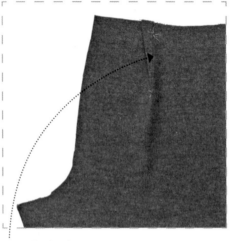

2 **Make the darts** (see p.91) in the trouser back and **press towards the CB** (centre back).

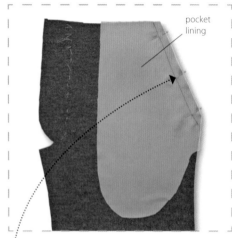

pocket lining

3 **Place the pocket lining to the trouser front,** RS (right side) to RS. **Pin and machine** in place.

topstitching

4 **Clip the seam allowance**. Turn the pocket lining to the inside and press. **Top-stitch to secure.**

side front

5 On the RS, **pin the trouser front to the side front**, matching the markings. Pin securely.

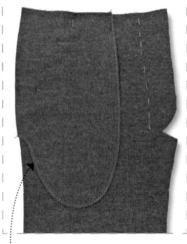

6 On the WS (wrong side), **pin and stitch around the pocket bag**. Neaten using a 3-thread overlock stitch or a small zigzag stitch (see pp.84–85). Be careful not to sew through the trouser front.

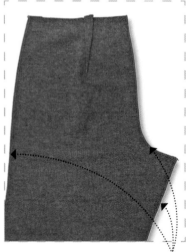

7 **Neaten the side, crotch and inside leg seams** of the front and back trouser legs using a 3-thread overlock stitch or a small zigzag stitch.

8 **Join a front leg to a back leg** at the outside and inside leg seams to make each leg. Press the seams open.

9 **Join the crotch seams,** RS to RS, stopping at the tailor's tack at the CF.

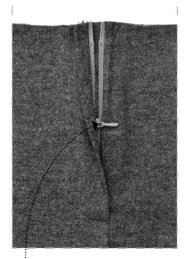

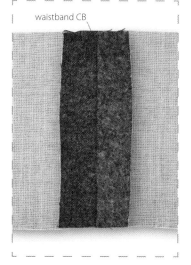

waistband CB

layered seam allowance

10 Insert a faced fly-front zip (see p.121) at the CF.

11 Attach medium-weight **fusible interfacing** (see p.94) to one set of waistbands. **Join each set of waistbands** at the CB and press the seams open.

12 Attach the waistband to the trousers, matching at the CB seams. **Layer the seam allowance** by trimming the trouser side of the seam to half its width (see p.89). Press towards the waistband.

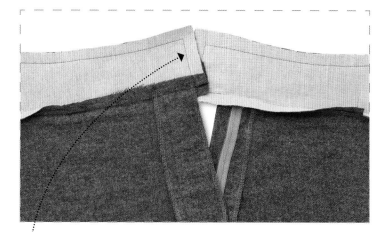

clipped end

13 Place the remaining waistband to the interfaced waistband RS to RS and **stitch around the waistband.**

14 Clip the ends of the waistband to reduce bulk. Turn the waistband to the RS, fold under the raw edge, **pin and handstitch** in place to the trouser-to-waistband seamline.

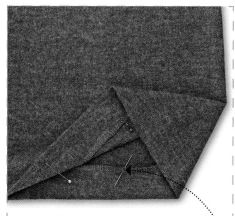

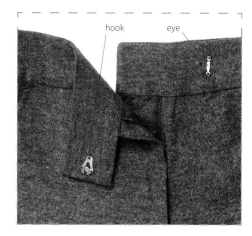

hook   eye

15 The finished waist at the CF from the RS.

16 Neaten the hem edge of the trouser legs by overlocking (see p.116). Turn up a 4cm (1½in) **hem and handstitch** in place.

17 Attach a trouser hook to the waistband extension **and an eye** to the other end of the waistband.

TROUSER PATTERN

>> p.204

>> p.209

the tailored trousers

TAPERED CAPRI TROUSERS

The trouser pattern has been altered to make cropped trousers. To decide the length you want, measure from your waist down. You can finish the trousers just above your ankle or on your calf, as here. These trousers are ideal to take on holiday.

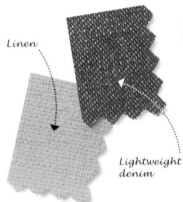

Linen

Lightweight denim

These trousers are made in cotton chambray but linen or lightweight denim would work just as well.

BEFORE YOU START

YOU WILL NEED
- 2.2m (87in) x 150cm (59in) fabric
- 30cm (12in) x 150cm (59in) lining
- 1 x reel matching all-purpose sewing thread
- 1 x reel contrasting all-purpose sewing thread for pattern marking
- 50cm (20in) x medium-weight fusible interfacing
- 1 x 18cm (7¼in) trouser zip
- 1 x trouser hook and bar

PREPARING THE PATTERN
- These trousers are made using Trouser Pattern One (see pp.294–295)
- Follow the instructions (see pp.278–279) to copy or download the pattern in your size

GARMENT CONSTRUCTION

The cropped trousers have a flat front with a fly-front zip opening, slanted pockets on the hip, and a shaped waistband that sits just below the natural waistline. The hem of the leg is tapered and there is a split in the side seam for added comfort.

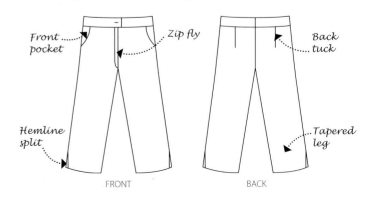

Front pocket

Zip fly

Hemline split

FRONT

Back tuck

Tapered leg

BACK

HOW TO MAKE THE TAPERED CAPRI TROUSERS

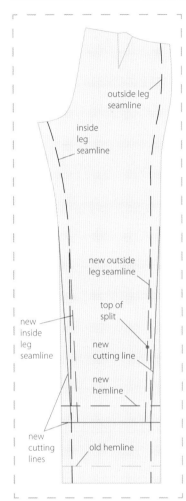

1 **Copy the back leg pattern and mark the seamlines and hemlines.** Measuring upwards from the hemline draw a line for the new hemline. Measure 4cm (1¹/₂in) below this line and mark a new hem cutting line. **To taper the legs**, on the new hemline mark a point 2cm (⁵/₄in) from the inside leg seamline. Join this point to the seamline in the thigh area, and to the new hem cutting line. On the outside leg, mark a point 1.5cm (⁵/₈in) along the new hemline and join this point to the new hem cutting line and to the seamline in the thigh area. To mark the position of the split, mark a point 10cm (4in) above the new hemline on each leg.

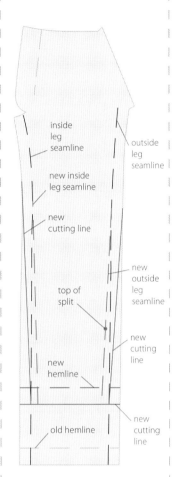

2 Repeat step 1 on the front leg pattern.

3 **Cut out the fabric using the new pattern pieces.** Mark the darts and the CF (centre front) lines.

4 Make up as for the Classic Tailored Trousers steps 2–7.

5 **Join a front leg to a back leg on the inside and outside leg seams,** stopping at the marking for the split on the outside leg. Press the seams open.

6 Continue making up as for the Classic Tailored Trousers steps 9–15.

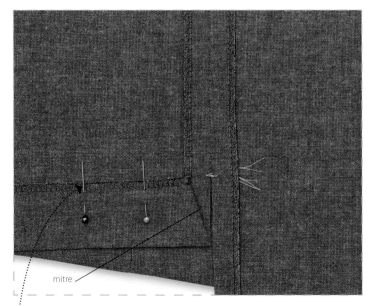

7 Neaten the lower edge of the trousers (see pp.116–117), and turn up a 4cm (1¹/₂in) hem. **Mitre the hem** at the bottom of the split and **pin in place.**

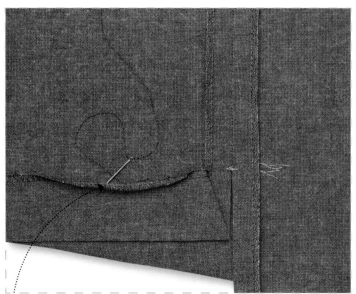

8 **Handstitch the mitre** and the remainder of the hem **and press.**

These flowing palazzo trousers epitomize 40s filmstar glamour

Medium-weight denim ....

.... Crepe

We made our trousers in linen, but you could try a crepe for evening, or a medium-weight denim or printed linen for daywear. Medium-weight fabrics give maximum impact for this style.

TROUSER PATTERN

2

>> p.212

>> p.216

the wide-leg trousers

CLASSIC PALAZZO TROUSERS

Wide-leg, or palazzo, trousers are very flattering when worn with a fashionable high heel. These retain their smooth-leg look by having discreet in-seam pockets. Choose the pattern size by your full hip measurement (see p.55) and be sure to check your crotch measurements against the pattern. It is recommended to make the pattern in calico first. These trousers would look fabulous in fine wool crepe for evening wear or in linen or heavy cotton – even in lightweight denim – for a more casual look.

BEFORE YOU START

YOU WILL NEED

- 2.7m (106¼in) x 150cm (59in) fabric
- 30cm (12in) x 150cm (59in) lining fabric
- 1 x reel matching all-purpose sewing thread
- 1 x reel contrasting all-purpose sewing thread for pattern marking
- 1m (39¼in) x fusible waistband interfacing
- 1 x trouser hook and eye
- 1 x 18cm (7in) trouser zip

PREPARING THE PATTERN

- These trousers are made using Trouser Pattern Two (see pp.296–299)
- Follow the instructions (see pp.278–279) to copy or download the pattern in your size

GARMENT CONSTRUCTION

These wide-leg trousers have a fly-front zip opening and a fitted waistband. Belt loops on the waistband take a narrow belt. The trousers feature in-seam pockets and front and back tucks at the waist.

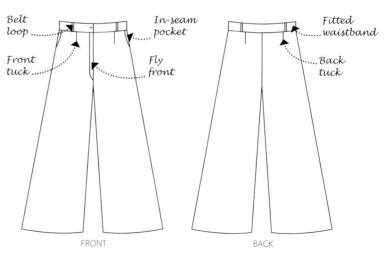

Belt loop

In-seam pocket

Front tuck

Fly front

Fitted waistband

Back tuck

FRONT

BACK

HOW TO MAKE THE CLASSIC PALAZZO TROUSERS

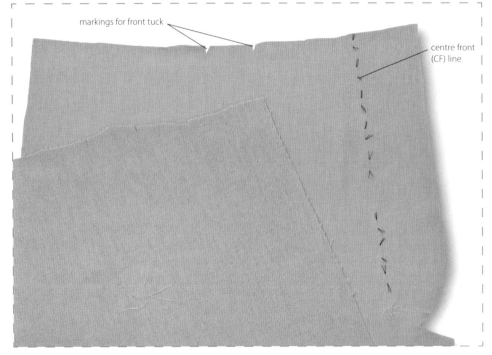

markings for front tuck

centre front (CF) line

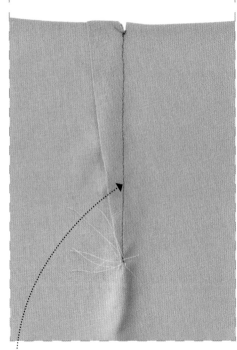

1 **Cut out the fabric** and transfer all the pattern markings (see pp.76–77). **Mark the CF (centre front) line, the front tuck, and the pocket opening** with trace tacks (see p.76).

2 **Make the darts** (see p.91) in the trouser back and press towards the CB (centre back).

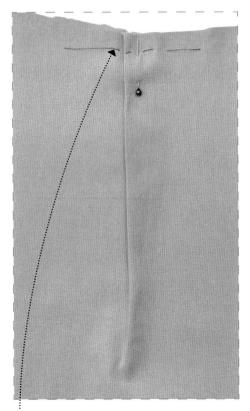

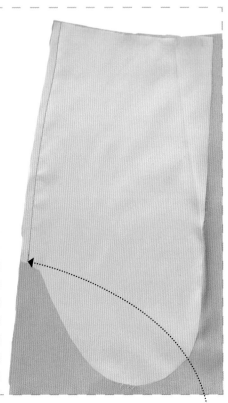

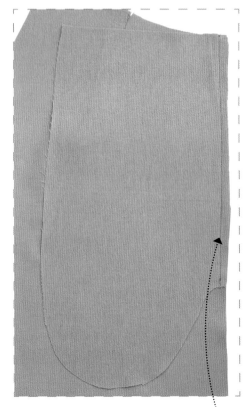

3 **Make the tucks in the trouser front** by bringing the tuck lines at the waist edge together RS (right side) to RS. **Pin and tack** across the top.

4 **Place the pocket lining to the trouser front**, RS to RS. **Pin and machine** in place with a 1cm (³∕₈in) seam allowance.

5 **Place the fabric pocket** to the trouser back, RS to RS. **Pin and machine** in place with a 1cm (³∕₈in) seam allowance.

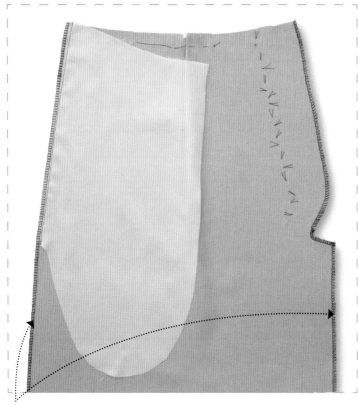

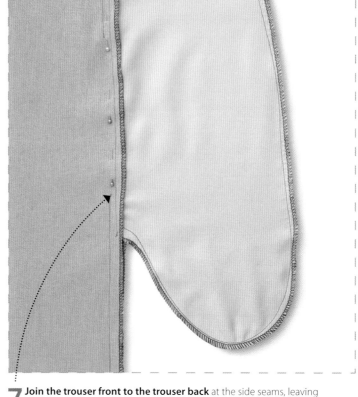

6 **Neaten the side seams, the inside leg seam, and the CF and CB crotch seams** using a 3-thread overlock stitch or a small zigzag stitch (see pp.84–85).

7 **Join the trouser front to the trouser back** at the side seams, leaving open above the point marked for the pocket opening. **Stitch around the edges of the pocket bag** and neaten.

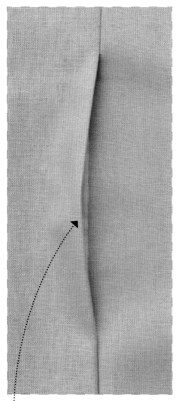

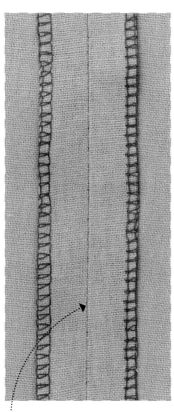

faced fly front zip

8 On the RS, **press the side seam open** and press the pocket towards the trouser front.

9 **Join the legs together** at the inside leg seam. Press the seam open.

10 **Join the crotch seam**, stopping at the marked dot on the CF. **Insert a faced fly-front zip** (see p.121).

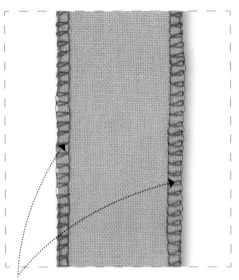

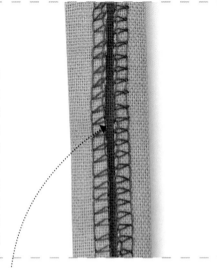

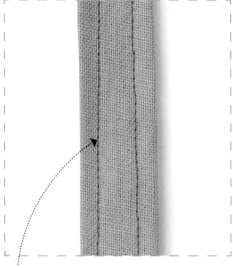

11 **Neaten the edges** of the belt carrier strip using a 3-thread overlock stitch or a small zigzag stitch.

12 **Fold the edges of the belt carrier strip** to the centre, WS (wrong side) to WS, and press.

13 Working from the RS, **topstitch either side** of the belt carrier strip.

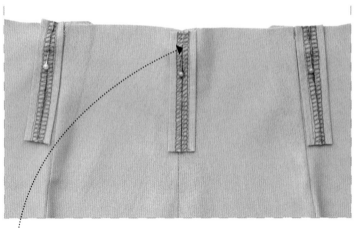

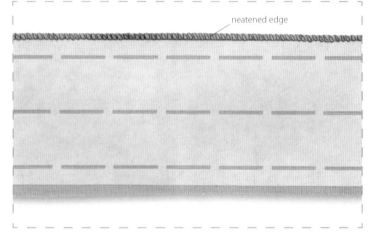

neatened edge

14 **Cut the belt carrier strip into five pieces** as indicated on the pattern. Pin, then stitch a belt carrier to each tuck, to each back dart, and to the CB seam.

15 **Attach fusible interfacing (see p.94) to the waistband.** Neaten one long edge using a 3-thread overlock stitch or a small zigzag stitch.

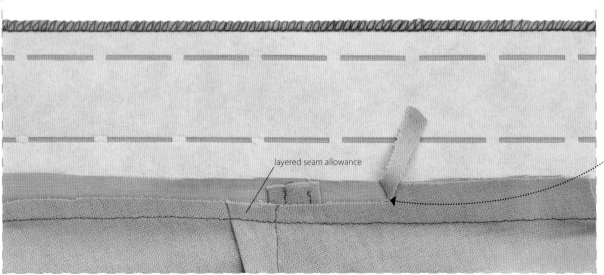

layered seam allowance

16 **Attach the other edge of the waistband to the trousers**, RS to RS, stitching over the ends of the belt carriers. **Layer the seam allowance** by trimming the waistband side of the seam to half its width (see p.89). Press towards the waistband.

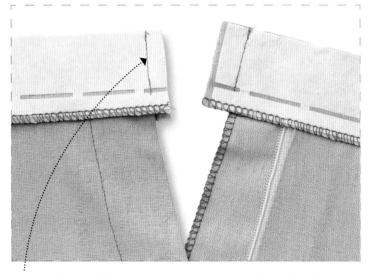

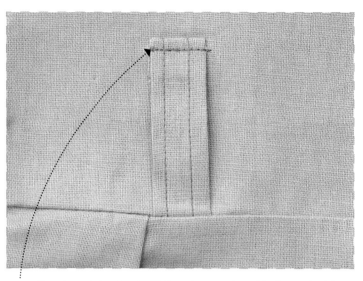

17 **Fold the waistband along the crease** in the interfacing RS to RS. At the CF, stitch along the ends of the waistband.

18 Turn the waistband to the RS. **Turn the raw edge** of the free ends of the belt carriers under and **topstitch in place.**

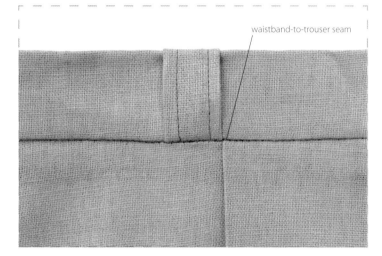

waistband-to-trouser seam

19 **Fold the waistband WS to WS. Pin the free edge of the waistband** to the waistband-to-trouser seam. Working from the RS of the trousers, **stitch in the ditch** – the line produced by the waistband-to-trouser seam – through all layers to secure the waistband in place.

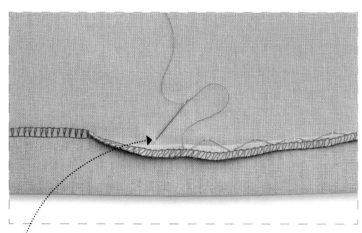

20 **Neaten the hem edge** by overlocking (see p.116). Turn up a 4cm (1½in) hem and handstitch in place.

hook

eye

21 **Attach a trouser hook and eye** to the waistband.

Trouser Pattern Two Variation

WIDE-LEG SHORTS

Here the palazzo trousers have been shortened and their front tucks widened to give more fullness. The result? A pair of shorts that are super-comfortable to wear. We made ours in cotton with a small spot print, but almost any lightweight fabric would work for this summery style.

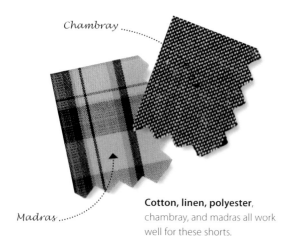

Chambray

Madras

Cotton, linen, polyester, chambray, and madras all work well for these shorts.

TROUSER PATTERN

2

>> p.210   >> p.217

the wide-leg trousers

BEFORE YOU START

YOU WILL NEED

- 1.20m (47¼in) x 150cm (59in) fabric
- 30cm (12in) x lining fabric
- 1 x reel matching all-purpose sewing thread
- 1 x reel contrasting all-purpose sewing thread for pattern marking
- 1m (39¼in) x fusible waistband interfacing
- 1 x 18cm (7¼in) trouser zip
- 1 x button

PREPARING THE PATTERN

- These shorts are made using Trouser Pattern Two (see pp.296–299)
- Follow the instructions (see pp.278–279) to copy or download the pattern in your size.

GARMENT CONSTRUCTION

The wide-leg shorts have a fly-front zip opening and a fitted waistband. The trousers feature in-seam pockets. There are generous front and back tucks at the waist for comfort.

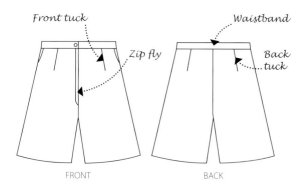

Front tuck

Zip fly

Waistband

Back tuck

FRONT

BACK

HOW TO MAKE THE WIDE-LEG SHORTS

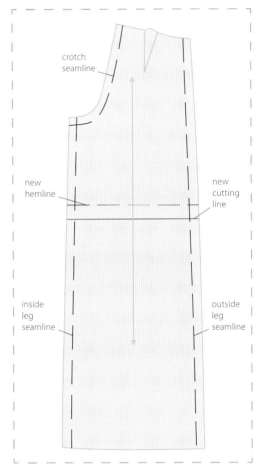

crotch seamline

new hemline

new cutting line

inside leg seamline

outside leg seamline

1 **Copy the trouser back pattern and mark the seamlines.** Mark a point 21cm (8½in) below the crotch seamline on the inside leg seam. Draw a horizontal line across the leg from this point to make a new hemline, keeping it at 90 degrees to the grain line.

2 **Measure a 4cm (1½in) seam allowance** from this line and mark a new cutting line.

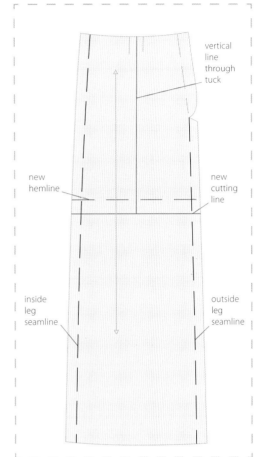

vertical line through tuck

new hemline

new cutting line

inside leg seamline

outside leg seamline

3 **Copy the trouser front pattern** and repeat step 1. Make sure the side seams are the same length.

4 On the trouser front pattern, **draw a vertical line** through the centre of the tuck to the new hemline.

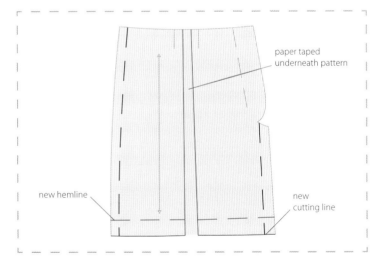

paper taped underneath pattern

new hemline

new cutting line

5 **Cut through the vertical line, place paper underneath, and spread the cut pattern pieces apart** by 2cm (¾in) at the waist and 3cm (1¼in) at the hem to make the shorts fuller at the front. Tape the pattern pieces to the paper. (For sizes over a size 14 or for fuller thighs, you may need to increase this measurement by 50 per cent.)

6 **Cut out and make the shorts** as for the Classic Palazzo Trousers, steps 1–18. You can add belt carriers if you wish.

7 **Machine a** 2cm (¾in) **double-turn hem** (see p.118). Press.

8 **Make a buttonhole** (see p.125) on the waistband overlap and attach a corresponding button (see p.123) to the underlap.

the TOPS

A quick change of shirt or top can transform a skirt or pair of trousers from an outfit for the office into one to wear at a weekend in the country or at a smart party. The two basic styles here form the basis for five different looks.

1

Top pattern one
Classic shell top
>> p.220

Top pattern one variation
Tie-neck top
>> p.224

Top pattern one variation
Long-sleeved tunic
>> p.226

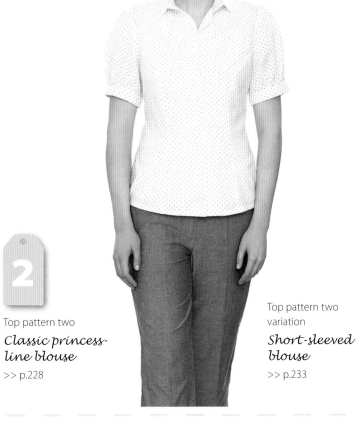

2

Top pattern two
Classic princess-line blouse
>> p.228

Top pattern two variation
Short-sleeved blouse
>> p.233

The ultimate shell top, this versatile little number is great with a skirt or trousers, tucked in or worn out

TOP PATTERN

1

>> p.222

>> p.224

>> p.226

the shell tops

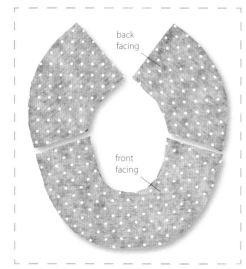

9 Attach lightweight fusible interfacing to the neck facing pieces (see p.94).

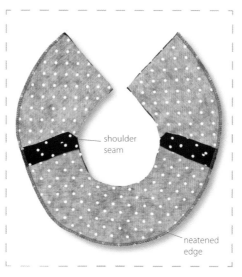

10 Join the facings at the shoulder seams and press the seams open. **Neaten the lower edge** (see pp.95–97).

11 Place the facings to the neck edge of the top RS to RS, matching the shoulder seams. **Pin and machine.**

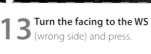

12 Layer the seam allowance by trimming the facing side of the seam to half its width. **Notch the seam allowance** to reduce bulk (see p.89).

13 Turn the facing to the WS (wrong side) and press.

14 At the CB, fold the edge of the facing in to meet the zip tape. **Pin and handstitch** in place.

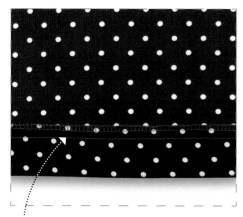

15 Neaten the lower edge of the top. Pin up 4cm (1¹/₂in) on the top and 3cm (1¹/₄in) on the sleeves. **Press and machine** in place.

16 Topstitch around the neck, using stitch length 3.5.

Top Pattern One Variation

TIE-NECK TOP

The shell top has now become a top with a slightly lower neckline, a tie neck, and a gathered sleeve. The back no longer features a zip but is cut in one piece. This neckline flatters the face and is easy to wear with a skirt, trousers, or jeans.

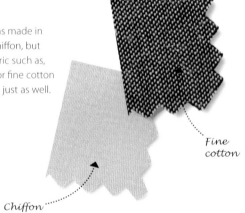

This top was made in polyester chiffon, but any soft fabric such as, georgette, or fine cotton would work just as well.

Fine cotton

Chiffon

TOP PATTERN

1

>> p.220

>> p.225

>> p.226

the shell tops

BEFORE YOU START

YOU WILL NEED

- 2m (79in) x 150cm (59in) fabric
- 1 x reel matching all-purpose sewing thread
- 1 x reel contrasting all-purpose sewing thread for pattern marking
- 50cm (19²/₃in) x 2cm (³/₄in) wide elastic

PREPARING THE PATTERN

- This top is made using Top Pattern One (see pp.300–301)
- Follow the instructions (see pp.278–279) to copy or download the pattern in your size

GARMENT CONSTRUCTION

This blouse has bust darts, a self-bound neck opening, a tie neck, and sleeves that are elasticated to fit the wrist.

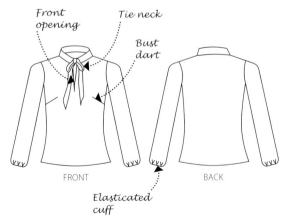

Front opening

Tie neck

Bust dart

FRONT

BACK

Elasticated cuff

HOW TO MAKE THE TIE-NECK TOP

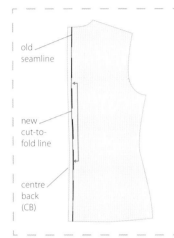

labels: old seamline, new cut-to-fold line, centre back (CB)

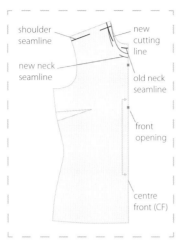

labels: shoulder seamline, new neck seamline, new cutting line, old neck seamline, front opening, centre front (CF)

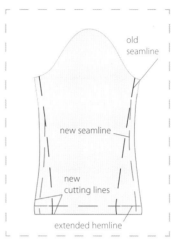

labels: old seamline, new seamline, new cutting lines, extended hemline

1 To cut the back as one piece, **copy the pattern back and mark the CB (centre back) seamline**. Put a ruler along the seamline and rule a new straight line in its place. This line will be placed to a fold for cutting.

2 **Copy the pattern front and mark the seamlines**. Mark a point on the CF (centre front) 3.5cm (1³⁄₈in) below the neck seamline. From here, **draw a new neck seamline** to the point where the neck and shoulder seamlines meet. Measure a 1.5cm (⁵⁄₈in) seam allowance from the new neck seamline and **mark a new cutting line**. On the CF, mark a point 16cm (6¹⁄₃in) below the new neck seamline.

3 To widen the sleeve, **copy the sleeve pattern and mark the seamlines.** Extend the hemline by 6cm (2³⁄₈in) on each side. **Draw a slightly curving line** from these two points to join them to the sleeve seamlines in the upper arm area. **Draw new cutting lines** 1.5cm (⁵⁄₈in) below the new hemline and at either side of the new sleeve seamlines.

4 **Cut out the fabric** using the new pattern pieces. **Mark the darts** using tailor's tacks (see p.77). **Make the darts** (see p.91) and **press** towards the waist.

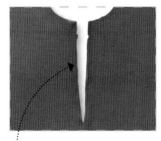

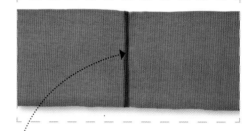

5 Make up as for the Classic Shell Top steps 5–8, using the seam for sheer fabrics method (see p.86).

6 **Slash the CF of the blouse front** to the point marked. Cut a piece of bias fabric 4cm (1¹⁄₂in) wide.

7 Use the bias fabric to bind the slashed opening (see p.109).

8 To make the necktie, **cut two strips of fabric** 12cm x 100cm (5in x 39¹⁄₄in) on the straight grain. **Join them together** at the short end, RS (right side) to RS. Press the seam to one side.

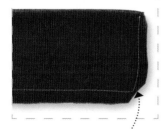

9 **Place the seam in the tie** at the CB of the blouse, RS to RS. Machine around the neck edge. **Clip the seam allowance** and press towards the necktie.

10 **Fold the tie**, RS to RS. Starting at the slash in the neck, **stitch the sides of the tie together**, pivoting at the corners (see p.87). **Clip the corners.**

11 **Turn the tie** to the RS. **Fold the raw edge of the tie** under along the neck edge. Pin and handstitch in place.

12 **Machine a 3cm (1¼in) double-turn hem** (see p.118) in the ends of the sleeve. Press. Insert elastic to fit the wrist (see p.108).

13 Complete as for the Classic Shell Top step 15.

Top Pattern One Variation

LONG-SLEEVED TUNIC

This time our pattern has been altered to make an A-line tunic with a deep, topstitched V-neckline and a wide sleeve. It is quick and simple to make, and you will learn how to cut a neck facing. A tunic like this makes ideal casual or holiday wear.

Acrylic knit

Cotton

This top has been made in printed linen, perfect for wearing over jeans or leggings. Alternatively, try it in a cotton for summer or in a knitted fabric for autumn.

TOP PATTERN

1

>> p.220

>> p.224

>> p.227

the shell tops

BEFORE YOU START

YOU WILL NEED

- 2.20m (87in) x 150cm (59in) fabric
- 1 x reel matching all-purpose sewing thread
- 1 x reel contrasting all-purpose sewing thread for pattern marking
- 60cm (24in) x lightweight fusible interfacing
- 1 x zip

PREPARING THE PATTERN

- This top is made using Top Pattern One (see pp.300–301)
- Follow the instructions (see pp.278–279) to copy or download the pattern in your size

GARMENT CONSTRUCTION

This A-line, V-necked tunic has wrist-length, set-in sleeves. The faced neckline features topstitching and the tunic and sleeve hems are also machined in place. There is a CB (centre-back) zip.

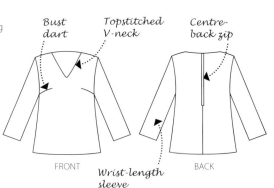

Bust dart

Topstitched V-neck

Centre-back zip

FRONT

BACK

Wrist-length sleeve

HOW TO MAKE THE LONG-SLEEVED TUNIC

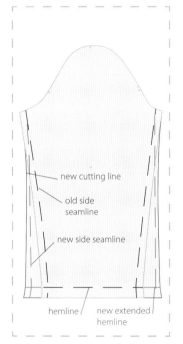

1 Copy the sleeve pattern and mark the side seamlines and the hemline. Measuring from the side seamlines, extend the hemline by 4.5cm (1³⁄₄in) each side to widen the bottom of the sleeve. Join these points to the old side seamlines just under the arm. Measure a 1.5cm (⁵⁄₈in) seam allowance from the new side seamlines and mark new cutting lines.

2 Copy the pattern front and mark the seamlines. Mark a point on the CF (centre front) 17cm (6¹⁄₂in) below the neck seamline and another point 4cm (1¹⁄₂in) from the neck seamline along the shoulder seamline. Join the points for the new V-neck seamline. Measure a 1.5cm (⁵⁄₈in) seam allowance from this new line and mark a new cutting line.

3 At the waist add 2cm (³⁄₄in) to the side seamline. At the hem edge, extend the side seamline 12cm (5in) to make the top longer. Join these two points to make a new side seamline and taper from here to the side seamline just below the bust dart. Measure a 1.5cm (⁵⁄₈in) seam allowance from this new line and from the new hemline and mark new cutting lines.

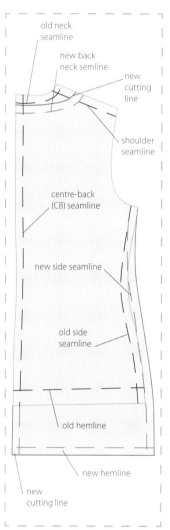

4 Copy the pattern back and mark the seamlines. Add to the side seamline and the hem to match the front. Mark a point on the CB (centre back) 2.5cm (1in) below the neck seamline and another point 4cm (1¹⁄₂in) from the neck seamline along the shoulder seamline. Join the points for the new back neck seamline. Measure a 1.5cm (⁵⁄₈in) seam allowance from this new seamline and mark a new cutting line.

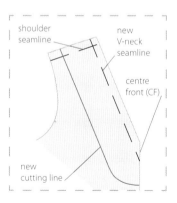

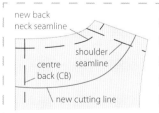

5 To make the new patterns for the facings, copy the neck area from the new pattern front and back. Copy the new neck seamlines. On the front, measure 7cm (2³⁄₄in) from the new neck seamline and mark a new cutting line, curving at the CF as shown.

6 Make the back neck facing to match.

7 Cut out the fabric using the new pattern pieces and mark the darts using tailor's tacks (see p.77). Make up as for the Classic Shell Top steps 2–10.

8 Place the facings to the neck edge of the tunic RS (right side) to RS, matching the seams. **Pin and machine**, pivoting at the CF (see p.87). **Layer the seam**. Turn the facing to the WS (wrong side) and press.

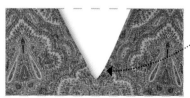

9 Topstitch around the neck.

10 Continue as for the Classic Shell Top step 15, remembering that the hem allowance on the tunic is now 1.5cm (⁵⁄₈in).

A crisp blouse is a must-have for every girl's wardrobe. This princess-line version has a subtle slimming effect

TOP PATTERN

2

>> p.230

>> p.233

the princess-line tops

Top Pattern Two

CLASSIC PRINCESS-LINE BLOUSE

This stylish blouse is very versatile. It will look efficient at the office in a plain fabric or a stripe, or is perfect for a country weekend in a cotton check. The princess lines at the front have a slimming effect that many women will appreciate. Choose the pattern by your bust measurement; you should also check your neck measurement to make sure the blouse is comfortable. Making this blouse will teach you some advanced sewing techniques, such as how to apply a yoke, collar, and cuffs.

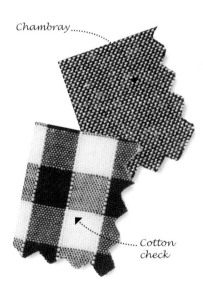

Chambray

Cotton check

Made in striped cotton shirting, this blouse is very suitable for office wear, but in printed viscose, cotton check , or a chambray it will happily accompany you on a weekend in the country.

BEFORE YOU START

YOU WILL NEED

- 2.4m (94in) x 150cm (59in) fabric
- 1 x reel matching all-purpose sewing thread
- 1 x reel contrasting all-purpose sewing thread for pattern marking
- 75cm (30in) x lightweight fusible interfacing
- 9 x 7mm (¹¹⁄₄₀in) diameter buttons

PREPARING THE PATTERN

- This blouse is made using Top Pattern Two (see pp.302–303)
- Follow the instructions (see pp.278–279) to copy or download the pattern in your size

GARMENT CONSTRUCTION

The long-sleeved, button-through blouse has princess-line seams at the front, deep darts at the back, and a one-piece collar. It also features a shoulder yoke which is top-stitched to match the topstitched collar and buttoned cuffs.

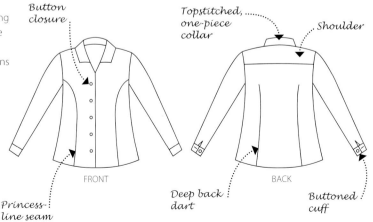

Button closure

Topstitched, one-piece collar

Shoulder

FRONT

BACK

Princess-line seam

Deep back dart

Buttoned cuff

HOW TO MAKE THE CLASSIC PRINCESS-LINE BLOUSE

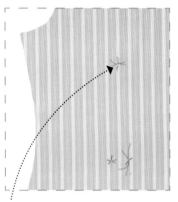

1 **Cut out the fabric** and transfer all the pattern markings (see pp.76–77).

2 **Make the darts** in the back (see p.91) and press towards the CB (centre back).

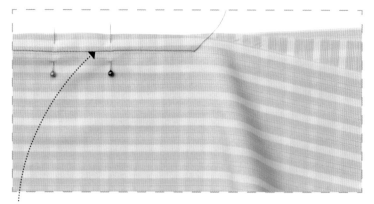

3 **Place one yoke to the back**, RS (right side) to RS. **Pin the other yoke** – the yoke lining – RS of the yoke to WS (wrong side) of the back. The back is now sandwiched between the yoke and the yoke lining. **Pin and machine** in place. If using a striped fabric, machine along a stripe.

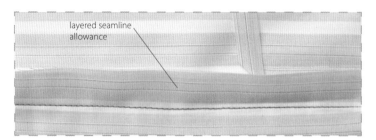

layered seamline allowance

4 **Layer the seam allowance** by trimming the yoke lining side to half its width (see p.89).

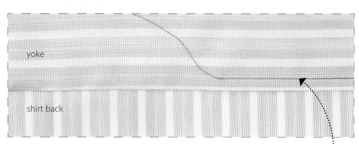

yoke

shirt back

5 **Press the seam allowances** towards the yoke. **Topstitch** using a slightly longer stitch length.

6 **Attach lightweight fusible interfacing** (see p.95) to the blouse fronts. **Neaten the edges** using either a 3-thread overlock stitch or a small zigzag stitch (see pp.84–85).

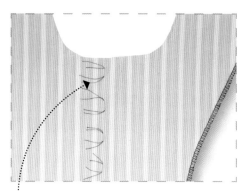

7 On the blouse fronts, **mark the CF** (centre front) with trace tacks (see p.76).

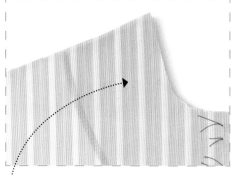

8 **Press the facing** back into position.

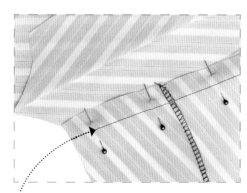

9 **Pin the blouse front** to the yoke front, RS to RS, and machine.

10 Turn under the seam allowance on both fronts of the yoke lining. **Pin and tack.**

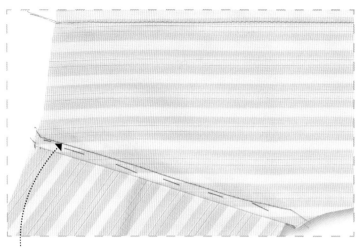

11 **Topstitch** to match the yoke back (see step 5).

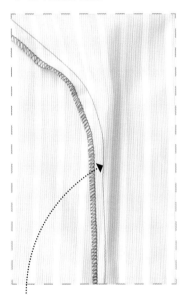

12 **Attach the side front** to the blouse front. **Neaten the seam allowances** together using either a 3-thread overlock stitch or a small zigzag stitch. Press towards the side.

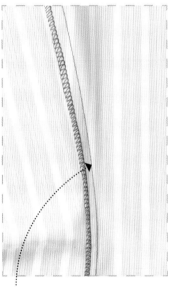

13 **Join the front to the back** at the side seams. **Neaten the seam allowances** together using either a 3-thread overlock stitch or a small zigzag stitch. Press towards the back.

tailor's tack

14 Attach lightweight fusible interfacing to both collar pieces and **mark the location of the button and the buttonholes** with tailor's tacks.

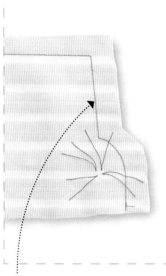

15 Place the collar pieces together, RS to RS. **Pin and stitch**, leaving the neck edge free.

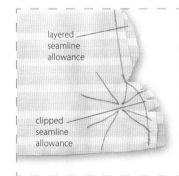

layered seamline allowance

clipped seamline allowance

16 **Layer the seam allowance** by trimming one side to half its width. **Clip the seam allowances** around the curves.

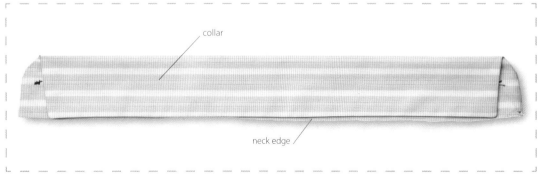

collar

neck edge

17 **Turn the collar** through to the RS and **press**. Fold the top half of the collar down towards the neck edge and press again.

18 **Attach the edge of the collar** to the neck edge of the blouse, RS to RS, matching the pattern markings.

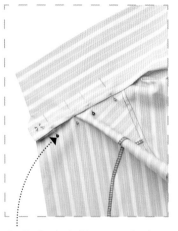

19 On the inside, turn under the raw edge of the collar, **pin and handstitch** in place to the collar-to-neck seam.

20 **Make a bound opening** at the wrist of the sleeve as marked (see p.109).

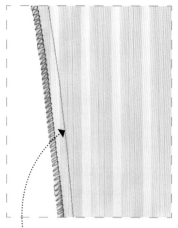

21 **Stitch the sleeve seam** and neaten the seam allowances together using either a 3-thread overlock stitch or a small zigzag stitch.

clipped end

22 Attach lightweight interfacing to the whole cuff. **Pin and machine** one edge of the cuff to the sleeve end, RS to RS (see p.111). Turn the cuff RS to RS and **stitch the short ends**. Clip and turn.

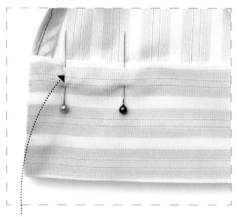

23 **Turn under the raw edge of the cuff** and pin. **Handstitch in place** to the sleeve-to-cuff seamline.

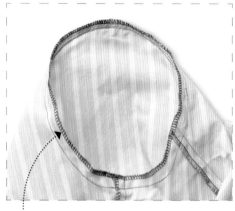

24 Using the longest stitch available, **machine two rows of ease stitches** through the sleeve head (see p.105). **Insert the sleeve into the armhole**, RS to RS (see p.105), pin and stitch. **Neaten the seam allowances** together.

25 **Topstitch** the collar to match the yoke back (see step 5).

26 **Make** six evenly spaced **horizontal buttonholes** on the CF of the right side as worn, as marked on the pattern, one on the collar, and one on each of the cuffs (see p.125). **Attach buttons** to correspond (see p.123).

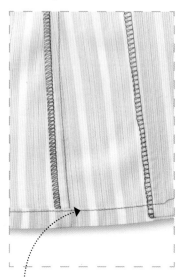

27 **Machine** a 1.5cm (⁵⁄₈in) double-turn hem along the bottom of the blouse (see p.118). **Press.**

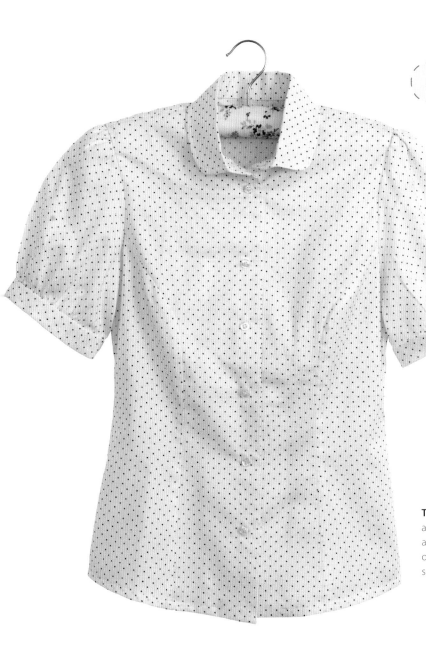

Top Pattern Two Variation

SHORT-SLEEVED BLOUSE

In this variation, the blouse pattern has been altered to eliminate the yoke, the sleeve has been shortened and widened to make a puffed sleeve, and the points of the collar have been rounded. This pretty little blouse would be good to wear in the summer with jeans or as summer workwear.

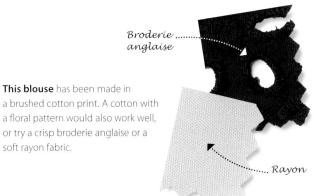

This blouse has been made in a brushed cotton print. A cotton with a floral pattern would also work well, or try a crisp broderie anglaise or a soft rayon fabric.

Broderie anglaise

Rayon

TOP PATTERN

2

>> p.228

>> p.234

the princess-line tops

BEFORE YOU START

YOU WILL NEED

- 2m (79in) x 150cm (59in) fabric
- 1 x reel matching all-purpose sewing thread
- 1 x reel contrasting all-purpose sewing thread for pattern marking
- 75cm (30in) x lightweight fusible interfacing
- 7 x 7mm ($^{11}/_{40}$in) diameter buttons

PREPARING THE PATTERN

- This blouse is made using Top Pattern Two (see pp.302–303)
- Follow the instructions (see pp.278–279) to copy or download the pattern in your size

GARMENT CONSTRUCTION

The button-through blouse is fitted at the back with long back darts. It has a short puff sleeve finished with a band, and a collar with rounded ends.

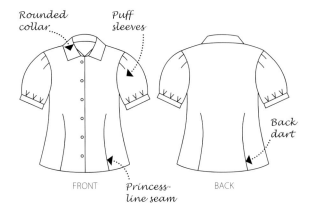

Rounded collar

Puff sleeves

Back dart

FRONT

Princess-line seam

BACK

HOW TO MAKE THE SHORT-SLEEVED BLOUSE

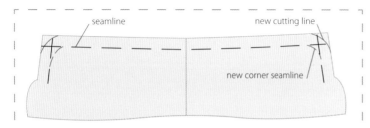

1 **Copy the collar and mark the seamlines**. Using a tin or cup as a guide, round the corners of the collar to give new seamlines. Measure a 1.5cm (⁵⁄₈in) seam allowance from the new seamline and mark a new cutting line.

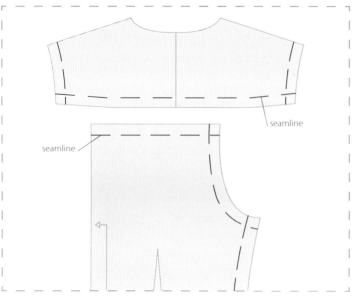

2 **Copy the yoke and blouse back** and mark the seamlines.

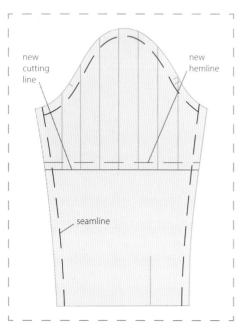

4 To shorten the sleeve, copy the sleeve and mark the seamlines. **Mark a point either side of the sleeve and 10cm (4in) below the armhole seamlines.** Join these points together to make a new hemline. Draw a new cutting line 1.5cm (⁵⁄₈in) below the new hemline.

5 To widen the sleeve, draw six vertical lines approximately 4cm (1¹⁄₂in) apart from the sleeve head to the new cutting line.

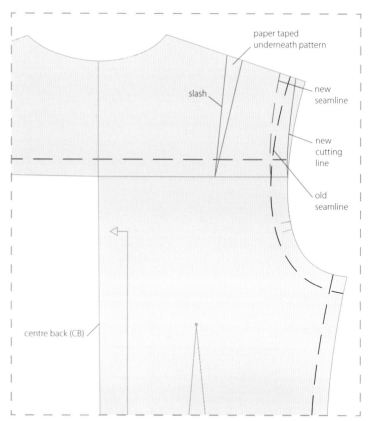

3 **To remove the yoke from the pattern, overlap the yoke-to-back seamlines, matching at the CB (centre back)**. As the yoke is slightly shaped, slash the yoke through the shoulder so the seamlines lie on top of each other. Tape the pattern pieces together. The shoulder seam now needs shortening by the width of the slash. Measure this amount along the shoulder seam and draw in a new seamline. Measure a 1.5cm (⁵⁄₈in) seam allowance from the new seamline and mark a new cutting line.

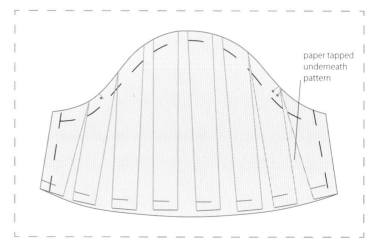

6 **Cut through the vertical lines, place paper underneath, and spread the cut pattern pieces apart** leaving a gap of 2cm (³⁄₄in) between the three middle sections at the sleeve head and 3cm (1¹⁄₄in) at the lower edge between all sections. **Tape the pattern pieces to the paper**. Mark dots between the notches to indicate where the gathers are to go.

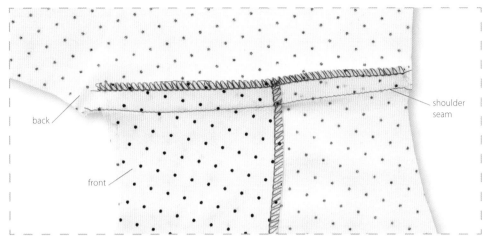

back

front

shoulder seam

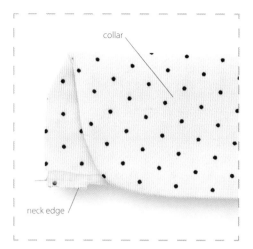

collar

neck edge

7 Cut out the fabric and transfer all the pattern markings (see pp.76–77). Make up as for the Classic Princess-Line Blouse steps 2, 6, 7, and 8.

8 Join the front to the back at the shoulder seams and neaten the seam allowances together, using either a 3-thread overlock stitch or a small zigzag stitch (see pp.84–85).

9 Continue as for the Classic Princess-Line Blouse steps 12–14.

10 Make and attach the collar as for the Classic Princess-Line Blouse steps 15–19.

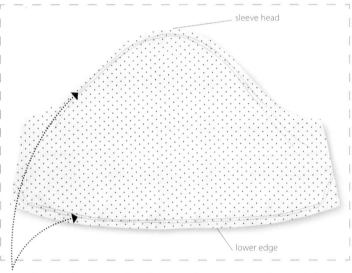

sleeve head

lower edge

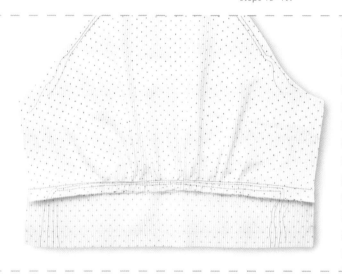

11 Using the longest stitch available, **machine two rows of ease stitches** through the sleeve head and along the lower edge (see p.105).

12 Cut a band of fabric, 9cm (3¹/₂in) wide with its length equal to the upper arm measurement plus 3cm (1¹/₄in). Attach lightweight interfacing to the strip and place to the lower edge of the sleeve, RS (right side) to RS. Pull up the ease stitches to fit the edge of the sleeve to the band. Pin and stitch in place. Press the gathers towards the band.

sleeve seam

13 Fold the sleeve, RS to RS, and machine the sleeve seam right through the band. Fold the band in half, WS (wrong side) to WS. Turn the edge of the band under by 1.5cm (⁵/₈in), pin and handstitch in place to the band-to-sleeve seamline.

14 Insert the sleeve into the armhole, RS to RS (see p.105).

15 Complete the garment as for the Classic Princess-Line Blouse steps 25–27.

the
JACKETS

The finishing touch for any outfit is the jacket. The four styles here prove that you do not have to be a tailor to create a head-turning look. Making these jackets will also add to the repertoire of sewing skills you have now acquired.

Jacket pattern one

Classic boxy jacket

>> p.238

Jacket pattern one variation

Boxy jacket with collar

>> p.242

Jacket pattern two

Classic shawl collar jacket

>> p.246

Jacket pattern two variation

Lined shawl collar jacket

>> p.251

HOW TO MAKE THE CLASSIC BOXY JACKET

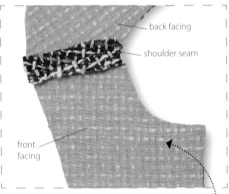

back facing

shoulder seam

front facing

1 Cut out the fabric. If working with a check fabric see pp.74–75.

2 Attach medium-weight fusible interfacing to the front and back facings. Join the facings together at the shoulder seam and press.

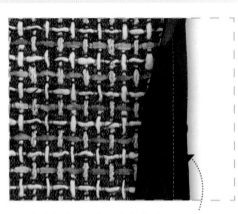

3 Bind the long edge of the facing using a Hong Kong finish (see p.86) and 2cm (³⁄₄in) bias binding. Place the binding to the facing, RS (right side) to RS, and machine stitch in the creaseline of the binding.

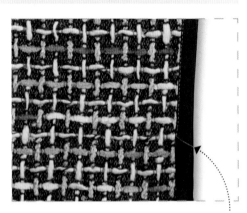

4 Wrap the binding round the raw edge of the fabric and secure by machining from the RS through the edge of the binding. Press.

side seam with Hong Kong finish

5 Join the back jacket to the side back, the side back to the side front, and the side front to the front. Neaten the seams with a Hong Kong finish. Press the seams open.

shoulder seam with Hong Kong finish

6 Join the front to the back at the shoulders and neaten the seams with a Hong Kong finish.

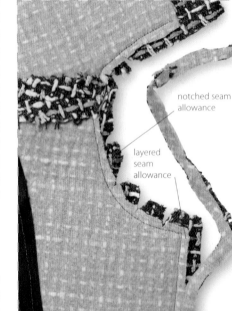

notched seam allowance

layered seam allowance

front facing

ease stitches

sleeve seam

7 Machine the sleeve seams, neaten with a Hong Kong finish, and press the seams open. Using stitch length 5, machine two rows of ease stitches through the sleeve head (see p.105)

8 Fit the sleeve into the armhole, RS to RS (see p.105). Join the armhole seam allowances together, wrapping them in bias binding and handstitching the long free edge of the binding to secure (see p.99).

9 Attach the facing to the edge of the jacket, RS to RS. Pin and stitch. Layer the seam allowance by trimming the facing side of the seam to half its width. Notch the seam. Turn the facing to the WS (wrong side) and press.

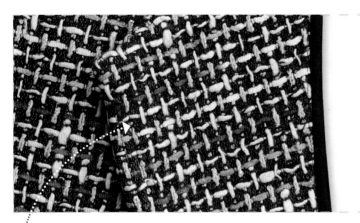

10 **Understitch** the seam allowances to the facing (see p.90).

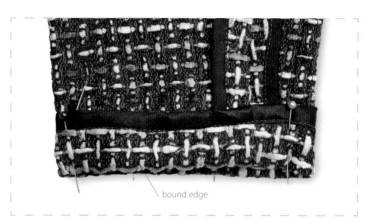

bound edge

11 **Bind the bottom edge of the sleeve** using a Hong Kong finish. Pin up a 2cm (³⁄₄in) hem and handstitch in place. Press.

12 **Bind the bottom edge of the jacket** but not of the facing, using a Hong Kong finish. **Turn up a 4cm (1½in) hem on the jacket**, pin, and handstitch in place. At each CF (centre front), turn under the lower edge of the facing, pin, and handstitch in place. Press.

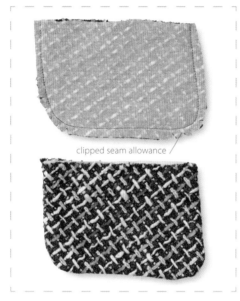

clipped seam allowance

13 **Attach medium-weight fusible interfacing** (see p.94) to one half of a pocket flap and place one interfaced flap and one non-interfaced flap together, RS to RS (see p.112). **Stitch together around lower edges** using a ¹⁄₂cm (¹⁄₄in) seam allowance. Clip, turn the flap to the right side, and press.

folded corner

14 **Pin decorative ribbon trim to the CF**, around the neck, and around the pocket flap. Fold or mitre the trim at the corners. **Topstitch** in place close to each edge of the trim. Press.

15 **Trim flap to match.** Press.

16 **Pin the jacket flap to the jacket front,** RS to RS, in a position of your choosing. **Machine along the raw edge** of the flap.

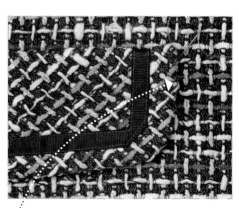

17 **Press the flap into place and handstitch** at each side to secure.

Jacket Pattern One Variation

BOXY JACKET WITH COLLAR

This version of the jacket is lined and has a heavy fringed trim. It would look great with a straight tailored skirt or maybe with the palazzo trousers on pages 210–215. There are no alterations to the pattern pieces but this time the collar and lining pattern pieces are used.

Gabardine

Traditional tweed

To get this exact look, use a tweed-type fabric. This jacket has been made in a check tweed. Other tweeds as well as wool suiting would also work well.

JACKET PATTERN

1

>> p.238

>> p.243

the boxy jackets

BEFORE YOU START

YOU WILL NEED

- 2.20m (86¹/₂in) x 150cm (59in) fabric
- 1.5m (59in) x 150cm (59in) lining fabric
- 2 x reels matching all-purpose sewing thread
- 1 x reel contrasting all-purpose sewing thread for pattern marking
- 1m (39¹/₃in) x medium-weight fusible interfacing

PREPARING THE PATTERN

- This jacket is made using Jacket Pattern One (see pp.304–307)
- Follow the instructions (see pp.278–279) to copy or download the pattern in your size

GARMENT CONSTRUCTION

This edge-to-edge lined jacket with wrist-length, set-in sleeves has princess-line styling. The pocket flaps have been omitted and a collar and fringing added instead. The jacket would also work without the fringing.

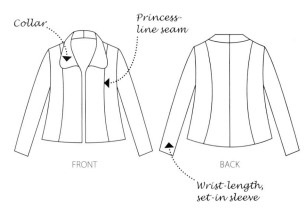

Collar

Princess-line seam

FRONT

BACK

Wrist-length, set-in sleeve

HOW TO MAKE THE BOXY JACKET WITH COLLAR

1 **Cut out the pattern pieces** from both the fabric and the lining. If using a check fabric see pp.74–75. **Transfer all the pattern markings to the lining** (see pp.76–77).

2 **Make the darts** (see p.91) and stitch along the tuck lines.

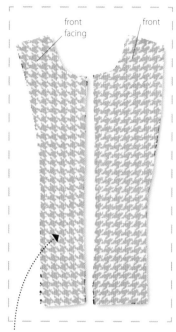

3 **Attach medium-weight fusible interfacing** to the front, front and back facings, and collar (see p.94).

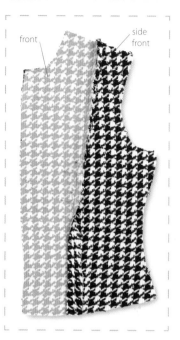

4 **Join the jacket sections** as for the Classic Boxy Jacket steps 5 and 6, omitting the seam neatening. **Match the checks by pinning** as shown. Press the seams open.

5 **Make up the sleeve** as for steps 7 and 8, omitting the seam neatening. The jacket should now be joined together.

6 **Attach a 3cm (1¼in) wide strip of medium-weight fusible interfacing** to the lower edge of jacket on the WS (wrong side). Clip to fit as required.

7 **Join the front facing to the front lining.** Press the seam to one side.

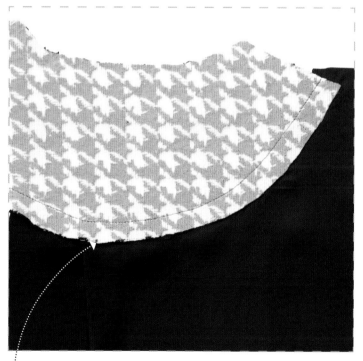

8 **Join the back facing to the back lining** and press the seam towards the lining.

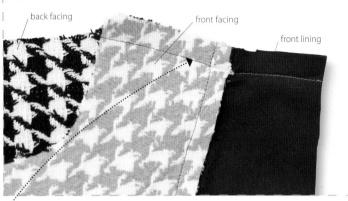

back facing front facing front lining

9 **Join the lining/facings at the shoulder seam** and press open.

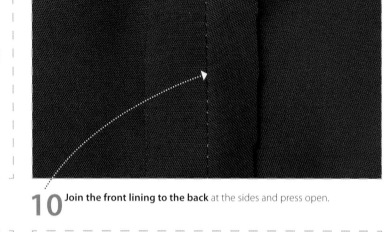

10 **Join the front lining to the back** at the sides and press open.

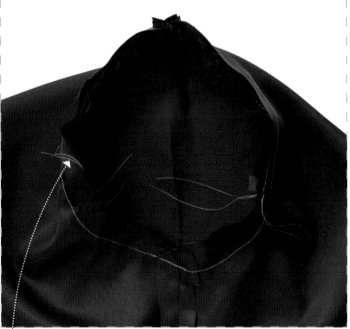

11 **Make up the lining sleeve** as for the Classic Boxy Jacket step 7, omitting the seam neatening. **Fit the lining sleeve into the lining armhole**, RS (right side) to RS.

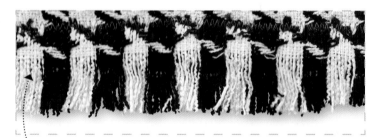

12 **To make the fringing, cut strips of fabric** approximately 10cm (4in) wide from selvedge to selvedge or along the straight grain – it depends on the weave of the fabric as to which produces the best-looking fringe. **Fold the strips in half, WS to WS, and zigzag** with stitch width 5 and length 2 close to the fold.

13 **Fray the fabric along the raw edge**, making enough fringing to go around the collar, around the hem of the sleeves, and around the lower edge and up the front of the jacket.

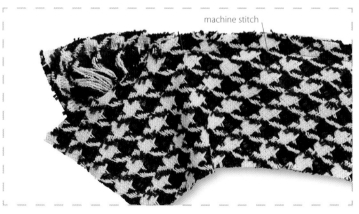

14 **Pin the fringing** to the RS of the interfaced collar, making a tight curve at the corners. **Pin and tack** in place.

machine stitch

15 **Place the RS of the non-interfaced collar over the fringing** and machine using a 1.5cm (⁵⁄₈in) seam allowance.

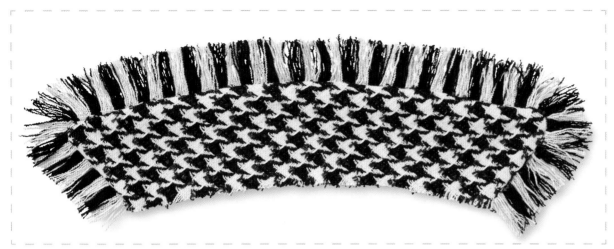

16 **Clip the seam allowances** around the curves and turn the collar to the RS.

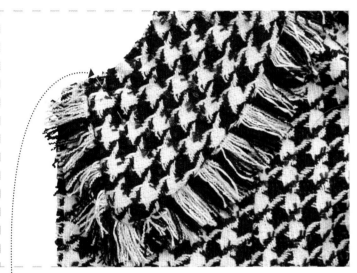

17 **Attach the collar to the neck edge of the jacket**, WS of collar to RS of jacket. **Pin and tack** in place.

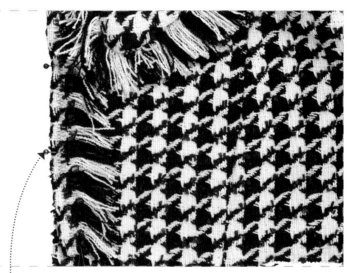

18 **Pin more fringing around the hem of the sleeves** and around the lower edge and up the front of the jacket. Tack in place.

19 **Place the lining/facings to the jacket,** RS to RS, on top of the fringing. Stitch all around the edge leaving an 18cm (7in) gap at the CB (centre back). **Layer the seam allowances** (see p.89) and **clip the seam**. Turn the jacket to the RS through the gap in the CB and press.

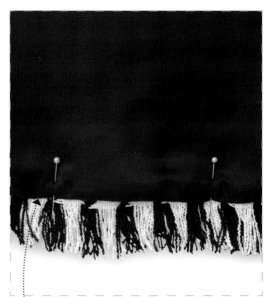

20 At the CB opening, **fold under the raw edge of the lining** to meet the top of the fringing. **Pin and handstitch** in place.

A relaxed, wear-anywhere-and-with-anything shawl collar jacket is always a success

JACKET PATTERN

2

>> p.248

>> p.251

the shawl collar jackets

Jacket Pattern Two

CLASSIC SHAWL COLLAR JACKET

This waist-length, unlined jacket with a simple shawl collar has a relaxed feel; it is almost like wearing a cardigan. The jacket is secured at the centre front with just a single button, but if you prefer, you could have two or three. Choose your pattern according to your full bust measurement (see p.54). The shoulder pads make the jacket slightly more structured, helping to balance the width of the shoulders to the hips. A wide choice of fabrics underlines this jacket's versatility.

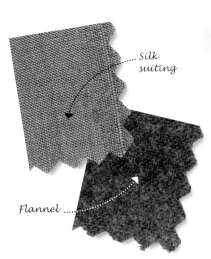

Silk suiting

Flannel

We made our jacket in a chunky wool boucle fabric, but it would also look good in a flannel or a silk suiting.

BEFORE YOU START

YOU WILL NEED

- 2m (79in) x 150cm (59in) fabric
- 1 x reel matching all-purpose sewing thread
- 1 x reel contrasting all-purpose sewing thread for pattern marking
- 1m (39in) x lightweight fusible interfacing
- 1 x pair shoulder pads
- 1 x 2.5cm (1in) button

PREPARING THE PATTERN

- This jacket is made using Jacket Pattern Two (see pp.308–311)
- Follow the instructions (see pp.278–279) to copy or download the pattern in your size

GARMENT CONSTRUCTION

The unlined, waist-length shawl collar jacket features front and back darts to fit it to the waist. There is a CB (centre-back) seam and the wrist-length, set-in sleeve has a shoulder pad. The jacket has a single-button closure.

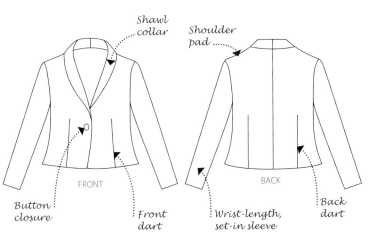

Shawl collar

Shoulder pad

FRONT

BACK

Button closure

Front dart

Wrist-length, set-in sleeve

Back dart

HOW TO MAKE THE CLASSIC SHAWL COLLAR JACKET

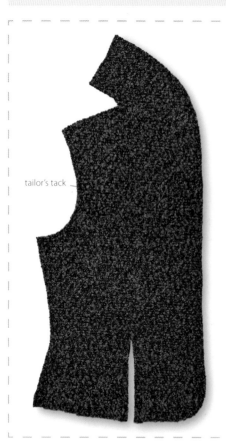

tailor's tack

1 **Cut out the fabric and mark the pattern markings** using tailor's tacks (see p.77).

2 **Make all the darts** (see p.91). Press open the slashed dart on the front and press its point to the CF (centre front). **Stitch the front shoulder dart** only as far as the shoulder seamline.

3 **Neaten the seam allowances** on the CB (centre- back) seams and on the back shoulder and side seams, using either a 3-thread overlock stitch or a small zigzag stitch (see pp.84–85). On a chunky boucle fabric, overlock stitches may look uneven; this is not a problem.

neatened front
shoulder seam

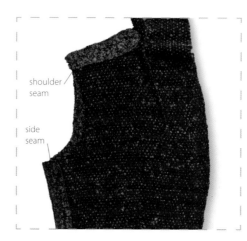

shoulder
seam

side
seam

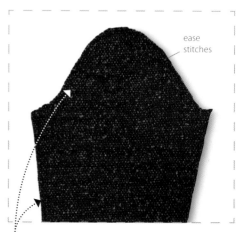

ease
stitches

4 **Clip the fabric** at the end of the front shoulder dart as shown. **Neaten the front shoulder seam** using either a 3-thread overlock stitch or a small zigzag stitch.

5 **Join the CB seam and join the front to the back** at the side seams and the shoulder seams. Press the seams open.

6 **Neaten the sleeve seam and lower edge of both sleeves** using either a 3-thread overlock stitch or a small zigzag stitch. **Machine the sleeve seam** and press it open. Using the longest stitch available, machine two rows of ease stitches through the sleeve head (see p.105).

7 **Insert the sleeve into the armhole**, RS (right side) to RS (see p.105). **Neaten the seam allowances** together using either a 3-thread overlock stitch or a small zigzag stitch. Turn up a 2cm (³/₄in) hem and stitch in place.

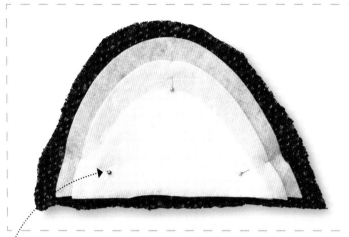

8 As this jacket is unlined, the outside of each shoulder pad needs to be covered. **Cut a piece of fabric** larger than the pad on the bias (see p.70). **Pin to the pad.**

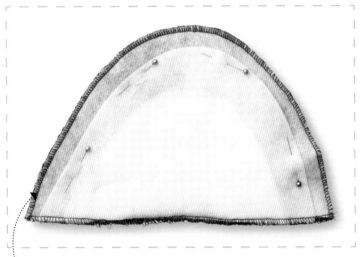

9 **Stitch the fabric to the pad** using either a 3-thread overlock stitch or a small zigzag stitch.

10 **Place the covered shoulder pad** to the sleeve-to-shoulder seam. **Pin and handstitch** in place along the armhole seam.

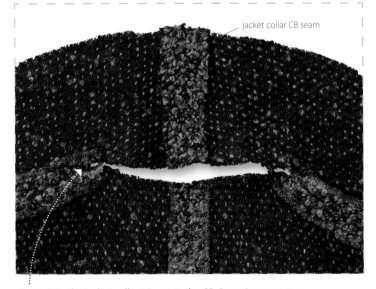

jacket collar CB seam

11 **Join the jacket collar pieces at the CB**. Press the seam open.

12 **Place the collar to the jacket,** RS to RS, matching the CB seams. Pin and stitch. Press the seam open.

13 **Attach lightweight fusible interfacing** to the hem facing, the front facing, the collar facing, and the back facing (see pp.94–95).

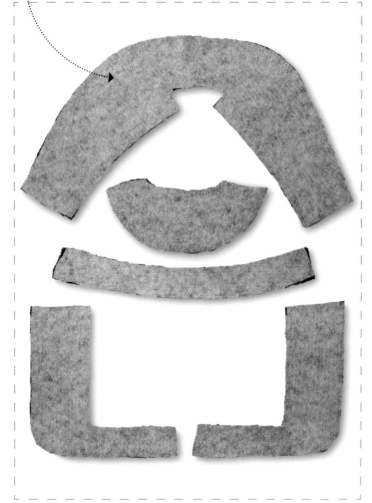

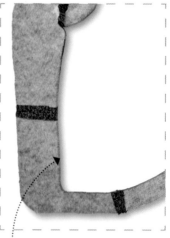

14 **Clip the front facing** at the marked dots. **Join the back facing to the front facing,** RS to RS, and stretch to fit. **Stitch**, pivoting (see p.87) at the clips.

15 **Join the lower front facing and the back hem facing to the front facing.** Neaten the outer edge using either a 3-thread overlock stitch or a small zigzag stitch.

16 **Join the completed facing to the edge of the jacket,** RS to RS. Pin and stitch.

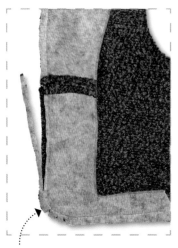

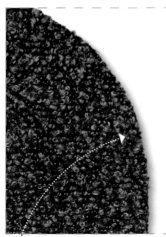

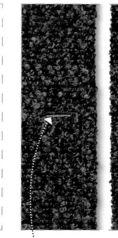

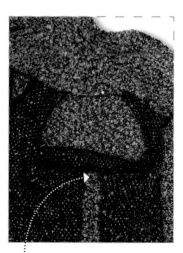

17 So the collar will roll back, **layer the facing side of the seam** (see p.89) below the seam in the facing, and layer the jacket side of the seam above the seam in the facing. Clip, turn to the RS, and press.

18 **Top-stitch** around the outer edges of the jacket.

19 On the RH (right hand) side of the jacket (as worn), **make a horizontal buttonhole** as marked (see p.125). Attach a corresponding button (see p.123). **Turn up the sleeve hems** by 3cm (1¼in) and **handstitch** in place.

20 **On the inside of the jacket,** handstitch the seams on the facings to the jacket seams and secure the end of each shoulder pad to the shoulder seam.

>> p.246

>> p.252

JACKET PATTERN

2

the shawl collar jackets

Jacket Pattern Two Variation

LINED SHAWL COLLAR JACKET

This version of the jacket in a fine, boiled wool has been lined, patch pockets have been added, and these and the collar edge have been trimmed with braid. The result is a more formal jacket that would look good with a matching skirt.

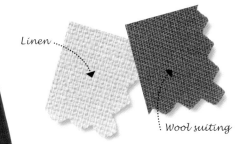

Linen

Wool suiting

We made our jacket in a very fine boiled wool, but you could try a linen for the summer or a wool suiting for the office.

BEFORE YOU START

YOU WILL NEED

- 2m (79in) x 150cm (59in) fabric
- 1.5m (59in) x 150cm (59in) lining fabric
- 1m (39in) x medium-weight fusible interfacing
- 2 x reels matching all-purpose sewing thread
- 1 x reel contrasting all-purpose thread for pattern marking
- 1 x pair shoulder pads
- 5m (197in) x decorative braid
- 1 x 2½cm (1in) button

PREPARING THE PATTERN

- This jacket is made using Jacket Pattern Two (see pp.308–311)
- Follow the instructions (see pp.278–279) to copy or download the pattern in your size

GARMENT CONSTRUCTION

This lined, waist-length, shawl collar jacket has front and back darts. There is a CB (centre-back) seam and the wrist-length, set-in sleeve has a shoulder pad. The jacket has a single-button closure and patch pockets trimmed with braid to match the collar.

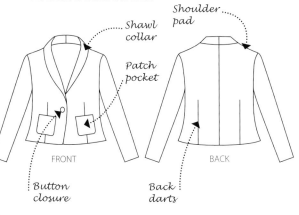

Shawl collar

Shoulder pad

Patch pocket

FRONT

BACK

Button closure

Back darts

HOW TO MAKE THE LINED SHAWL COLLAR JACKET

1 **Cut out the pattern pieces** from both the fabric and the lining.

2 **Mark the pattern markings** on both the lining and the fabric using tailor's tacks (see p.77). Make all the darts in both fabrics (see p.91) as for the Classic Shawl Collar Jacket step 2.

3 **Make up the fabric** as for the Classic Shawl Collar Jacket steps 5–7 and 11–15, omitting the seam neatening.

4 **Pin a shoulder pad to the sleeve-to-shoulder seam** and attach with a large running stitch.

5 **Make the lined patch pockets** (see p.113).

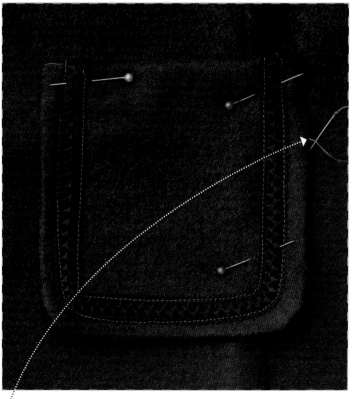

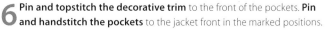

6 **Pin and topstitch the decorative trim** to the front of the pockets. **Pin and handstitch the pockets** to the jacket front in the marked positions.

7 **Make the darts in the back lining** and pin the tuck in the front lining. **Join the lining at the side and shoulder seams** and press the seams open.

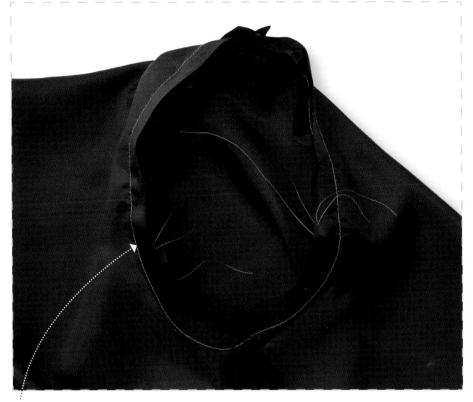

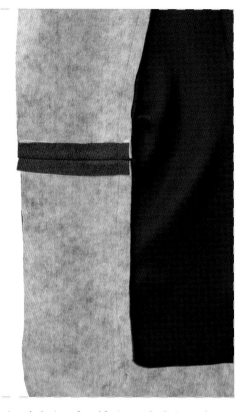

8 **Make up the lining sleeve and insert it into the lining jacket** in the same way as for the Classic Shawl Collar Jacket steps 6–7.

9 **Attach the interfaced facing to the lining jacket,** RS (right side) to RS, matching at the shoulder seams. **Do not attach the hem facing to the lining**. Remove the pins in the tucks. Press the seams towards the lining.

10 **Continue as for the Classic Shawl Collar Jacket** steps 16 and 17.

11 **Turn up the raw edge of the lining** 1.5cm (⁵/₈in) and pin it to overlap the jacket facing. Allow a tiny pleat to form at the CB (centre back) of the lining to ensure the lining does not pull on the jacket. Handstitch in place. **Turn up the sleeve lining and the sleeve hem** to match.

12 **Add a decorative trim to the collar**, as you did on the pocket. **Topstitch the front and bottom edges of the jacket** and the end of the sleeves.

MENDING & REPAIRS

It is always useful to know how to do some basic repairs to your clothes. Just a few minutes' work can extend their life by years. The old saying "a stitch in time saves nine" is very true, so do repairs as soon as they are needed.

MENDING

Repairing a tear in fabric, patching a worn area, or fixing a zip or a buttonhole can add extra life to a garment. Repairs like these may seem tedious, but they are very easy to do and well worthwhile. For some of the mending techniques shown here, a contrast colour thread has been used so that the stitching can be seen clearly. However, when making a repair, be sure to use a matching thread.

UNPICKING STITCHES
LEVEL OF DIFFICULTY **

All repairs involve unpicking stitches. This must be done carefully to avoid damaging the fabric because the fabric will have to be restitched. There are three ways you can unpick stitches.

SMALL SCISSORS

Pull the fabric apart and, using very small, sharply pointed scissors, snip through the stitches that have been exposed.

SEAM RIPPER

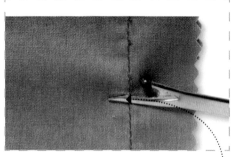

Slide a seam ripper carefully under a stitch and cut it. Cut through every fourth or fifth stitch, and the seam will unravel easily.

PIN AND SCISSORS

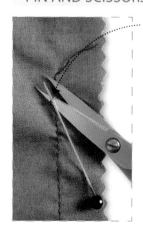

On difficult fabrics or on very small, tight stitches, slide a pin under the stitch to lift it away from the fabric, then snip through with a pair of sharply pointed scissors.

DARNING A HOLE
LEVEL OF DIFFICULTY **

If you accidentally catch a piece of jewellery in a sweater or other knitted garment, it may make a small hole. A moth could make a hole, too. It is worth darning the hole, especially if the sweater was expensive or is a favourite. Holes can also occur in the heels of socks; these can be darned in the same way.

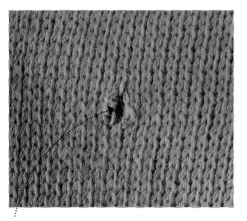

1 Even if the hole is small, the sweater will be unwearable.

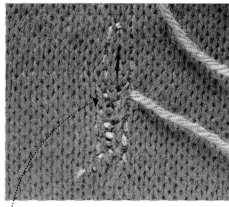

2 Work several rows of running stitches vertically around the hole.

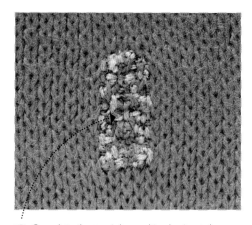

3 Complete the repair by working horizontal rows of running stitches through the vertical stitches.

REPAIRING FABRIC UNDER A BUTTON

LEVEL OF DIFFICULTY **

A button under strain can sometimes pull off a garment. If this happens, a hole will be made in the fabric, which needs fixing before a new button can be stitched on.

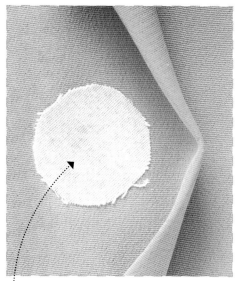

1 On the right side of the fabric, the hole where the button has pulled off is clearly visible.

2 Turn to the wrong side and apply a patch of fusible interfacing over the hole.

3 Work straight machine stitches over the hole on the right side to strengthen the fabric.

4 Stitch the button back in place.

REPAIRING A DAMAGED BUTTONHOLE

LEVEL OF DIFFICULTY **

A buttonhole can sometimes rip at the end, or the stitching on the buttonhole can come unravelled. When repairing, use a thread that matches the fabric so the repair will be invisible.

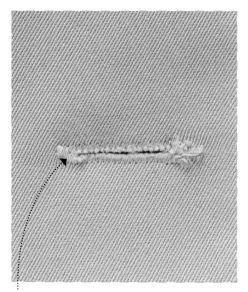

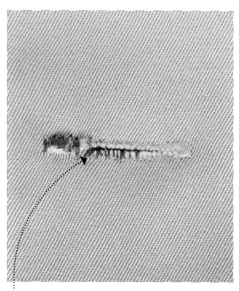

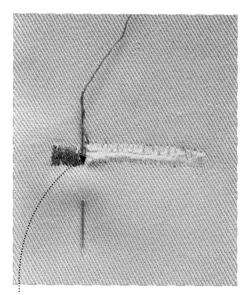

1 On the right side of the fabric, the edges of the buttonhole stitching have torn and come unravelled.

2 Stitch over the torn edges by hand using a buttonhole stitch.

3 Reinforce the ends using small over-sewing stitches.

MENDING A SPLIT IN A SEAM

LEVEL OF DIFFICULTY **

A split seam can be very quickly remedied with the help of some fusible mending tape and new stitching.

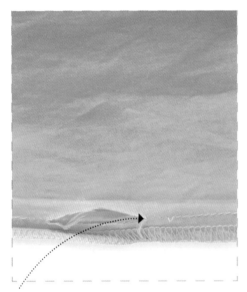

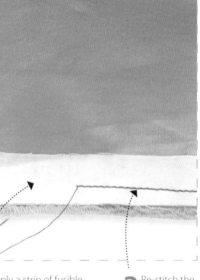

1 Where the split has occurred in the seam, unpick the stitching on either side. Press the fabric back into shape.

2 Apply a strip of fusible mending tape over the split and the seam on either side of the split.

3 Re-stitch the seam using a thread colour to match the fabric.

4 The repair will not be visible on the other side.

MENDING A TEAR WITH A FUSIBLE PATCH

LEVEL OF DIFFICULTY *

Tears easily happen to clothing, especially children's wear. There are several methods for mending a tear. Most use a fusible patch of some kind, which may or may not be seen on the front.

FUSIBLE APPLIQUÉ PATCH

1 Place a fusible appliqué over the tear and pin in place.

2 Apply heat to fuse the decorative patch in place.

FUSED PATCH ON THE RIGHT SIDE

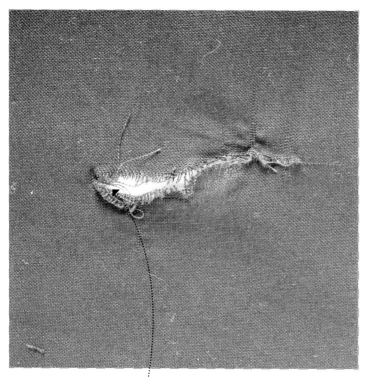

1 Measure the tear in the fabric.

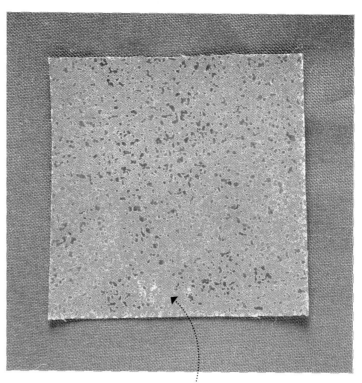

2 Cut a piece of fusible mending fabric that is slightly longer and wider than the tear.

3 Fuse the fabric in place on the right side.

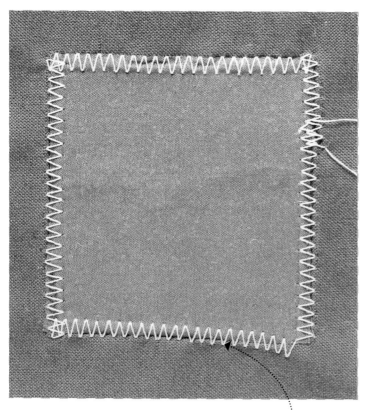

4 Using a zigzag stitch, machine all around the edge of the patch on the right side of the work.

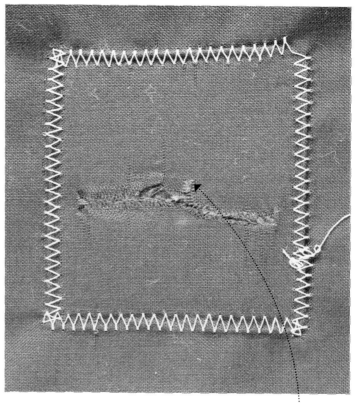

5 On the reverse side of the fabric, the tear will be firmly stuck to the mending patch, which will prevent the tear getting any bigger.

FUSED PATCH ON THE WRONG SIDE

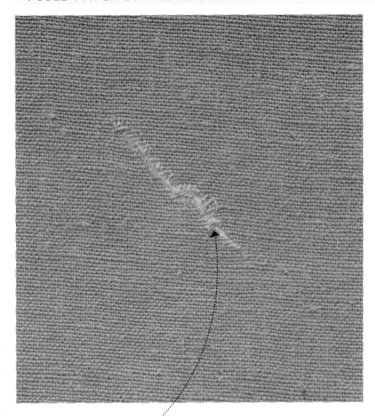

1 Measure the length of the tear.
Cut a piece of fusible mending tape to fit.

2 On the wrong side of the fabric,
fuse the mending tape over the tear.

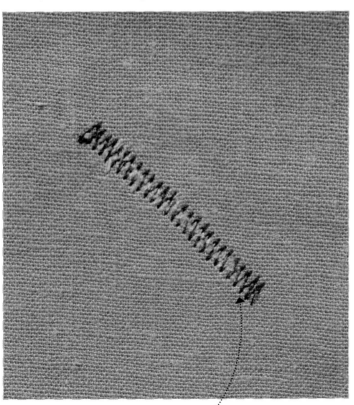

3 Using a zigzag stitch, width 5.0 and length 0.5,
stitch over the tear on the right side of the fabric.

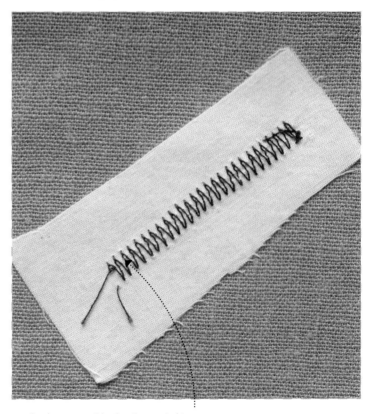

4 On the wrong side, the zigzag stitching
will have gone through the fusible tape.

REPAIRING OR REPLACING ELASTIC

LEVEL OF DIFFICULTY *

Elastic can frequently come unstitched inside the waistband, or it may lose its stretch and require replacing. Here is the simple way to re-insert elastic or insert new elastic.

Old elastic

1 Carefully unpick a seam in the elastic casing.

2 Pull the old elastic through the gap in the seam and cut through it.

3 Attach new elastic to the old with a safety pin. Pull the old elastic through the casing. It will pull the new elastic with it.

4 Secure the ends on the new elastic.

5 Hand stitch the unpicked seam back together.

REPAIRING A BROKEN ZIP

LEVEL OF DIFFICULTY **

Zips can break if they come under too much strain. Sometimes the zip has to be removed completely and a new zip inserted. However, if only a few teeth have been broken low down on the zip and it can still be opened sufficiently, you can make this repair.

Broken teeth

1 Where there are broken teeth on the zip, the zip pull will be attached to one side only. Move the pull up so it is alongside the gap in the teeth on the other side.

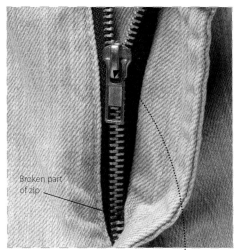

Broken part of zip

2 Carefully feed the teeth on the broken side into the top of the zip.

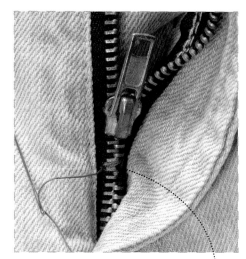

3 Just above the broken area, hand stitch over the zip teeth using double thread. This makes a stop for the zip pull. The zip will now have an extended life.

CUSTOMIZING

If you have a favourite garment that is looking tired, there is no need to throw it out.

This section is full of quick and easy ideas for revamping and updating the clothes

you already have, or any you may find at a knock-down price in a thrift shop.

LENGTHENING A SKIRT WITH A CONTRAST BAND

Is last season's skirt just too short this year? Do you want to coordinate a skirt with a new jacket or with a top you have made? This simple technique shows you how to add a deep contrast band to the hem of a simple A-line or straight skirt.

Simple A-line skirt

BEFORE YOU START

YOU WILL NEED

- Skirt
- 50cm (20in) contrasting fabric of similar weight to the skirt
- 1 x reel matching all-purpose sewing thread

Add a splash of colour with a contrast band at the bottom of a simple skirt and perhaps complete your ensemble with a jacket or cardigan to match

HOW TO LENGTHEN A SKIRT WITH A CONTRAST BAND

1 To make this project really easy, you will **work on the front and back of the skirt separately, then join them at the side seams**. Start by unpicking the skirt hem and 5–8cm (2–3¼in) of the side seams.

2 For the skirt front, **cut a piece of contrasting fabric 22cm (9in) wide** and at least 3cm (1¼in) longer than the front of the skirt is wide. Do the same for the back of the skirt. **Fold the two pieces** in half and press.

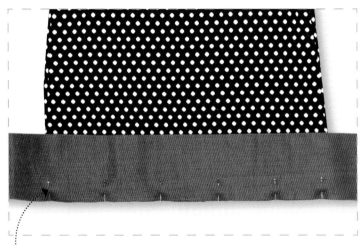

3 **Pin the raw edges of the doubled contrast bands** to the front and back hems of the skirt, RS (right side) to RS. Don't worry if the bands overhang at the sides of the skirt.

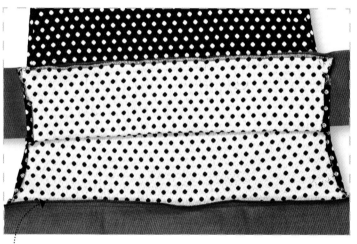

4 **Machine the strips** to the front and back hems. **Neaten the seams** using a 3-thread overlock stitch or a small zigzag stitch (see pp.84–85).

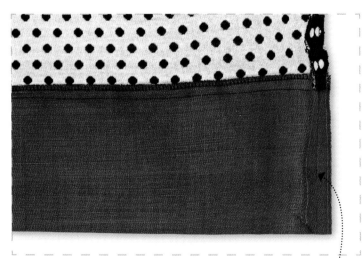

5 **Machine the skirt** together at the sides, WS (wrong side) to WS, following the line of the original side seams.

6 **At the hem edge**, pin under the ends of the seam allowances. **Handstitch** in place.

TURNING JEANS INTO A SKIRT

Turning old jeans that are too short or have ripped legs into a little skirt is so easy. You don't even have to make a hem; a row of stitches at the bottom edge is enough to stop it fraying. Wear it with a T-shirt for a casual yet trendy holiday outfit.

Old pair of jeans

BEFORE YOU START

YOU WILL NEED

- Pair of jeans
- 1 x reel topstitching sewing thread to match topstitching on jeans

Don't throw out those old jeans. Just a few cuts and topstitched seams will give you a nifty casual skirt in no time at all

HOW TO TURN JEANS INTO A SKIRT

1 Decide the length you want for your skirt and **measure down from the waist of the trousers** by that amount. Add 3cm (1¼in) allowance for the hem, and **cut through each leg** at that point.

2 **Carefully unpick** the inside leg seams and the curved section of the crotch seam.

3 **Cut off the curved part of the crotch seam** on the front and back.

4 **Cut through the side seams** on one of the leg sections that you removed in order to make a single layer of fabric.

5 **Place a piece of this leg fabric under each of the unpicked sections**, front and back, to fill in the gap created by cutting away the crotch seam. Pin in place.

6 **Starting at the crotch** and matching the stitching lines, topstitch together using a longer machine stitch. **Turn under a double-turn hem (see p.118), pin, and topstitch.**

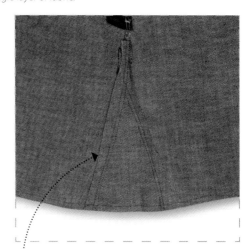

7 **Remove any surplus fabric** on the inside.

ADDING A COLLAR AND POCKETS TO A DRESS

It's easier than you think to add a contrasting collar to a simple round-necked dress. You can really push the boat out if you add a pair of fake pockets too. Try this on a simple cotton print dress for a retro look.

Simple dress

BEFORE YOU START

YOU WILL NEED

- Dress
- 50cm (20in) contrasting fabric for collar and pockets
- 1 x reel matching all-purpose sewing thread
- See-through non-woven fabric
- 50cm (20in) lightweight fusible interfacing
- 50cm (20in) x 2cm (¾in) bias binding

Give a plain shift dress a new lease on life with a neat little Peter Pan collar and oh-so-simple fake pockets

HOW TO ADD A COLLAR AND POCKETS TO A DRESS

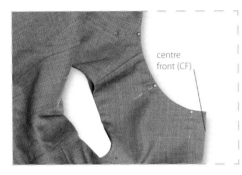

1 Fold the dress in half, pin around the neck and **mark the CF** (centre front) with a thread marking.

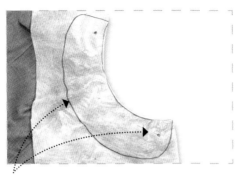

2 **Pin some see-through non-woven fabric** to the neck edge and draw on the shape of your collar. We made our collar 6cm (2³⁄₈in) deep.

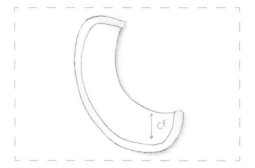

3 Remove the drawing and **add seam allowances** of 1.5cm (⁵⁄₈in). Do not add a seam allowance at the neck edge. **Draw in the grain line at the CF.**

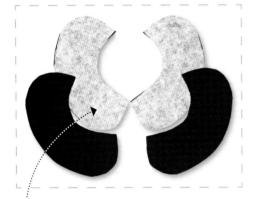

4 Using this as your pattern, **cut two left and two right collars. Attach lightweight fusible interfacing** to one pair.

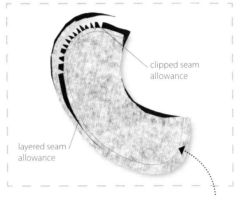

5 **Place the collars together** RS (right side) to RS and **stitch around the outside edges. Layer the interfaced side of the seam and clip.**

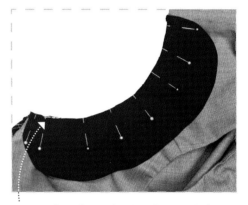

6 **Turn the collar to the RS and press. Pin the collar to the neck,** raw edge to finished dress neck edge.

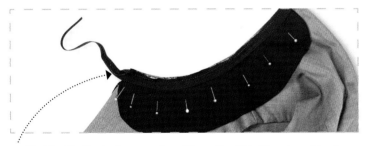

7 **Pin bias binding to the raw edge of the collar,** RS to RS, and **machine in place.** Wrap the binding to the WS (wrong side) and handstitch.

8 To make the false pockets, **cut two pieces of fabric** 20cm (8in) wide by 14cm (5³⁄₄in) deep and **interface with lightweight fusible interfacing.** Fold in half, RS to RS, along the length and **machine the short ends. Clip the corners. Turn to the RS and press.**

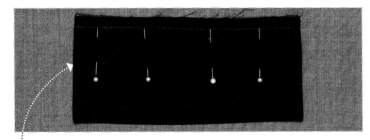

9 Try the dress on to determine the position of the false pockets, then **pin and stitch them in place** working from the RS.

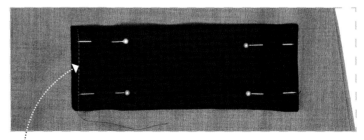

10 **Turn the pocket upwards** over the stitching. **Pin in place then stitch down the ends.** The effect will be one of a pocket that is open at the top.

EMBELLISHING A DRESS WITH SEQUINS AND BEADS

This is a fabulously simple and inexpensive way to bling up a day dress and turn it into a cocktail outfit in just an hour or so. All the sewing is done by hand, so settle down in a comfy chair with some soothing music and get creative!

Plain dress

BEFORE YOU START

YOU WILL NEED

- Plain dress
- Assorted sequins, pearls and beads
- 1 x reel matching all-purpose sewing thread

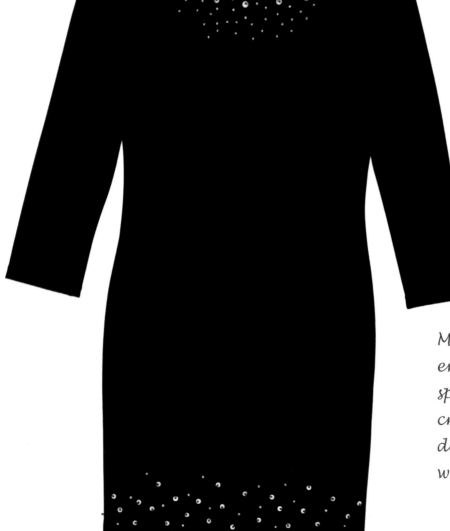

Make a grand entrance in this sparkly little number created from a simple day dress. Cinderella will go to the ball!

HOW TO EMBELLISH A DRESS WITH SEQUINS AND BEADS

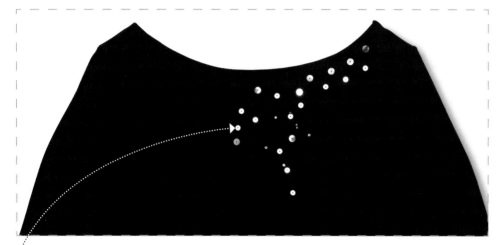

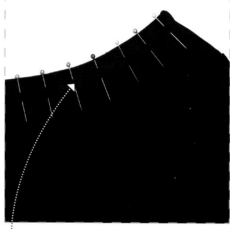

1 **Choose some beads, pearls, and sequins** that you like and **scatter them** on the dress to see which show up best.

2 **Mark the placement of the row of embellishment** at the neck edge with pins. Ensure the pins are evenly spaced.

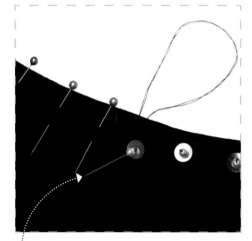

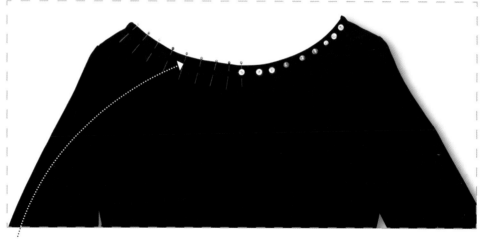

3 **Handstitch** a sequin at each pin and **add a small bead** on top of each sequin.

4 **Continue adding sequins and beads** all the way round the neck edge of the dress at the marked positions.

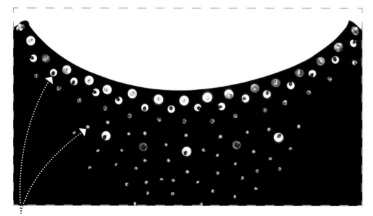

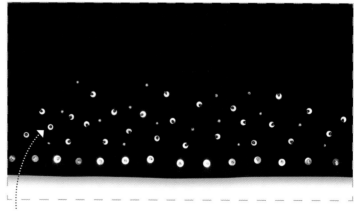

5 **Add a scattering of beads and sequins to form a panel** below the neck edge. **Stitch from bead to bead** without finishing the thread after each one, but don't attach more than 10 beads with one thread in case the thread breaks.

6 **Add beads and sequins** in the same way to create a border at the bottom of the dress.

EMBELLISHING A T-SHIRT WITH FLOWERS

For an up-to-the minute look, try this idea to breathe new life into a tired old long-sleeved T-shirt. The sleeves have been cut up to make a dainty flower corsage for the neckline. The flowers are so simple you'll want to make more and embellish other garments too.

Long-sleeved T-shirt

BEFORE YOU START

YOU WILL NEED

- Long-sleeved T-shirt
- Paper
- 1 x reel matching all-purpose sewing thread

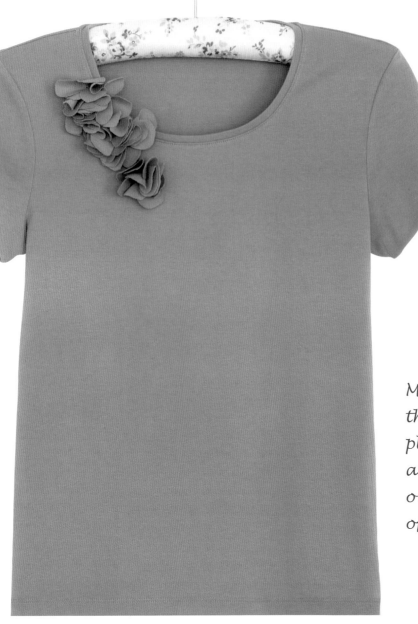

Matching flowers at the neckline turn a plain T-shirt into a pretty-as-a-picture one with just a couple of hours' work

HOW TO EMBELLISH A T-SHIRT WITH FLOWERS

1 **Cut the sleeves off your T-shirt** – we cut ours to leave a small cap sleeve.

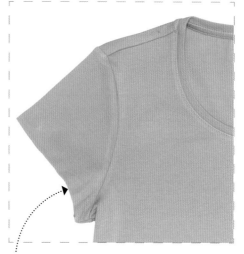

2 **Make a 1cm (⅜ in) hem** at the bottom of each sleeve and handstitch in place.

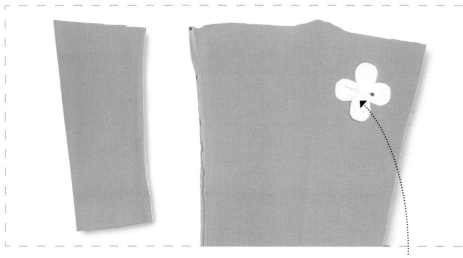

3 **Cut through the side seams** of the sleeves that you removed in order to make single layers of fabric. **Draw a flower shape** onto paper to use as a template. Cut it out, and use it to cut flowers from the sleeve.

4 **To make a flower**, pinch the centre to bring the petals together. Secure with a stitch.

5 **Scatter the flowers** on the front of the T-shirt to help you decide where to position them. Pin them in place.

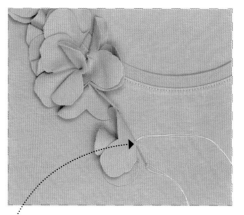

6 **Stitch each flower down** using a small stitch: this will be hidden by the petals.

ADDING A RIBBON TRIM TO A CARDIGAN

Is your cardigan looking tired and dull? If so, why not add a pretty ribbon trim to the front edges and some decorative buttons? This technique could be applied to any style of cardigan. You could even embellish the neck and cuffs of a jumper in the same way, in which case you won't need the snap fasteners.

Plain cardigan

BEFORE YOU START

YOU WILL NEED

- A cardigan
- 2m (79in) firm ribbon, the width of the button band
- 15–20 assorted buttons
- Snap fasteners
- 1 x reel matching all-purpose sewing thread

An assortment of buttons and a glam ribbon trim together give a tired old cardigan a quirky, handmade look

HOW TO ADD A RIBBON TRIM TO A CARDIGAN

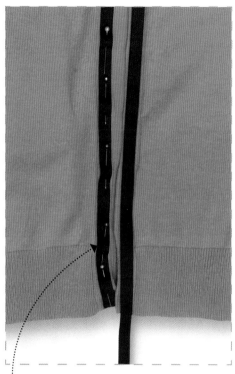

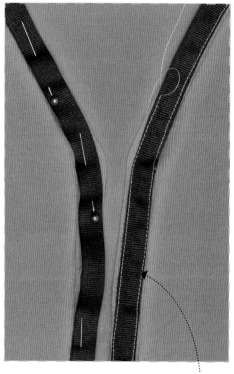

1 **Carefully remove the buttons** using sharp scissors. Take care not to cut the fabric.

2 Taking care not to stretch the cardigan, **pin a single length of ribbon**, wide enough to cover the button band, from the hem of one front up, round the neck, and down to the other hem.

3 **Machine carefully along both sides** of the ribbon to hold it in place.

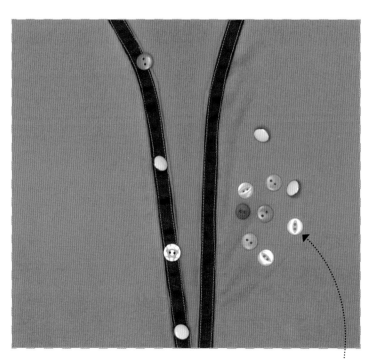

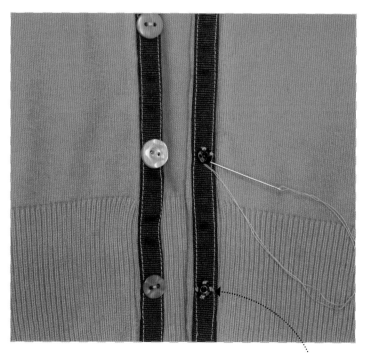

4 **Evenly space assorted buttons**, with a diameter no wider than the ribbon, along the length of the ribbon, leaving it free of buttons where the two fronts will join. Stitch in place.

5 **Where the two fronts are to join**, stitch one half of a snap fastener beneath each button and the other half in the corresponding position on the other side of the ribbon trim.

the PATTERNS

This section contains all the fabulous patterns that are needed to make the garments in this book. The patterns come in a range of sizes, enabling you to choose the size that suits you best. Full instructions explain how to transfer the patterns to paper.

USING THE PATTERN SECTION

To create any of the garments in this book, you will first need to transfer the pattern to paper. You can do this in one of three ways: download it from our website, draw the pattern by hand onto pattern paper, or enlarge it on a photocopier. Before you begin, you will also need to find the correct size for you.

FIND YOUR SIZE

Find your size by taking your bust, waist, and hip measurements and finding the closest set of measurements in the table below. If you are between sizes, choose the larger of the two.

Size	6-8	8-10	10-12	12-14	14-16	16-18	18-20	20-22	22-24
Bust	82cm (32¼in)	84.5cm (33¼in)	87cm (34¼in)	92cm (36¼in)	97cm (38in)	102cm (40in)	107cm (42in)	112cm (44in)	117cm (46in)
Waist	62cm (24½in)	64.5cm (25¼in)	67cm (26¼in)	72cm (28¼in)	77cm (30¼in)	82cm (32¼in)	87cm (34¼in)	92cm (36¼in)	97cm (38 in)
Hip	87cm (34¼in)	89.5cm (35¼in)	92cm (36¼in)	97cm (38in)	102cm (40in)	107cm (42in)	112cm (44in)	117cm (46in)	122cm (48in)

VARIED SIZES

You may have noticed that your size in the table differs from what you would buy in a store. In general, dressmaking sizes tend to be smaller than store sizes. It is always a good idea to make a garment in a toile first (see pp.68–69) to make sure that the size is right and the garment fits.

SEAM ALLOWANCE

Seam allowance is the amount of fabric that is taken up by the seam. It is usually given as the distance between the cutting line and the stitching line.

The patterns in this section include 1.5cm (⅝in) seam allowance. This means that to make a garment that is the correct size and shape, you will need to cut along the line on the pattern, and stitch 1.5cm (⅝in) inside the cutting line. An easy way to remember to do this is to mark a stitching line onto the pattern pieces before you begin.

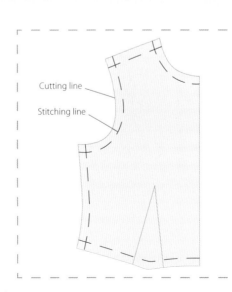

Cutting line

Stitching line

PATTERN MARKINGS

The following markings are used on the patterns in this section.

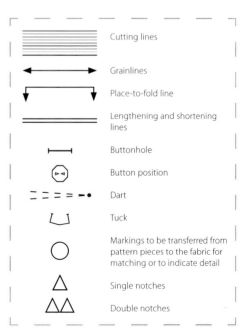

Cutting lines

Grainlines

Place-to-fold line

Lengthening and shortening lines

Buttonhole

Button position

Dart

Tuck

Markings to be transferred from pattern pieces to the fabric for matching or to indicate detail

Single notches

Double notches

DOWNLOAD OR COPY YOUR PATTERN

METHOD 1: DOWNLOADING FROM THE INTERNET

 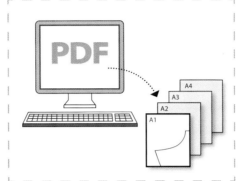 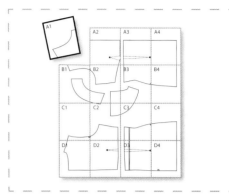

1 Start by checking which pattern is needed to make the garment or variation. This is listed on the first page of the instructions. Then go to the website **www.dk.co.uk/dressmaking**.

2 Find the correct PDF for your garment and your size. Download the PDF to your computer, and print it out. The pages will be labelled in the order that they fit together.

3 Trim the white margins from the printed pages, and tape the pages together, using the letters and gridlines as a guide. Cut out the pattern pieces.

METHOD 2: DRAWING THE PATTERN BY HAND

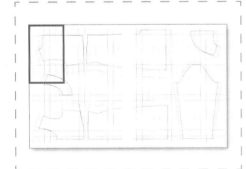 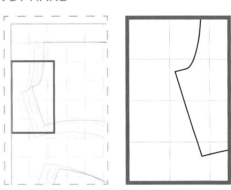 

1 Each grid square in the patterns represents a 5cm square at full size. To enlarge the patterns by hand, you will need pattern paper with either a 1cm or 5cm grid.

2 Begin by finding the coloured line for your size in the pattern. Enlarge the pattern onto your paper, mapping each square of the pattern onto a 5cm square on the pattern paper.

3 Depending on the size of your pattern paper, you may need to stick together several sheets to fit all the pieces for a single pattern. Once you have copied all the pieces, cut them out.

METHOD 3: PHOTOCOPYING

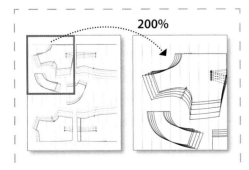 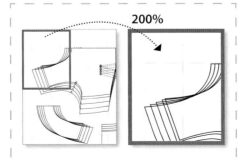 

1 To enlarge the pattern on a photocopier, begin by copying it at 100%. Find your size in the table, and draw along the line for your size in marker or pen. Enlarge the pattern by 200%.

2 Enlarge the pattern pieces again by 200% to reach full size. If you are using a photocopier that has a 400% setting, you can use this setting to enlarge the pieces in one step.

3 Once you have enlarged all parts of the original page, piece them together using the gridlines as a guide, and tape them down. Cut around your size.

SKIRT PATTERN ONE

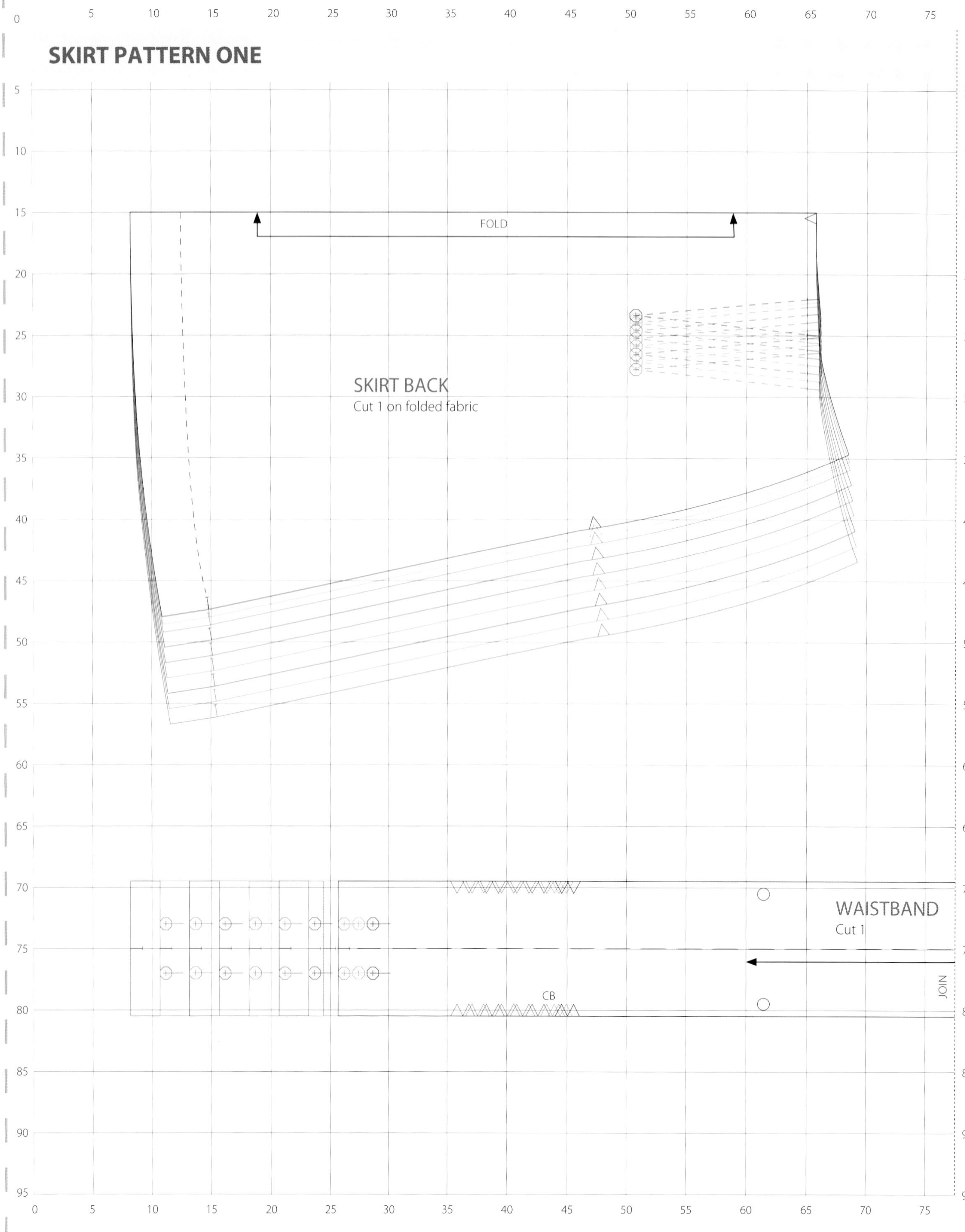

FOLD

SKIRT BACK
Cut 1 on folded fabric

WAISTBAND
Cut 1

CB

JOIN

SKIRT PATTERN ONE

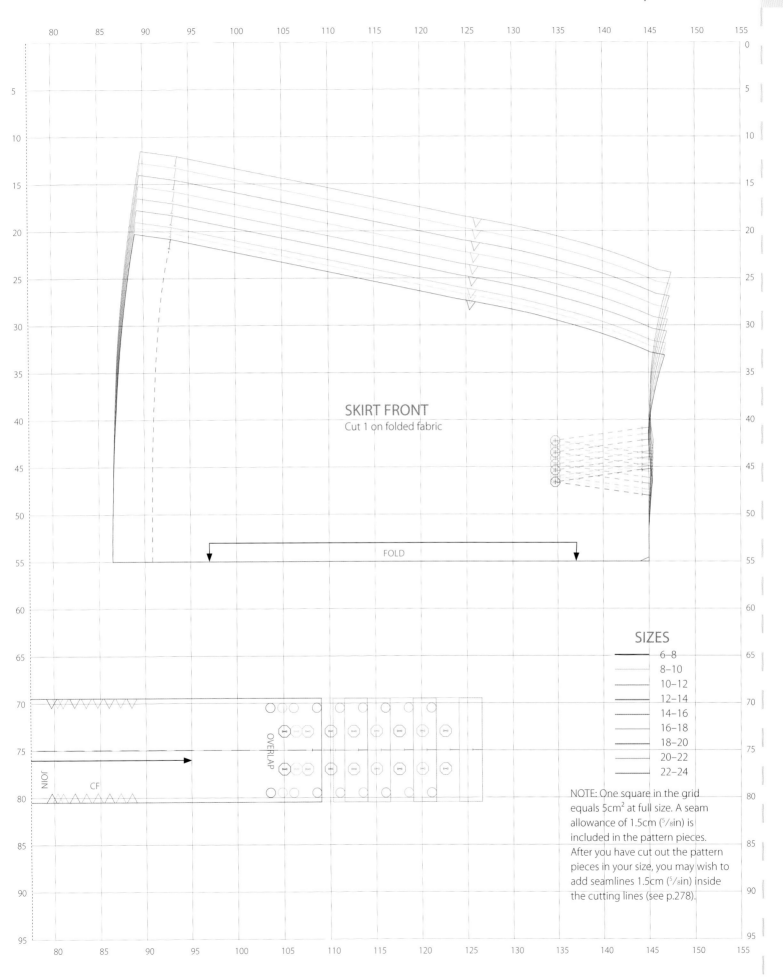

SKIRT FRONT
Cut 1 on folded fabric

FOLD

JOIN CF OVERLAP

SIZES
6–8
8–10
10–12
12–14
14–16
16–18
18–20
20–22
22–24

NOTE: One square in the grid equals 5cm² at full size. A seam allowance of 1.5cm (⅝in) is included in the pattern pieces. After you have cut out the pattern pieces in your size, you may wish to add seamlines 1.5cm (⅝in) inside the cutting lines (see p.278).

SKIRT PATTERN TWO

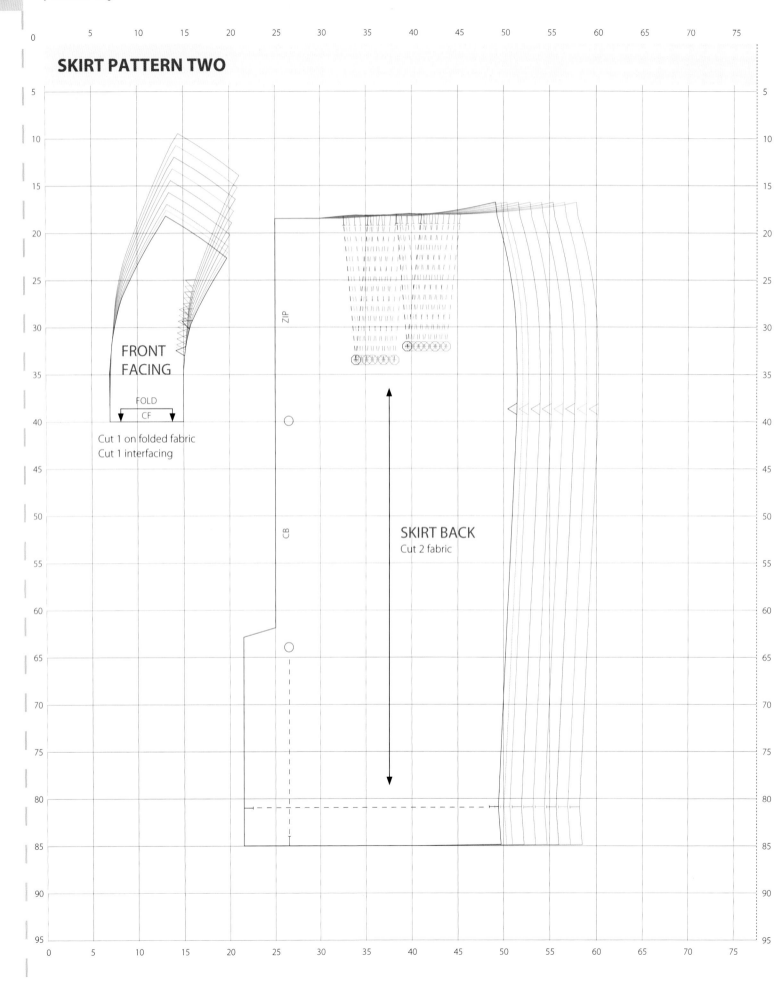

FRONT
FACING

FOLD

CF

Cut 1 on folded fabric
Cut 1 interfacing

ZIP

CB

SKIRT BACK
Cut 2 fabric

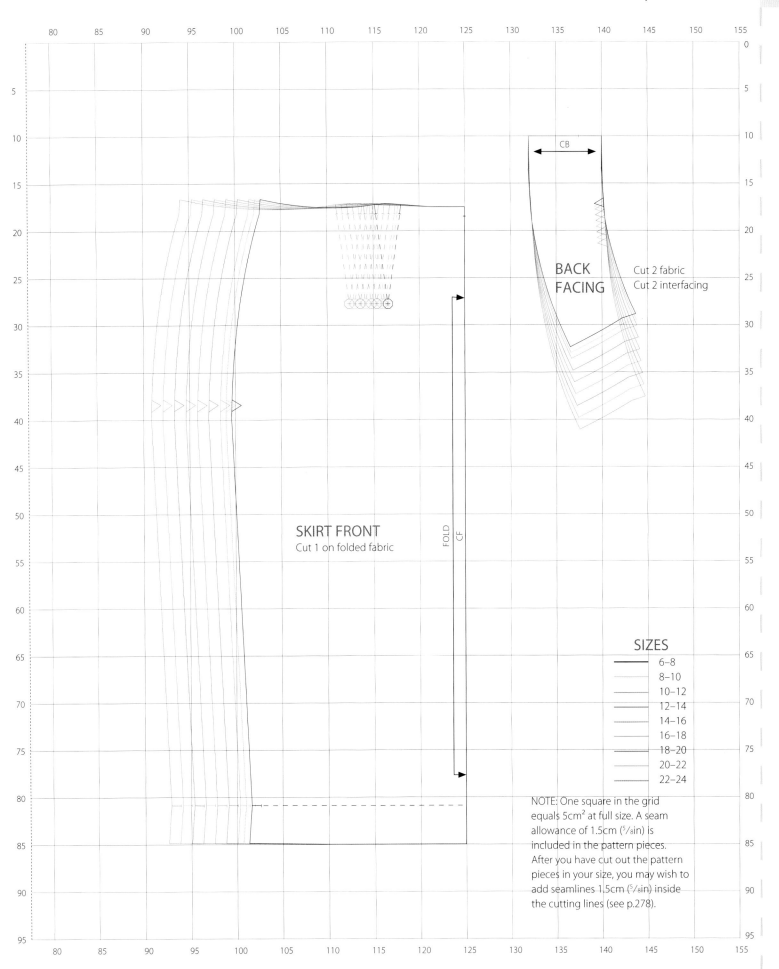

BACK
FACING

Cut 2 fabric
Cut 2 interfacing

CB

SKIRT FRONT

Cut 1 on folded fabric

FOLD CF

SIZES

———	6–8
———	8–10
———	10–12
———	12–14
———	14–16
———	16–18
———	18–20
———	20–22
———	22–24

NOTE: One square in the grid
equals 5cm² at full size. A seam
allowance of 1.5cm (⅝in) is
included in the pattern pieces.
After you have cut out the pattern
pieces in your size, you may wish to
add seamlines 1.5cm (⅝in) inside
the cutting lines (see p.278).

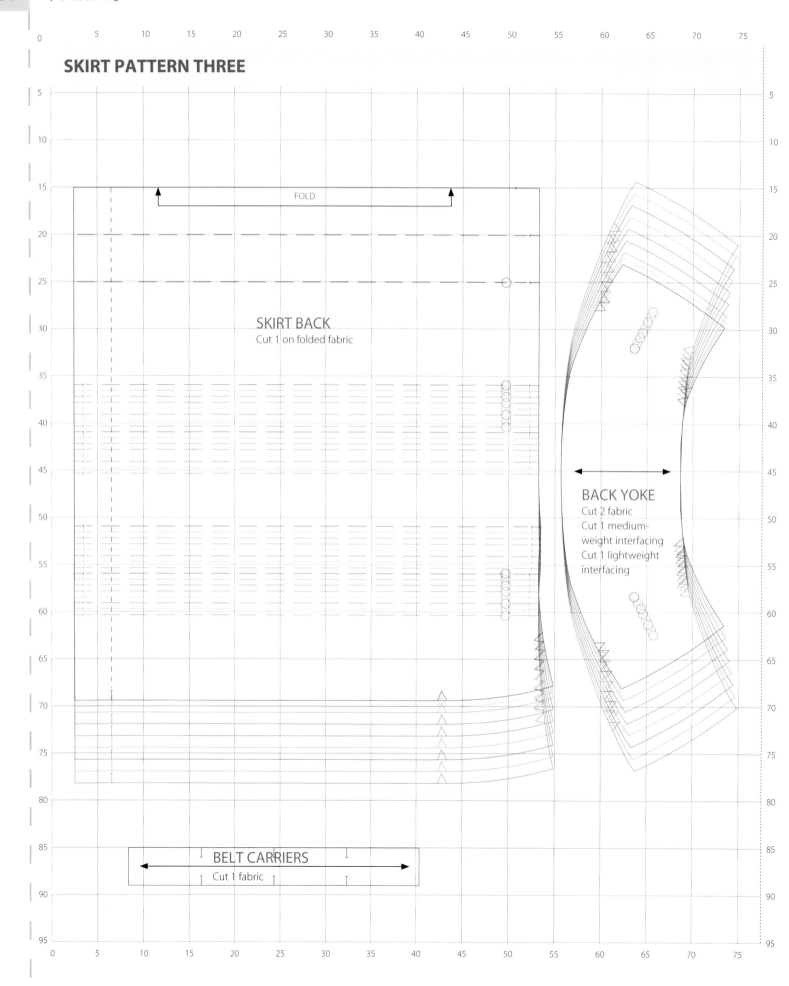

SKIRT PATTERN THREE

FOLD

SKIRT BACK
Cut 1 on folded fabric

BACK YOKE

Cut 2 fabric
Cut 1 medium-
weight interfacing
Cut 1 lightweight
interfacing

BELT CARRIERS
Cut 1 fabric

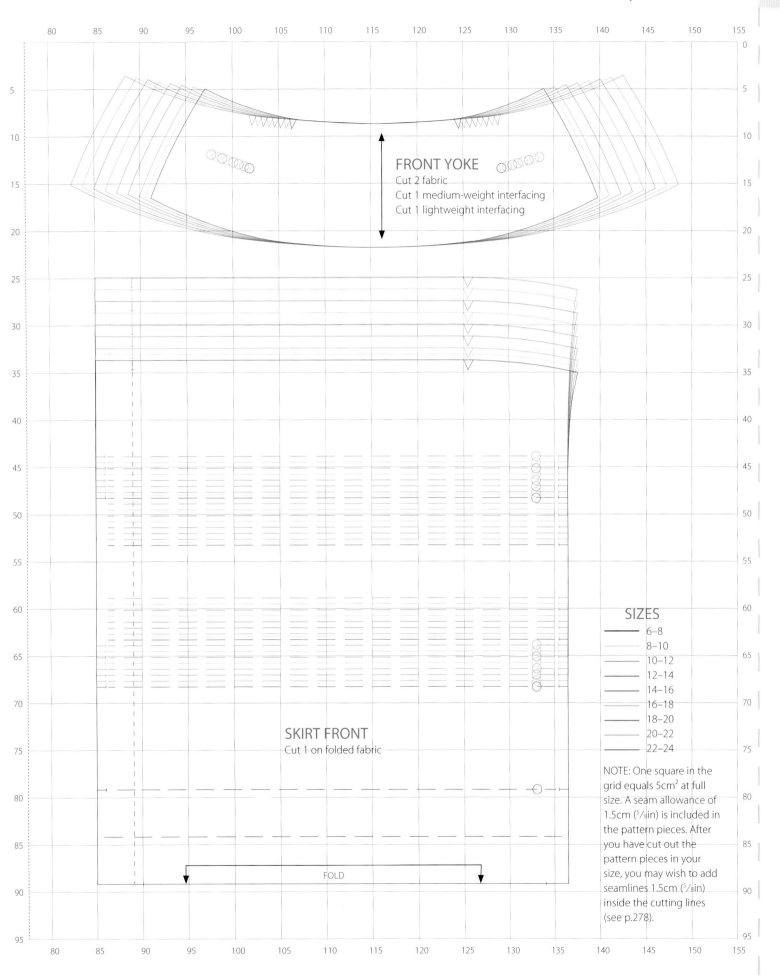

FRONT YOKE
Cut 2 fabric
Cut 1 medium-weight interfacing
Cut 1 lightweight interfacing

SKIRT FRONT
Cut 1 on folded fabric

FOLD

SIZES

——	6–8
——	8–10
——	10–12
——	12–14
——	14–16
——	16–18
——	18–20
——	20–22
——	22–24

NOTE: One square in the grid equals 5cm² at full size. A seam allowance of 1.5cm (⅝in) is included in the pattern pieces. After you have cut out the pattern pieces in your size, you may wish to add seamlines 1.5cm (⅝in) inside the cutting lines (see p.278).

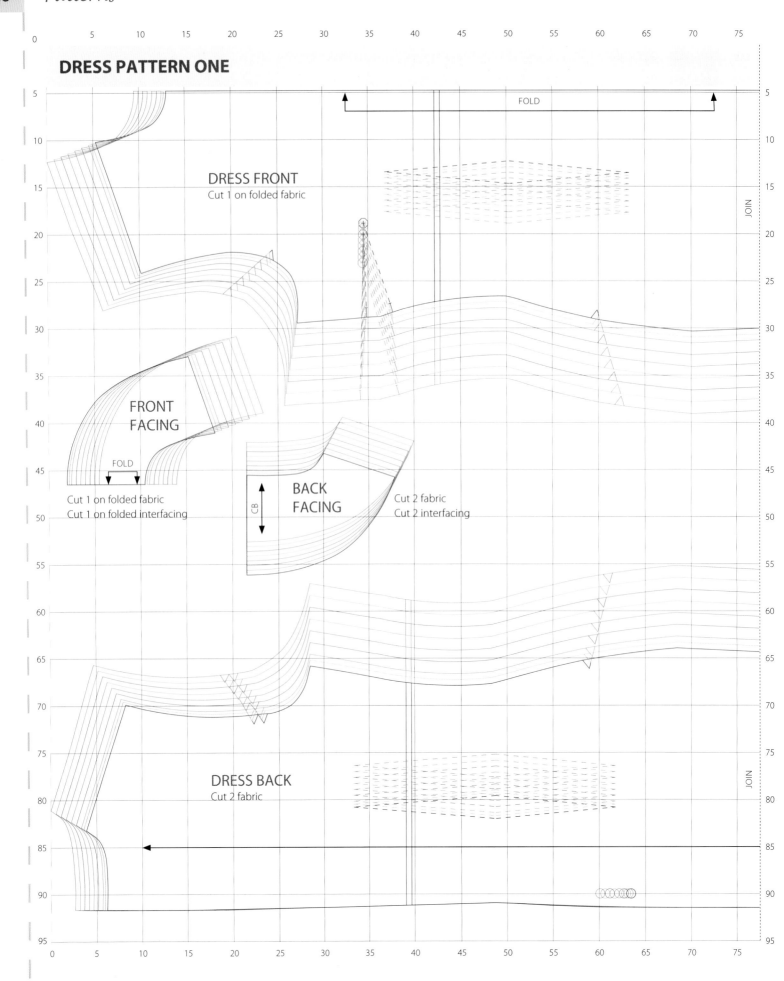

DRESS PATTERN ONE

FOLD

DRESS FRONT
Cut 1 on folded fabric

FRONT FACING

FOLD

Cut 1 on folded fabric
Cut 1 on folded interfacing

CB

BACK FACING

Cut 2 fabric
Cut 2 interfacing

DRESS BACK
Cut 2 fabric

JOIN

JOIN

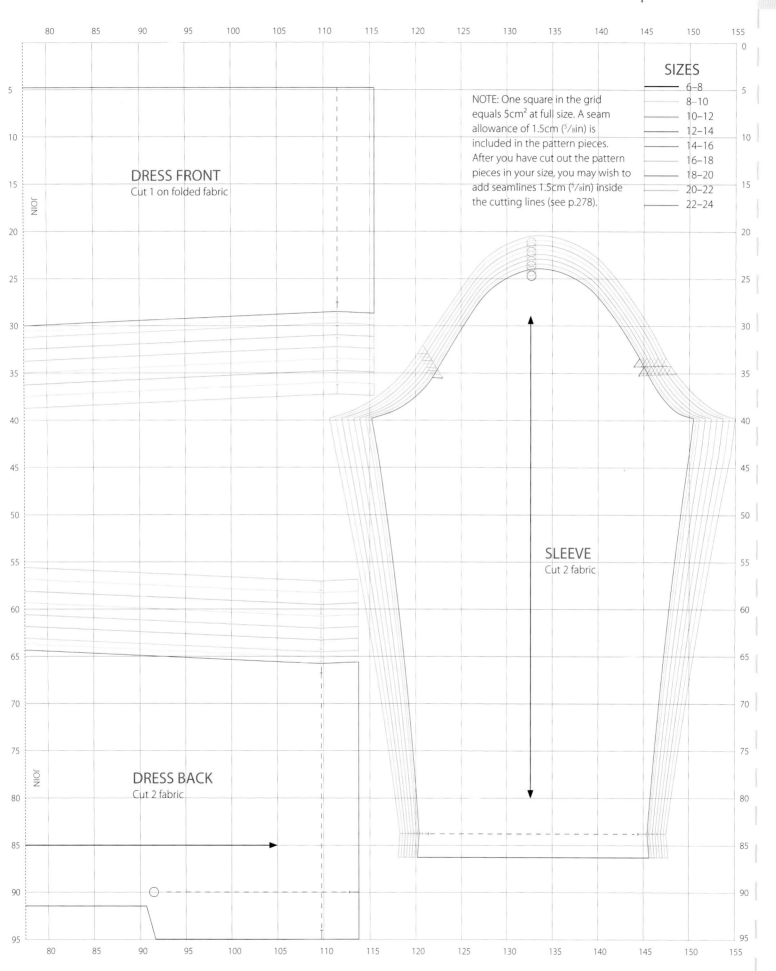

DRESS FRONT
Cut 1 on folded fabric

NOTE: One square in the grid equals 5cm² at full size. A seam allowance of 1.5cm (⅝in) is included in the pattern pieces. After you have cut out the pattern pieces in your size, you may wish to add seamlines 1.5cm (⅝in) inside the cutting lines (see p.278).

SIZES

—	6–8
—	8–10
—	10–12
—	12–14
—	14–16
—	16–18
—	18–20
—	20–22
—	22–24

SLEEVE
Cut 2 fabric

DRESS BACK
Cut 2 fabric

JOIN

DRESS PATTERN TWO

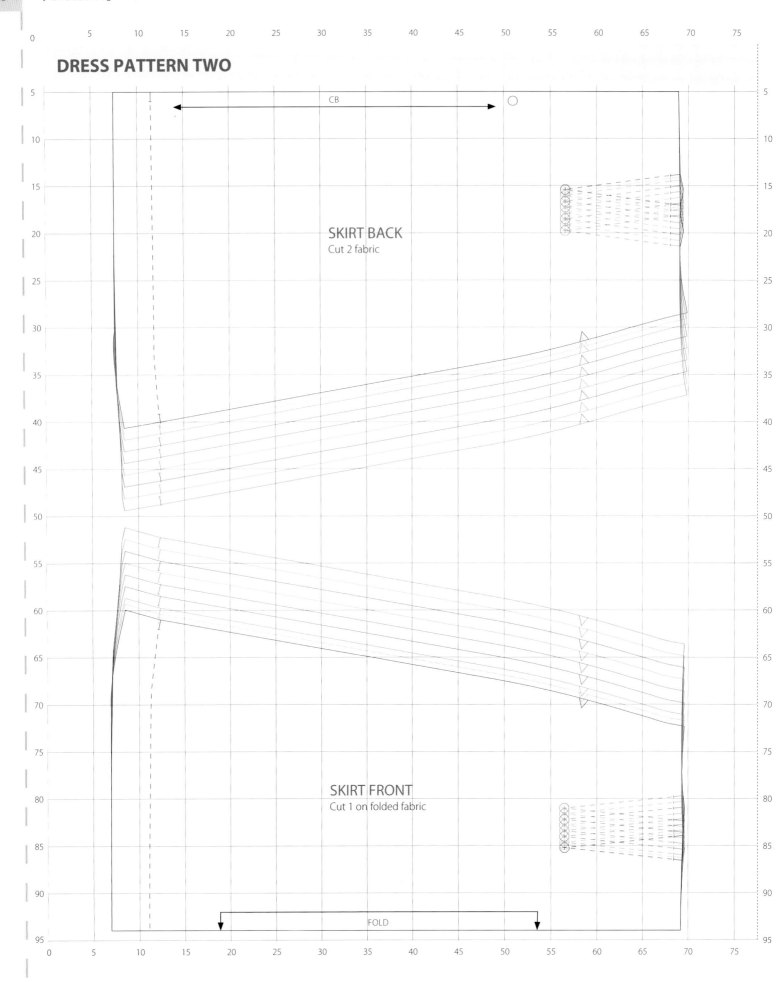

CB

SKIRT BACK
Cut 2 fabric

SKIRT FRONT
Cut 1 on folded fabric

FOLD

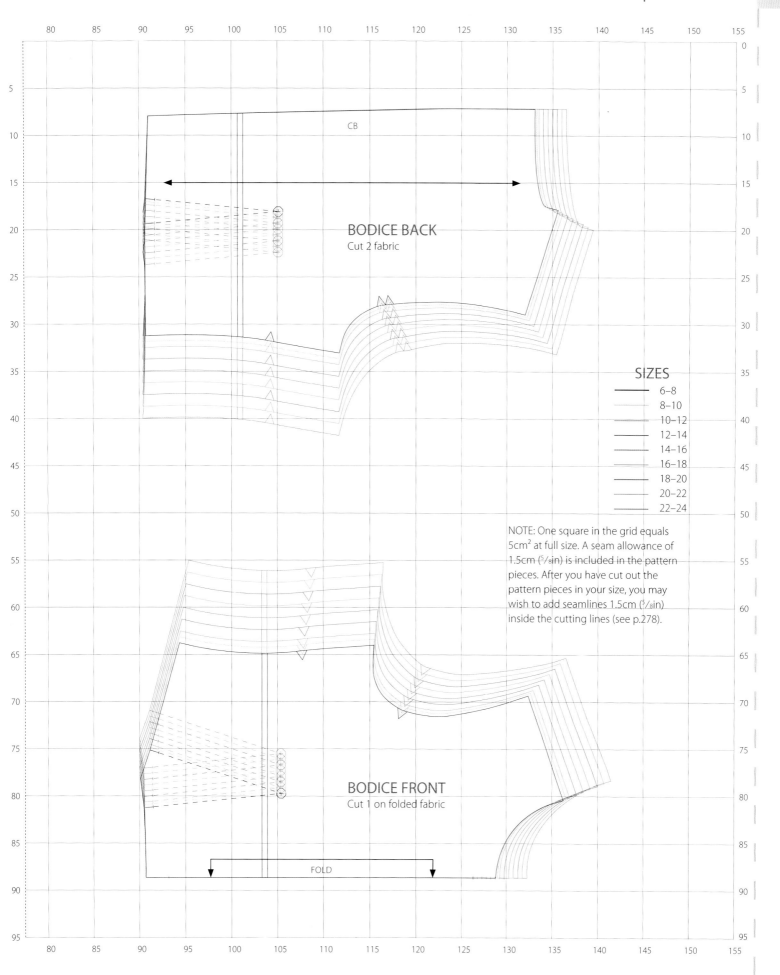

BODICE BACK
Cut 2 fabric

CB

SIZES
— 6–8
— 8–10
— 10–12
— 12–14
— 14–16
— 16–18
— 18–20
— 20–22
— 22–24

NOTE: One square in the grid equals 5cm² at full size. A seam allowance of 1.5cm (⅝in) is included in the pattern pieces. After you have cut out the pattern pieces in your size, you may wish to add seamlines 1.5cm (⅝in) inside the cutting lines (see p.278).

BODICE FRONT
Cut 1 on folded fabric

FOLD

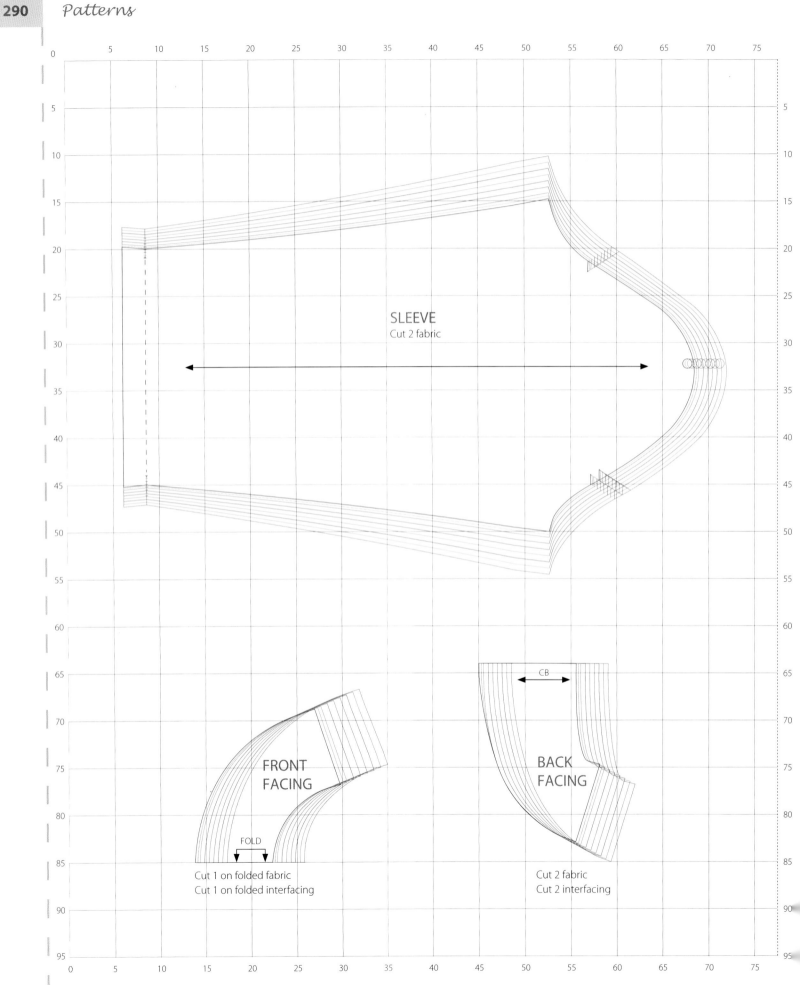

SLEEVE
Cut 2 fabric

FRONT
FACING

FOLD

Cut 1 on folded fabric
Cut 1 on folded interfacing

CB

BACK
FACING

Cut 2 fabric
Cut 2 interfacing

DRESS PATTERN THREE

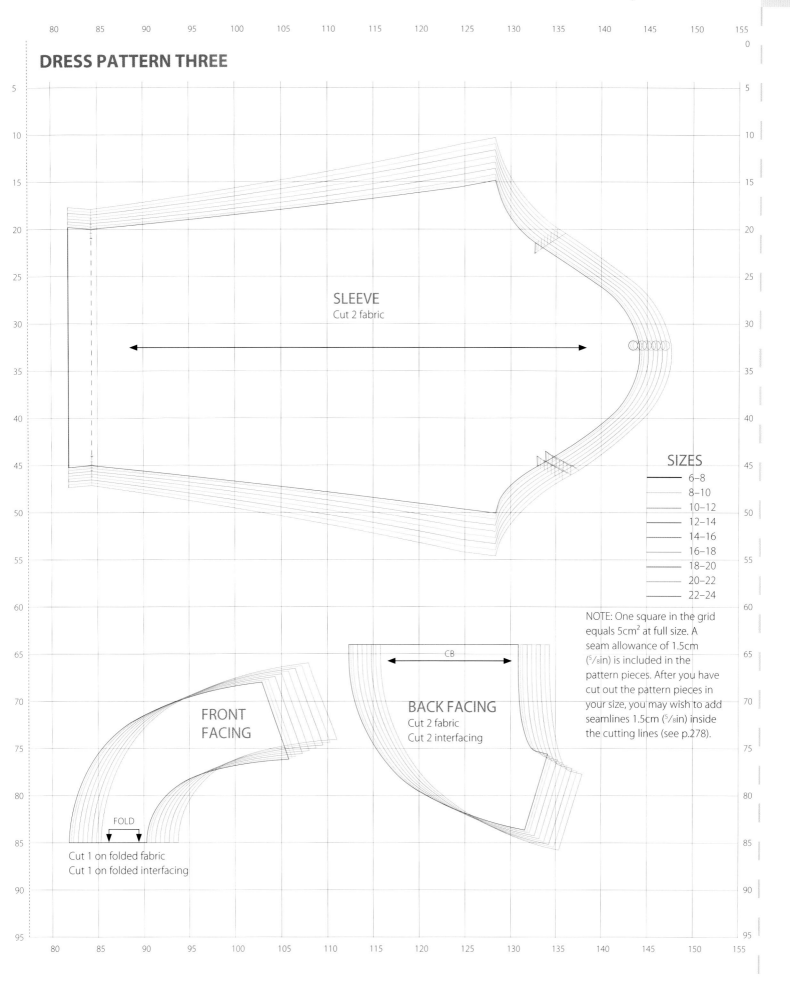

SLEEVE
Cut 2 fabric

SIZES
— 6–8
— 8–10
— 10–12
— 12–14
— 14–16
— 16–18
— 18–20
— 20–22
— 22–24

NOTE: One square in the grid equals 5cm² at full size. A seam allowance of 1.5cm (⁵⁄₈in) is included in the pattern pieces. After you have cut out the pattern pieces in your size, you may wish to add seamlines 1.5cm (⁵⁄₈in) inside the cutting lines (see p.278).

FRONT FACING

CB

BACK FACING
Cut 2 fabric
Cut 2 interfacing

FOLD

Cut 1 on folded fabric
Cut 1 on folded interfacing

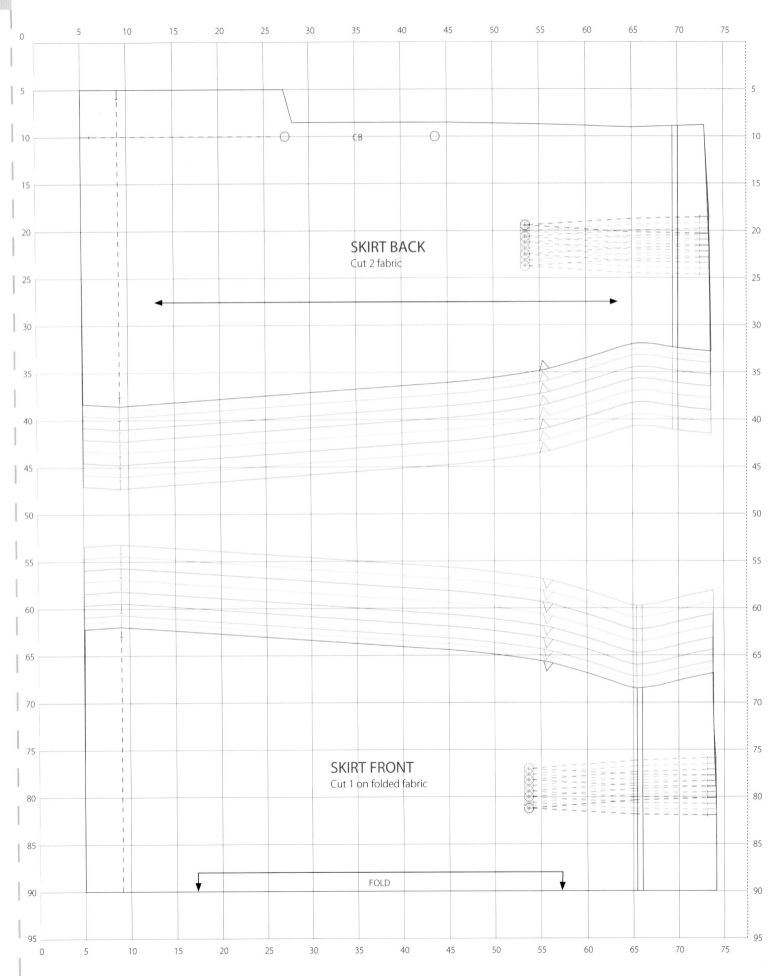

SKIRT BACK
Cut 2 fabric

CB

SKIRT FRONT
Cut 1 on folded fabric

FOLD

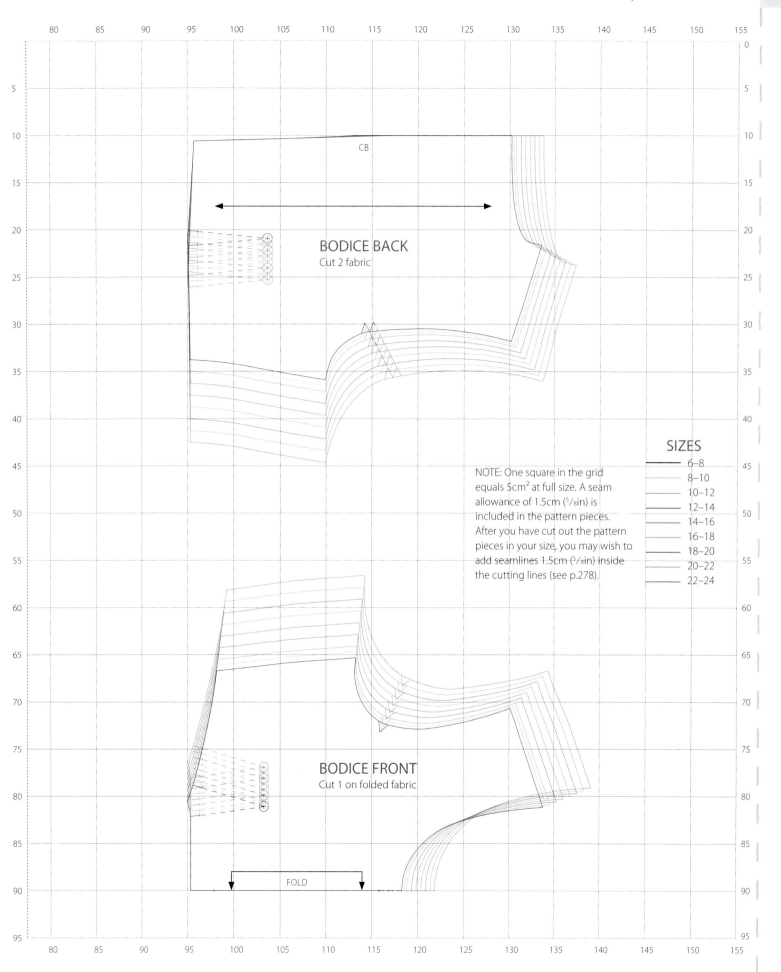

CB

BODICE BACK
Cut 2 fabric

NOTE: One square in the grid equals 5cm² at full size. A seam allowance of 1.5cm (⁵⁄₈in) is included in the pattern pieces. After you have cut out the pattern pieces in your size, you may wish to add seamlines 1.5cm (⁵⁄₈in) inside the cutting lines (see p.278).

SIZES

———	6–8
———	8–10
———	10–12
———	12–14
———	14–16
———	16–18
———	18–20
———	20–22
———	22–24

BODICE FRONT
Cut 1 on folded fabric

FOLD

TROUSER PATTERN ONE

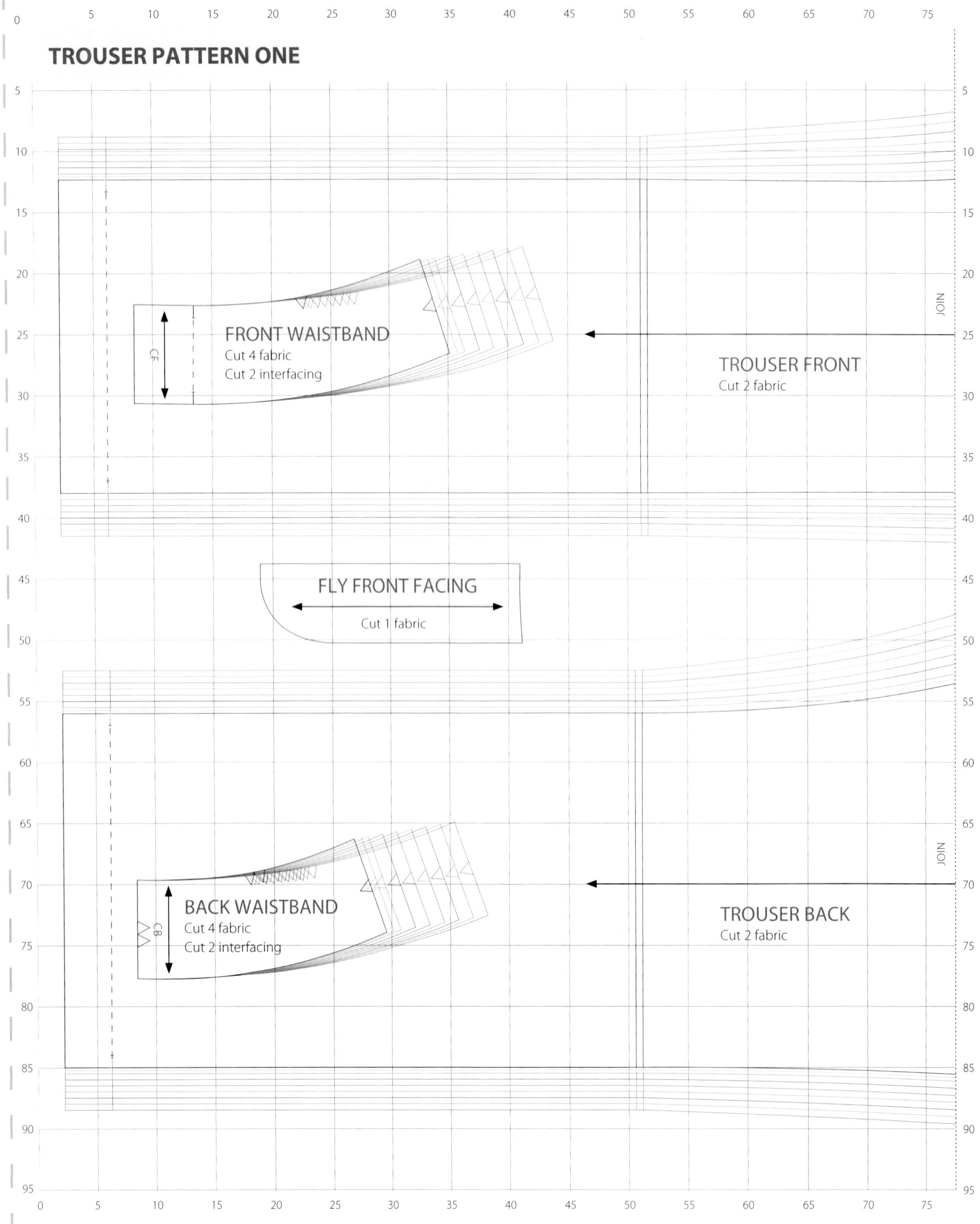

FRONT WAISTBAND
Cut 4 fabric
Cut 2 interfacing

CF

TROUSER FRONT
Cut 2 fabric

JOIN

FLY FRONT FACING
Cut 1 fabric

BACK WAISTBAND
Cut 4 fabric
Cut 2 interfacing

CB

TROUSER BACK
Cut 2 fabric

JOIN

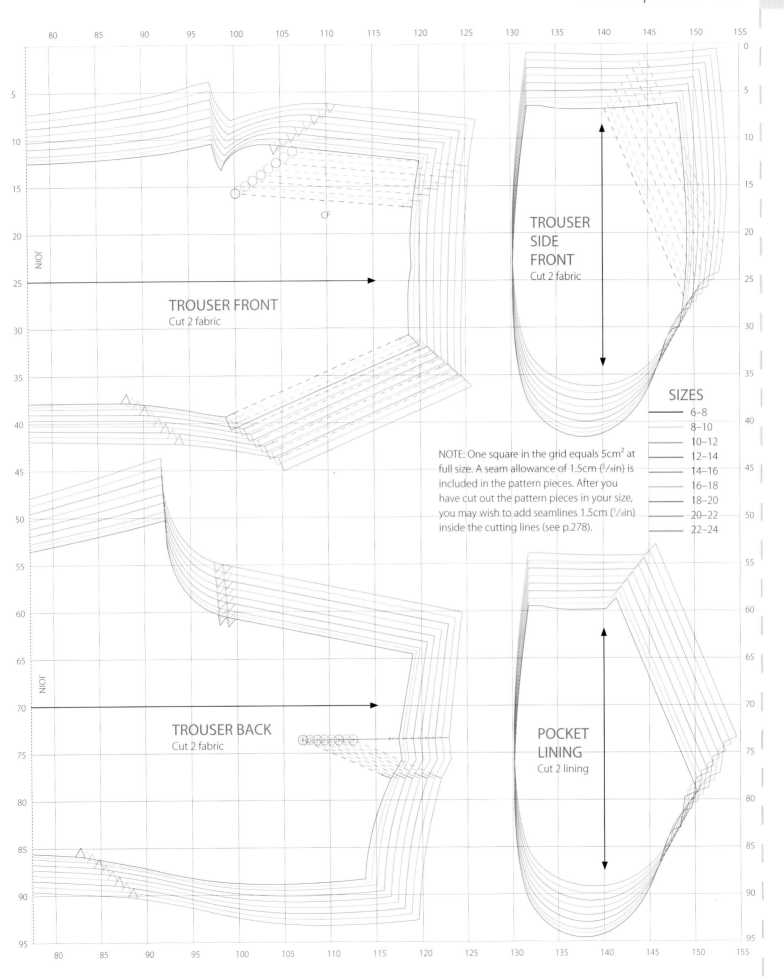

TROUSER SIDE FRONT
Cut 2 fabric

CF

JOIN

TROUSER FRONT
Cut 2 fabric

SIZES

— 6–8
— 8–10
— 10–12
— 12–14
— 14–16
— 16–18
— 18–20
— 20–22
— 22–24

NOTE: One square in the grid equals 5cm² at full size. A seam allowance of 1.5cm (⁵⁄₈in) is included in the pattern pieces. After you have cut out the pattern pieces in your size, you may wish to add seamlines 1.5cm (⁵⁄₈in) inside the cutting lines (see p.278).

JOIN

TROUSER BACK
Cut 2 fabric

POCKET LINING
Cut 2 lining

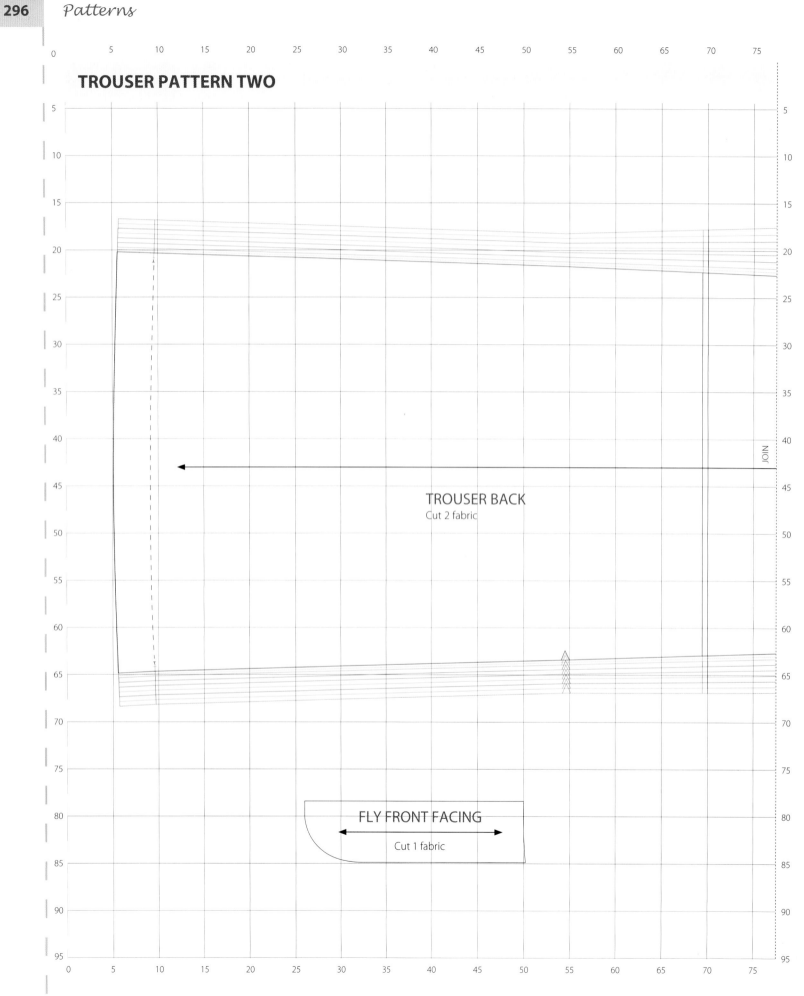

TROUSER PATTERN TWO

JOIN

TROUSER BACK
Cut 2 fabric

FLY FRONT FACING
Cut 1 fabric

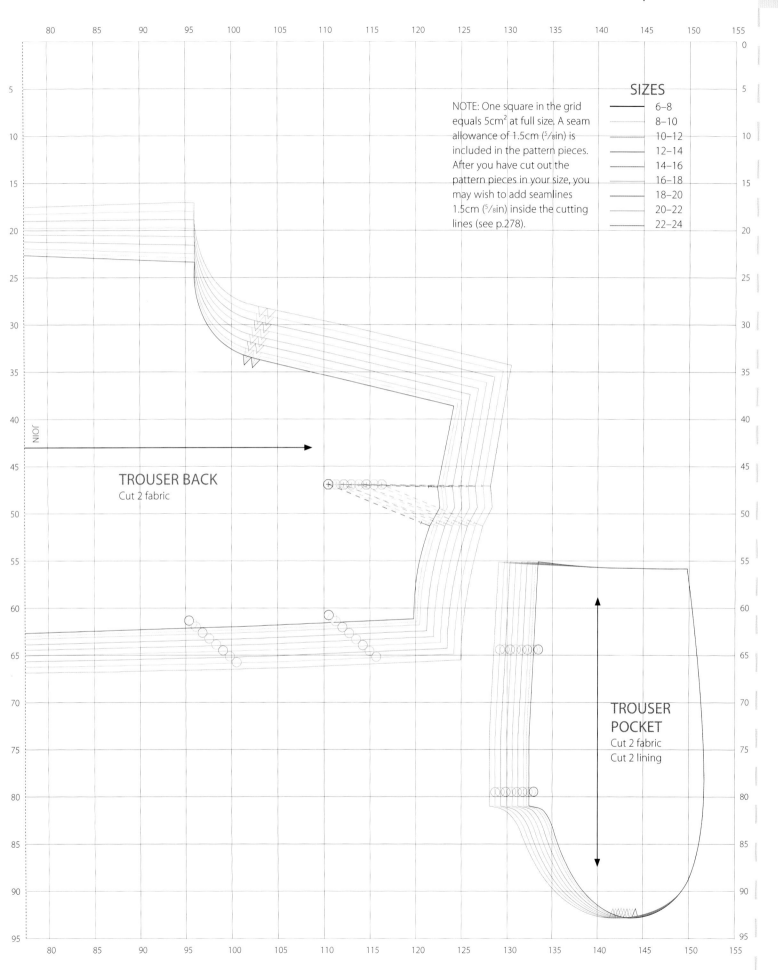

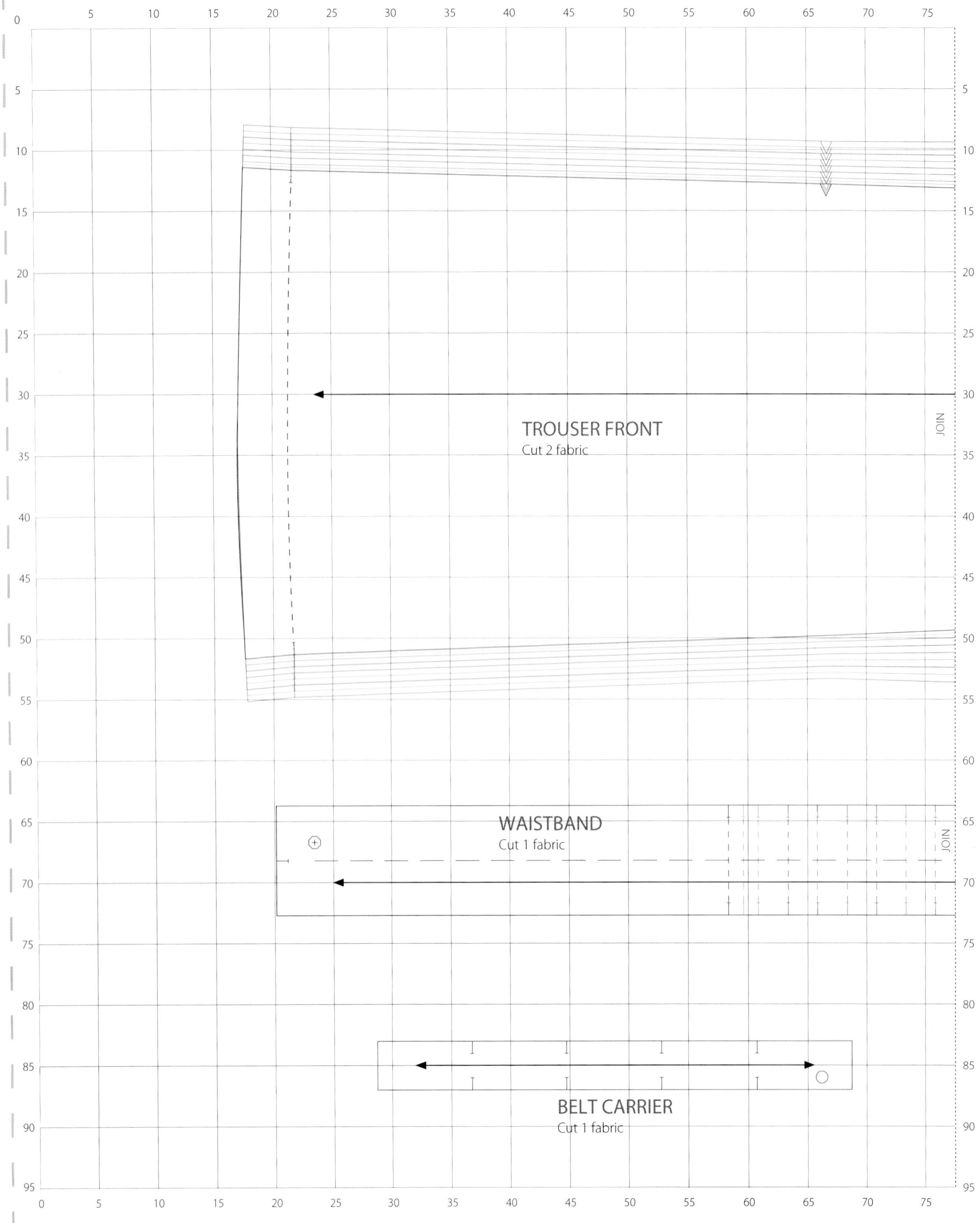

TROUSER FRONT
Cut 2 fabric

JOIN

WAISTBAND
Cut 1 fabric

JOIN

BELT CARRIER
Cut 1 fabric

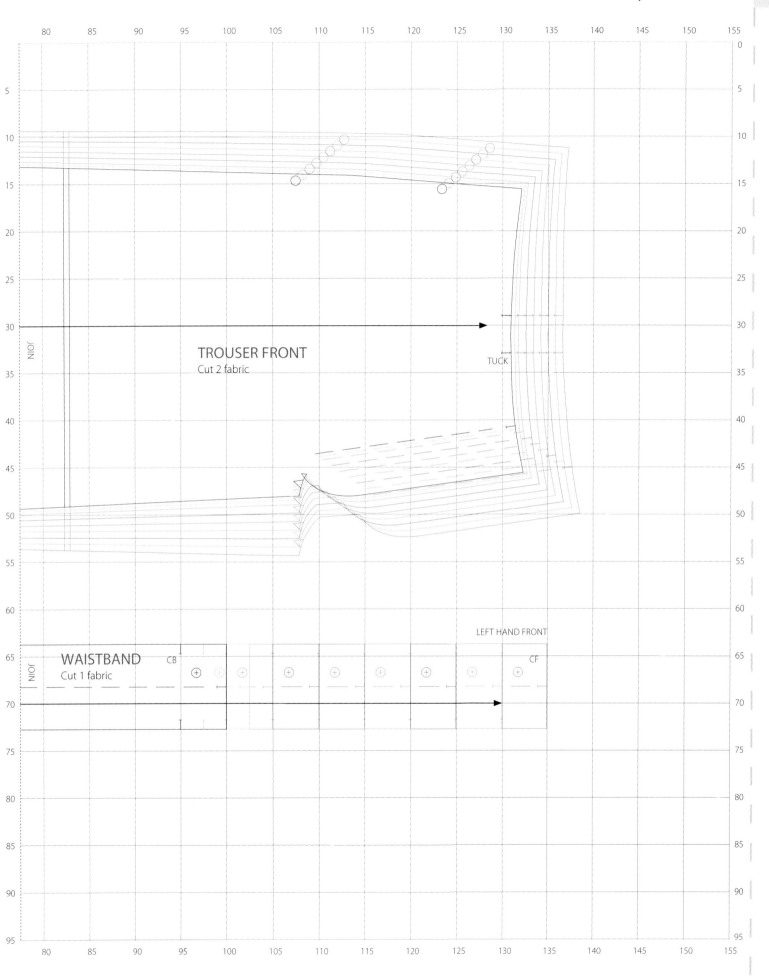

TROUSER FRONT
Cut 2 fabric

JOIN

TUCK

LEFT HAND FRONT

WAISTBAND   CB
Cut 1 fabric

JOIN

CF

TOP PATTERN ONE

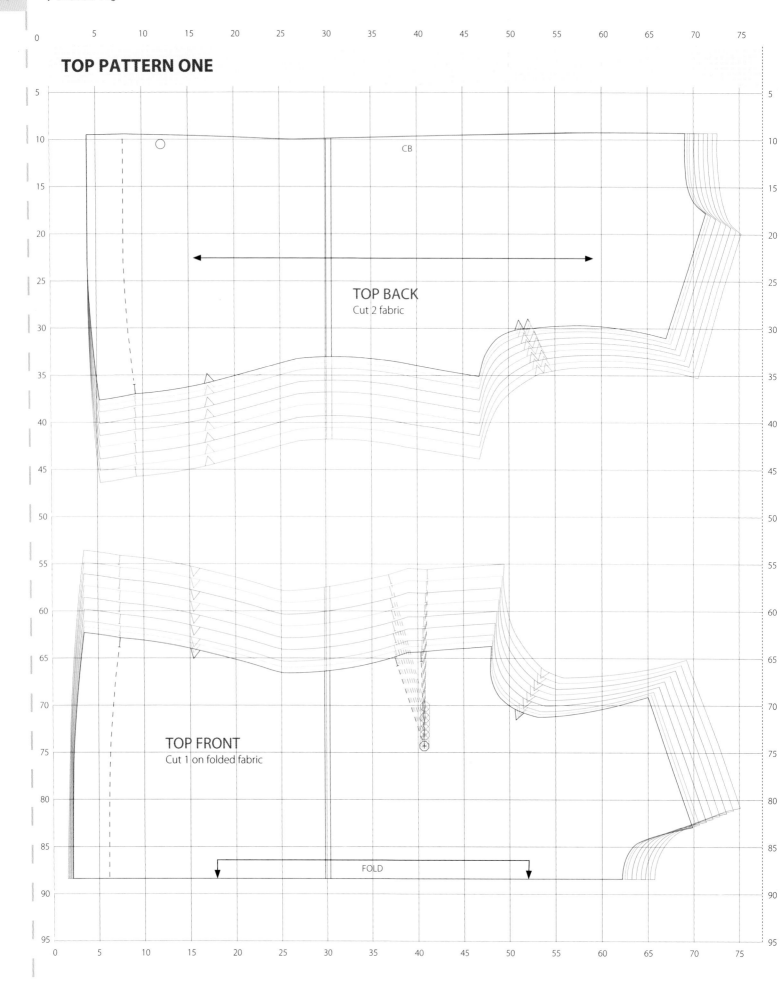

TOP BACK
Cut 2 fabric

CB

TOP FRONT
Cut 1 on folded fabric

FOLD

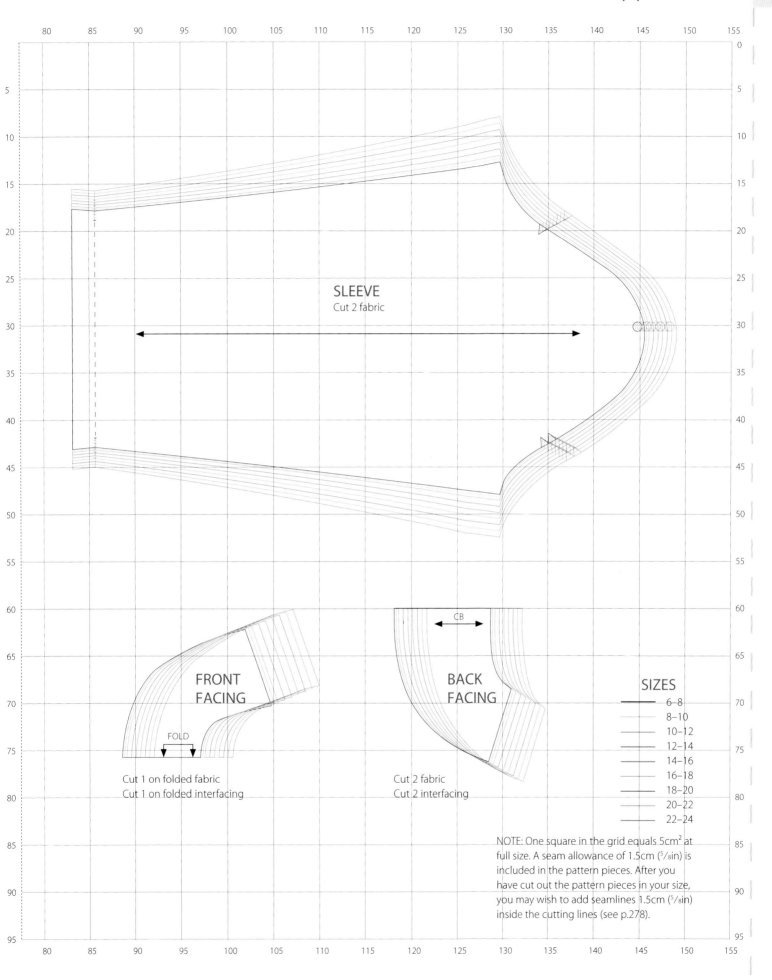

SLEEVE
Cut 2 fabric

FRONT
FACING

FOLD

Cut 1 on folded fabric
Cut 1 on folded interfacing

BACK
FACING

CB

Cut 2 fabric
Cut 2 interfacing

SIZES

———	6–8
———	8–10
———	10–12
———	12–14
———	14–16
———	16–18
———	18–20
———	20–22
———	22–24

NOTE: One square in the grid equals 5cm² at full size. A seam allowance of 1.5cm (⅝in) is included in the pattern pieces. After you have cut out the pattern pieces in your size, you may wish to add seamlines 1.5cm (⅝in) inside the cutting lines (see p.278).

TOP PATTERN TWO

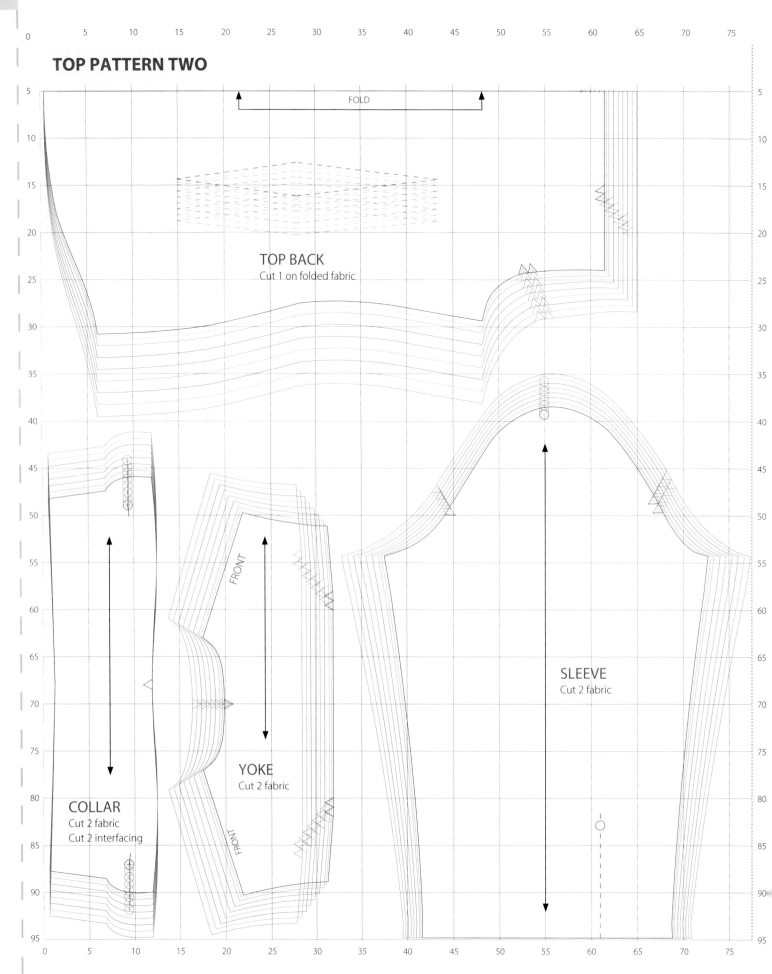

FOLD

TOP BACK
Cut 1 on folded fabric

FRONT

SLEEVE
Cut 2 fabric

COLLAR
Cut 2 fabric
Cut 2 interfacing

YOKE
Cut 2 fabric

FRONT

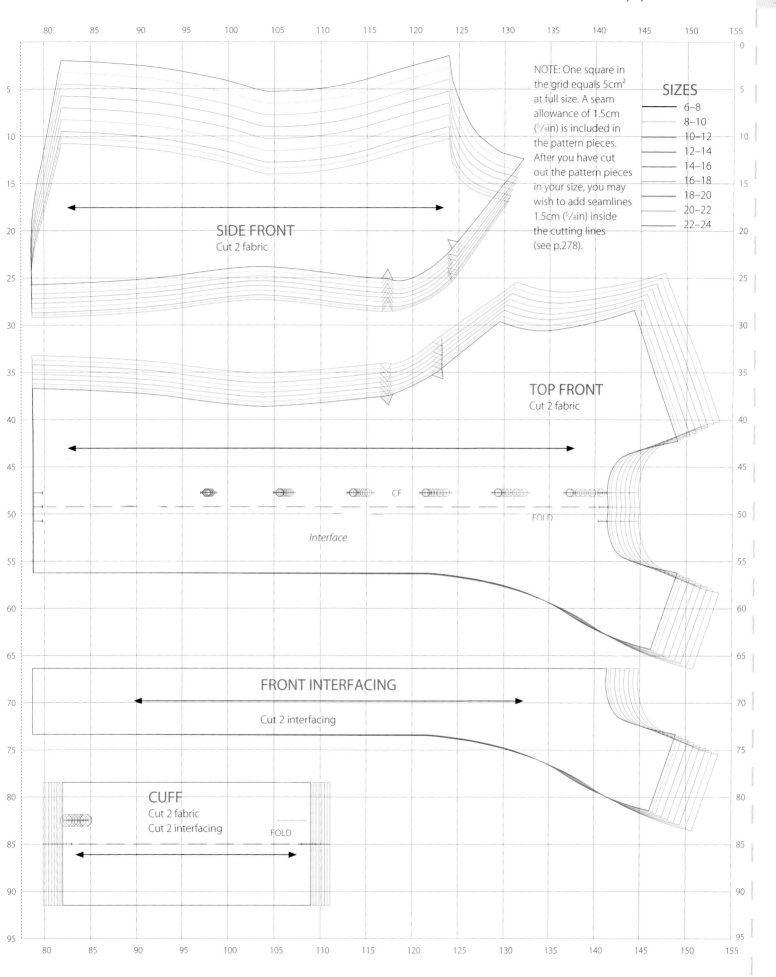

NOTE: One square in the grid equals 5cm² at full size. A seam allowance of 1.5cm (⁵⁄₈in) is included in the pattern pieces. After you have cut out the pattern pieces in your size, you may wish to add seamlines 1.5cm (⁵⁄₈in) inside the cutting lines (see p.278).

SIZES
— 6–8
— 8–10
— 10–12
— 12–14
— 14–16
— 16–18
— 18–20
— 20–22
— 22–24

SIDE FRONT
Cut 2 fabric

TOP FRONT
Cut 2 fabric

CF

FOLD

Interface

FRONT INTERFACING

Cut 2 interfacing

CUFF
Cut 2 fabric
Cut 2 interfacing

FOLD

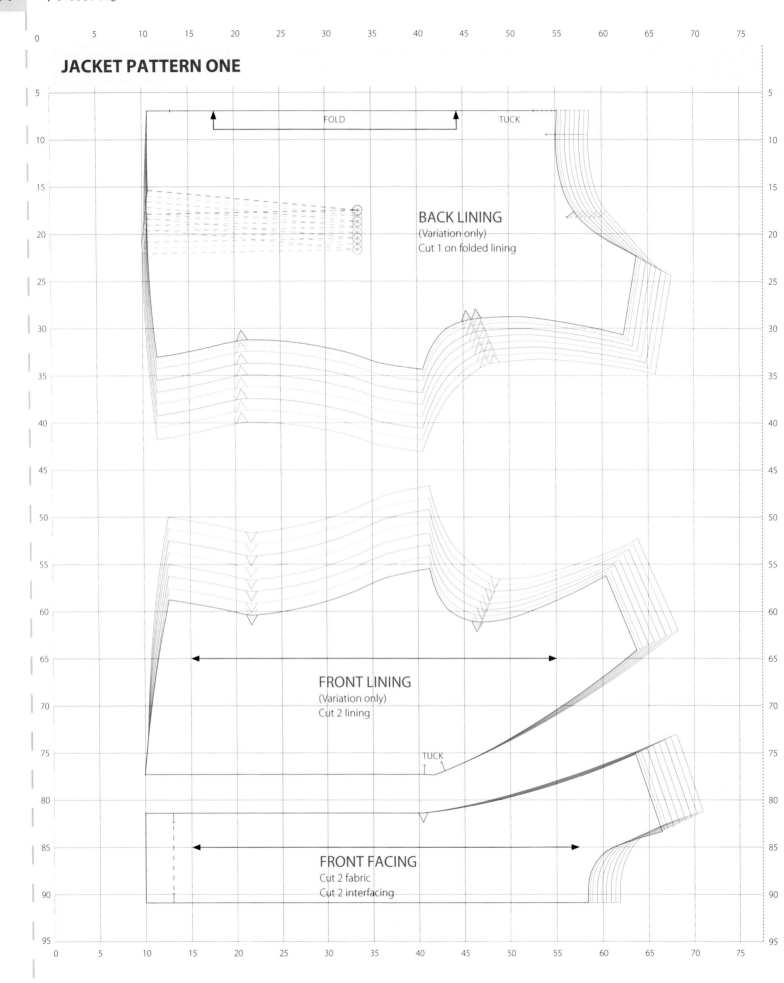

JACKET PATTERN ONE

FOLD

TUCK

BACK LINING
(Variation only)
Cut 1 on folded lining

FRONT LINING
(Variation only)
Cut 2 lining

TUCK

FRONT FACING
Cut 2 fabric
Cut 2 interfacing

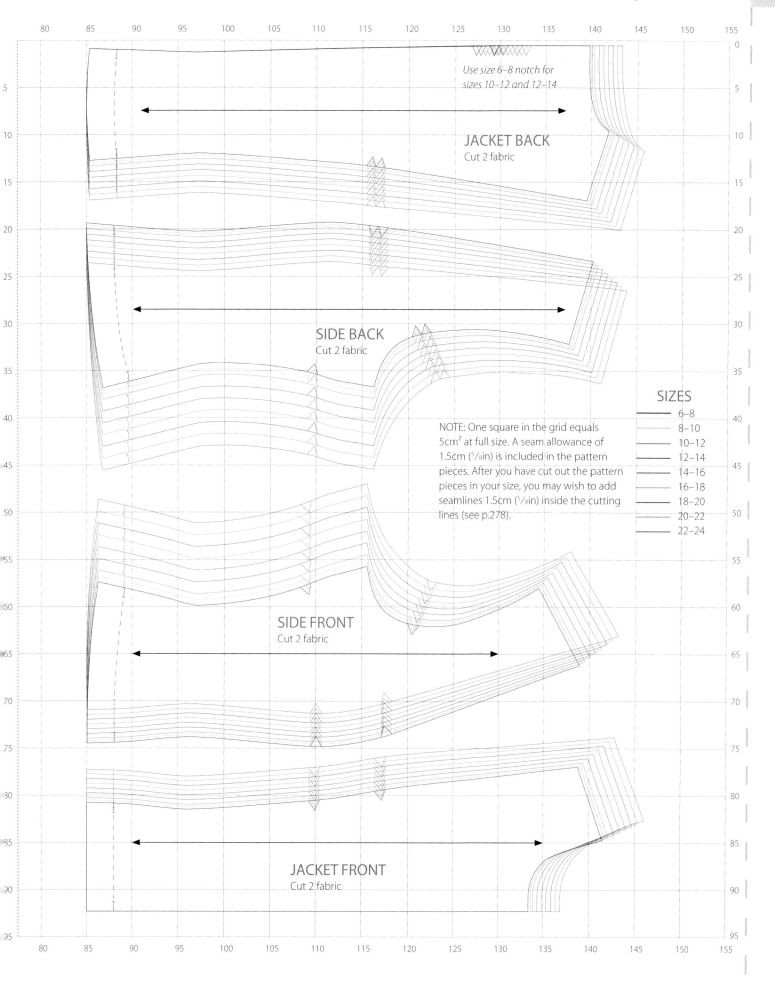

JACKET BACK
Cut 2 fabric

*Use size 6–8 notch for
sizes 10–12 and 12–14*

SIDE BACK
Cut 2 fabric

SIDE FRONT
Cut 2 fabric

JACKET FRONT
Cut 2 fabric

NOTE: One square in the grid equals
5cm² at full size. A seam allowance of
1.5cm (⁵⁄₈in) is included in the pattern
pieces. After you have cut out the pattern
pieces in your size, you may wish to add
seamlines 1.5cm (⁵⁄₈in) inside the cutting
lines (see p.278).

SIZES
—— 6–8
—— 8–10
—— 10–12
—— 12–14
—— 14–16
—— 16–18
—— 18–20
—— 20–22
—— 22–24

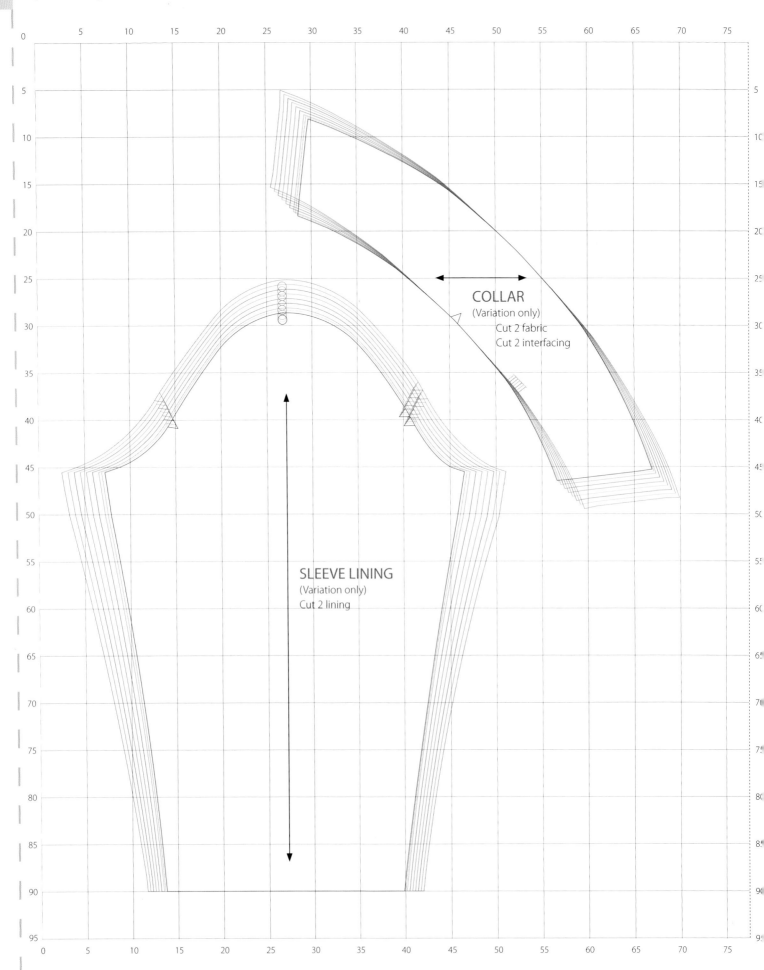

COLLAR
(Variation only)
Cut 2 fabric
Cut 2 interfacing

SLEEVE LINING
(Variation only)
Cut 2 lining

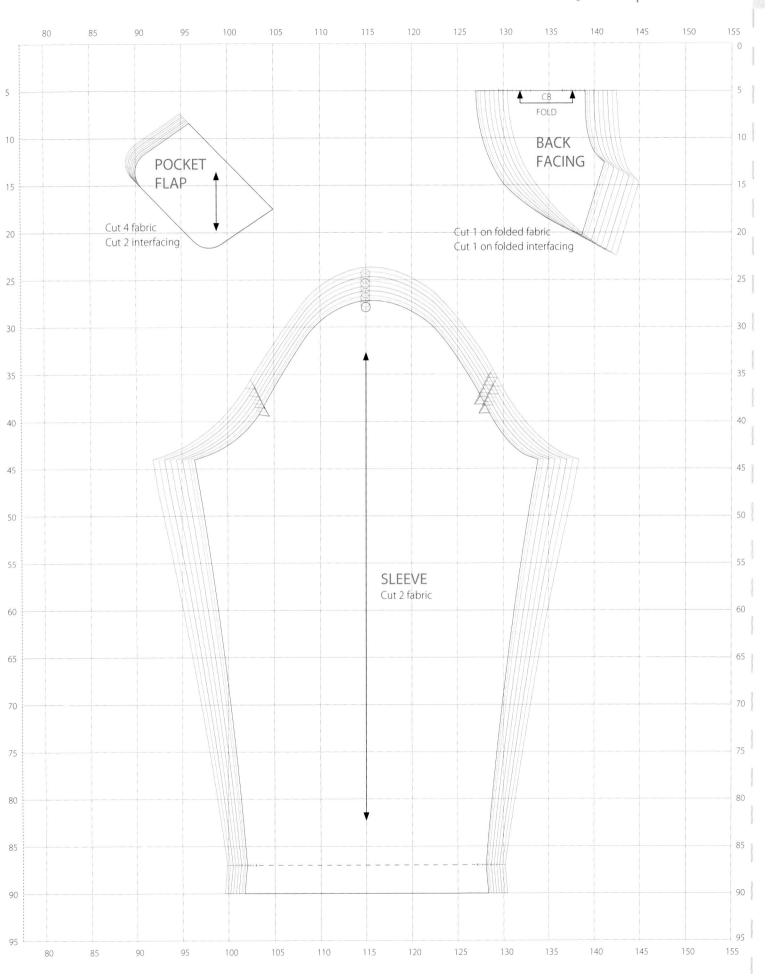

POCKET
FLAP

Cut 4 fabric
Cut 2 interfacing

CB
FOLD

BACK
FACING

Cut 1 on folded fabric
Cut 1 on folded interfacing

SLEEVE
Cut 2 fabric

JACKET PATTERN TWO

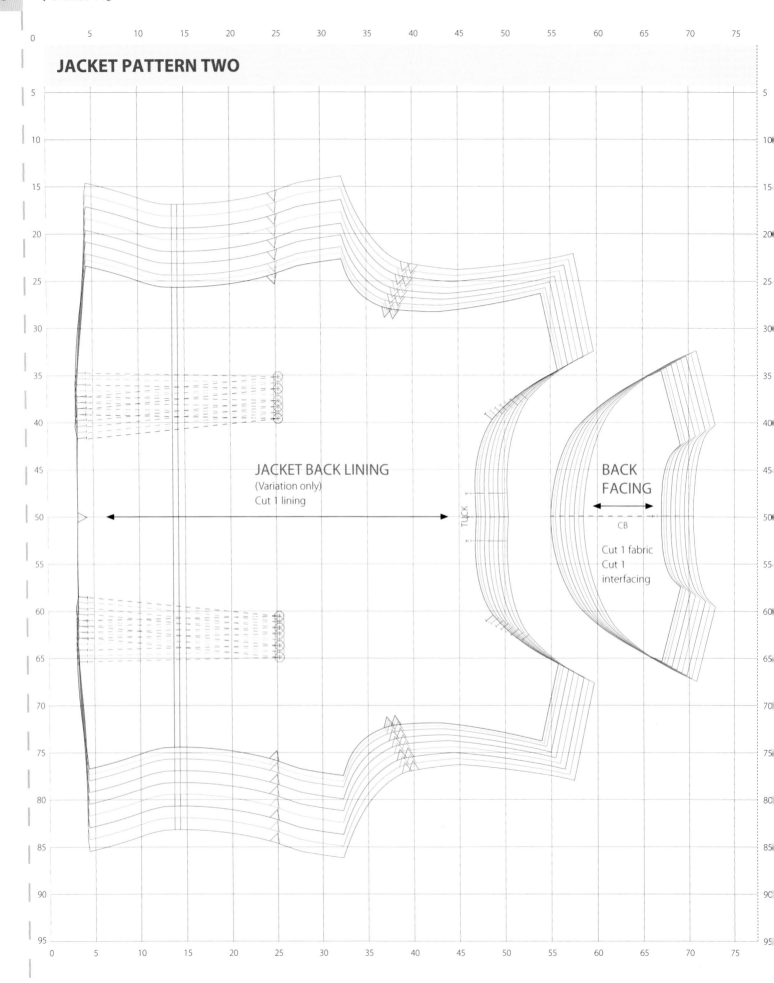

JACKET BACK LINING
(Variation only)
Cut 1 lining

TUCK

BACK
FACING

CB

Cut 1 fabric
Cut 1
interfacing

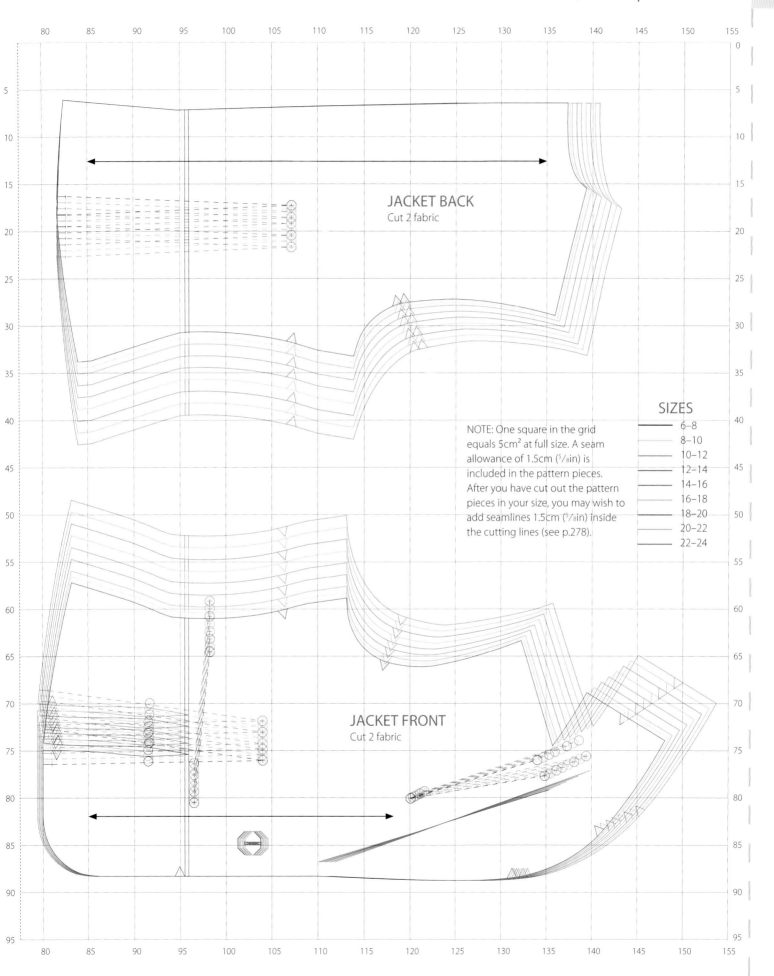

JACKET BACK
Cut 2 fabric

NOTE: One square in the grid equals 5cm² at full size. A seam allowance of 1.5cm (⅝in) is included in the pattern pieces. After you have cut out the pattern pieces in your size, you may wish to add seamlines 1.5cm (⅝in) inside the cutting lines (see p.278).

SIZES
6–8
8–10
10–12
12–14
14–16
16–18
18–20
20–22
22–24

JACKET FRONT
Cut 2 fabric

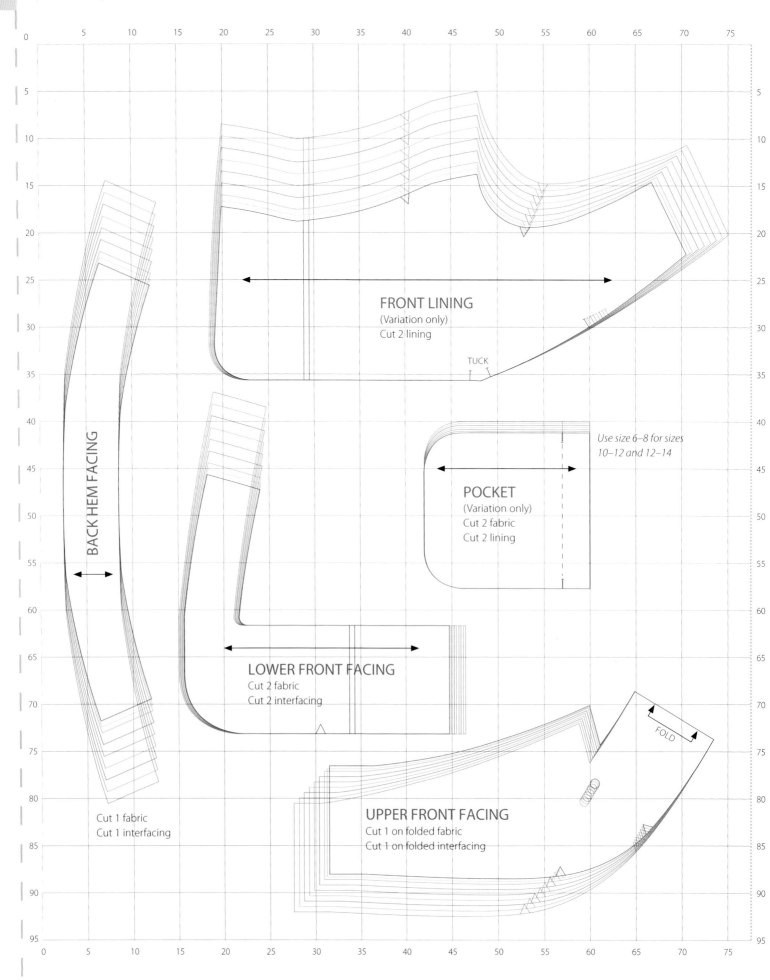

FRONT LINING
(Variation only)
Cut 2 lining

TUCK

BACK HEM FACING

POCKET
(Variation only)
Cut 2 fabric
Cut 2 lining

Use size 6–8 for sizes
10–12 and 12–14

LOWER FRONT FACING
Cut 2 fabric
Cut 2 interfacing

Cut 1 fabric
Cut 1 interfacing

FOLD

UPPER FRONT FACING
Cut 1 on folded fabric
Cut 1 on folded interfacing

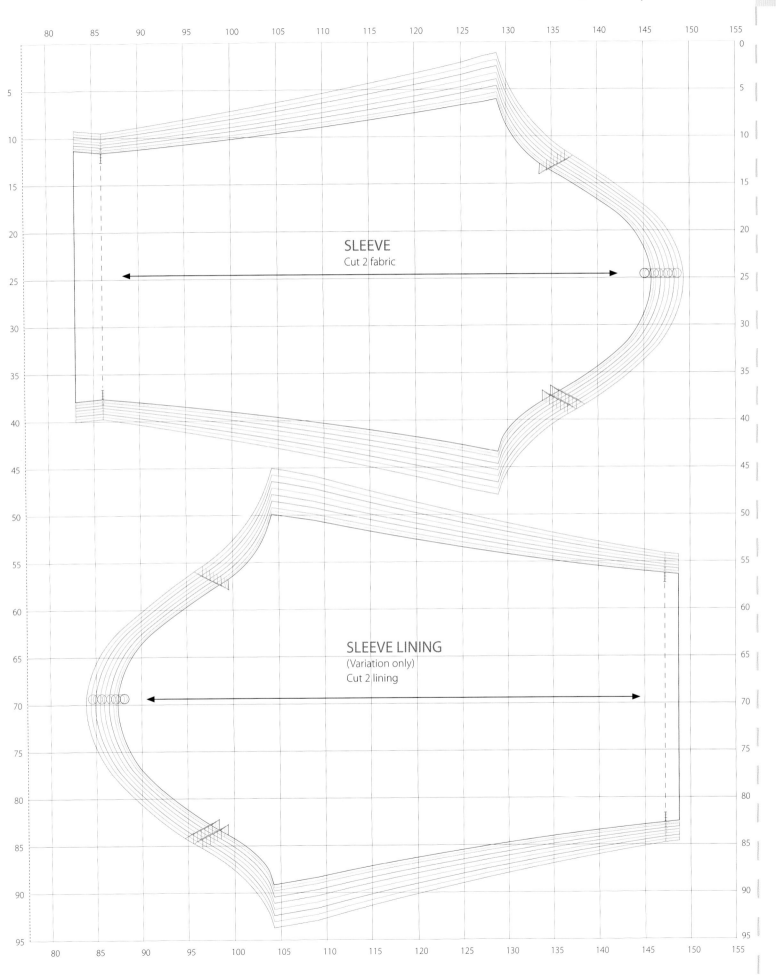

SLEEVE
Cut 2 fabric

SLEEVE LINING
(Variation only)
Cut 2 lining

GLOSSARY

Acetate Man-made fabric widely used for linings.

Acrylic Man-made fabric resembling wool.

Armhole Opening in a garment for the sleeve and arm.

Back stitch A strong hand stitch with a double stitch on the wrong side, used for outlining and seaming.

Belt carrier Loop made from a strip of fabric, which is used to support a belt at the waist edge of a garment.

Bias 45-degree line on fabric that falls between the lengthways and the crossways grain. Fabric cut on the bias drapes well. *See also* Grain.

Bias binding Narrow strips of fabric cut on the bias. Used to give a neat finish to hems and seam allowances.

Binding Method of finishing a raw edge by wrapping it in a strip of bias-cut fabric.

Blanket stitch Hand stitch worked along the raw or finished edge of fabric to neaten, and for decorative purposes.

Blind hem stitch Tiny hand stitch used to attach one piece of fabric to another, mainly to secure hems. Also a machine stitch consisting of two or three straight stitches and one wide zigzag stitch.

Bobbin Round holder beneath the needle plate of a sewing machine on which the thread is wound.

Bodice Upper body section of a garment.

Boning Narrow nylon, plastic, or metal strip, available in various widths, that is used for stiffening and shaping close-fitting garments, such as bodices.

Box pleat Pleat formed on the wrong side of the fabric, and fuller than a knife pleat. *See also* Pleat.

Broderie anglaise A fine plain-weave cotton embroidered to make small decorative holes.

Buttonhole Opening through which a button is inserted to form a fastening. Buttonholes are usually machine stitched but may also be worked by hand or piped for reinforcement or decorative effect.

Buttonhole chisel Very sharp, small chisel that cuts cleanly through a machine-stitched buttonhole.

Buttonhole stitch Hand stitch that wraps over the raw edges of a buttonhole to neaten and strengthen them. Machine-stitched buttonholes are worked with a close zigzag stitch.

Button shank Stem of a button that allows room for the buttonhole to fit under the button when joined.

Calico A plain weave, usually unbleached fabric.

Cashmere The most luxurious of all wools.

Casing Tunnel of fabric created by parallel rows of stitching, through which elastic or a drawstring cord is threaded. Often used at a waist edge. Sometimes extra fabric is required to make a casing; this can be applied to the inside or outside of the garment.

Catch stitch *See* Slip hem stitch.

Centre back The vertical line of symmetry of a garment back piece. Often marked as CB.

Centre front The vertical line of symmetry of a garment front piece. Often marked as CF.

Challis Fine woollen fabric with uneven surface texture.

Chambray A light cotton with a coloured warp thread.

Chiffon Strong, fine, transparent silk.

Clapper Wooden aid that is used to pound creases into heavy fabric after steaming.

Contour dart Also known as double-pointed dart, this is used to give shape at the waist of a garment. It is like two darts joined together. *See also* Dart.

Corduroy A soft pile fabric with distinctive stripes.

Cotton Soft, durable, and inexpensive fabric widely used in dressmaking. Made from the fibrous hairs covering the seed pods of the cotton plant.

Crease Line formed in fabric by pressing a fold.

Crepe Soft fabric made from twisted yarn.

Cross stitch A temporary hand stitch used to hold pleats in place and to secure linings. It can also be used for decoration.

Cutting line Solid line on a pattern piece used as a guide for cutting out fabric.

Darning Mending holes or worn areas in a knitted garment by weaving threads in rows along the grain of the fabric.

Dart Tapered stitched fold of fabric used on a garment to give it shape so that it can fit around the contours of the body. There are different types of dart, but all are used mainly on women's clothing.

Darted tuck A tuck that can be used to give fullness of fabric at the bust or hip. *See also* Tuck.

Denim Hard-wearing twill weave fabric with coloured warp and white weft.

Double-pointed dart *See* Contour dart

Drape The way a fabric falls into graceful folds; drape varies with each fabric.

Dressmaker's carbon paper Used together with a tracing wheel to transfer pattern markings to fabric. Available in a variety of colours.

Duchesse satin Heavy, expensive satin fabric.

Dupion Fabric with a distinctive weft yarn with many nubbly bits; made from 100 per cent silk.

Ease Distributing fullness in fabric when joining two seams together of slightly different lengths, for example a sleeve to an armhole.

Ease stitch Long machine stitch, used to ease in fullness where the distance between notches is greater on one seam edge than on the other.

Edge to edge A garment, such as a jacket, in which the edges meet at the centre front without overlapping.

Enclosed edge Raw fabric edge that is concealed within a seam or binding.

Facing Layer of fabric placed on the inside of a garment and used to finish off raw edges of an armhole or neck of a garment. Usually a separate piece of fabric, the facing can sometimes be an extension of the garment itself.

Filament fibres Very fine synthetic thread, manufactured using plant materials and minerals.

Flannel Wool or cotton with a lightly brushed surface.

Flat fell seam *See* Run and fell seam.

Flat fell stitch A strong, secure stitch used to hold two layers together permanently. Often used to secure linings and bias bindings.

French dart Curved dart used on the front of a garment. *See also* Dart.

French seam A seam traditionally used on sheer and silk fabrics. It is stitched twice, first on the right side of the work and then on the wrong side, enclosing the first seam.

Fusible tape Straight grain tape used to stabilize edges and also replace stay stitching. The heat of the iron fuses it into position.

Gabardine Hard-wearing fabric with a distinctive weave.

Gathers Bunches of fabric created by sewing two parallel rows of loose stitching, then pulling the threads up so that the fabric gathers and reduces in size to fit the required space.

Gingham Two-colour, checked cotton fabric.

Grain Lengthways and crossways direction of threads in a fabric. Fabric grain affects how a fabric hangs and drapes.

Grosgrain Synthetic, ribbed fabric often used to make ribbons.

Haberdashery Term that covers all the bits and pieces needed to complete a pattern, such as fasteners, elastics, ribbons, and trimmings.

Habutai Smooth, fine silk originally from Japan.

Hem The edge of a piece of fabric neatened and stitched to prevent unravelling. There are several methods of doing this, both by hand and by machine.

Hem allowance Amount of fabric allowed for turning under to make the hem.

Hemline Crease or foldline along which a hem is marked.

Herringbone stitch Hand stitch used to secure hems and interlinings. This stitch is worked from left to right.

Herringbone weave A zigzag weave where the weft yarn goes under and over warp yarns in a staggered pattern.

Hong Kong finish A method of neatening raw edges particularly on wool and linen. Bias-cut strips are wrapped around the raw edge.

Hook and eye fastening Two-part metal fastening used to fasten overlapping edges of fabric where a neat join is required. Available in a wide variety of styles.

Interfacing A fabric placed between garment and facing to give structure and support. Available in different thicknesses, interfacing can be fusible (bonds to the fabric by applying heat) or non-fusible (needs to be sewn to the fabric).

Interlining Layer of fabric attached to the main fabric prior to construction, to cover the inside of an entire garment to provide extra warmth or bulk. The two layers are then treated as one. Often used in jackets and coats.

Jersey Cotton or wool yarn that has been knitted to give stretch.

Keyhole buttonhole stitch A machine buttonhole stitch characterized by having one square end while the other end is shaped like a loop to accommodate

the button's shank without distorting the fabric. Often used on jackets.

Layering Trimming one side of the seam allowance to half its width to reduce bulk at the seam.

Linen Natural fibre derived from the stem of the flax plant, linen is available in a variety of qualities and weights.

Lining Underlying fabric layer used to give a neat finish to an item, as well as concealing the stitching and seams of a garment.

Locking stitch A machine stitch where the upper and lower threads in the machine "lock" together at the start or end of a row of stitching.

Madras Brightly coloured, unevenly checked cotton fabric from India.

Matka A silk suiting fabric with uneven yarn.

Mitre The diagonal line made where two edges of a piece of fabric meet at a corner, produced by folding. *See also* Mitred corner.

Mitred corner Diagonal seam formed when fabric is joined at a corner. Excess fabric is cut away before or after stitching.

Mohair Fluffy wool yarn cloth used for sweaters, jackets, and soft furnishings.

Multi-size pattern Paper pattern printed with cutting lines for a range of sizes on each pattern piece.

Muslin Fine, plain, open-weave cotton.

Nap The raised pile on a fabric made during the weaving process, or a print pointing one way. When cutting out pattern pieces, ensure the nap runs in the same direction.

Needle threader Gadget that pulls thread through the eye of a needle. Useful for needles with small eyes.

Notch V-shaped marking on a pattern piece used for aligning one piece with another. Also V-shaped cut taken to reduce seam bulk.

Notion An item of haberdashery, other than fabric, needed to complete a project, such as a button, zip, or elastic. Notions are normally listed on the pattern envelope.

Organza Thin, sheer fabric made from silk or polyester.

Overedge stitch Machine stitch worked over the edge of a seam allowance and used for neatening the edges of fabric.

Overlocker Machine used for quick stitching, trimming, and edging of fabric in a single action; it gives a professional finish to a garment. There are a variety of accessories that can be attached to an overlocker, which enable it to perform a greater range of functions.

Overlock stitch A machine stitch that neatens edges and prevents fraying. It can be used on all types of fabric.

Pattern markings Symbols printed on a paper pattern to indicate the fabric grain, foldline, and construction details, such as darts, notches, and tucks. These should be transferred to the fabric using tailor's chalk or tailor's tacks.

Pile Raised loops on the surface of a fabric, for example velvet.

Pinking A method of neatening raw edges of fray-resistant fabric using pinking shears. This will leave a zigzag edge.

Pinking shears Cutting tool with serrated blades, used to trim raw edges of fray-resistant fabrics to neaten seam edges.

Pivoting Technique used to machine stitch a corner. The machine is stopped at the corner with the needle in the fabric, then the foot is raised, the fabric turned following the direction of the corner, and the foot lowered for stitching to continue.

Placket An opening in a garment that provides support for fasteners, such as buttons, snaps, or zips.

Plain weave The simplest of all the weaves; the weft yarn passes under one warp yarn, then over another one.

Pleat An even fold or series of folds in fabric, often partially stitched down. Commonly found in skirts to shape the waistline, but also in soft furnishings for decoration.

Pocket flap A piece of fabric that folds down to cover the opening of a pocket.

Polyester Man-made fibre that does not crease.

Presser foot The part of a sewing machine that is lowered on to the fabric to hold it in place over the needle plate while stitching. There are different feet available.

Pressing cloth Muslin or organza cloth placed over fabric to prevent marking or scorching when pressing.

Prick stitch Small spaced hand stitch with large spaces between each stitch. Often used to highlight the edge of a completed garment.

Raw edge Cut edge of fabric that requires finishing, for example using zigzag stitch, to prevent fraying.

Rayon Also known as viscose, rayon is often blended with other fibres.

Reverse stitch Machine stitch that simply stitches back over a row of stitches to secure the threads.

Right side The outer side of a fabric, or the visible part of a garment.

Rouleau loop Button loop made from a strip of bias binding. It is used with a round ball-type button.

Round-end buttonhole stitch Machine stitch characterized by one end of the buttonhole being square and the other being round, to allow for the button shank.

Run and fell seam Also known as a flat fell seam, this seam is made on the right side of a garment and is very strong. It uses two lines of stitching and conceals all the raw edges, reducing fraying.

Running stitch A simple, evenly spaced straight stitch separated by equal-sized spaces, used for seaming and gathering.

Satin A fabric with a satin weave.

Satin weave A weave with a sheen, where the weft goes under four warp yarns, then over one.

Seam Stitched line where two edges of fabric are joined together.

Seam allowance The amount of fabric allowed for on a pattern where sections are to be joined together by a seam; usually this is 1.5cm ($^5/_8$in).

Seam edge The cut edge of a seam allowance.

Seamline Line on paper pattern designated for stitching a seam; usually this is 1.5cm ($^5/_8$in) from the seam edge.

Seam ripper A small, hooked tool used for undoing seams and unpicking stitches.

Seam roll Tubular pressing aid for pressing seams open on fabrics that mark.

Selvedge Finished edge on a woven fabric. This runs parallel to the warp (lengthways) threads.

Set-in sleeve A sleeve that fits into a garment smoothly at the shoulder seam.

Sewing gauge Measuring tool with adjustable slider for checking small measurements, such as hem depths and seam allowances.

Sharps General purpose needle used for hand sewing.

Shirting Closely woven, fine cotton with coloured warp and weft yarns.

Silk Threads spun by the silkworm and used to create cool, luxurious fabrics.

Slip hem stitch Similar to herringbone stitch but is worked from right to left. It is used mainly for securing hems.

Snaps Also known as press studs, these fasteners are used as a lightweight hidden fastener.

Snips Spring-loaded cutting tool used for cutting off thread ends.

Staple fibres These include both natural and manufactured fibres such as cotton, wool, flax, and polyester. They are short in length, and relatively narrow in thickness.

Stay stitch Straight machine stitch worked just inside a seam allowance to strengthen it and prevent it from stretching or breaking.

Stitch in the ditch A line of straight stitches sewn on the right side of the work, in the ditch created by a seam. Used to secure waistbands and facings.

Stitch ripper *See* Seam ripper.

Straight stitch Plain machine stitch, used for most applications. The length of the stitch can be altered to suit the fabric.

Stretch stitch Machine stitch used for stretch knits and to help control difficult fabrics. It is worked with two stitches forwards and one backwards so that each stitch is worked three times.

Tacking stitch A temporary running stitch used to hold pieces of fabric together or for transferring pattern markings to fabric.

Taffeta Smooth plain-weave fabric with a crisp appearance.

Tailor's buttonhole A buttonhole with one square end and one keyhole-shaped end, used on jackets and coats.

Tailor's chalk Square- or triangular-shaped piece of chalk used to mark fabric. Available in a variety of colours, tailor's chalk can be removed easily by brushing.

Tailor's ham A ham-shaped pressing cushion that is used to press shaped areas of garments.

Tailor's tacks Loose thread markings used to transfer symbols from a pattern to fabric.

Tape maker Tool for evenly folding the edges of a fabric strip, which can then be pressed to make binding.

Tape measure Flexible form of ruler made from plastic or fabric.

Tartan Fabric made using a twill weave from worsted yarns. Traditionally used for kilts.

Thimble Metal or plastic cap that fits over the top of a finger to protect it when hand sewing.

Toile A test or dry run of a paper pattern using calico. The toile helps you analyse the fit of the garment.

Topstitch Machine straight stitching worked on the right side of an item, close to the finished edge, for decorative effect. Sometimes stitched in a contrasting colour.

Top-stitched seam A seam finished with a row of top-stitching for decorative effect. This seam is often used on crafts and soft furnishings as well as garments.

Trace tacking A method of marking fold and placement lines on fabric. Loose stitches are sewn along the lines on the pattern to the fabric beneath, then the thread loops are cut and the pattern removed.

Tracing wheel Tool used together with dressmaker's carbon paper to transfer pattern markings on to fabric.

Tuck Fold or pleat in fabric that is sewn in place, normally on the straight grain of the fabric. Often used to provide a decorative addition to a garment.

Tweed Traditional tweed is a rough fabric with a distinctive warp and weft. Modern tweed is a mix of chunky and bobbly wool yarns, often in bright colours.

Twill weave Diagonal patterned weave.

Understitch Machine straight stitching through facing and seam allowances that is invisible from the right side; this helps the facing to lie flat.

Velvet Luxurious pile-weave fabric.

Waistband Band of fabric attached to the waist edge of a garment to provide a neat finish.

Warp Lengthways threads or yarns of a woven fabric.

Warp knit Made on a knitting machine, this knit is formed in a vertical and diagonal direction.

Weft Threads or yarns that cross the warp of a woven fabric.

Weft knit Made in the same way as hand knitting, this uses one yarn that runs horizontally.

Welt Strip of fabric used to make the edges of a pocket.

Wool A natural animal fibre, available in a range of weights, weaves, and textures. It is comfortable to wear, crease-resistant, and ideal for tailoring.

Wool worsted A light, strong cloth made from good quality fibres.

Wrong side Reverse side of a fabric; the inside of a garment or other item.

Yoke The top section of a dress or skirt from which the rest of the garment hangs.

Zigzag stitch Machine stitch used to neaten and secure seam edges and for decorative purposes. The width and length of the zigzag can be altered.

Zip Fastening widely used on garments consisting of two strips of fabric tape, carrying specially shaped metal or plastic teeth that lock together by means of a pull or slider. Zips are available in different colours and weights.

Zip foot Narrow machine foot with a single toe that can be positioned on either side of the needle.

INDEX

ABOUT THE AUTHOR

Alison Smith trained as an Art and Fashion Textile Teacher before becoming Head of Textiles at one of the largest secondary schools in Birmingham. Alison left mainstream teaching to have a family, but missed teaching so much that she soon established the Alison Victoria School of Sewing. The school is now the largest of its kind in the UK with students attending from all over Europe and beyond. Alison specialises not only in teaching Dressmaking but also Tailoring and Corsetry. In addition to her own school, Alison lectures at Janome in Stockport, and various sewing shows across the UK. Alison has brought her passion for sewing to TV on series such as *From Ladette to Lady*. Alison lives in Leicestershire with her husband Nigel and has two adult children.

ACKNOWLEDGMENTS

AUTHOR'S ACKNOWLEDGMENTS

No book could ever be written without a little help. I would like to thank the following people for their help in making all the garments: Jackie Boddy, Averil Wing, Jenny Holdam, Christine Scott, Angela Paine, and Joan Culver. My darling husband Nigel and our children Kathryn and Oliver for all their support and endless cups of tea! Thanks must also go to the companies who have continued to support me: Janome UK, Coats Crafts, Fruedenberg –nw, Fabulous Fabric, and MIG. Thank you to my editors Laura Palosuo – and Hilary Mandleberg, who I think I have inspired to take up sewing again!

DK ACKNOWLEDGMENTS

DK would like to thank all the people who helped in the creation of this book: Alison Shackleton for art direction, and Paula Keogh for her skills as sewing technician on the first photo shoot; Jane Ewart for art direction on the second photo shoot, Ruth Jenkinson and her assistant Carly for photography, and Rebecca Fallowfield for production assistance. We are immensely grateful to our models Kate and Charlotte. A big thank you goes out to Bob at MIG for demystifying the art of pattern creation. Finally, we would like to thank Claire Cross for editorial assistance, Angela Baynham for proofreading the book, and Marie Lorimer for creating the index.